D1106432

THE ART IN TEACHING ART

THE ART IN TEACHING ART

*

MANFRED L. KEILER

UNIVERSITY OF NEBRASKA PRESS • LINCOLN • 1961

Library of Congress catalog card number 61-5497.

MANUFACTURED IN THE UNITED STATES OF AMERICA
BY AMERICAN BOOK–STRATFORD PRESS, INC.

To Inge

PREFACE

The real purpose of a book
is to trap the mind into
doing its own thinking.
Christopher Morley

When he writes a book on a given subject, an author includes what he believes to be most pertinent. If he has done his job properly, his book will speak for him—no further exposition of its content is necessary. By way of preface, however, he may wish to say why he has presented the material in the manner he did and what impelled him to write the book.

In my case, the impetus came first of all from my students—their eagerness to learn and the difficulty they had in assimilating the widely assorted facts and ideas presented by art educators, pedagogues, psychologists, philosophers, artists, and art historians. Then, also, in the course of my work I met many educators and administrators who were interested in knowing more about the field of art education and in understanding its aims and practices. And finally I found that a surprising number of artists and parents appeared to have only the vaguest notion of the contribution which might be made by art education to the student's development, to art, and to society. In different ways all these people inspired the writing of this book.

Since understanding a problem (and the teaching of art can be considered a large problem) means to be aware of it in its entirety, not merely of a single segment, I decided to discuss briefly the various aspects of art education in the elementary school before focusing on the subject of teaching art in the high school. Some of the material reviewed belongs to the realm of general pedagogy, but it bears on art teaching, and I have included it particularly for the benefit of beginning teachers.

The arrangement of the material in Part III may at times strike the reader as unconventional. Elements of art history are considered along with methods of presentation and technique—but then the teaching of art is often an amalgamation of all three. For the sake of convenience in illustrating or clarifying certain points, I have divided the entire field of visual art into three broad categories. Admittedly these categories are not mutually exclusive; in numerous instances they overlap. Similarly with regard to such subjects as perspective, design, and composition. Though they belong to all forms of visual expression and all approaches to it, they are not treated in a separate section but in conjunction with those categories with which, from an educational point of view, they appear to have the closest affinity.

Among the considerations which prompted the organization of this book, perhaps the strongest stems from my belief that before anyone can understand and practise the applications of an art or craft he must see it in its historical context and have some cognizance of its significant relationships as well as being acquainted with the basic ideas and facts pertaining to its immediate function. Since it is also my conviction that only "cardinal points" and dogmas can be stated in absolutes, I have made no attempt to synthesize the aims and concepts of art education and encapsulate them in a pat, easily digestible formula. A philosophy does not come prepackaged for mass distribution: it can be acquired by the individual only gradually through exposure to many ideas. Their effect on him is something which another person can neither determine nor experience on his behalf.

In the pages which follow I have set forth some ideas. If they should provide the reader with food for thought and discussion—possibly even for contemplation—this book will have achieved its primary purpose.

In preparing this book I have been guided by the notations of those who read one or more versions of the manuscript. I am deeply indebted to my colleagues Professors Philipp Fehl and Duard Laging for their careful evaluation and criticism, and to Mrs. Shirley Kreissman and Mrs. Jeanne Fosnot for their unstinting assistance during my work. I am also under special obligation to the University of Nebraska Research Council and to Norman Geske, Director of the University Art Gallery, for aiding me in securing material for the illustrations.

MANFRED L. KEILER

April 1960
Lincoln, Nebraska

CONTENTS

List of Illustrations

THE ART IN TEACHING ART

PART ONE

AIMS AND CONCEPTS

Moral education is impossible without the habitual vision of greatness.
Alfred North Whitehead

Any serious consideration of the teaching of art in our high schools involves three distinct complexes: teaching, art, and the high school. These in turn are made up of such components as students, teachers, subject matter and its organization, techniques, and equipment. Before analyzing the more specific components of the concept "high school," our attention first must be given to the two other essential elements, art and teaching. Insight into these fundamentals is necessary before they can be evaluated and related to the total problem, the teaching of art in high school.

Since the terms "teaching" and "art" comprise a multiplicity of meanings, they are difficult to use with precision. The verb "to teach," for example, may mean to make aware, to guide, to inculcate, to make known, to direct, to discipline, to impart knowledge. The term "art" also embraces a variety of concepts. In present usage its primary meaning denotes superior skill based on knowledge and practise; once it also meant technical or professional proficiency. Both these ideas are still vaguely implied in the term "fine arts."

In principle, the fine arts include all the concrete manifestations of man's imagination and creative effort which are directed towards representing an aspect of aesthetic values. But not all creative endeavors have as their end beauty or aesthetic virtues, and therefore one must recognize at least one other criterion for fine arts: the intentional or unintentional absence of utilitarian purpose. Even with these qualifications, however, the term "fine arts" is still too broad to be related to the teaching of art. In the first place, the term does not refer to the visual arts alone—it includes music, poetry, literature, drama, and the dance. The visual arts deal only with those forms of art expression which are perceived or observed by our eyes, and which also appeal directly to our touch sensations. Like all the other branches of the fine arts, the visual arts are a particular mode of interpretation and not a pure representation of nature.

In search of ways of clarifying art's nature and possible function, one encounters at least three basic approaches to art. They are closely related, overlap at many points, and are not mutually exclusive. One approach presents art primarily as a device for elucidating and symbolizing nature, as a medium for expressing ideas and ideals, and as an instrument with which to excite man's sensibilities. A quite different approach emphasizes its social and educational aspects: art as related to morality and religion. A third focuses on the psychological impulses of the artist and the spectator, relating art to feelings, imagination, and sensations. It also distinguishes between the spectator's and the creator's point of view. This third approach is less concerned with the basic values of art than with its final issues or essential nature. It is generally applied in criticism, in evaluation, and in the analysis of art.

There are a host of additional reasons for continuing the examination of the terms "art" and "teaching" with their many implications. Obviously something more than a broad understanding of these terms is not merely desirable, it is imperative for anyone seriously concerned with art education. A more detailed study, it is hoped, will lead the reader to develop basic concepts of art and—more important—of art's function in the education of young people; it also should enable him to recognize both the strength of art education and its limitations. The final aim of this discussion is to provide the wherewithal from which he will be able to develop fundamental convictions in regard to the teaching of his chosen field.

The foundation of all teaching is sincere conviction. Without it a teacher will be adrift in a sea of educational fads and fashions, lacking rudder and compass. He is unable to evaluate, accept, or reject innovations which are often advocated after only brief experimentation. He will fall an easy victim to outside pressures, because without firm convictions based on knowledge, reasoning, contemplation, and confidence he is incapable of withstanding them. He will be impressed by students' works which are spectacular or conspicuous, and will require his own students to duplicate them without first having investigated the genuine educational values of such assignments. In contrast, teachers who have acquired a clear and firm conviction in regard to their teaching are unlikely to fall prey to such dangers. They are able to make decisions and adhere to them until they find valid reasons for changing. Their teaching is directed towards definite ends—ends which are not vague, unrealistic, or pompous, nor based on convenience or trends.

Aims should be the logical consequences of convictions, and curricula the blueprints for attaining these goals. Since within the art education area no rigid courses of study, only basic directions, can ever be advocated or meaningfully stated, setting goals and organizing procedures must remain the responsibility of each individual art teacher. If they are to carry out this responsibility, art teachers must first develop convictions based on a penetrating analysis of their field. They must understand the nature of visual art and its possible function within the educational process. They must be familiar with the many diverse art techniques, and must know their possible contributions and limitations.

Unquestionably, art teachers need to have a deep understanding of young people and their growing relationship with visual art. They must recognize that this relationship is comprised of two parts: active participation in the creative process, and the development of attachments to great works of art. Such attachments should gradually lead to the formation of ideals, and culminate in a "vision of greatness." There is no reason to believe that one part of the relationship is superior to the other. They are equals in principle and must be given equal attention, particularly since many young people have little opportunity to participate in the creative process after leaving high school. For this reason the second part of the relationship (attachments to great works of art) often becomes the more significant of the two in their adult life. The frequently stated concept that participation in the creative process is not only the best but the only way to develop affinities for art is a questionable one. Countless people who listen to music, read books and poems, attend plays, and view works of art are able to form strong attachments to art expression without their ever having truly experienced the formulation and execution of creative thoughts. In order to understand these factors more fully, we must return to the original question: What is art and how can it perform an educational function?

I The Manifold Aspects of Art

Art as Communication

One of the commonest definitions of visual art is that it is a mode of communication. The term "communication" is very much overworked in current educational literature and has been given such a variety of meanings that it has lost all precision. "Communication" primarily designates an exchange of thoughts or ideas. Yet in art no *direct* exchange of thought takes place; rather it can be asserted that art is a carrier or transmitter of impressions, thoughts, or feelings.[1] The painter, for instance, imparts facts, thoughts, and feelings to a piece of linen, and thus the canvas is converted into a transmitter. In this context, the term "feelings" denotes emotional responses to a thing or event, whereas "facts" designates dispassionate statements of things or events. It is a characteristic of visual art that feelings and facts are transmitted regardless of cultures, language barriers, and time. But since facts are also preserved in and conveyed by many media other than art expression, one can single out the preservation of feelings as a major characteristic of art. Inasmuch as feelings and emotions are essentially fleeting, only art gives them permanence.

The expression of feelings embedded in any genuine piece of art is also a manifestation of truth—not an objective or factual truth, but a truth in regard to feelings and reactions to experiences. The relationship between "truth as to fact, so far as art is concerned, is above all the truth of our own sensations, of our own sentiments. It is truth as we see it, as it appears modified by our own temperaments, preferences, and physical organs."[2] That is why every genuine work of art reflects the artist's subjective point of view towards that particular aspect of reality he wishes to transmit, and why it can never be an objective factual statement. "A work of art reproduces its original, not as it is in itself, but as it appears to the senses. Art addresses itself not to the abstract reason but to the sensibility and image-making faculty; it is concerned with outward appearances; it employs illusions; its world is not that which is revealed by pure thought; it sees truth, but in its concrete manifestations, not as an abstract idea."[3] It is exactly this tangibility of art which sets it far

---

[1] Tolstoy said: "Speech, transmitting the thoughts and experiences of men, serves as a means of union among them, and art acts in a similar manner. The peculiarity of this latter means of intercourse, distinguishing it from intercourse by means of words, consists in this, that whereas by words a man transmits his thoughts to another, by means of art he transmits his feelings." Leo Tolstoy, "What Is Art?" (London: Oxford University Press, 1950), p. 121.

[2] Eugene Véron, "Aesthetics," in *A Modern Book of Esthetics,* Melvin M. Rader (ed.) (New York: Henry Holt & Co., 1947), p. 97.

[3] S. H. Butcher, *Aristotle's Theory of Poetry and Fine Art* (Dover Publications, Inc., 1951), p. 127.

apart from abstract reasoning and philosophical deliberations. The concrete revelations of thoughts and feelings manifested in art forms are intelligible without strenuous intellectual discourse. "Philosophy is said to begin in wonder and end in understanding. Art departs from what has been understood and ends in wonder,"[4] John Dewey said. The cause of this wonder can be defined as the manifestations of man's genius illustrated through art, and man's ability to preserve emotions so effectively that they will not lose their power to incite or stimulate others, regardless of time or environment.

Both of these definitions refer in a large degree to an appeal to our emotions. Our emotional responses to persons, objects, and events influence our actions at least as much as do our intellectual faculties. This is particularly noticeable in the realm of visual art where vividness and directness of emotional responses are generally utilized and retained.[5] The way to retain these responses is to give them permanent expression. The act of externalizing emotions in a concrete and constructive manner is an essential part of creative activity. On this very point art and education converge. Our present high school curriculum offers very little opportunity for the adolescent to transform emotion into a productive force; indeed the art course is often the only one which provides such an occasion. There is no justification from any educational point of view for this lack of opportunity for transmitting thoughts and emotions in an orderly and constructive manner. It is common knowledge that adolescents in particular are frequently in need of such emotional outlets, and that if properly motivated, they may derive inner satisfaction from such a release. Art sessions should bring students in contact with works of men who expressed emotions powerfully, because these contacts not only act as additional stimuli for students' creative undertakings, but can help them to find comfort in expressing their personal feelings and thoughts.

This brings us to the questions: Are all thoughts and feelings worthy of expression? Is art's only value in being a catharsis of emotions? Such queries immediately evoke a larger problem: What are the values of art?

Art as Value

We have seen that art may be defined as a mode of communication or form of transmission; it also may be defined in terms which can be summarized as "art—a manifestation of values." These values are contained in every true piece of art, they are in no way related to the ordinary material values of an object, and they do not serve any direct practical purpose.[6] Even when a piece has been created with utilitarian intent, if it is then revered for its own sake, independent of its original prac-

---

[4] John Dewey, *Art as Experience* (New York: Minton, Balch & Co., 1934), p. 270.

[5] "We may say then, by way of general definition, that art is the manifestation of emotion, obtaining external interpretation, now by expressive arrangements of line, form or color, now by a series of gestures, sounds, or words governed by particular rhythmical cadence.

"If our definition is exact, we must conclude, from it, that the merit of a work of art, whatever it may be, can be finally measured by the power with which it manifests or interprets the emotion that was its determining cause, and that, for a like reason, must constitute its innermost supreme unity." Eugene Véron, "Aesthetics," in Rader, *A Modern Book of Esthetics,* pp. 86–87.

[6] "Great art is the arrangement of the environment so as to provide for the soul vivid, but transient, values. Human beings require something which absorbs them for a time, something out of the routine which they can stare at. But you cannot subdivide life, except in the abstract analysis of thought. Accordingly, the great art is more than a transient refreshment. It is something which adds to the permanent richness of the soul's self-attainment. It justifies itself both by its immediate enjoyment, and also by its discipline of the inmost being. Its discipline is not distinct from enjoyment, but by reason of it. It transforms the soul into the permanent realization of values extending beyond its former self." Alfred North Whitehead, *Science and the Modern World* (New York: The Macmillan Co., 1948), pp. 290–291.

tical purpose, it is transformed into a work of art. In such instances, the particular values which we admire and which are characteristic attributes of any work of art are, in fact, those which humanity has held in high esteem for an infinite time. They seem to comprise truth and honesty, mastery and perfection, beauty, dedication, and individuality. Man recognizes the realizations of these values as the highest attainable and most worthy to be striven for. With these ideals he can raise himself above his everyday existence, above his ego-centered horizon; with them he can fill his mind and soul and become attuned to greatness and universality. It is exactly this difference which sets him apart from any other creature on earth.

This value concept of art is probably one of the most important concepts, if not the most important, in regard to art education on the high school level; it implies that absorption in art is a form of preoccupation with moral principles.[7] (It should be noted here that not everyone who paints is occupied with art!) Consequently, education in art can, in a sense, be considered a moral education. The scope of art education extends beyond the narrow concept of learning skills and performing aimless exercises in ego-centered self-expression. The term "moral" in this context should not be construed as referring to a narrow code of behavior but rather understood in its broadest meaning, that of preoccupation with issues which are both aesthetic and ethical, such as honesty, purity, and sincerity. As Santayana expressed it, ". . . when the conscience is formed, and right principles acquire an immediate authority, our attitude to these principles becomes aesthetic also. Honour, truthfulness, and cleanliness are obvious examples. When the absence of these virtues causes an instinctive disgust, as it does in well-bred people, the reaction is essentially aesthetic, because it is not based on reflection and benevolence, but on constitutional sensitiveness. This aesthetic sensitiveness is, however, properly enough called moral, because it is the effect of conscientious training and is more powerful for good in society than laborious virtue, because it is much more constant and catching."[8]

The preceding discussion presupposes an acceptance of adolescents as spiritual creatures. Their education, therefore, must of necessity be twofold. One part should deal with practicalities which equip them for material survival in society; the other should develop a need and desire for timeless spiritual values. Whitehead said: "You cannot, without loss, ignore in the life of the spirit so great a factor as art. Our aesthetic emotions provide us with vivid apprehensions of value. If you maim these, you weaken the force of the whole system of spiritual apprehensions. The claim for freedom in education carries with it the corollary that the development of the whole personality must be attended to. You must not arbitrarily refuse its urgent demands. In these days of economy, we hear much of the futility of our educational efforts and of the possibility of curtailing them."[9]

The practice of curtailing those high school courses which do not contribute towards immediate material comfort or security is all too noticeable. Even a casual survey of high school English teaching over the past thirty years reveals this trend. Creative writing, poetry, and literature have been de-emphasized, and subjects like business English and journalism given greater importance. We can detect a similar tendency in the recent teaching of visual art. Painting, drawing, sculpture, and art history are often given less prominence than commercial arts, applied arts, and

---

[7] Hegel said, "Art fulfills its highest task when it has joined the same sphere with religion and philosophy and has become a certain mode of bringing to consciousness and expression the divine meaning of things, the deepest interest of mankind, and the most universal truth of the spirit." J. Lowenberg (ed.), *Hegel Selections* (New York: Charles Scribner's Sons, 1929), p. 314.

[8] George Santayana, *The Sense of Beauty* (New York: Charles Scribner's Sons, 1936), p. 25.

[9] Alfred North Whitehead, *The Aims of Education* (New York: The Macmillan Co., 1929), pp. 63–64.

crafts. This narrow and frequently rather materialistic approach towards art can easily deprive high school students of their most important educational opportunities, those which help them to develop strong moral and creative qualities. An art educator who advocates only a limited "practical" approach to art appears to have little understanding of, and even less trust in, art or art education's positive effect on young people. After all, genuine art provides us with a sense of greatness, and "the sense of greatness is the groundwork of morals."[10]

"Just as physical life cannot exist without the support of a physical environment," Dewey said, "so moral life cannot go on without the support of a moral environment."[11] The art room is a most fitting place for providing this moral environment; it should also be a place where the adolescent has the opportunity to become familiar with his cultural heritage and with the culture of his day. Particularly during his formative years, his moral and cultural environment often determine his character and his attitude toward aesthetic and intellectual refinements. It is the fine arts which exemplify and symbolize this refinement as well as the culture of a society: "The final measure of the quality of culture is the arts which flourish."[12] Education of young people which does not provide constant contact with significant art and opportunities for creativeness is failing in one of its fundamental functions: to educate youngsters so that they will become not trained savages but civilized men.

Art as Order

Another common definition of art is "to bring order out of chaos." While order has many meanings, in this context it can be defined either as a systematic arrangement or as a condition in which everything is so organized as to play its proper part. These two definitions are quite similar; and both can be applied to man and to objects. For instance, we can systematically arrange our thoughts and, to some degree, our feelings. Inasmuch as chaos can exist inside as well as outside of man, order applies to both his internal and external worlds. The definition of art as bringing order out of chaos may also be stated as "Art reflects an established order" or "Art facilitates the establishment of order."

The reflection of order can also be called harmony. Harmony in visual art is achieved by combining parts with each other so that an aesthetically pleasing effect is attained. The most obvious principles for attaining this harmony are balance, rhythm, and unity. The first problem of any painter consists of finding a satisfactory solution for integrating various distinctly different forms, shapes, colors, and textures into a single unit. If he fails and unity is absent, the spectator will see not a wholeness but unconnected entities. This lack of harmony conveys disorder which, like any other form of disorganization, is disturbing as well as confusing. Hence one can say that a vital quality of a work of art is order or harmony.

Man's desire for order affects all phases of his life, and in his attempts to attain it he also turns to art. Much of the satisfaction he derives from art is a result of having momentarily satisfied his longing for order. This inner need arises as soon as the child becomes consciously aware of the world he lives in. He is bombarded by bits of unrelated information which he receives through his senses. He attempts to establish a kind of system in which all random information and accidental facts are related and arranged in an order. This process also characterizes one of the most common principles of learning, and we can find an analogous principle within the creative process as well. The innumerable visual facts and impressions which man

---

[10] Whitehead, *The Aims of Education,* p. 107.
[11] Dewey, *Art as Experience,* p. 345.
[12] *Ibid,* p. 345.

is constantly receiving, and his own emotional responses to them, are without apparent order. But as soon as he attempts to transform them into a creative whole, he must establish order both within his undertaking and within his mind or he will be unable to create. It can be claimed that the creative urge has its origin partly in a desire for order. The chaotic mixture of impressions and sensations derived from the external world and the confusing impulses and feelings or reactions of man's inner life are disentangled during any creative process.

The creative urge in its beginning is rather nebulous. A very young child begins to create by forming single thoughts or single reactions to which he may then add other unrelated ideas. These isolated formulations are without order. Gradually, as the child matures, he starts to relate, rather vaguely still, more complex thoughts and reactions to each other, and order begins to emerge. As soon as the child expresses himself in visual form, relating several facts and his reaction to them in a logical arrangement, he begins to establish order. His logic may be quite different from an adult concept of connecting facts, impressions, and reactions; nevertheless there is an innate consistency. For instance, if a child represents an object as very large, it means that the object is very important to him; if it is represented as very small, it is unimportant; and if there is an omission, it means that the omitted part is totally insignificant to the child *at the time of his drawing*. This form of expressing facts and feelings represents order, in spite of the fact that it is quite different from the one which adults commonly establish.

When the child grows older he will change the principle of order. Most adolescents wish to express order in close resemblance to standards which are generally accepted by adults; and these standards demand that size relationships, distances, and colors correspond to those found in reality. However, some young people prefer to express order in a strongly subjective manner. To them the visual reality is of secondary importance; it is their own emotional reactions to environment and experiences which are of primary significance. These adolescents will distort forms, colors, and arrangements in a manner similar to contemporary expressionists, thereby achieving order in their emotions as well as in their visual expression.

As already indicated, the concept of "art as order" has educational implications. First, it helps us understand certain underlying reasons for young people's art expression. Second, it assists us in comprehending how the art activity helps children establish order in their minds and therefore in their work. The larger educational implications of this thought will become clear as soon as we relate it to a broader frame of reference: without order man is confused and hampered in his actions and thinking. This confusion is a basic cause for indecision and tension. On the other hand, order relieves us and permits us to act constructively and creatively.

Art as Illusion

Art is also a concept in which stature is given to the world of make-believe or illusion. To be sure, this concept is applicable to all branches of the fine arts, but it can be most clearly demonstrated within the realm of visual art. The more accomplished a piece of art, the less our awareness of being victimized by an illusion. The painting we admire, rich in colorful forms and pleasing in movements, is in fact nothing more than a length of material covered with countless spots. The graceful marble statue is merely white limestone from which someone has chipped away countless pieces. The thing that impresses us so much is neither the spotted canvas, nor the chipped then polished limestone, but the illusion created with them by the artist. This legitimate form of deception is largely effective only with man. No hungry dog will react to even the most exquisitely painted steak, nor will an ape show fear in front of the most naturalistically depicted lion. Creating visual deception is a unique ability of man, and he is most successful in victimizing himself and his fellow men.

The basis for the effectiveness of illusion in the realm of art is a combination of several human qualities: specifically, man's capacity to retain facts and to recall experiences, to imagine tangibles and situations, and to project himself into situations which he has not literally experienced. The spectator as well as the creator of art relies on these three different capabilities whenever he is in contact with visual art. In paintings, for instance, the artist produces certain suggestions with the help of lines, forms, and colors, and these suggestions usually recall to the mind familiar forms or experiences. The definiteness or vagueness of these suggestions will in part determine the artist's style. For example, Cézanne frequently employed simple, basic, geometric shapes to suggest many forms found in nature. A Cézanne tree is neither a scientific observation delineating and recording facts, nor an attempt to imitate a tree; rather it is a carefully planned suggestion which reminds us vividly of a tree. If we had never seen a tree, this suggestion could not be effective. We would see nothing but what is actually on the canvas: an array of geometric shapes.

Some works of art—and this is particularly true of much contemporary work—are not immediately effective because their visual suggestions fail to lead many spectators to a recalling of familiar forms or situations. Without a proper frame of reference the spectator cannot submit to an illusion, hence will be easily irritated: indeed, seeing facts without illusion can produce a spontaneous dislike. "I see only lines and colors; it does not make sense!" In some such words one often hears an annoyed onlooker give vent to his reaction. However, while his assertion that sense or meaning are absent in the work may be the result of total unfamiliarity with the depicted suggestion, it may simply indicate an impatient attitude—he has not been willing to devote enough time to the work of art to become accustomed to or affected by the entailed illusion. Not every illusion created in art has immediate, direct reference to the commonplaces of life. For instance, many illusions impart thought complexes which are expressed in symbols. Not all of these symbols are widely known; indeed, many are rather esoteric and cannot be understood without special knowledge. Frequently the spectator is not fully aware that what he perceives on a canvas may perhaps be symbols as well as representations of objects. Nor does he realize that each individual form often represents more than appears to the eye, and may actually stand for a particular thought. For example, the portrayal of a yellow apple can be a pleasing, colorful, circular shape, representing exactly what it is: a common fruit. But in a particular context the same apple may symbolize man's downfall, referring to his expulsion from the Garden of Eden. In another context it may represent discord, the symbolic meaning in this instance deriving from Paris' famous judgment which led to the Trojan War. Anyone unfamiliar with Homer's epic would be at a loss in front of a painting utilizing an apple as a symbol of discord.

There is one more reason for the possible ineffectiveness of a depicted illusion: A work of art may force the spectator into a frame of reference which is only most superficially related to the perceivable illusion and is, in fact, totally foreign to the artist's intent and to the concept represented. If, for instance, a colorful nonrepresentational painting accidentally reminds a spectator of a piece of printed material, he will claim that he sees nothing but a glorified and framed textile design. His mind is made up, and it is impossible for him to be affected by the created illusion. Even worse, being under the impression that he has understood the painting, he will leave without having perceived the illusion. Since illusions are suggestions which frequently are based on associations, misunderstandings can easily occur.

Up to this point "art as illusion" has been discussed from a general point of view only, without particular reference to that form of visual art in which illusions are deliberately created to trick the eye and, as a result, the mind. This mode of expression is known as "trompe-l'oeil" (literally: fools the eye) and as "magic realism." The latter pertains mostly to modern easel painting, whereas the former is also used in connection with other forms of painting and three-dimensional works.

The history of optical illusion, or trompe-l'oeil, is a long one. The technique was employed by the Greeks and Romans; some good early examples have been found in Pompeii and Herculaneum. This form of deliberate optical deception originated in conjunction with architecture. The walls of many ancient chambers were covered with large murals on which painters had used perspective in such a way as to make the room appear much larger. With the renewed application of the laws of perspective during the Renaissance, there was fresh interest in creating optical illusions. Murals, ceiling paintings, stage settings, easel paintings, and sculpture were utilized for the purpose of fooling men's eyes. At times, trompe-l'oeil, in a whimsical fashion, became a series of stunts.[13]

THE BLACKBOARD
Kenneth Davies
oil on canvas

University Collection, University of Nebraska

As a rule, only four media are employed in the creation of these optical illusions: perspective, light, shadow, and texture. The execution of such works demands a high degree of technical proficiency which not infrequently has degenerated into a

---

[13] "Along with facility in rendering the illusion of spatial volume, the sixteenth century developed virtuosity at creating puzzles with a trick point of view, perhaps in order to keep a meaning secret." "The Grand Illusion," *Art News Annual,* 1953, Part II, p. 151.

kind of ostentatious display of skills. Trompe-l'oeils are still being produced today. They are part of the school of "magic realism," of the German school of "Neue Sachlichkeit" (new factualism), and of the movement known as surrealism. Trompe-l'oeil holds an especially great fascination for adolescents: they tend to take the excessive display of skills in magic realism and in surrealism as the only valid criterion for greatness in visual art. Still, their admiration for this form of expression can be utilized effectively by the art teacher: it can serve to motivate their learning the basic skills, and to help them realize that such skills are essential to the execution of any significant work of art. Their admiration should also be used as a means for correcting a common misconception in regard to creativity in art—that art is the product of genius, and that genius or talent precludes the necessity for any learning. As a corollary to this, many people think that in creating art nothing can be acquired by learning. Trompe-l'oeil lends itself well to disproving and correcting these misconceptions.

One more issue bearing on the concept of illusion in art requires clarification: the difference between illusion and imitation. In principle, imitations in art are artificial likenesses void of any suggestion or illusion. They force a spectator, in quasi-dictatorial manner, to see facts and nothing but facts. (An exception is the mechanical reproduction of an original work of art.) Medical and scientific illustrations are legitimate examples of imitations, but if an imitation is exhibited as an object of art, it merely displays a kind of counterfeit or trickery. This holds true even though an imitation can be an example of considerable skill, obviously referring to a known frame of reference. But the spectator will not be aroused beyond the point of noticing factual information, and his imagination and emotions will usually remain dormant. Accordingly, we can conclude that two major points differentiate art from imitation: one is humility, as expressed by the artist's subordination to the subject; the other is truthfulness beyond the surface appearance. "The artist should not content himself with a superficial glance at his object, but he must try to penetrate its inner structure. His task is faithful interpretation, not slavish imitation."[14] Rendering a faithful interpretation, however, is possible only if the individual carefully investigates the particular nature and character of what he intends to portray as well as its outward appearance. These investigations are synthesized and formulated visually and the result is illusion.

This process has significant educational implications. It implies that thorough investigation should precede the creation of illusion. In this context investigation and learning are clearly synonymous. Both mean observing, examining, and inquiring patiently; hence, in art learning and creating are fused. Whenever the desire to create illusion is sufficiently motivated, an acquisition of knowledge, not to mention skills, almost automatically takes place.

Symbols and Art

As previously indicated, illusion in art is closely related to the concept of art as an expression in symbols. The core of this concept is the recognition that form can and frequently does serve as a representation of ideas. Goethe's statement on the essence of symbolism in art should clarify this concept more fully: "Symbolism transforms the phenomenon into the idea, and the idea into an image in such a fashion that in the image the idea remains infinitely active and incommensurable, and if all languages were used to express it, it would still remain inexpressible."[15]

---

[14] W. J. Verdenius, *Mimesis* (Leiden: E. J. Brill, 1949), p. 21.
[15] *Goethe, Wisdom and Experience,* selections by Ludwig Curtis (New York, Pantheon Books, 1949), p. 260.

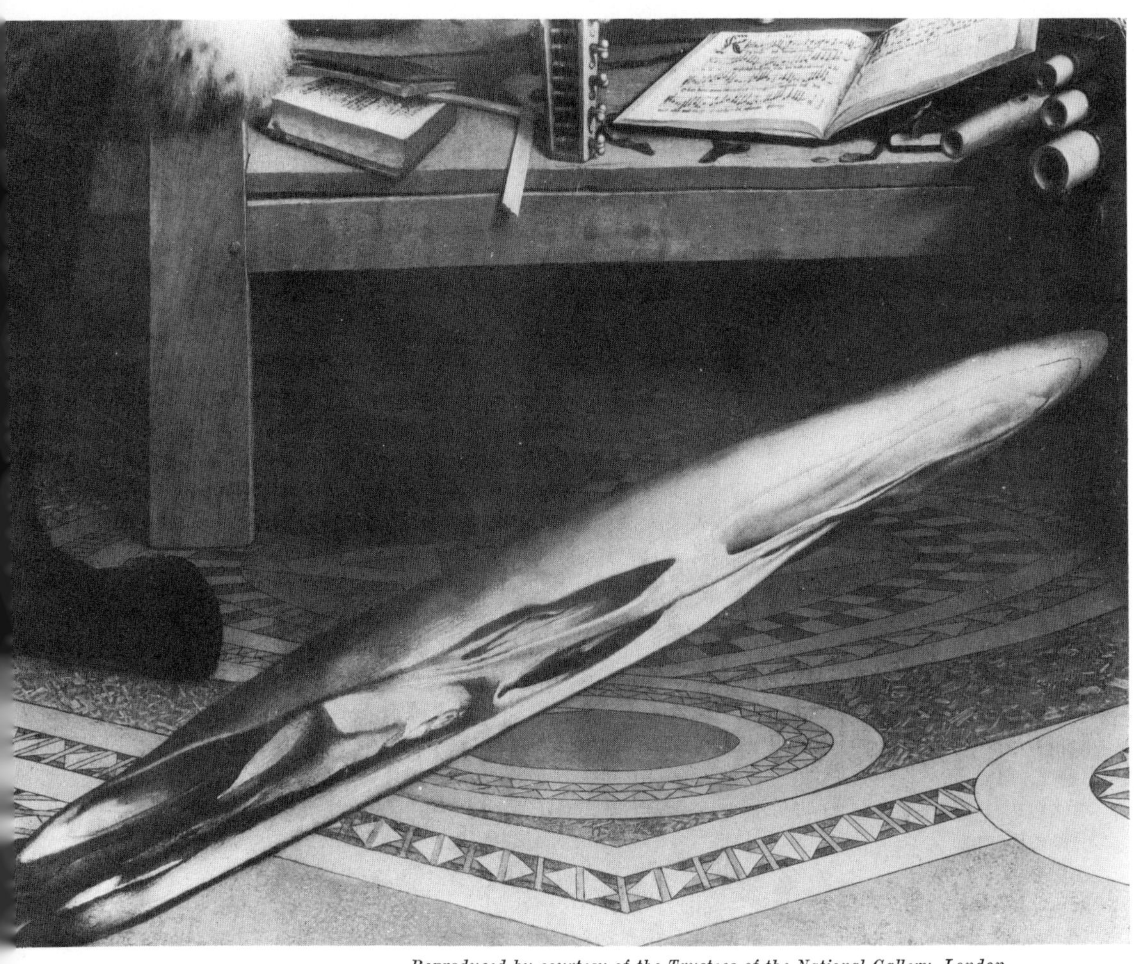

skull detail from
THE AMBASSADORS
Hans Holbein

Symbolism is as old as humanity; for as far back as we can discover, man has employed symbols to communicate his thoughts. But although symbols are not limited to art or to visual forms, visual art expression has frequently exploited the symbolic meanings of forms. Many works of art take on additional significance as soon as we become conscious of their symbols. For instance, in Leonardo da Vinci's painting *Virgin and Child with St. Ann and the Infant St. John,* the infant is playing with a young lamb. The joyful scene immediately takes on added meaning if we realize that the lamb symbolizes meekness. Contrasting with this is Hans Holbein's painting *The Ambassadors* showing a skull in an amorphic perspective in the center of the canvas: the skull is certainly a symbol, but here it stands for a thought not definitely known.[16] To avoid later misunderstandings, the latter example has been given to demonstrate that not all symbols convey their meanings clearly or according to a fixed code based on tradition or convention. Sometimes symbols lose their precise meaning; at other times, their connotations cease to have application and are forgotten. In Hieronymus Bosch's *Altar of the Last Judgment* a great variety of symbols are portrayed, but the meanings of many have been lost and have not yet been rediscovered.

---

[16] ". . . Holbein's skull must be held level with the eye, along the line of their attenuation, to be read in normal terms. Holbein's skull is a disguised memento mori, or reminder of human mortality, within these portraits of transitory power and splendor." *Art News Annual, loc. cit.*

Symbols often change their meanings in the course of time. The swastika is an extreme example of such a change: in ancient times it was a symbol for good fortune and luck; in our time it came to mean oppression, hatred, and subjugation. Then again the symbolic meaning of an object may vary: a pearl in a painting may simply represent what it is, a precious gem. But it can also be a symbol for tears and sadness, for rain and fertility, for purity and chastity. Almost every generation has invented new symbols; nowadays, for instance, a combination of globoid figures with straight or spherical lines has become a symbol for the atom, the atomic age, space awareness, total destruction, and future progress.

Many spectators will accept and understand a symbol without consciously realizing that it is not only a representation of an object, but also a kind of code which conveys a message. A symbol's effectiveness is contingent on more than the spectator's familiarity with its meaning; it depends in part on his willingness to become fully engrossed in the work of art. If symbols are seen only as isolated forms out of context with the whole piece, they may well lead the spectator to a misunderstanding or to a sort of puzzle game, and he never makes contact with the work as a whole.

It should be noted that it is an artist's privilege to invent symbols, and that he is under no obligation to employ only those already in existence. All known forms have significance beyond their obvious appearance, and these connotations may be utilized by any artist. He establishes new symbols by emphasizing or exploiting the implied meanings of forms in his works. For instance, a cigarette is a pleasure-giving commodity, but since it is also a medium through which people may form an enslaving addiction, it can become a symbol of slavery. Furthermore, since nicotine is a poison which can cause sickness and death, a cigarette may stand as a symbol for self-destruction. A colloquial term for cigarettes, "coffin nails," is a case in point. Depending on how an artist portrays these narrow, white, cylindrical shapes on his canvas, they will be transmuted into symbols or will simply represent images of cigarettes.

Consciously conceived symbols, based either on tradition and convention or on recognition of meanings entailed in forms beyond their immediate external appearance, have significance in the teaching of art. In most high school art rooms one finds examples of adolescent work in which conscious symbols are represented. These symbols are as legitimate a part of students' visual expression as they are of mature art. It is desirable that high school students utilize symbols, provided that they originate in a search for genuine expression of thought or feeling. But if symbols are merely employed as thoughtless substitutes or pretenses for thought or feeling, they are most objectionable. The stereotyped bells typifying Christmas, the trite three-pointed, petaled tulips symbolizing spring, the isolated musical notes representing gaiety are characteristic examples of insensitive, thoughtless, and therefore undesirable symbols. Whenever they are encountered, a teacher should recognize that the student is only pretending to express himself, that he is substituting platitudes and banalities for thoughts and emotions. On the other hand, the adolescent who varies conscious symbols, shapes them into a personal expression, or invents new signs to convey meaning, should be encouraged and made aware that he is utilizing one of the most significant forms of visual art.

Up to this point, only those symbols have been discussed which were conceived or given meaning from a rational or conscious point of view. However, there exists an entirely different category of symbols, embracing all those which are definitely the creation of the unconscious. For purposes of clarification, this form of symbolism can be divided into two classes. The first comprises symbols whose visual manifestations are casual, lack precision, and are somewhat vague in appearance, design, and meaning. These symbols, often found in contemporary abstractions, stand for broad

BLIND BEAST
James Boynton
oil on canvas

Reproduced by courtesy of the artist

or not sharply definable concepts. As an example: a strange dark shape with various appendages might convey something unpleasant, evoking fear, nightmares, terror, or panic. When it induces this notion in the spectator's mind, the dark shape assumes the status of a symbol, a symbol representing not a precise thought but a mood or feeling.[17] The other division embraces symbols which are more definite in form and usually are related to subconscious feelings or particular moods. The person who is portraying these symbolic shapes is, for the most part, unaware of conveying a thought or a notion, hence his symbols are based neither on preconceived ideas nor on a conscious desire to state precise thoughts. Frequently they are not even directly related to the expressed theme. The archaic sun symbol, for example, often appears isolated and independent of the pictorial idea, as in the paintings of small children depicting, for instance, night or a stormy day. The unconscious symbols seen in

---

[17] "The artist . . . becomes a man gifted with the capacity to project symbols from his unconscious, which symbols are of general validity—that is to say, they are symbols which other people might project if they had the capacity, and which, when projected for them, they can immediately accept. This act of acceptance replaces the feeling of pleasure which is the reaction in the case of a normal work of art. We might even go further and say that the value of such a type of art can be gauged by a new test of universality: universality of the plane of the unconscious." Herbert Read, *Art Now* (New York: Pitman Publishing Corp., 1948), p. 117.

works of adolescents, which at times resemble parts of the body, not infrequently the reproductive organs, are equally unrelated.[18]

In relation to the art teaching of normal adolescents, unconscious symbols have no marked importance, nor should they be considered of vital consequence. The meaning of the symbols as such, and their relationship to the individual, are of significance *only* to psychologists and of very little value to the art teacher. Still, just as an art teacher should have some knowledge of anatomy, so also should an acquaintance with unconscious symbolism be part of his basic equipment. But just as his extremely limited knowledge of anatomy would never entitle him to practice medicine, so his superficial acquaintance with depth psychology should never be regarded as adequate preparation for the practice of clinical psychology. Moreover, unconscious symbols as portrayed by adolescents are *extremely personal* and involuntary disclosures. The unconscious self-revelations which a teacher may notice in students' art works should be regarded by him as a sacred trust, whose content he has no right to reveal to anyone, *including* the originator of the symbols. If the teacher disregards this sacred trust and reveals to the student the existence and/or meaning of the symbols, he risks totally frustrating the pupil's creative ability. Fearing he may again reveal some secret aspects of his inner life, the student will, at best, only go through the motions of expressing himself, and will put on paper only the most impersonal observations or trite expressions. The one positive conclusion an art teacher may legitimately draw from the appearance of unconscious symbols is that he has been able to establish a very desirable working relationship with the students, and that in his presence they feel free to be truly themselves.

Free Art versus Servile Art

The different aspects of art thus far discussed still leave one important problem wide open: where does art end, and where do the more practical applications of visual art techniques and principles begin?

This question harks back to the old controversial issues involved in ranking the different fields of visual art in order of superiority and inferiority, of distinguishing between fine versus applied arts, or minor versus major arts. "The distinction between the 'Fine' and 'Applied Arts' is hardly defensible, for as someone remarked: if a product is not 'fine' it is not art."[19]

Still, not all "fine" or accomplished art products should automatically be considered fine art. Pursuing this point further, we might compare an effective, excellently designed poster with an important painting by a renowned artist. Let us assume that in both instances superior skill and good taste are of the highest order. The question now arises: Where does the exact difference lie between the poster and the painting? Because Hegel distinguishes between "free" and "servile" art, his thoughts on art may help in finding a sound answer. Whenever art is employed for predominantly material or practical purposes, as in the decorative and commercial

---

[18] "I have given the name of *dream-work* to the process which, with the cooperation of the censorship, converts the latent thoughts into the manifest content of the dream. It consists of a peculiar way of treating the preconscious material of thought, so that its component parts become *condensed,* its psychical emphasis *displaced,* and the whole of it is translated into visual images or dramatized, and completed by a deceptive *secondary revision.* The dream-work is an excellent example of the processes occurring in the deeper, unconscious layers of the mind which differ considerably from the familiar normal processes of thought. It also displays a number of archaic characteristics, such as the use of a symbolism (in this case of a predominantly sexual kind) which it has since also been possible to discover in other spheres of mental activity." *The Standard Edition of the Complete Psychological Works of Sigmund Freud,* trans. James Strachey (London: The Hogarth Press, 1959), Vol. XX, p. 45.

[19] Ray Faulkner, Edwin Ziegfeld, and Gerald Hill, *Art Today* (New York: Henry Holt & Co., 1949), p. xxvi.

arts, Hegel classifies it as servile. "In this mode of employment art is indeed not independent, not *free* but *servile*. But what we mean to consider is the art which is [as] free in its end as in its means. . . . Free art is not real art till it is in this sense free, and only achieves its highest task when it has taken its place in the same sphere with religion and philosophy."[20] According to Hegel, no particular form, medium, or technique is characteristic of either the free or the servile arts. Therefore any creative work, be it a painting, a poster, or a piece of ceramics, can belong to either category. A painting which maintains its appeal and derives its effectiveness primarily from conveying a literary message is, according to Hegel, not free but servile. Such a painting draws on thoughts and associations which are neither innate in nor essential to visual art. There are religious paintings, for example, whose peculiar function is to describe events that might as well, or better, have been expressed in words. In these instances paintings are converted into story-telling vehicles, and the entire effectiveness of such works depends on their literary message.[21] On the other hand, if a religious theme is painted so that it can exist independently of its particular message, and can hold the attention of a spectator who brings to the painting neither historical knowledge nor preconceived admiration—then such a work belongs to the "free" arts. Typical examples of such "free" art are the *Isenheim Altar* by Grünewald, and the sculptured portrait of Egyptian queen Nefertiti. Both works exist independently of their subject matter and can be enjoyed and admired as works of art, not merely as religious or historic artifacts.

Ordinary posters usually depend strongly on their literal message and are effective only within the narrow confinement of their utilitarian function. However, numerous commercial art works continue to be publicly shown even after having lost their original function because they are now regarded as significant creative achievements. Typical examples are most of the Toulouse-Lautrec posters which are even yet admired and cherished not as vehicles of a particular message, but as forceful creative expressions, free and independent of all extraneous thoughts.[22]

The concept of free versus servile art can be further elucidated by examples from the field of pottery. A pot is essentially a functional implement produced to serve a utilitarian purpose, but if it becomes an object of admiration and enjoyment independent of utilitarian functions—that is to say, if its form and surface become a source of aesthetic enjoyment—then it changes its status from servile or applied art to free or fine art. The essence of these deliberations can be stated as follows: a work of art that is "free" exists independent of any considerations other than stimulation of strongly felt emotions through the eye, the touch, and the mind.

In principle, these approaches toward free or servile art are closely related to the purpose which a work of art should serve. A piece of servile art is effective and appreciated only within a limited utilitarian frame of reference, whereas a work of free art radiates outside of any practical considerations in a sphere of our spiritual or emotional life. "Art has accordingly two stages," Santayana said, "one mechanical or industrial, in which untoward matter is better prepared, or impeding media are overcome; the other liberal, in which perfectly fit matter is appropriated to ideal

---

[20] Introduction to Hegel's *Philosophy of Fine Art,* Bernard Bosanquet, trans. (London: K. Paul, Trench and Co., 1905), p. 48.

[21] "It is true, when a literary subject is so well known the artist can treat it and yet expect to be understood. Yet it is better, in my opinion, that the works of painters and sculptors should contain all their interest in themselves. Art can offer thought and imagination without recourse to literature. Instead of illustrating scenes from poems, it need only use plain symbols which do not require any written text." Rodin, quoted by Paul Gsell in *Art by Auguste Rodin,* Mrs. Romilly Fedden, trans. (New York: Hodder and Stoughton, 1912), p. 172.

[22] "Productions in which an aesthetic value is or is not supposed to be prominent take the name of fine art; but the work of fine art so defined is almost always an abstraction from the actual object, which has many non-aesthetic functions and values." George Santayana, *The Life of Reason* (New York: Charles Scribner's Sons, 1954), p. 303.

uses and endowed with a direct spiritual function. . . . This spiritual fruition consists in the activity of turning an apt material into an expressive and delightful form, thus filling the world with objectives which by symbolising ideal energies tend to strengthen and refine them."[23]

The question now arises: Which of the two aspects should be emphasized in the education of adolescents, the "free" or the "servile," the "spiritual" or the "utilitarian"? As pointed out before, the utilitarian application of education is given major importance in our public schools today. Many subject areas, such as natural and social sciences or industrial and commercial arts, are taught with the aim of equipping young people for the practicalities of life. Yet all educators agree that the objectives of high school education should not be limited, but should embrace all aspects of man. It appears then that the visual arts are entrusted with the major responsibility of developing the moral, aesthetic, and spiritual qualities in adolescents. But if greater emphasis in art teaching is placed on the utilitarian or servile aspects of the arts, these obligations cannot be fulfilled. Teachers, therefore, should make every effort to cross the narrow border between free and servile art so that students will become intimately acquainted with significant art, which may or may not have had its origin in the more practical applications of visual art techniques and principles.

In the foregoing, the object has been to highlight some of the most significant meanings which are generally attached to the human phenomenon called art. Since it is obviously impossible to give a single, clear, all-embracing definition for the term "art," only those concepts were treated which have an immediate bearing on the education of adolescents. There was no attempt to unify these diverse concepts and to present the reader with a ready-made theory of art. On the contrary, the intention of the preceding discussion is to be thought-provoking and to assist in finding, or redefining, one's own concepts in regard to the teaching of art.

II The Creative Process

A number of other pertinent factors relating to the education of young people need serious consideration before one attempts to shape a final conviction about art education. Several of these factors will become apparent through a careful analysis of the creative process, with its numerous educational implications. For the purposes of the present discussion, the process is simplified and divided into three major complexes: perception, imagination, and experience. This artificial separation is permissible only for the sake of comprehensibility, for these complexes not only are closely knit but overlap. Nonetheless, each has a distinct function, and without the presence of all three we are severely hampered artistically although we may be capable of imitating or reproducing. A close examination of each in turn should lead to a more precise understanding of the creative process, and to a disclosure of its educational implications and contributions.

---

[23] *Ibid.*, p. 309.

Perception

In order to understand the complex of perception with its many different aspects, the term itself must first be classified. Most often "perception" refers to the significant impression which an object or an event produces on the mind through the various senses. It also implies that although an individual is consciously aware of the external world, he simultaneously—even if largely subconsciously—judges and exercises discrimination in what he perceives. This form of discrimination occurs because in any given situation our sensibilities will be more impressed by *one* particular aspect of perceived reality than by any other, and we will perceive more acutely those aspects which have a strong effect on us. This inherent characteristic of perception is of significance because it differentiates between perceiving and looking, and also, to some degree, between perceiving and observing.[24]

The term "observation" generally implies an objective gathering of data and facts, and therefore excludes any emotional reactions. We may ask, then, what is the essential difference between perception and observation? Why is it not enough merely to observe the external appearance of objects? After all, we can identify them and obtain much relevant information by simple observation. Yet observation as such often implies not more than noticing an incidental or accidental occurrence. Even if it is intentional, as it may be in any art room, mere observation will not immediately result in perception. "External objects usually affect various senses at once, the impressions of which are thereby associated. Repeated experiences of one object are also associated on account of their similarity, hence a double tendency to merge and unify into a single percept, to which a name is attached, the group of those memories and reactions which in fact had one external thing for their cause. But this percept, once formed, is clearly different from those particular experiences out of which it grew. It is permanent, they are variable. They are but partial views and glimpses of it. The constituted notion therefore comes to be the reality, and the materials of it merely the appearance. The distinction between substance and quality, reality and appearance, matter and mind, has no other origin."[25]

William James explains that the law of perception consists of two parts: one part of what we perceive comes through our senses from the object before us; the other part always comes out of our mind.[26] The mind recalls previous experiences which figure in our reaction to what the senses convey to the brain. The compound of reactions and collected sense-data is termed "perception." In addition, perception always implies that part of what has been noticed has left a distinct imprint on the mind. Alfred Adler defines perception thus:

> The impressions and stimuli which arise in the outer world are transmitted by means of the sense organs to the brain where certain traces of them may be retained. On these vestiges are built the world of imagination and the world of memory. But a perception is never to be compared with a photographic image because something of the peculiar and individual quality of the person who perceives is inextricably bound up with it. One does not perceive everything that one sees. No two human beings react in quite the same way to the identical picture; if we ask them what they have perceived they will give very diverse answers. A child perceives only that in his environment which fits into a behavior pattern previously determined by a variety of causes. The perceptions of

---

[24] "The ability and the quality of what is seen are not the same in all individuals even though they may have equally effective eyesight. The totality of perception goes beyond 'seeing' and involves comprehension. For examples of this fact one might consider the significance of such popular phrases as 'seeing through' something, or the existence of 'more than meets the eye.' Such phrases imply the sensing of time, space, and meaning of objects." Italo L. De Francesco, *Art Education, Its Means and Ends* (New York: Harper & Brothers, 1958), p. 100.

[25] Santayana, *The Sense of Beauty,* p. 36.

[26] William James, *Psychology* (New York: Henry Holt & Co., 1920), p. 329.

> children whose visual desire is especially well developed have a predominantly visual character. The majority of mankind is probably visual-minded. Others fill in the mosaic picture of the world which they have created for themselves with predominantly auditory perceptions. These perceptions need not be strictly identical with actuality. Everyone is capable of reconfiguring and rearranging his contacts with the outer world to fit his life pattern. The individuality and uniqueness of a human being consists of *what* he perceives and *how* he perceives.[27]

It is exactly at this point—with regard to what is perceived and how it is perceived—that education and art enter into the complex of perception. The "what" implies a kind of selection, the "how" indicates the dominance of one of the senses over the others. Most schools of psychology agree that in different individuals one sense may be more acutely developed, from a perceptual point of view, than any other. Adler, for instance, asserts that the majority of us react most strongly towards visual stimuli. Yet there is a sizable minority which is quite insensitive towards the visual world, and acutely aware of sound. These people can be separated into two groups: one which intensely perceives tone and rhythm (music); and a second which senses and feels keenly the configuration of sounds and/or verbal images (poetry, drama, and literature).

A basic knowledge of the various spheres of primary perceptions should be helpful to art teachers, particularly since their work is mostly directed towards individuals with pronounced visual perception. It has not been determined whether art instruction can be effective for those students who have predominantly auditory perception. The fact that many individuals are endowed with both acute visual and auditory perception further complicates the issue. Painters like Ingres, Doré, Klee, and Feininger also had strong *auditory* perception and were accomplished musicians. Composers like Mendelssohn and Schoenberg had pronounced *visual* perception, and left behind many drawings and paintings. The sculptor Barlach and the painter Blake had strong *verbal* perception and wrote plays and poetry. A great number of poets had keen visual perception, as is attested in their descriptive passages. Thus it would be a gross oversimplification to assume that we can divide students into auditory and visually perceptive groups, and provide art instruction only for the latter. At the time of writing, the available research on this point is too inconclusive to allow of any definite statement as to whether or not the spheres of perception can be altered with exposure or training. Until we have developed the means for accurately measuring the intensity of the different spheres of perception in individuals, it seems that we will have to accept the student's bias as a reliable indicator of his most acutely developed primary perception.

"*What* is perceived" needs still further elaboration. It implies a form of selection by means of which the teacher guides his students, as they are exposed to visual experiences.[28] In principle, the teacher should select every work of art to produce fresh and vigorous perceptual experiences. This selection is in itself a form of guidance. But still more important, each creative activity should be aimed at giving adolescents new and intense perceptions. There are two different means for achieving this aim. One is to expose students to carefully planned visual experiences. Precise verbal explanations will usually stimulate students to an intense awareness of the many different visual qualities confronting them. Texture, form, light and

---

[27] Alfred Adler, *Understanding Human Nature,* W. B. Wolfe, trans. (Philadelphia: Chilton Co., 1928), pp. 47–48.

[28] "A poem and picture present material passed through the alembic of personal experience. They have no precedents in existence or in universal being. But, nonetheless, their material came from the public world and so has qualities in common with the material of other experiences, while the product awakens in other persons new perceptions of the meaning of the common world." Dewey, *Art as Experience,* p. 82.

shadow, and size and color relationships need to be pointed out, and further explanation often is necessary to ensure that students will have a thorough comprehension of what they are viewing.

The other means for achieving intensified perception is to provide and encourage tactile experiences. When drawing, painting, or modeling the human figure (and also in many cases still lifes), students should be encouraged to employ touch perception. Actually feeling muscles, joints, and bones, either on the model or on their own bodies (or, with still lifes, touching the objects) should add considerably to the total perceptual experience. Also, whether he is a spectator or a creator, the individual must spend some time contemplating what he is perceiving, if he is to have fresh and significant perceptions.[29] "At first sign, 'contemplation' appears to be about as inept a term as could be selected to denote the excited and passionate absorption that often accompanies experience of a drama, a poem, or a painting. Attentive observation is certainly one essential factor in all genuine perception including the esthetic."[30]

As already indicated, there is still another type of perception which is directly related to the creation of visual art, hence to the teaching of art. This is perception by touch. The importance of tactile perception becomes apparent if one calls to mind the usual behavior of little children. The very small child touches indiscriminately any object within reach in order to examine and verify what he has seen. The same process takes place when adults are exposed to new forms, textures, or materials. Here again visual perception appears inadequate, and is often supplemented with tactile perception. Typical examples of the utilization of tactile perception can be observed in a department store where shoppers, moving from counter to counter, touch whatever is on display, often even without looking.

There are probably two major reasons why we rely strongly on tactile perception. First, visual perception excludes a number of significant sense-data. Vision does not tell us with any degree of certainty the hardness or softness of a material, or the weight or temperature of an object. Generally it is only by touch that we obtain this information. The second reason is that our visual perception often cannot be depended upon. In instances where the eye is easily fooled, tactile perception proves to be more reliable. Clever and/or faithful imitations of textures, materials, and forms many times can be detected only through touch.

Visual perception, when exposed to powerful experience, will frequently stimulate tactile perception—as is demonstrated by the need for "Do not touch" signs in museums. Within the realm of sculpture, tactile perception plays a most significant part. The attraction of three-dimensional creations, however, is based on visual as well as tactile perception. In principle, a work of sculpture affects us by its shape and the texture of its surface. The form appeals directly to the sense of vision, and the surface chiefly to the sense of touch. Until lately, sculptors spent much time and effort in achieving a surface pleasing to the touch as well as in creating an expressive form. In contrast, very recent welded metal sculptures confront us with a strange discrepancy between form and surface: by and large, these pieces are attractive to the eye and repulsive to the touch. Such a marked separation is an extremely sophisticated approach to the creation of three-dimensional forms and is

---

[29] "Gazing is such a wonderful thing, of which we still know so little; with it we are turned completely outward but just when we are most so, things seem to be going on in us that have waited longingly to be observed, and while they, untouched and curiously anonymous, achieve themselves in us *without us,*—their meaning is growing up in the object outside, a name convincing, strong, the only one possible for them, in which we blissfully and reverently recognize the event within us . . . ." *Letters of Rainer Maria Rilke,* Jane Bannard Greene and M. D. Herter Norton, trans. (New York: W. W. Norton & Co., 1945), p. 266.

[30] Dewey, *Art as Experience,* p. 82.

unprecedented in the history of art. From a perceptual point of view, surface and form have never befòre been sharply divorced, and this concept is foreign to most beginners of sculpture. The adolescent's interest in modeling and sculpturing is commonly divided equally in attention to form and surface.

Modeling, sculpturing, and pottery-making are the activities in which touch perception is an indispensable prerequisite. Many students who have strongly developed visual perception also will react keenly to tactile perception. This group will profit particularly by working in three dimensions and will establish a strong affinity for this form of creative expression. Frequently their appreciation for it is enhanced when their hands can feel the play of forms and the treatment of the surface.

From a perceptual point of view, great art works of the past lend themselves to division into several broad groups. One group consists predominantly of products of the imagination, another is composed of creations of fantasy, and a third embraces all works which are immediate results of direct perceptual experiences. (For further explanation of these terms see pp. 24–35.) Included in the last group are the many visual creations which are generally termed "works from nature." It should be emphasized that study from nature does *not* force individuals into a narrow channel which restricts their choice or mode of expression.[31] This is evident from the great variety of styles, concepts, and techniques employed by significant artists, which at once suggest that responses to fresh visual perceptions vary considerably. If we compare portraits painted from models, we see plainly that freedom of choice and expression exists even though the theme is very narrow and rich in objective facts. As another example, we might cite the landscape paintings of southern France by Cézanne, Van Gogh, and Derain; or the paintings of Paris by Monet, Van Gogh, and Utrillo. Most of these works are the result of immediate perceptions, and each artist attempted to be completely faithful to the truth in portraying his surroundings, but nonetheless these paintings are utterly different from one another and in fact have little in common.

While the creative process is largely based on the ability to perceive intensely, it does not matter whether the perceptual experience is *immediately* transformed into a creative statement or collected and retained and expressed at a later time. Retained perceptions provide the raw material for the imagination, and imagination plays a significant part in the creative process. Finally, it should be pointed out that the enjoyment of visual art is fundamentally a perceptual experience. By contrast, observation—which need not be synonymous with enjoyment—is essentially conceptual, for it recognizes and classifies only in terms of form, size, material, color, style, subject matter, and purpose.

Empathy

Empathy is akin to perception and plays a prominent part within the creative process. The term "empathy" (a vague equivalent for the German word "Einfühlung," whose approximate literal translation is "feeling one's way into") signifies

---

[31] "A distinction is made between artists who work directly from nature and those who work purely from their imagination. I think neither of these methods should be preferred to the exclusion of the other. Often both are used in turn by the same man; sometimes he needs tangible objects to provide him with sensations and thus excite his creative power; at other times when his pictorial sensations are already present in his mind he needs contact with reality before he can organize them into a picture. However, I think that one can judge of the vitality and power of an artist when after having received impressions from nature he is able to organize his sensations to return in the same mood on different days, voluntarily to continue receiving these impressions (whether nature appears the same or not); this power proves he is sufficiently master of himself to subject himself to discipline." Henri Matisse, *Notes of a Painter* (New York: Museum of Modern Art, 1931), p. 35.

the ability to project oneself into anything outside of one's self. Empathy can also be described as self-identification with perception.

> Empathy occurs in the moment one human being speaks with another. It is impossible to understand another individual if it is impossible at the same time to identify oneself with him. Drama is the artistic expression of empathy. Other examples of empathy are those cases in which someone has a strange feeling of uneasiness when he notices another in danger. This empathy may be so strong that one makes involuntary defense movements, even though there is no danger to oneself. We all know the well known gesture which is made when someone has dropped his glass! . . . A common expression is the involuntary application of imaginary brakes by the occupants of a motor car whenever they feel that they are in danger. . . . In the theater particularly we can hardly avoid identifying ourselves with the players, or prevent ourselves from acting the most varied roles within ourselves. Our entire life is very much dependent upon the faculty of identification. If we seek for the origin of this ability to act and feel as if we were someone else, we can find it in the existence of an inborn social feeling. This is, as a matter of fact, a cosmic feeling and a reflection of the connectedness of the whole cosmos which lives in us; it is an inescapable characteristic of being a human being. It gives us the faculty of identifying ourselves with things which are quite outside our own body.[32]

This "faculty of identifying ourselves with things which are quite outside our own body" is a vital component of the creative act. Without empathy we may well be able to *imitate* what has been observed, but we are hardly capable of *creating.* As stated previously, recorded observations are not creations. The uniqueness of any creation is mostly a compound of reflected perception and empathy. In essence, ". . . a work of art is not the record of a bare matter of fact, but the projection of the artist's inspiration, his emotions, preferences, or sense of value."[33]

It is not difficult to understand how empathy enters into the relationship of man to man, or how it affects an artist's creative representation of a human being. Regardless of whether such a representation results from a study of a living model or is done from memory, many artists are bound to project part of themselves into their creations. Similarly, students working in an art class mimic the model's pose or facial expression without being aware of it. But it is harder to comprehend how an artist or a spectator can project himself into an inanimate object.[34] "The work of art, however concrete and objective, is not constant or inevitable in its effect: it demands the cooperation of the spectator, and the energy which the spectator 'puts into' the work of art has been given the special name of 'empathy'. . . ."[35]

Countless works of visual art impress the spectator as "lifelike" or "real," and he tends to forget that what he actually sees is a lifeless, inert object. This "real," "lifelike," or expressive quality is felt by the spectator because he projects himself into the inanimate creation. Visualizing a large building in one's mind, for example, one may wonder how a person could experience empathy in relation to such a structure. The German psychologist Theodor Lipps states: "In viewing a large hall I feel an inner 'expansion,' my heart 'expands;' I have this peculiar sense of what is happening within me. Connected with it are muscle-tensions, perhaps those involved in the expansion of the chest. To be sure, they do not exist for my consciousness, so

---

[32] Adler, *Understanding Human Nature,* pp. 60–61.
[33] Rader, *A Modern Book of Esthetics,* p. xv.
[34] "In varying degrees, artists tend to project their own experiences into an unfinished work of art. For example, the sculptor imagines his block of stone as possessed of inner life and muscular tensions. Van Gogh projected his own emotional agitations into his paintings of trees, clouds, rocks, and houses." Thomas Munro, *Art Education, Its Philosophy and Psychology* (New York: The Liberal Arts Press, 1956), p. 95.
[35] Herbert Read, *Education through Art* (New York: Pantheon Books, 1945), p. 24.

long as my attention is directed to the spacious hall. But it is possible that this fact may not prevent an esthetician from confusing the feeling of inner expansion with this sensation of the body expanding with its muscle tension."[36]

This raises the question: To what degree is empathy related to kinesthetic feelings? ("Kinesthetic" means muscular sensations stimulated by any of our senses and/or emotional tensions.) The main difference between empathy and kinesthetic feelings is that empathy need not necessarily result in physical sensations, although it frequently does. How far kinesthetic sensations enter into empathy depends on how intensely an individual becomes absorbed in the object he is viewing, and how far his self remains in his foremost consciousness. "Empathy simply means the disappearance of the two-fold consciousness of self and object, and the enrichment of experience that results from this interpenetration. So completely is the self transported into the object that the contemplator of a statue, for example, may unconsciously imitate its posture and implied movement by definite muscular adjustments."[37] These unconscious imitations of the posture of a statue well demonstrate to what an extent kinesthetic sensations may enter into the whole complex of empathy.

There still remains the important question: To what degree does empathy contribute to the development of creativity in adolescents? The ability to identify oneself with something other than one's own body or one's own achievement is, according to Adler, poorly developed in very young children. "Cases of cruelty to animals which we see in childhood," Adler says, "were impossible without an almost total absence of the social feeling, and the ability to identify with other living beings."[38] Empathy apparently develops more slowly than other mental faculties. Young children are often unable to project themselves into anything with which they are not intimately acquainted and which is not part of their immediate environment. This limited ability to experience empathy is one of the principal reasons why grade school children so often remain unaffected by great works of visual art.

It is characteristic for adolescents, on the other hand, that their ability to identify themselves with others is already developed to a considerable degree; we have cause to believe that their preoccupation with the creative activity strengthens their capability to experience empathy. The more willing a student is to immerse himself in creative work, and the more he identifies himself with what he is creating, the more intensely he experiences empathy. This not only augments his creative ability, but strengthens him as a social being. The creative activity helps accustom him to utilizing empathy in a constructive manner.

To sum up: The capacity to put oneself into another's place, to identify oneself with one's fellow man—which is empathy—is an essential for effective and adjusted social behavior. Here again, we can find a direct connection between the art activity and the total education of adolescents.

Imagination

The development of creativity and the ability to perceive within and around oneself is directly related to one's capacity for conceiving mental images. Mental images are the product of the imagination, based on sense-data collected largely through perception and retained by the memory. "By imagination we mean the reproduction of a perception without the presence of the object itself which gave rise to it. In other words, imagination is reproduced perception:—another evidence of the creative faculty of the soul. The product of imagination is not only the repe-

---

[36] Rader, *A Modern Book of Esthetics,* p. 302.
[37] *Ibid.,* p. 288.
[38] Adler, *Understanding Human Nature,* p. 62.

tition of perception (which in itself is a product of the creative power of the soul), but it is an entirely new and unique product built upon the basis of the perception, just as the perception was created on the basis of physical sensations."[39]

Before discussing imagination in relation to the creative process, it may be wise to give some thought to its whole function, which extends beyond the limited aspect of artistic creation. Imagination is a fundamental necessity for man's progress, and a primary aid for his survival. To demonstrate this we need only ask what the result would be if an individual were to lose his faculty to imagine. Being unable to envision anything pertaining to his future, his drive and initiative would cease to exist, and his capacity to plan would be annihilated. These capacities depend on the ability to form mental images, for without them we would be incapable of "seeing" ourselves pursuing some goal, or performing in a "tomorrow." Whenever the following day becomes a reality in our minds, we are automatically employing our powers of imagination.

A great deal of misunderstanding exists in regard to the function of imagination. The two most prevalent misconceptions are that imagination is either a substitute for reality or an escape from it. People rarely stop to consider that most great ideas, important inventions, and enduring artistic creations first were conceived as *intangible* images in the mind of man. Visionary images rising in the imagination led to the search for ways of translating them into reality, which finally resulted in their physical existence. For example, man imagined for centuries that he could fly, an image based on his perception of birds in flight. Scores of ancient fables tell how man transformed himself into birdlike creatures, and this concept, which can be traced back to the legendary Icarus with his bird's wings, culminated in Leonardo da Vinci's "Flying Machine." However, in spite of many attempts man did not succeed in translating this mental image into a practicable, tangible equivalent before our century. There we have demonstrated one aspect of the relationship between perception, empathy, imagination, and creation.

It would be wrong to suppose that imagination is synonymous with mental images alone or that it manifests itself solely in visual terms. William James distinguishes plainly between visual, tactile, and aural imagination. There are many examples of aural imagination in accounts by great authors who claim to have merely recorded conversations heard in their mind's ear. Tales told by small children also reflect strongly the flow of auditory or verbal imagination. In many cases these stories are more elaborate, in terms of imagination, than their corresponding visual images on paper. Hypothetical explanations for this discrepancy are not hard to find. One is that externalizing the imagination in pictorial form demands a lucid comprehension of precise fact and a more pronounced logical structure than the verbal expression of imagination, if it is to appear credible. This is true even though the visualized imagination is represented in broad and simple generalizations, such as one sees in art works of very young children. Another explanation is that verbalized imagination is fleeting and without permanency, whereas the depicted imagination is tangible and permanent, accessible to scrutiny and evaluation by both the creator and the spectator. It seems likely that the fleeting and vague quality of verbalized imagination permits the child to take liberties which he would not dare to take in his two- or three-dimensional works.

The older a child becomes the more restricted he will feel in formulating his visual imagination adequately, both for the reasons already stated and because simplified generalizations no longer satisfy him. This is partly caused by his awareness of his limited command of skill, which inevitably comes during some phase of the maturing process, and which not only hampers him in expressing his imagination

[39] *Ibid.*, p. 49.

but is often another source of dissatisfaction. With older students, therefore, we need to distinguish between the *range* of their imagination and their ability and willingness to transfer it into visual expression. We are confronted by two distinct entities, one being the imagination and the other the skill needed to express what the mind envisions. Since any creative process requires some degree of skill during the act of externalizing the imagination, one can fairly claim that it is part of the art teacher's obligation to equip adolescents with sufficient skill to express their mental images. Obviously the need for skill increases with the maturity and experience of the individual.

Sudden manifestations, or spurts, of creative thoughts and images also belong to the realm of imagination. They are what is commonly called "artistic inspiration," and are frequently nothing but a conscious awareness of flashes of the imagination. They may be the result of the frenzied working of the intellect freed from the confines of words. They may consist of a mixture of factual information, retained perceptions, and the emotional reactions to both.

To sum up, the imagination is largely constituted of an array of different perceptions which are reassembled in our minds in such a manner as to continue to bear valid semblance to reality.[40] This same point relates to the distinction between imagination and fantasy.

Fantasy

The term "fantasy" implies the assembling of perceptions which no longer bear close resemblance to reality, but are freely grouped and fused in an unprecedented manner. Many paintings by Bosch, Klee, and Chagall, and a large segment of the graphic works of Goya, exemplify this unparalleled and often denaturalized aggregation of various perceptions. As opposed to their works of fantasy, Michelangelo's murals in the Sistine Chapel are products of the imagination. Other typical examples are Rembrandt's paintings and etchings depicting Biblical themes, many Delacroix and Daumier paintings and lithographs, and most works by recent expressionists. Although different perceptions are fused in all these creations, they remain closely related to that aspect of reality which originally aroused the artist's imagination. None of these artists intentionally violated laws of nature in their representations, nor did they depict forms in a manner dissimilar to nature.

In essence, fantasy is a variable of imagination and is another significant factor in the creative process. Adler points out that it is impossible to lay down exact rules for what belongs strictly to the realm of imagination and what pertains only to fantasy. Certainly traces of fantasy can be found in every sphere of the imagination. "Fantasy is but another creative faculty of the soul. . . . Just as the projection of certain memories into the sharp focus of consciousness, or the erection of the bizarre superstructure of the imagination, fantasy and day-dreaming are to be considered part of the creative activity of the soul. . . . Fantasy is bound up with the mobility of the human organism and is indeed nothing more than a method of pre-

[40] "Imagination is sometimes misunderstood as the inventions of new subject matter. In that view an imaginative artist is one who creates situations of which no one else has thought before or which have never existed or never could exist. Actually the achievement of artistic imagination could be described more correctly as the finding of new form for old content, or—if the handy dichotomy of form and content is not used—as a fresh concept of an old subject. The invention of new things or situations is valuable only to the extent to which they serve to interpret an old—that is universal—topic of human experience. In fact artistic imagination reveals itself most strikingly in the presentation of common objects and well-worn stories. There is more imagination in the way Titian paints a hand than in hundreds of surrealist nightmares depicted in a dull, conventional manner." Rudolf Arnheim, *Art and Visual Perception* (Berkeley: University of California Press, 1954), pp. 113–114.

vision and prescience. The fantasies of children and grown-ups, sometimes called day-dreams, are always concerned with the future, the 'castles in the air' are the goal of their activity, built up in fictional form as models for real activity."[41] In this context fantasy is linked with unrealized accomplishments. Very often frustrated ambitions, wishes for achievement and personal success, and desires for changed situations find expression in fantasy. The "daydream"—a not infrequent form of fantasy—is the least constructive. Like any dream, it is fleeting and illusory, and often has a depressing aftereffect on the individual.

Still, to a large degree, fantasy is a creative force, provided it is channelled into constructive outlets and given expression and permanence. In such instances it will elate rather than depress the normal individual.

> There is, in fact [says Freud], a path from phantasy and back again to reality, and that is—art. . . . The way back to reality is found by the artist thus: he is not the only one who has a life of phantasy; the intermediate world of phantasy is sanctioned by a general human consent, and every hungry soul looks to it for comfort and consolation. But to those who are not artists, the gratification that can be drawn from the springs of phantasy is very limited; their inexorable repressions prevent the enjoyment of all but the meager day-dreams which can become conscious. A true artist has more at his disposal. First of all he understands how to elaborate his day-dreams, so that they lose that personal note which grates upon strange ears and becomes enjoyable to others; he knows, too, how to modify them sufficiently so that their origin in prohibited sources is not easily detected. Further, he possesses the mysterious ability to mold his particular material until it expresses the ideas of his phantasy faithfully; and then he knows how to attach to this reflection of his phantasy-life so strong a stream of pleasure that, for a time at least, the repressions are out-balanced and dispelled by it. When he can do all this, he opens out to others the way back to the comfort and consolation of their own unconscious sources of pleasure, and so reaps their gratitude and admiration; then he has won—through his phantasy—what before he could only win in phantasy: action, achievement and recognition.[42]

It is uncertain to what extent the average high school student is willing to give expression to his fantasy. For one thing, many aspects of fantasy deal with topics which are socially unacceptable or too involved to lend themselves to visual representation. For another, genuine fantasy is a highly personal facet of the imagination, and adolescents often shy away from revealing publicly such intimate creative images. Also, students frequently resort to one of the many stereotyped forms of fantasy, as for example the flying carpet, or Superman, or Pogo-like animals. In such instances already existing forms of fantasy are employed as substitutes for genuinely *new* fantastic creations.

On the other hand, fantasy is an aspect of the imagination over which the individual has no control. It is therefore quite unreasonable to believe that a teacher could force or stimulate the mind of a student to produce objects of fantasy on demand. Although any trained art teacher should be able to stimulate students' minds to recall, rearrange, and relive past perceptions and experiences, something more than verbal stimulation seems to be required to induce fantastic imagery. This "something more" is a particular mood which must take possession of the entire individual. Since students are rarely able to become totally involved in the creative process during a sandwiched-in art session in an ordinary school day, they encounter great difficulties in portraying aspects of genuine fantasy. Even subjects which actually deal with fantasy seldom produce new and original free assembling of facts and memorized perceptions. In our day "men from Mars," for instance, have become as stereotyped as the Falstaffian figure of Santa Claus. Still, now and then an art

---

[41] Adler, *Understanding Human Nature,* p. 57.
[42] Sigmund Freud, *A General Introduction to Psycho-Analysis,* trans. Joan Riviere (New York: Liveright Publishing Corp., 1935), pp. 327–28.

instructor does find a strange, bizarre, capricious, or dreamlike work created by a student, and when this happens he should protect the youngster from unwarranted criticism from his peers. He may also consider such a work a token of personal success, for it symbolizes a pupil's confidence and trust in his teacher.

Experience

Another important element in the creative process requiring further comment is that which is generally referred to as experience. The German language recognizes two distinct meanings in this term and assigns a word to each. The word "Erfahrung" denotes a useful knowledge gained empirically through experiments or accidental happenings; the word "Erlebnis," which derives from "Leben" (life), means an event that moves us, leaves a marked impression, and is retained by the mind. In English these two quite different ideas are expressed by the same word, "experience," which in itself creates confusion. Moreover, in current usage the term is applied so liberally and indiscriminately that it has all but lost its meaning. It is used to infer that one has learned—in an informal way—almost anything; it even serves as a substitute for "being alive." Expressions like "living experience," "daily experience," and "social experience" are cases in point. Yet mere existence is not synonymous with experience! Every day we are exposed to, and participate in, myriad happenings which leave no marked impression or are not consciously registered by our minds, and certainly cannot constitute experience. Unthinking scribbling on a piece of paper is not an "art experience" any more than walking down a crowded sidewalk, rubbing elbows with other pedestrians, is a "social experience." In Dewey's words, "It is possible to be efficient in action and yet not have a conscious experience. The activity is too automatic to permit of a sense of what it is about and where it is going. It comes to an end but not to a close or consummation in consciousness."[43]

Life is dynamic, a continuous flow of events, happenings, and changes. By contrast, experience is static, a process in which an event becomes separated from a chain of happenings and is arrested and retained by the mind as an isolated occurrence. It is static regardless of whether its quality is vital and dramatic or poetic and lyrical, and no matter how weak or strong its aftereffect on the mind. A major characteristic of experience is that the events which precede and succeed the experienced occurrence are largely forgotten by the individual who undergoes it.

Whenever the term "experience" is used to signify the acquisition of knowledge, it means knowledge gained as a result of trial and error. But not all of our knowledge stems from firsthand experience. In many learning situations we are exposed to the results of the trials and errors of others, and our mind retains these findings or conclusions. Laws of composition or perspective are typical examples of this form of secondhand experience. In addition, there are many kinds of knowledge which are not based on *either* direct or indirect experiences. By reading an out-of-doors thermometer from inside the house, for instance, we learn the outside temperature without having an actual physical experience with the atmosphere. Our knowledge of light years or of the circumference of the moon is based chiefly on calculations and is not the result of direct experience. Nor is Einstein's theory of relativity the outcome of tangible experience. In this instance, thought came first and experience afterwards, and it was many years before Einstein found proof in physical reality of the correctness of his reasonings and calculations.

To believe, therefore, that acquiring knowledge is identical with experience would seem to be an oversimplification of what is involved in the act of learning, and adds to the confusion over the meaning of the term "experience." It is, however,

---

[43] Dewey, *Art as Experience,* p. 38.

valid to say that through firsthand experience one can gain knowledge, even though most of it is acquired in an informal and unplanned manner. For example, a curious little child touches hot water in a white vessel and feels a pain in his hand. From this hurtful experience he may have learned either that white vessels can cause painful burns or that hot water in a vessel is the cause of unpleasant sensations. In other words, it is possible to draw the wrong conclusion from an isolated experience. Therefore, when speaking of "learning by experience," we usually refer to numerous experiences of a similar nature which have been unified. Our actual learning consists of the conclusion reached after several experiences whose consequences were similar, and from which we finally extracted a general principle.[44] In the case cited, this would be that hot water, not white vessels, can cause pain.

Certain forms of experimentation also can result in experience; in fact, until recent times the two words "experience" and "experiment" were synonyms. Today the term "experiment" still generally applies to an empirical form of learning, or learning by trial and error. All of us have learned that leaving an egg in boiling water for a number of minutes will result in changing the albumen from a liquid to a firm substance. This knowledge is empirical, and does not entail an understanding of the cause of the change, nor provide us with the biochemical explanation for the transformation of albumen in different temperatures. Learning by experience acquaints us with the effects and results of certain actions or processes, but it leaves the explanation of the cause which produces these results to quite a different branch of learning—one which is not based on direct experience but on additional examination, reasoning, induction, deduction, and reflective thinking.[45]

So far only those experiences have been discussed which pertain to forms of learning. But of equal or greater significance to the creative process are those experiences which relate to powerful emotional reactions and impressions derived from persons, objects, or events. When we speak of "having had an experience," we are generally referring to an incident which has had an immediate and strong impact on our emotions and at least momentarily has captured our *total* attention. This attention is twofold: one part is focused on ourself, particularly on the emotions and reactions which immediately take possession of our consciousness; the other part is centered on those facts which are intensely perceived and leave indelible impressions on our mind. For example, we unwittingly witness an accident where a child is hurt. We see the crying youngster and simultaneously feel an emotional shock. Later on we will remember both what we saw and how we felt seeing it. Another distinctive feature of emotional experience is that all peripheral sensations and happenings are obliterated, and that the event as such and our intense emotional responses to it remain foremost in our memory.

Usually we connect emotional experiences with pleasurable or painful feelings, joyful or sorrowful ones, expressible in definable concepts such as anger, fear, joy, elation. We are likely to believe that such experiences must always be spectacular or dramatic. In actuality, many incidents which constitute significant emotional ex-

---

[44] "The essence of knowledge is *generalization.* That fire can be produced by rubbing wood in a certain way is a knowledge derived by generalizing from individual experiences; the statement means that rubbing wood in this way will *always* produce fire. The art of discovery is therefore the art of correct generalization. What is irrelevant, such as the particular shape or size of the piece of wood used, is to be excluded from the generalization; what is relevant, for example, the dryness of the wood, is to be included in it. The meaning of the term 'relevant' can thus be defined: that is relevant which must be mentioned for the generalization to be valid. The separation of relevant from irrelevant factors is the beginning of knowledge." Hans Reichenbach, *The Rise of Scientific Philosophy* (Berkeley: University of California Press, 1957), p. 5.

[45] "The perceptible world is like the shadows on the wall of the cave. Thought alone can reveal to us the existence of a higher reality, of which visible objects are but poor images." *Ibid.*, p. 253.

periences are not dramatic, nor do they force us into the few general, recognizable groups of emotional responses. For instance, if an artist looks intently at a decayed piece of wood, he may be fascinated by many minute forms and colors. He may discover subtle shades, unusual textures, and pronounced rhythmical patterns. All of these visual properties arouse emotions in him. Yet these emotions cannot be generalized, labeled, or verbally described. The only way for the artist to express what he sees and experiences is to formulate it visually so that it will arouse a similar emotion in the spectator. A conscientious artist is satisfied with his work only if he feels that it can kindle in another individual the emotions that inspired it. In order to judge success or failure by this criterion, the artist becomes, quasi-automatically, the first spectator of his own work.

One other major characteristic of emotional experience is that it produces a strong desire for action, most commonly verbal. But as already indicated, countless emotional experiences can be expressed only in media other than words: numerous paintings and musical compositions as well as works of literature stem from this desire for action and for giving form to emotional experiences. In many instances it is possible for us to trace the exact connection between an emotional experience and the resulting creative work. This does not mean, however, that these forms of artistic expression are immediate, echolike reactions. Often considerable time passes between the actual experience and the creative expression which it motivated. As a rule, emotional experiences can be vividly recalled without difficulty, and when this occurs the original urge for action or expression also is revitalized. Art teachers often can stimulate students to relive in their minds past emotional experiences; these, in turn, remotivate their desire for expression.

The two meanings of the term "experience" ("learning" and "being moved by") have in common that we attempt to draw general conclusions or to extract valid principles from both types. Having learned from several analogous experiences that certain happenings frequently have the same effects or results, we form conclusions which we retain and reapply in comparable situations. In a manner similar to the learning experience, we frequently carry over the effects of previous emotional experiences to related situations. We draw conclusions from emotional experiences, and these influence our attitude towards or during new experiences. For instance, when we listen to a Beethoven symphony for the first time, the music may stimulate us and temporarily take total possession of our minds; it may satisfy certain aesthetic impulses and leave with us the desire to hear more. From such a rewarding emotional experience we usually draw the general conclusion that we enjoy Beethoven's music, meaning that we expect to delight in *all* his works. But as has been pointed out before, these generalizations commonly are valid only if based on a number of homogeneous experiences; a single experience may well lead to misconceptions and prejudices. It may turn out that we do not like all of Beethoven's works, finding no pleasure, for example, in his chamber music. Similarly, a painting of a particular style or with a particular subject may arouse a spontaneous aversion, which we may transfer to works of a like nature, or it may turn us against all paintings by a particular artist.

In these examples, the object has been to illustrate how emotional experiences subsequently lead to generalizations, and how these generalizations in turn influence our actions and choices. Here, specifically, learning experience and emotional experience overlap.

Up to this point the nature of experience has not been discussed. Essentially, it is an intensive form of perception from which, almost simultaneously, generalizations are made and conclusions are drawn. To state it another way, experience is intensive perception fused with immediate emotional reactions and conclusions.

The main difference between perception and experience is that perception is an intensive absorption of reality, whereas experience includes the *reaction* to the perception from an emotional as well as from an intellectual point of view. In many instances reactions to experience, or conclusions derived from it, are of more significance than the occasion which evoked them, because the reactions are preserved much longer in the mind of an individual. Numerous likes and dislikes, preferences and rejections, are based on past experiences which left a deep impression on the mind. The experiences themselves slowly fade from memory, and only the reaction to them or their effects linger on. These reactions and effects often influence the artist's point of view, determining not only his approach to reality but his representation of it. For instance: on a visit to the cathedral at Chartres, an artist was overwhelmed at the sight of the beautiful stained glass windows of this medieval church. What he felt and perceived there left a strong impression; he underwent a powerful experience. The brilliant colors in filigree-like arrangement embedded in a network of black lines were retained so vividly in his mind that he later used this combination in his own work without consciously remembering his previous experience.

This example illustrates only one aspect of the many-faceted relationship between experience and its lingering effects. As already implied, the more lasting effects figure prominently in the relationship between experience and creativity. To understand this relationship more fully, we must distinguish among three major kinds of experience connected with the creative process: the experience which *precedes* the creative act and gives rise to the creative impulse; that which occurs *during* the actual formulation of the creative thought; and that which takes place immediately *after* the completion of the creative work.

"Experience is the source of every work of art—experience as a fund of material from which the artist, eliminating what is irrelevant, selects, emphasizes and reorganizes the phases which interest him, and creates out of them a characteristic personal form."[46] Unquestionably, innumerable experiences, predominantly of an emotional nature, must have taken place before an individual is able to create. They must have been sufficiently intense to be recollected; and, more important, they must have been of such a nature as to instill the desire for expression.

In the final analysis, any artistic creation is a particular generalization based on one or several experiences. What makes one work of art so different from any other (even from those of a similar nature or on a similar subject) is the artist's personal experience embedded in the work. When he portrays aspects of his world, he not only states what he perceives, but also imbues it with the related experience. For, as John Dewey said, "The poem, or painting, does not operate in the dimension of correct descriptive statement but in that of experience itself."[47]

Many fallacies exist about those experiences which must take place before an individual is able to create. One of the commonest misconceptions, encountered even among art teachers, is that experience presupposes a concrete physical involvement. But in the realm of creativity an individual makes use of many kinds of experiences other than those in which he literally participated. His imagination and fantasy provide him with innumerable experiences which occur only in his mind; these experiences, often consisting of vivid visions, leave powerful images in the recesses of his memory and inspire his will to create. Other sources of similar "imaginary" emotional experiences are passages of novels, short stories or the Bible, poems, and musical compositions. Modern mass communication media provide countless opportunities for listeners and spectators to undergo strong experiences. For example,

---

[46] Albert C. Barnes and Violette de Mazia, *The Art of Henri-Matisse* (New York: Charles Scribner's Sons, 1933), p. 43.
[47] Dewey, *Art as Experience,* p. 85.

through empathy a spectator may experience intensely the terror and panic of a volcanic eruption, an earthquake, or a forest fire without ever literally having lived through such situations. The historic past and the imaginary future also are ever-present sources for experiences independent of those we may encounter during our daily affairs.

Our everyday experiences are frequently casual, and many persons as they mature become increasingly more callous towards them. By contrast, the reaction of small children to everyday events is much like that of adult visitors in a foreign land: what is quite common and of no particular interest to the native they find exciting and new. The uniform of a mailman, the color and shape of a bus, even a tramway ticket may be invested with glamour for the tourist in a strange country. Similarly, daily happenings to which the older child and the adult have become quite indifferent still hold many new and exciting experiences for younger children. That the creative artist too is sensitive to the many familiar events which occur during the day is attested by the numerous sketches by important artists, in which they have recorded almost indiscriminately, but with great delicacy, seemingly insignificant details of their ordinary surroundings. Usually a creative person remains sensitive even to diverse "minor" experiences.

Finally—and this is the key to understanding the relationship between creativity and experience—the creative person is plagued by neither apathy nor lassitude, and continues to respond to ordinary as well as to extraordinary experiences, to real as well as to imaginary ones. He recognizes that all these experiences are the raw materials from which we create.

An entirely different set of experiences is encountered as soon as an individual attempts to transform previous experiences into concrete creative expression. At the very beginning of such an undertaking his actions and their immediate results are the source of new experiences. The first line or brush stroke on a clean flat surface immediately triggers a burst of new sensations which frequently are transformed into experiences. These experiences are twofold: one aspect refers to the learning process which automatically takes place during the formulation of the creative thought, and the other to the emotional impact of the creative act on the creator. The emotional impact, again, consists of two parts: one derives from recalling previous experiences which led to the creative impulse, and the other is the outcome of the animation which results from participation in the creative act. This animation or excitement is commonly most pronounced during the initial phases of the creative undertaking, but it often recurs strongly when the work nears completion. It is a necessary part of the creative act, and a teacher's stimulation should be aimed at producing this form of excitement.

The whole process of formulating experiences and thoughts into creative expression can be divided into three basic phases. In the initial stage the rudiments of creative concepts are roughly defined and delineated. The subsequent development of or elaboration on the initial effort is the intermediate stage, leading to the last phase in which the work is refined. It is during this final phase that most artists try to recapture the freshness of their first attempts.

The beginning work on any creative project is of vital importance since it often determines future success or failure. During the brief span while the creator comes to grips for the first time with hitherto undefined creative thoughts, his initial outline or rough sketch many times seems to possess a hypnotic quality—a quality which apparently makes him forget other possibilities for developing his creative idea and forces his imagination into a narrow path which restricts his freedom of choice. The sudden materialization of definite thoughts and visions which were intangibles only moments ago has still other important implications; it can act either as a stimulator or an inhibitor. Not surprisingly, the initial stage is frequently characterized by a significant emotional experience in which hopes are high or frustrations endured.[48] During this phase the artist often plays a dual role: he is both the creator and the spectator watching the unfolding of his own creative thoughts. For this brief period any form of outside interference is most detrimental to the artist or student, and endangers the success of his work.

All this is changed in the second phase when the initial attempts of the creative work are developed. These initial attempts, the first sketchy outlines, are, so to speak, expositions of a self-imposed problem, and the ensuing development equals a search for the problem's solution. During this phase most artists or students are primarily occupied with intellectual considerations; relationships between forms, colors, and space become objects of conscious concern. Previous experiences with materials and techniques enter prominently into the creative act, and difficulties with media and expression are acutely experienced. The teacher usually has an excellent opportunity to exercise guidance during this stage.

The form his guidance will take depends on the nature of the difficulty and on the individual student's background and experience with art expression. One of the student's commonest difficulties during the working out of a creative problem is born of his sudden bewilderment and indecision. His sketchy lines, scantily applied colors, and vaguely defined forms and shapes become a perplexing sight in his eyes, and he feels that he is caught in a maze from which he cannot escape. Nothing looks right to him, but he is unable to put his finger on what is wrong. The teacher's approach in such cases should be rather direct, consisting of sympathetic but pointed questions which should enable the student to determine his difficulty, thereby narrowing his problem into specifics. Help of this kind usually gives him the means to overcome the obstacle and to go on with the work unassisted. When this approach appears inadequate, there are several alternatives. One is to show and analyze reproductions of works by important artists which depict different approaches to a similar pictorial problem. The analysis should be aimed at stimulating the student's thinking in the proper areas so that he will discover a way to surmount his difficulty. Such an approach fuses great art and learning in a most efficient and meaningful manner. Another alternative is to re-expose the student to perceptual experiences similar to the one he is attempting to express. Intensively restudying forms, colors, and their relationships as they can be found in the immediate surroundings often produces answers to the student's problem.

However, it cannot be sufficiently emphasized that one approach which should never be used is to present the student with a ready-made solution to his problem. Only by sheer coincidence could such a solution be the very one for which the student is searching; moreover, a pupil who would blindly accept and carry out such a random solution would learn nothing save how to become a dependent follower.

During this second phase of creative activity the teacher is given an excellent opportunity for spontaneous guidance. Even more important, he can discover the exact need of each one of his students and thus plan succeeding lessons most effectively.

In the brief period immediately preceding the completion of a creative work, the differences between the experienced or professional artist and the beginner or student become most pronounced. During this short, final stage the accomplished artist will exert considerable effort to unify the many different elements in his composition. Usually he does this by simplifying lines and shapes, by accentuating some forms and colors, by eliminating details which have acquired undue prominence, or by re-emphasizing minute parts which have become indistinct. But above all, the artist knows when he has arrived at the point where he should stop working. This

---

[48] "It is a question as to whether one is more thrilled at beginning a work than at finishing it. I think beginning is the more exciting. The finished work—well, there it is." Jacob Epstein, *Let There Be Sculpture* (New York: G. P. Putnam's Sons, 1940), p. 138.

knowledge is the result of many creative experiences. It is a common occurrence that students, lacking experience, either will relinquish their work without this last effort, or else will continue to labor until it has altogether lost its freshness and immediacy, and reflects nothing but sweat and strain. Sometimes not knowing when to stop or when to continue robs students of the deep enjoyment derived from having achieved a satisfactory piece of work. This inner satisfaction is one of the most important experiences related to the creative process. There is no stronger incentive to further creative achievements than a spontaneous feeling of having succeeded. It is evident, therefore, that the art teacher should concentrate on helping students attain this inner gratification by careful guidance during the last phases of executing a creative idea. The teacher also should do everything in his power to make the completed work so presentable that students will truly experience their deserved success.

The experiences related to or immediately resulting from the completion of a creative work differ markedly from those which occur before or during any creative act. It is a characteristic of this type of experience that it is unique: it does not exist in any other comparable form nor result from any other activity. Its intensity depends on the degree of effort exerted by the creator during the execution of the work. Assuming that an artist, or student, exerted great effort to achieve what he intended to accomplish, the experience of suddenly finding himself confronted by his completed work can have both elating and depressing effects.

The depressing effect is due largely to having been intensely occupied for a considerable period of time with the problem of expressing thoughts and feelings creatively and convincingly, and then all at once being faced by the solved problem. For a moment the artist, or student, is without direction. He feels somewhat at a loss; nothing seems left to be done. Perhaps he is beset by doubts; he feels uncertain; he questions himself as to how far he has actually succeeded. He may gaze at his accomplishment, wondering what he should have avoided or what he could still do to improve his work. This doubt and emptiness, this temporary feeling of being in a vacuum, constitutes an experience which belongs with the creative process. It is frequently followed by a creative pause—what could be termed an emotional rest period. This kind of pause should be respected by every art teacher. It appears in many art rooms many times, even if rarely in such pronounced form as described here. These emotional rest periods are often the explanation for the unevenness of students' work. A careful study of each student's various products frequently reveals a pattern of achievement and creative pause.

The immediate emotional reaction experienced by a creator when he finally faces his finished work can also be elating. A pleasant feeling of relief, an optimistic notion of having done something really well, may produce an experience which also is an inherent part of the creative process. Studying every detail of his work, the artist, or student, may see not only what is there, but even *more* than is factually represented or expressed. The mental image of what he set out to accomplish and the finished product have become indistinguishable in his mind. This combination of reality and imagination can easily persuade the creator that he really and truly attained what he set out to accomplish.

Many experienced artists, aware of this trick of the imagination, of their capacity for self-deception, will set aside a finished work until they feel they can view it in a relatively objective manner. However, a student is rarely able or permitted to exert this form of self-control. In many instances he is carried away by a temporary elation, thus satisfying an inner need for self-assurance. A teacher who lacks understanding of this need and at once expresses his well-meaning, analytical criticism can be most harmful to his students. Such wrongly timed criticism is not only deflating and shocking but is also ineffective, since the student has not gained the necessary perspective of his own work. The teacher's comments will be based on objective facts which the student is not yet able to see or comprehend. Later on, when he begins to see his work as it factually appears to the eye, when he attempts to take a more objective point of view, when doubts set in, then it is the teacher's obligation to help him evaluate his work. Such an evaluation should be based on a detailed analysis of each achievement and should single out any provable progress as well as clarifying any weaknesses.

Finally, it should be emphasized that both types of experience—learning experiences as well as those resulting from an emotional impact—play a most important part in any creative process. They are the inspiration for *what* we create, the basis from *which* we create, and the deciding factor in *how* we create.

Skill

Closely connected with the creative process, but not really a part of it, are the skills which are needed for transferring a creative idea into concrete expression. Since the term "skill" suggests various capabilities and forms of knowledge, it may at first seem rather confusing or inept. The commonest meaning of skill is manual dexterity developed through training and/or experience. But the term also denotes the possession of varied technological information, as in "knowing how" to etch, or how to print an etched plate. In regard to art products, skill is frequently synonymous with the craftsmanship which implies the knowledge and expertness of an accomplished artisan. In relation to creative work, however, the term "skill" does not necessarily imply expertness. As a rule, it indicates merely the knowledge and experience needed for the execution of a work of art.

Obviously no work of art can be created without utilizing some form of skill. It may be quite limited, as in the drawings of very young children, or fully accomplished, as in the works of great masters. A relative relationship exists between skill and maturity. A small child who begins to express himself in visual terms will utilize chiefly the manual skill he has acquired during earlier physical activities. Playing with toys and taking care of everyday needs usually develop youngsters' muscular coordination and manual dexterity sufficiently so that they have little difficulty in handling their easily manageable art materials.

It is quite different with high school students who are exposed to materials and tools which demand special knowledge and dexterity. Creating with wood and chisels, for example, requires both technical information and a special skill which can be acquired only through specific manual exercises; a simple transfer of previously learned skills generally proves inadequate. "But as desire for expression grows in the student there develops also a desire for the techniques and skills by which the expression is to be achieved. When the student realizes this need, the skills should be emphasized, and then only in relation to that need. In this way technique is recognized and developed not as a desideratum in itself but as a necessity inherent in the art process."[49]

Purely theoretical information—a prerequisite for the understanding of many working processes—usually does not equip an individual to use a given tool efficiently or to handle a material appropriately. Manual experiences are commonly just as necessary as the comprehension of theoretical facts. For instance, a thorough knowledge and understanding of the mechanical operation of an automobile will not equip a person to manipulate and control a car in motion; he still must learn through practical, physical experience to coordinate his hands and feet in a definite and unaccustomed way. Only then will he be able to translate his theoretical knowledge into the skill which will enable him to drive. Similarly, the skills needed to ex-

---

[49] A report of the Committee on the Function of Art in General Education, *The Visual Arts in General Education* (New York: D. Appleton-Century Co., 1940), pp. 69–70. By permission of Appleton-Century-Crofts, Inc.

press a creative idea visually cannot be learned by theory alone. To a large degree these skills are acquired only through arduous practice. It frequently happens that the underlying theoretical reasons and facts pertaining to the execution of a creative work become meaningful only *after* practical experience with media and tools.

The most significant aspect of skill in relationship to creativity, however, is not its effect on the actual execution of a creative work, but its intimate connection with creative thoughts. The possession or lack of skill is often the factor which decides whether or not an individual will continue to nurture a creative idea for more than a very brief time. Untold creative thoughts have been blocked off almost at the moment of conception in the minds of persons who realize they lack the skill to translate such thoughts and images into tangible form. Such individuals suddenly become very conscious of the gulf between thought and action, concept and performance. What usually bridges the gulf is the self-confidence derived from skill. Skill in this case is the force which gives self-assurance to the creator, and which enables him to evaluate his projected task in terms of facility or difficulty. Also, an individual in possession of skills knows from experience that many anticipated problems solve themselves during the working process, or that they will be solved by means discoverable only during the actual execution.

The relationship between skill and self-confidence has many educational implications. Limited or superficial instruction in techniques and skills makes students aware only of the labor and difficulties involved in executing a creative idea. It will not equip them to employ skills freely, nor help them to develop the inner security which would enable them to face with equanimity new or unsolved creative problems. For instance, a student who has had little or no experience with carving a stone rarely will form a creative idea concerning stone carving, nor will he dare to speak of a wish to express himself creatively in this medium. He may have a vague urge to shape a piece of stone, but he will not pursue this impulse further because of his unfamiliarity with the skill, his lack of experience with the material, and his dread of possible failure.

This situation can be avoided only if teachers abstain from introducing too many skills. Unless each skill is developed to the point where the student feels that he can manipulate the medium freely, he will not be able to form new creative ideas. "All living, all doing, all artistic creation presupposes craftsmanship, which can be acquired only by self-limitation. To know and to practice one thing right bestows a higher education than is achieved by dabbling in a hundred spheres of interest."[50]

Most skills are acquired slowly. Study of the creative growth of renowned artists will reveal the long time they needed to master the skills for competent handling of their chosen media. Many skills falsely convey the impression that they can be learned without much effort in a short time. However, as soon as the student attempts anything beyond the simplest application of these skills, he discovers his own lack of command. This lack cannot be overcome by jumping from one technique and medium to another, but only through continuous and concentrated work within a very limited range of activities. A student who senses that his skill is increasing because he feels that he is gaining control over medium and technique, will become more prolific and creative and will enjoy both his work and the results of his endeavors.

Skill plays still another significant part in creativity. Only through skills can an individual become truly familiar with a medium and its various possibilities, and this familiarity will help him find the very medium, or media, in which he can express himself most adequately. The relationship between media, skills, and creative imagination is a reciprocal one. Frequently love for a medium, and the command of a

---

[50] Goethe, *Wilhelm Meister's Journeyings,* I.

F. M. Hall Collection, University of Nebraska

DESPARATES GENERAL
Francesco Goya
aquatint etching

Collection of the Nebraska Art Association, University of Nebraska Art Galleries

TAOS MOUNTAIN
John Marin
watercolor

skill needed to manipulate it, will inspire or arouse new or latent creative ideas. For example, an artist may be looking at the grain of a smooth plank of wood. Since he loves to express himself in blockprints, he studies this piece of wood with the greatest interest, for he has acquired not only the skill but also a feeling for the medium and this type of graphic expression. The texture of the wood is inspiring; it suggests shapes and lines, and without further hesitation he begins to work on a new woodcut.

This intimate relationship between skill, feeling for a medium, and expression in it is demonstrated in many works of art. For example, if we study intently the blockprints by Munch, the aquatint etchings by Goya, or the watercolors by Marin, we must become aware of the extent to which skill is an integral part of each work. In all these examples the skills involved are inseparable from the whole; they are a deciding factor not only for what is expressed, but also for how it is expressed. Unity between medium and expression, between form and substance, can be achieved only through a superior command of skill.

Significantly, most important artists have mastered only a few skills and media in their lifetimes. Among the hypothetical explanations, one is that every artist develops an affinity for certain media corresponding to his particular temperament and background. Inevitably, he learns the skills which enable him to exploit these media to the fullest. The freedom derived from a command of skill and familiarity with media can be so satisfying that it frequently precludes further search for new or different means of expression.

Theoretically, the whole realm of visual art can be divided into three very broad but distinct categories. One pertains to expression in monochromes (including graphics and black and white), the second comprises all pictorial manifestations in two or more colors, and the third includes all forms of three-dimensional creations. Within these three groups, each artist must make his choice. It is noteworthy that very few have developed an equally strong affinity for all three groups of visual art and competence in their skills and techniques. The great majority of artists have limited themselves to two groups, and a sizable minority have cultivated an active interest in and command of the skills needed for only one group. However, it has never mattered in how many different ways an artist can express himself; his greatness has never been determined by the number of techniques, skills, or media at his command. In the realm of art, versatility is not a sign of excellence, or of profundity, or of a creative gift. "In self-limitation the master shows himself," said Goethe. This applies to any artist as well as to any competent teacher, and it entails definite and often difficult decisions.

From a selection of many different techniques and skills an art educator, for instance, must choose those few which can be considered basic. "Basic techniques and skills" in this context mean those which are fundamental because they are essential in learning others more complex. The teacher must decide the sequence in which they should be introduced to students, and the length of time to be devoted to each. The importance of this decision becomes clear when one recalls how little time an adolescent spends in the art class during the school year. A student who takes art daily for one hour during the full school year spends between 180 and 200 actual hours in the art room. Considering that a school day consists of six hours, this total approximates only a month and a half of instruction. Even a high school student who is enrolled in art for four years will have no more than a total of six months of art training. This is an extremely short time for learning any skill well.

Under these circumstances it is obvious that a conscientious teacher must devote much thought to *what* should be taught, *when* it should be taught, and *how* it should be taught. "What should be taught" constitutes a problem in itself, since it requires self-limitations and decisions, and it is made more difficult because it involves a conflict of principles. On one hand is the obligation of the art teacher to help students develop basic skills to the point where they are able to exercise choices and express themselves freely and adequately—a time-consuming procedure. On the other hand, the teacher also must allow his students to gain enough experience with a considerable variety of media and skills so that they can eventually choose among them intelligently on the basis of their aptitudes and individual personalities. Meaningful exposure to a great variety of skills and media is also very time-consuming; if only a little time can be devoted to them, the result will tend to be negative, as previously pointed out. Superficial contact with skills and media produces misconceptions and fears rather than affinities. Unfortunately there is no clear and simple way out of this dilemma. No proved methods exist which can be applied to most high school art classes comparable to those which have been developed for certain academic subjects. The problem must be solved anew each time, each semester, for every art class by the individual teacher. The solution must not only be consonant with his conviction, training, and experience, but must also be suited to his students in their particular environment and school situation.

The foregoing discussion brings us to the questions: Is it possible to single out any basic contributions of art education in the realm of the general education of adolescents? How can the training of art be beneficial to high school students who have neither a pronounced aptitude nor a special interest in the visual arts?

The Function of Art in General Education

The questions asked at the end of the previous chapter introduce the basic problems of defining and clarifying the function of art within a general high school educational process. Probably the most fundamental and accurate statement in regard to this problem was made by Aristotle when he spoke "slightingly of the pleasures of the mass of men who 'can form no idea of the noble and the truly pleasant whereof they have never tasted'. . . ."[51] Accordingly, we can assert that one objective in the teaching of art is simply to afford students the opportunities to taste "the noble and the truly pleasant," for art often embraces one or both of these qualities. In sum, a basic function of art education in the high school is to acquaint future citizens intimately with great art.

There are two possible approaches to the development of this acquaintanceship: one is through guided exposure which should lead gradually to an appreciation and admiration of art; the other is through actual participation in the creative process. It is of prime importance that these approaches are not kept separate but are employed in conjunction so that one fosters the other.

For a better understanding of this, we might compare the recent changes in art education with the development of contemporary art expression during the past fifty years. In this period we have become increasingly susceptible to art expression

[51] Butcher, *Aristotle's Theory of Poetry and Fine Art,* p. 204.

other than naturalistic or realistic. Also idealization, perfection, and harmony are no longer considered the only valid criteria for art, hence the classical concept of beauty has become somewhat obsolete. Today we demand powerfully or provocatively expressed emotions, and accept anomalies like pain and pleasure, tenderness and brutality, refinement and coarseness in one and the same work of art. The contemporary criteria are whether these conflicting elements have been fused and, even more important, whether new and meaningful statements have been made. The liberation of art from the narrow confines of the classical approach (the idealization and glorification of man and nature) has significantly influenced the teaching of art. Yet before we can understand their influence, we have to be aware that most contemporary aesthetic theories have one common denominator: the acceptance of art as a means for expressing emotions and reactions, regardless of external appearance in form or style.

The acceptance of emotional expression as a legitimate and significant part of visual art provides the link between the education of adolescents and the teaching of art. To understand this point completely, it is necessary to recall the inflexible rules to which artists, and sometimes high school students, were forced to adhere until very recent times. Anatomy, perspective, drawing, proportion, and color theory often were taught as unrelated, isolated units in accordance with rigid laws, and any deviation was strictly prohibited. During their training period, they spent considerable time in the mechanical memorization and exercise of the contents and laws of these subjects. This approach often led to an ostentatious display of isolated skills, or —in the case of adolescents—left them unable to put to use their newly acquired facility in work outside of the classroom.

When art education entered our public schools more than a hundred years ago, the subjects cited above dominated the art periods.[52] At the turn of the century, when artists broke entirely with the classical concept of visual art and adopted a wider range of approach, art teachers slowly began to discard the formalistic method of teaching and to develop the diverse potentialities of individual students. Conformity to rigid standards was abandoned and in its place greater importance was given to individual initiative, sensitivity to visual stimuli, and imagination. Externalized emotions took the place of rigid formulae, and the original expression of the individual superseded conformity. As time went by, art teachers realized that, historically, the first artistic manifestations of new visions, concepts, and thoughts often were executed in a somewhat clumsy or unsophisticated manner despite being profound and vital expressions. Powerful convictions rather than skills and techniques are dominant in these creations. Among many of the more recent well-known examples of this dualism are works of the initial phases of postimpressionism or expressionism. Characteristically, as soon as a new mode of expression becomes widely accepted and recognized as a particular style, it is analyzed, transposed into formulae, and becomes a convention or technique; it is then exploited by "experts" to the detriment of the originators who had "magnificent dreams. The work is clever and finished but lacks depth."[53]

To avoid this pitfall, the teaching of art techniques for their own sake and without definite aims should be excluded from high school art classes. Rather the emphasis should be on "the magnificent dreams" which though often hidden can still be discovered in many a student. Such "dreams" are made up of visions, notions, and feelings. If these elements stay dormant and are not translated into con-

---

[52] In its earliest beginnings public school art was known as "freehand drawing." According to Frederick M. Logan's extensive research on this subject, art education came into existence in this country between 1825 and 1838.

[53] *Dialogues of Alfred North Whitehead,* as recorded by Lucien Price (Boston: Little, Brown & Co., 1954), pp. 89-99.

crete forms, they must remain ineffective and unproductive. "Until art arises," says Santayana, "all achievement is internal to the brain, dies with the individual, and even in him spends itself without recovery, like music heard in a dream. Art, in establishing instruments for human life beyond the human body, and moulding outer things into sympathy with inner values, establishes a ground whence values may continually spring up . . . not only does the work of art thus perpetuate its own function, but the process of art is teachable."[54]

Santayana's reflections bring to mind the question: What is actually teachable within this "process of art"? Before attempting to answer this weighty question and before defining the role of the teacher, it should be pointed out that the term "teaching" subsumes two different meanings. The more familiar is: the guidance given by a person with superior knowledge of and skill in a particular subject. The other meaning refers to knowledge an individual may acquire through experience independent of any formal instruction. Therefore it may be wise to discuss first what kind of knowledge may be gained by students through creative activity, since significant aspects of learning occur during the execution of creative thoughts.

Creative activity compels any individual sincerely engaged in it to penetrate the outward appearance of visual reality. It induces the person to *investigate thoroughly* what he perceives since a casual or superficial contact would not enable him to make a valid statement or give a profound interpretation.[55] As soon as a student begins to draw, paint, or sculpture in earnest, he forces himself to study intensively whatever he intends to portray; he realizes that any visual statement which is to convey a message requires the enumeration of many facts. This need is demonstrated when we contrast a simple written or verbal statement with a visual one. The sentence, "I saw a tree," appears to convey clearly a definite thought. However, if the same thought is to be expressed in visual terms, much more detailed information is necessary for it to become meaningful. The visual statement would have to contain a combination of such facts as the height of the tree and the trunk in relationship to its width; the tree's size in comparison to that of man or an object; the trunk's proportion in relationship to its crown; the texture of the bark; the characteristics of the branches and their general direction; and finally the amount and distribution and texture of the foliage. Therefore, if a student wishes to present a clear and adequate visual formulation of a tree which he has seen, he is compelled either to recall the facts just enumerated, or else to perceive anew the same or a similar tree.

A true work of art is neither an imitation nor merely an objective record of facts. The painter August Macke said: "A work of art is an analogy to nature, not a copy."[56] It is the result of the experiences, interests, and preferences of an artist (or student) in regard to many particular aspects of the visual world. He expresses his thoughts, impressions, and feelings by his selection of forms and color, by his choice of subject matter and its arrangement, and by his utilization of distortions, omissions, or exaggerations of particulars. In order to achieve a convincing formulation, the artist (or student) must have perceived intensely all the pertinent facts related to the experience. If he has not done so, he will discover during the creative process that he is unable to express adequately his feelings and thoughts. In such a case, he is forced to re-examine or reinvestigate all the facts pertaining to the desired statement.

Reinvestigation induced by the creative activity is also a unique learning situa-

---

[54] Santayana, *The Life of Reason,* p. 302.

[55] "Expressive art demands a capability of being moved by many varying sentiments, demands the power to penetrate beneath outward appearances and to seize a hidden thought, the power to grasp either the permanent characteristic or the particular and momentary emotion . . . ." Véron in Rader, *A Modern Book of Esthetics,* p. 93.

[56] *Künstlerbekenntnisse,* Paul Westheim, ed. (Berlin: Propyläen Verlag, n.d.), p. 167.

tion because it is self-motivated and therefore often most effective. Simultaneously—and this is important from an art educator's point of view—the creative process takes possession of the whole person and demands his most concentrated attention. Hence it can be claimed that the creative activity strengthens a student's capacity to concentrate over a considerable span of time, and that this capacity, if developed, will also be operative in many situations other than those connected with creating visual art.

Various other important educational factors can be identified and related to the creative process. First of all, the creative act itself forces the individual to deal with and bring into focus vague and confused thoughts. Most creative thoughts or ideas are nebulous when first conceived, and usually remain so until they are expressed. Therefore when a student attempts to formulate these rather indefinite ideas in concrete terms, a clarification of his thoughts and visions must occur. This clarifying process is an essential part of the creative act and has important educational implications. Most young persons have little experience in translating their many vague creative ideas into realistic formulations or actions, and the art activity provides one of the most constructive opportunities for them.

At least two more equally important constituents of the creative process also have significant educational implications. One concerns learning to make decisions and the other to enjoy doing so. Each work of art represents innumerable decisions, since each line, form, or color set down by an artist or student is the tangible result of a choice. This is true whether or not a student is actually aware of having made these many decisions. During the art period high school students are usually confronted with more opportunities to make choices than in most other learning activities, as, for example, in academic courses where instruction is based mainly on the students' ability to comprehend and memorize facts. Although they are frequently asked to arrange or rearrange facts in a logical sequence, hardly ever are they required to choose or to select. The problem of selection is mostly solved for them by the subject matter itself, by the textbook, and by the teacher. Making decisions and choices constitutes a real problem in the lives of many people, and when there has been little or no experience in doing so, it often becomes a disturbing, even overwhelming task. Guided exercises in selecting and deciding should condition students for later life-situations. Not only are countless experiences in choosing and making decisions inherent in artistic activity, but there is the additional value that students are immediately faced with the results of their choice. Thus they may learn rapidly the relationship between cause and effect, whereas in most life-situations much time often elapses between a decision and its consequences. Moreover, high school students are rarely exposed to genuinely free choices outside of the art class, because of such factors as their age, dependency, and lack of experience. Hardly anywhere else can they select, make choices, and state and interpret their thoughts and feelings as freely as in front of a drawing board or sculpture stand. They are well able to create visually without having to know or adhere to inflexible rules, such as harmony and counterpoint in composing, or orthography and syntax in writing. In conclusion, it can be claimed that among several other educational functions art activity provides limitless opportunities to learn to choose and to make decisions, and to experience vividly immediate results.

Two other contributions of art education should be pointed out. One of them, being closely related to the complex of making decisions, pertains to learning how to solve problems. The other, also intimately linked to these forms of learning, concerns the preparation for living effectively with uncertainties.

In our high school curricula, many subject areas deal with facts which suggest that educated man lives in a world of absolute certainties. Indeed, most youngsters receive the impression that learning equals the accumulation of indisputable truth, and that the world which they will soon enter is filled with the same certainties as are most of their classroom hours. Mathematical theorems, laws of physics, chemical formulae, historical data, and grammatical rules are presented to students in terms of absolutes which leave no room for doubts. The students' days consist mainly of memorizing indisputable facts, and the only uncertainty they encounter is the result either of faulty memorization of these facts, or of an inability to relate them intelligently to a different or varied context. But here again the students' teachers will tell them with certainty what is right or wrong, and whether or not they have performed well. In this form of learning students are rarely confronted by problems which have more than a single solution.

Problems which permit a multitude of solutions are confusing to most students, because a strong element of uncertainty is present. "Psychologists explain the search for certainty as the desire to return to the early days of infancy, which were not troubled by doubt and were guided by the confidence in parental wisdom."[57] The adolescent frequently transfers some of his confidence in parental wisdom to his teachers. He expects the teacher to *know,* and "to know" means, to the student, to provide him with certainties. However, this form of education does not correspond to real life, in which man is almost constantly beset by uncertainties. And it is precisely in this respect that the art area simulates reality most closely. As in reality, the creative activity is charged with uncertainties: every creative undertaking consists of many steps into the unpredictable and the precarious; every creative thought leaves the known premise and ventures into something new and unknown, therefore uncertain. Becoming accustomed to living and working without certainties is as much a prerequisite to achievement as command of precise facts. The art teacher can help students realize that many significant areas of human endeavor are without known absolutes and without certainty, and that courage, vision, and the ability to pursue an aim steadfastly are as important to achievement as skill, techniques, and facts. Learning not to fear uncertainties and to work with them is another contribution which the art area can provide.

One other contribution which the creative activity can make to the education of adolescents concerns learning to solve problems. Exercises in this form of discipline are a part of most academic subjects. Among subjects which provide rich opportunities for problem solving, mathematics and the sciences come first to mind. On the high school level, however, laws and facts in these areas are generally presented in such a manner as to permit only a single, predetermined solution to a given problem. This is in many respects quite different from the creative area where no absolute "corrects" and "incorrects" exist, and where the student's problem is largely self-imposed and allows a variety of solutions. This is true no matter how rich a background the art teacher offers to his pupils, how many facts he introduces, or how strong a stimulus he provides. It is of the greatest importance that no topic, assignment, or stimulus is ever presented to high school students in such a narrowly conceived manner that it permits creative thoughts to be interpreted in only one particular way. At bottom, it does not matter whether the creative inspiration is motivated by someone other than the student (or the artist), or whether it is apparently self-inspired. The important thing is that the individual student be given the freedom to respond to the inspiration in accordance with his experience, his emotional sensibility, and his natural bent. This means that he should never be curtailed in freedom of expression, style, or approach, and that any creative theme should allow of more than a single formulation.

Creative and artistic problems cannot be solved by applying clearly formulated and inflexible laws or wholly objective facts. The essential problem in creative ex-

---

[57] Reichenbach, *The Rise of Scientific Philosophy,* p. 36.

pression is based on the desire to state convincingly an observation and/or emotional reaction to an experience, and to find a corresponding clear and meaningful formulation. Finding the most adequate expression constitutes a problem for which each artist (or student) has to discover a new solution every time; he will not be able to express creatively the identical situation twice in the identical manner. Therefore, no existing former solution can ever be reapplied in exactly the same way.

Solving self-imposed problems which are an essential part of the creative process requires a large degree of self-discipline. The value of self-discipline is so evident that no further discussion appears necessary. However, a more detailed analysis of the relationship between the creative process and self-discipline may be of use.

A study of average works by high school students discloses many failures which can be directly attributed either to the students' inability to attend to detail, or to their inability to carry out projects to their satisfactory conclusion. Every genuine work of art entails two basic elements: one is plain labor, and the other is a composite of inspiration and invention. Often it is possible to distinguish these elements in significant works of art after only a brief study. Yet not infrequently great masterpieces impress us as having resulted from a spontaneous creative outburst. Actually these "unlabored" creations may have called forth all the artist's skill to disguise his strenuous efforts, or they may be the result of years of arduous exertion. Whistler declared that "To say of a picture, as is often said in its praise, that it shows great and earnest labor, is to say that it is incomplete and unfit for view. . . . The work of the master reeks not of the sweat of the brow—suggests no effort—and is finished from its beginning."[58]

Untutored spontaneity is often present in the drawings of small children, and we rightly admire them for it. But a marked difference exists between the work of elementary school children and that of high school students. It is characteristic of adolescents, with their self-critical attitude, that they lose this desirable effortlessness. Thus the high school student, like any artist, must labor to the limit of his ability and then attempt to surpass it. Only considerable self-discipline will enable him to reach such a goal. The teacher's duty is to help develop this form of self-control by the constant use of persuasion and persistence, so that eventually the student will be able to exercise self-discipline at will. It is not unusual to find a teacher who believes that this or any other form of discipline trespasses freedom. But "freedom and discipline are the two essentials of education," said Whitehead. "The two principles, freedom and discipline, are not antagonists, but should be so adjusted in the child's life that they correspond to a natural sway, to and fro, of the developing personality. My main position is that the dominant note of education at its beginning and at its end is freedom, but that there is an intermediate stage of discipline with freedom in subordination."[59]

The importance of self-discipline and hard work in relation to creative efforts is often insufficiently well understood.

> We of today have little realization of the amount of labor expended on the long road from apprenticeship to mastery, whereon the world's artists have all had to travel in the past. The popular notion of genius, surviving probably from the Romantic movement, as an effortless and God-given illumination, descending like the Pentecostal dove on the chosen few, has corrupted our understanding of the artist's real nature and encouraged all manner of outrage, ranging from laziness to sheer impudence, in the self-chosen apostle of today, who has indeed a gift of tongues, but no other manifestation of divinity. Until recently, art has

---

[58] James McNeil Whistler, *The Gentle Art of Making Enemies* (New York: G. P. Putnam's Sons, 1923), p. 115.
[59] Whitehead, *The Aims of Education,* pp. 47–48.

been very hard work. It is still so for those who preserve any continuity with the Great Tradition.[60]

It is mainly self-discipline which enables the artist to travel the difficult road from the creative impulse and the spontaneous sketch to the finished work. Moreover, concentrated effort and self-discipline can result in re-vision which in turn will evoke new inspiration. These re-visions may then lead to new appraisals and new solutions which are sometimes superior to the initial attempts. Proof of this exists in the works of many important artists who repeated the same theme time and time again. (To name some of the more recent: Cézanne, Rouault, and Braque.) Most decidedly, these "repetitions" are not owing to a lack of inspiration; often they stem from the desire to refine and develop statements more fully.

It requires considerable self-discipline to be affected neither by lack of immediate success, nor by disappointments arising from a feeling of inadequacy. In fact, one of the most important prerequisites for any creative success is the capacity to pursue an aim steadfastly, regardless of whether rapid results are attained. This holds true in most working situations and is definitely not restricted to the art area. Certainly it is an obligation of any art educator to aid students in developing this trait. Three obvious ways he may do so are: first, by insisting on a satisfactory and complete execution of any creative idea; second, by leading students on to tackle more difficult solutions to their creative problems; and third, by exposing them frequently to the same or very similar problems, so that they will have opportunities to revise and improve their already formulated concepts.

Another aspect of self-discipline pertains to transforming a creative idea or inspiration into a concrete form or image, a process which requires a considerable degree of self-discipline. In this instance "self-discipline" is almost analogous to will power. Although will power as such has little relation to or influence over creative inspiration, it is often needed to bring a work to its conclusion. However, will power can neither stimulate the imagination nor revitalize experience, and functions only within the limited domain of execution. Therefore will power is external, whereas the desire to bring order into creative impulses is internal. The latter is akin to self-realization, and—though almost independent of any will power—can be remarkably benefited by self-discipline.

Inspiration cannot be forced into existence, but once present it demands the exercise of self-discipline to convert it into constructive and creative action. Impatience, impetuousity, fearfulness, and lack of confidence are deadly enemies of the creative process. Patience and trust in oneself are essential, and both can be developed through guided experiences in the art room. Patience, which is one form of self-discipline, plays a significant but often underestimated role within the creative process. Patience should lead to contemplation, and contemplation is a necessary and important part of any creative activity. As the result of internal discipline, contemplation permits the lighting up of imagination, allows perceptions to come into focus, and provides opportunity for experiences to crystallize in the mind and be transformed into creative action. During the average school day students are only too frequently compelled to produce instantly without being allowed any time for contemplation. A speedy demonstration of knowledge ranks as the highest attainable achievement in many subject areas. ("Knowledge" in this context means memorized information arranged in a logical sequence.) The ability to repeat memorized information on demand plays an important part in the affairs of the ordinary school day, and although it is needed to a limited extent in the mechanical

---

[60] Rhys Carpenter, *The Bases of Artistic Creation* (New Brunswick: Rutgers University Press, 1942), p. 35.

process of executing a creative idea, it has nothing in common with initial creative impulses and ideas.

One more aspect of self-discipline should be discussed in this context. The adolescent phase is one which is characterized by impatience; the adolescent's longing for immediate results stems from a temporary but typical insecurity. He will embark on a creative venture impetuously, in a haphazard manner, often with only the vaguest creative thought. The first minor difficulty will turn his whole undertaking into a sudden disappointment; lack of immediate results will frustrate him to the point of abandoning the whole project. Only self-discipline can help a student overcome such temporary frustrations, and where self-discipline is absent, the teacher's insistence and reassurance must serve as a substitute. Several successes usually produce sufficient self-confidence in the student so that he himself can exercise the necessary self-discipline without assistance from the teacher. Still, it is a difficult point to reach for both student and teacher; it takes a long time to learn not to give up at the first encounter with obstacles. "Follow through!" said Goethe. "The only attitude by which everything is accomplished, and without which nothing can be achieved—why is it so rarely sustained? Why is it so difficult to create in ourselves, and in those we try to influence?"[61]

To find answers to these questions, we must divide the creative process into its integrant parts, and also must study the problem of motivation in creativity. Creating may be taken to mean the act of formulating a new concept expressed in artistic and, in this context, predominantly visual terms. The creative process as such is one of constant change, evolutionary in character, the purpose of which is to transform thoughts and feelings into constructive action. While it is operating, our inventive mind is driven to finding new approaches which in turn lead to new works. Through the creative process we discover ourselves, our capacities, our weaknesses, our predilections, and our effectiveness in relation to others.

Motivation in this context can also be termed the *will* to bring into existence new, artistic ideas. A "new" idea can be a statement or formulation which has never existed before; or it can be something which is already in existence and widely known, but is being stated for the first time by an individual who believes his statement to be genuinely new. The latter commonly pertains to art works of high school students. Seldom do they find genuine, enduring, new, creative formulations, although many of their works display originality in a limited way. The term "originality" as it is generally used in connection with high school teaching designates the marked differences between several equally accomplished works of similar nature produced by students of approximately the same age level. But these dissimilarities are "new," "different," or "original" only in so far as they are unique to the individual student; they are not "new" in a larger concept of art, although they may still be most commendable and reveal imaginative power and creative thoughts. What is frequently called creative originality in adolescents is the particular intangible quality which cannot be directly attributed to a specific influence, such as teacher direction, and which is not present in imitations, copies, or tracings.[62]

The battle against copying and tracing in high school art education has almost been won. Nowadays one rarely encounters the old-fashioned filing cabinet filled with photographs and reproductions of two-dimensional art products, available to students for copying. However, art imitations still are widely considered a legitimate

---

[61] Goethe in a letter to Riemer, 1809. *Goethes Gespräche,* F. von Biedermann, ed. (Leipzig: F. W. von Biedermann, 1909), vol. 2, p. 45.

[62] "Anyone who observes school art exhibits in one American town after another is likely to become first annoyed and then amused by the constant claims of originality and spontaneity on the part of proud teachers, in spite of the obviously stereotyped imitativeness of much of the work." Munro, *Art Education, Its Philosophy and Psychology,* pp. 80–81.

part of the education of adolescents. Teachers, in their desire to have students produce "original" works, frequently permit or even force them to imitate contemporary art expression. It is not hard to find abstractions and stylizations manufactured by high school students who have neither an understanding of *any* abstract concepts (including those reflected in visual art), nor a knowledge of those principles underlying the simplifications which are the basis for stylization. Mass-manufacture of mobiles and stabiles in art rooms is a case in point. These three-dimensional art forms often degenerate into meaningless decorations without a single new thought or feature, assembled in a most haphazard manner, devoid even of the discipline needed for skillful execution. Since in reality they are imitations, the only possible justification for these undertakings by students is the opportunity afforded for acquiring skills and disciplines. But because an insistence on good workmanship could well result in unmasking the lack of understanding of the problem, and thereby lead to the exposure of blind imitation and pretended originality, teachers as well as students shy away from the practice of skills and the exercise of discipline. A more serious danger resulting from this kind of imitation is that students may leave the art room with the notion that art today has no standards of excellence, and that any mindless, undisciplined, and/or pretentious work is acceptable so long as the product does not superficially resemble any other, regardless of the reason for its seemingly different appearance.

It is certain that any good art instructor must influence his students. They are affected by his personality and by the instruction which exposes them to significant art, widening their horizons and acquainting them with artistic problems and their unique solutions. But influence has little to do with permitting or demanding imitation. Imitation is following implicitly someone else's thoughts or the documentation of these thoughts, disregarding or precluding any real understanding of them; it may also mean producing a semblance of an existing form without having penetrated or comprehended all the different aspects embodied in it.[63] Influence, on the other hand, changes an individual gradually, without apparent force. Imitation forces the individual to follow authoritative direction, whereas influence still permits him to exercise numerous choices and does not channel him into such a narrow position that he cannot help but follow a fixed, prescribed course.

Nevertheless, it would be unrealistic to assume that high school students can be motivated to the point where they will be able to create genuinely new visual concepts.[64] Setting up such ambiguous, unobtainable goals for art education would be both impractical and discouraging to students and teachers. An important, realistic aim of art education is to encourage, praise, and motivate adolescents so that they will have the courage to depart from the herdlike conformity in which they are so prone to take refuge, and which in so many instances is forced on them by their peers and by society at large. The desire to state something different, personal, and new needs constant stimulation in the case of adolescents. Fostering this desire should eventually produce a more self-confident being who will not be perpetually

---

63 "The imitator or maker of the image knows nothing of true existence; he knows appearances only." *Plato's The Republic,* B. Jowett, trans. (New York: Modern Library, n.d.), p. 369.

64 "Adult artists, too, often make excessive claims of complete originality. They feel it as an admission of inferiority to recognize that they have learned from their predecessors, and especially that they have learned from their contemporaries. To the trained observer, their indebtedness is usually quite apparent. But the basic error lies in the implication that any artist or any work of art can be completely original. All artists build upon the past, upon the traditions and recent tendencies in their field. There can be no justifiable stigma in admitting such debts; and the most any artist should presume to claim is that he has made some slight addition of his own, some relatively new adaptation of earlier achievements to a new situation, need, technique, or material." Munro, *Art Education, Its Philosophy and Psychology,* p. 81.

dependent on the ephemeral approval of unselected groups or persons. The student who develops the courage to think as an individual, independently and creatively, must finally achieve self-reliance, and this quality will prevent him from becoming a blind follower. In helping to develop these desirable traits, art education can make another significant contribution to the general education of adolescents.

Still another of its contributions can be labeled simply *learning to see* or *learning to perceive intensely and fully.* While perception has already been treated in another context (see pages 19–22), it is so important as to warrant mentioning here once again.

Scarcely any high school subject other than art demands, utilizes, and stresses the importance of fresh and genuine visual perceptions. Obviously many subjects may be learned and mastered without seeing anything intensely, fully, or anew. Even the natural sciences may be, and often are, taught without exposing students to genuine perceptual experiences. Recognition of visual facts is usually required, but recognition is not perception. "The difference between the two is immense. Recognition is perception arrested before it has a chance to develop freely. In recognition there is a beginning of an act of perception. But this beginning is not allowed to serve the development of a full perception of the thing recognized. It is arrested at the point where it will serve some *other* purpose, as we recognize a man on the street in order to greet or avoid him, not so as to see him for the sake of seeing what is there.

"In recognition we fall back, as upon a stereotype, upon some previously formed scheme. Some detail or arrangement of details serves as cue for bare identification."[65] This "bare identification" is commonly no more than placing visual facts into some broad or general categories. If we simply say, "This is an apple," it may be inferred that this apple is identical with all other existing apples; such variations as shape, size, and color are ignored. Generalizations of this kind are void of discrimination and are often the result of a most insensitive and superficial form of perception. To learn to see sharply or to perceive acutely, to become sensitive to minute visual differences, should be part of any art training.[66] Most students who say "I cannot draw" do not tell the objective truth, because the truth is that they *can* draw; they can move a tool intelligently and quite skillfully over any flat surface, leaving controlled marks. What these students cannot do is *see.* They are unaccustomed to perceiving what is in front of their eyes—as the Bible says, "They have eyes and see not." The quality of their drawings and paintings often reflects this lack of visual training and attention.

The common lack of genuine visual perception can be explained partly by the fact that our society is predominantly a verbal one. In primitive societies visual perception is given considerably more status; physical safety, food procurement, and survival in general depend to a great extent on acute visual perception. In modern society we are dependent chiefly on verbal communication. Our safety is almost wholly contingent upon oral or written agreements and laws rather than on visual signs (as, for instance, the footprints of a ferocious beast). Our food is obtained by buying and bargaining rather than by hunting. In short, visual perception has lost its preëminent status, in terms of survival, and verbal perception has taken its place. However, this should not mean that perception today is of less importance to the individual than before, but that in our present society more emphasis is placed on

---

[65] Dewey, *Art as Experience,* p. 52.

[66] "Observation is almost entirely an acquired skill. It is true that certain individuals are born with an aptitude for concentrated attention, and for the eye-and-hand co-ordination involved in the act of recording what is observed. But in most cases the eye (and the other organs of sensation) have to be trained, both in observation (directed perception) and in notation." Read, *Education through Art,* p. 206.

developing auditory, in particular verbal, rather than visual perception. Yet to see intensely, clearly, and sharply is still a major source of delight. Of even greater importance is the fact that we not only gain a wealth of information through visual perception, but are constantly stimulated to search for more knowledge.

That acute and thorough visual perception is of extreme significance to anyone, no matter what his vocational interest, is so obvious that the point need not be elaborated. However, here once more the distinction between verbalizing visual perception and portraying perception in visual terms should be pointed out. Words which are used to describe visually perceived facts are familiar abstract symbolic equivalents; they permit fluent, convincing descriptions of barely perceived facts. The consequent generalizations are accepted without thought because the listener is rarely aware that he is exposed to a shallow account. Moreover, eloquence and gestures often help to give the spoken word such a convincing quality that the lack of genuine perception remains unnoticed. Also, empathy often enters into verbal communication, whereas visual expression is without any such auxiliary means.

The main difference between visual and verbal accounts of what has been seen becomes apparent when an individual attempts to draw or to paint visually perceived facts. The art activity makes students quite aware that they are unaccustomed to seeing discerningly, for it forces them to take account of details which are often slurred over in a verbal statement. The art sessions challenge them to make thorough use of their eyes and to become less content with superficial glances.

Seeing sharply, vividly, and intensely is largely based on habit. As with any other habit, it can be cultivated by any person to varying degrees, and once acquired, is retained. In this respect no other subject can serve students so well as art. Helping them to perceive keenly, and training them really to use their eyes is another of art education's characteristic contributions to the total development of adolescents.

The inherent beneficial qualities unique to art education cannot be expected to manifest themselves automatically. They are not evoked simply by giving students the opportunity to work with art materials and encouraging them to use these as they please. Art education can fulfill its function only under the competent guidance of a well-trained art teacher.

IV The Art Teacher

What constitutes a well-trained art teacher? To begin with, he must be an educated person, widely read, and competent in the oral and written usage of English. He should have a thorough knowledge of the history of art, be creative, and have considerable studio experience.[67] In addition, he must be thoroughly familiar with the

---

[67] "Teachers of art in the schools below college level are being prepared with some technique and some educational methods, but often with little art history or theory, and little general cultural background, as evidenced by the small number of courses required in literature, history, and science. Teachers of professional art or craft instruction tend in their preparation to specialize on technique and to sacrifice all the other alternatives to some extent, except as they are forced to a broader preparation by certification requirements." Munro, *Art Education, Its Philosophy and Psychology*, p. 33.

processes of children's and adolescents' psychological development, especially in relation to their creative growth. Last but not least, he must have a deep understanding of art, and of the art of teaching.[68]

For teaching is an art, not a science. "Teaching is not like inducing a chemical reaction: it is much more like painting a picture or making a piece of music, or on a lower level like planting a garden or writing a friendly letter. You must throw your heart into it, you must realize that it cannot all be done by formulas, or you will spoil your work, and your pupils, and yourself."[69]

Teaching is an art because it is a creative process constantly producing something new and exciting. The trite is boring to students as well as to teachers. Even the well known can be restated freshly and creatively: for example, the mother-and-child theme has been used by many different artists for hundreds of years. Without becoming repetitious or boring, these artists often found ways to give us a new experience, a new insight, and a new point of view into this most familiar motif. But "new" also implies venturing into uncertainty, for certainty can be found only in the known and trite. Creative teaching consists of numerous courageous acts; it leaves the familiar and known and attempts to venture into the untried and unknown.

The uncertainty in creative teaching derives from two factors. First, the students themselves are largely unknown entities; second, any original approach to teaching in itself carries an element of precariousness. Even objective dates and facts are susceptible to more than one interpretation, and there is always the possibility of error because a teacher, not a machine, conveys them. In spite of our knowledge of the psychological structure and common behavior of adolescents, the teacher must look at each of his students as an individual unlike any other. After all, there is more that is unique about a human being than his fingerprints.

Educational training should develop a teacher's sensitivity even to the smaller but still important differences between students. A teacher should also realize that students' classifications, previous grades, records, and I.Q.'s are merely guiding aids.[70] They do not give a deep insight into the individual student nor do they constitute a genuine basis for understanding him; and as they can easily prejudice a teacher about a student, they must be used with great care. Without the exercise of such discretion a teacher cannot expect to discover what is truly unique in each student, and be able to adjust his instruction in accordance with individual needs. Here again, he must accept the fact that he is teaching in a realm of uncertainty. He can never be sure of "really knowing" a pupil or of having done "the right thing" for him. Time will tell, but unfortunately high school teachers are rarely given the opportunity to harvest the fruit of their teaching. Moreover, the immediate results of teaching are not a genuine indication of successful efforts—those seemingly splendid works produced by high school students are not positive proof of a teacher's effectiveness. His real effectiveness is not recorded in anything so immediate and

---

[68] "It is called *The Art of Teaching* because I believe that teaching is an art, not a science. It seems to me very dangerous to apply the aims and methods of science to human beings as individuals, although a statistical principle can often be used to explain their behavior in large groups and a scientific diagnosis of their physical structure is always valuable. But a 'scientific relationship' between human beings is bound to be inadequate and perhaps distorted." Gilbert Highet, *The Art of Teaching* (New York: Vintage Books, 1954), p. vii. Originally published by Alfred A. Knopf, Inc.

[69] *Ibid.*, p. viii.

[70] "Certainly some kind of classification is necessary. The wise teacher will set to work, with his very first class, to observe the commonest traits that show character, to look for hidden resemblances of personality even between pupils who seem quite different to the eye, and to test his findings both by checking back with earlier records, and by watching how his products turn out, years after they have left his class.

"But after he has learnt the main types and subspecies, some unclassifiable individuals will always remain. These are the joys, the sorrows, and the horseflies of the teacher's life." *Ibid.*, p. 41.

tangible. It manifests itself in the students' better understanding of art and their greater fondness for it, and in their increased ability to think independently and creatively. These effects of teaching are in harmony with one of the highest aims of education: to help a student lead a more useful life, useful to others and therefore to himself. What finally counts is how much a teacher has contributed toward helping his students reach this goal.

As in any other creative activity, teaching requires perception, imagination, empathy, factual knowledge, and courage. Courage to leave the trite, courage to attempt or to express something new, courage to make decisions. One characteristic of a poor teacher is his unwillingness or inability to make decisions and to assume the responsibility for them. Frequently he will defer to textbooks, administrators, or even his own students. If challenged, he will probably say that his actions or teaching are not his choice, that he is only following a curriculum or a textbook, or carrying out a superior's suggestion—in short, that his actions are based neither on his careful considerations nor on his free decisions. Possibly he may also say, "This is what the students like and want." Such a statement (or excuse) conceals both irresponsibility and ignorance. If a teacher does what the students like and want, he assumes that they know by instinct what is good for them and exactly what they will need to achieve the understanding and mastery of a particular subject or skill.

Unfortunately we have no proof that man is born with some kind of animalistic instinct which directs him only to what is good for him, or provides him with some sort of foresight, so that he knows instinctively how to prepare himself for his complex future. Even on the most primitive survival level man seems to have less instinct than any highly developed animal. A small child, for instance, will put anything into his mouth, wholly ignoring his physical safety. Our highways also give tragic evidence of man's inability to protect himself instinctively. If students' wishes were reliable indices of their needs, we would have to believe that they possessed a mystical second sight, giving them the foresight and insight which a teacher must acquire by years of rigorous and intensive training. We would have to believe that pupils have such a wide knowledge of the subject they are studying that they know what to learn and when to learn it. Clearly a teacher who accepts the students' wishes and desires as his guide for teaching is unaware that these wishes are mostly the result of casual influences, or a search for convenience, and of a fear of venturing into something new. More than that, such a teacher seems to forget that teaching can be made so inspiring and exciting that the students will lose sight of their preconceived ideas and will *want* to learn what is considered most significant for them at the time. The teacher's influence over his pupils should counterbalance their different motives and biases; he should be able to sway their tastes and desires so that they will prefer what is in their best interest. The ability to motivate students to *want* what they are being taught is a characteristic of a good teacher.

However, this should not be construed to mean that a teacher should be insensitive to his students' wishes and uninterested in them; on the contrary, he should know them well. But while their wishes and biases should not dictate his selection of subject matter, they should determine his approach to the presentation of each lesson. In addition, the teacher must be thoroughly familiar with his students' attitude toward a subject in order to decide how far he can incorporate or utilize their wants and wishes, and to what extent he must ignore them for their own benefit. This form of interaction between the students' wishes and the teacher's knowledge and pedagogical skill must take place before an instructor can discharge his obligations effectively. However, the final responsibility for the conduct of a course always rests with the teacher; no one else can carry this responsibility for him, least of all his students.

Part of this responsibility consists of decisions about the over-all teaching plan for every class, including when and how to present a certain lesson, assignment, or topic. Although curricula, textbooks, and superiors should serve as guides for and aids to a teacher, he must still assume the ultimate responsibility for these decisions. It is the teacher who is—or should be—most familiar with his students' interests, needs, and backgrounds; it is also he who should know how and what he can teach best.

The last is particularly important in art education. Although many techniques and subject areas are of equal educational value, hardly any school program can provide time for all of them. The art teacher is faced with the problem of what to select, when to present it, and how much time to devote to each area. This triple responsibility is rarely encountered by his colleagues in other fields. In a course of modern American history, for example, an instructor does not teach all periods of history but one specific and clearly established area. On the high school level the content of this subject is quite circumscribed, and the sequence in which the material is presented is usually chronological and does not require that the teacher make many choices. Moreover, the curriculum, textbooks, and established practices further eliminate the need for many pedagogical decisions.

All this is quite different in the teaching of art. Out of a wealth of material the art teacher must select what is most suitable for his students.[71] He must also decide in which sequence it should be introduced, and how much time should be provided for each lesson or topic. These decisions are made more difficult because many areas of art instruction have similar educational aims—to challenge creative imagination, to provide opportunities for the appreciation of great accomplishments, to offer many choices, and to permit a great degree of freedom of expression. Moreover, all require about the same amount of concentrated effort, of self-discipline, of precision, of will to overcome difficulties, and of manual skill.

The age, background, and experience of students, and such factors as the budget, materials, and equipment, often limit to some extent choices of subject matter. But even with fewer alternatives each art teacher still must choose among many of equal significance. Since numerous offerings in the art class are of the same educational value from an objective point of view, we must employ subjective criteria to find significant differences in these equivalents. Probably the most pronounced differences result from the individual teacher's attitude towards various art areas. Every art teacher who is creative in his own right develops strong feelings for certain media, techniques, and forms of expression. In the areas for which he has a genuine affinity he will probably be able to teach best and most inspirationally.

The art teacher should aim to help each student cultivate a particular fondness for at least one form of creative expression. It does not matter whether this is painting, sculpture, ceramics, or another of the many forms of visual art. What does matter is that the student who finishes a high school art course should have found at least one artist he truly admires, one type of creative work with which he would like to continue, and one work of art with which he would like to live.

As indicated, it should be evident that every art teacher ought to continue to be creative in his own right. The medium in which he prefers to work, and the manner or style in which he likes to express himself are of no consequence; the important thing is that he remain creative. Despite the fact that teaching days are long and strenuous, he must pursue his own artistic development.[72] Otherwise, it

---

[71] "The good school master is known by the number of valuable subjects that he declines to teach." Sir Richard Livingstone, *On Education* (New York: Macmillan & Co., 1944), p. 28.

[72] "He [the teacher] must have command of at least one medium of expression so that he may have experience of and feeling for the creative process which he is striving to promote, so that on this as a basis he may refine his own insight into the process of creating." *The Visual Arts in General Education,* p. 135.

will become increasingly difficult for him to convince his students that what he is teaching is truly significant. Moreover, by working creatively on his own, a teacher does not run so much risk of becoming boring and repetitious, and of having his teaching slide into a set routine. His creative work and his continuing interest in art will be a source of new thoughts, ideas, and approaches. He will remain alert to what is being accomplished in the art world, to new ideas which are being advocated, and to new interpretations of older ideas. All this will act as inspiration to his own work and, more important, will keep him enthusiastic in the classroom. His intellect and imagination will be stimulated and his teaching will be more inspiring; he will bring his students new ideas, show them new examples, and point out new ways.

There is still another reason for urging that every art teacher continue to work creatively in his own right. Scarcely any creative work is accomplished without friction; there is always a struggle between thought and expression, between the mental image and the tangible form. Most artists (including those teachers who continue to work creatively) experience again and again these almost inevitable difficulties. The experiences connected with surmounting obstacles will help the art teacher to remain sensitive and sympathetic to the difficulties of his students. He will not easily lose his understanding of their struggles and problems, and will be able to project himself readily into his students' situation. Moreover, out of his understanding he will be able to inspire his students for what he believes is worth doing.

Because he has this understanding, the art teacher will not be prone to believe or accept various vague, fashionable, or unsound ideas about his teaching and his own work. One of these ideas, often stated, is that many artistic experiences may be transferred into the realm of everyday living, hence art education has an immediate utilitarian value. This would mean that in the pursuit of visual art one unconsciously cultivates the sort of taste which determines choices pertaining to the home, clothing, or surroundings. Such a proposition postulates either that we have developed definite standards of taste, and that these standards are identical with aesthetic judgment; or that the same taste which is applied in everyday situations is equally applicable in the realm of art—and vice versa.

Such a proposition is questionable. The "pursuit of visual art" here means actual participation in a creative act or in the production of artistic works. "Taste is, however, merely a critical, not a productive faculty . . . ."[73] This probably explains why many artists in their *private* lives have paid so little attention to the accepted taste of their time. Hardly ever has the artist been a pacemaker for or representative of taste in clothing and housing. His mind was occupied with creating, not with critically judging the taste of the day.

The problem of taste is more complex than is commonly realized. To begin with we have to distinguish between aesthetic judgment, taste, fashion, and fads. Aesthetic judgment emphasizes permanent values, whereas in judgment applied to taste, the stress is on transitory values. Fashion is outside of any value considerations except purely material or social ones. What is regarded as good taste today may be in poor taste fifty years from now, and what was most acceptable fifty years ago is now often considered displeasing or unattractive. The dark, velour-curtained rooms of the Victorian era with their palm trees, oriental ornaments, metal curlicues, and cluttered walls were once in perfectly good taste. Today, while we might look at such a room with interest as a museum-piece or as a stage setting, we would resent having to incorporate its style into our present mode of life. Furthermore, we should be aware that taste always has been the concern chiefly of the educated. The ignoramus, the vulgarian, the philistine have never been troubled by questions of good

---

[73] *Kant's Critique of Aesthetic Judgment,* James Creed Meredith, trans. (Oxford: The Clarendon Press, 1911), p. 174.

or bad taste. The term "taste" as it is used here entails more than a judgment of artistic or useful objects. It implies an all-pervasive quality which finds expression in one's behavior in general. Taste enters not only into the way we dress or furnish our homes, but into our choice of words and gestures, in our selection of the music we hear, the artistic presentations we see, and the books we read.

It is in connection with this "all-pervasive quality" that taste and fashion may be most easily differentiated. Fashion is the style or vogue of the day which exploits man's desire for change. To a great extent it is forced on the individual from the outside, and—with rare exceptions—becomes acceptable through social pressure. On the other hand, taste is largely the expression of the inner man, reflected in most of his mundane choices. It endows him with the strength to resist outside pressure. It permits him to select sensitively and freely whatever he wishes even from what is fresh or new in his day.

The general undiscriminating reliance today on fads and fashion can be interpreted as a substitute for individual taste. Without having cultivated personal taste, the poorly educated individual finds certainty only in temporary fashion. Blindly accepting and following the mode of the day, he labors under the notion that what he acquires will certainly be socially pleasing or at least agreeable. The advocated fashion of the moment relieves him of the burden of deciding what is in good or bad taste. The question now arises: Have there ever been definite standards of good or bad taste?

This question can be answered only in relative terms. In all periods of history, tastes or aesthetic preferences are based on the prevailing ideals and thoughts of the time; whenever they change, the taste of the period changes also. The taste of early colonial days was strongly influenced by the Puritan mode of life. The Puritans discriminated against frills and ostentatiousness; in their personal lives they exemplified simplicity, restraint, and austerity, and these attributes characterize the taste of this period in America. Another example is Empire, the style of the Napoleonic era. It mirrored the ideals and thoughts of its time, which were strongly influenced by those of the Roman Empire. The characteristic elegance of a past culture was revived, but in an extravagant and pompous manner. The standard of taste was a mixture of refinement and coarseness, befitting the spirit of the day.

Our present standard of taste reflects our quest for certainty and honesty. The prevailing criterion is veracity in all forms of artistic expression, which bars pretense and embellishment. The same criterion is applied to the utilization of materials, be they words, sounds, colors, or wood. The more truthfully the manifold aspects of life are stated, the more the innate characteristics of a material are exposed, the more acceptable are they to our present taste.

Significantly, if instead of asking "What is good or bad taste?" one asks "What is good or bad fashion?", one finds oneself at a loss. The question does not make sense because fashion is outside moral considerations such as "good" or "bad." It can be neither good nor bad, merely more or less pleasing. Yet pleasing is not identical with good.[74] The red cheeks of a pale-faced girl suffering from tuberculosis may be pleasing, but not good. They are, in fact, symptoms of something evil.

"Good taste," said Santayana, "comes . . . from experience, in the best sense of that word. It comes from having united in one's memory and character the fruit of many diverse undertakings. Mere taste is apt to be bad taste, since it regards nothing but a chance feeling. Every man who pursues an art may be presumed to

---

[74] "The word and conception 'good' includes the conception of 'beautiful', but the reverse is not true, the conception 'beauty' does not include the conception 'good.' If we say 'good' of an article which we value for its appearance, we thereby say that the article is beautiful; but if we say it is 'beautiful,' it does not at all mean that the article is a good one." Tolstoy, *What Is Art?,* p. 88.

have some sensibility; the question is whether he has breeding, too, and whether what he stops at is not, in the end, vulgar and offensive. Chance feeling needs to fortify itself with reason and to find its level in the great world."[75]

Unquestionably, education plays a key role in changing "mere taste" into "good taste." Good taste results from experiences with the best of taste, as exemplified in all forms of great art, whether literature, poetry, music, painting, sculpture, or architecture. Great creative works reflect good taste, but good taste is not an automatic result of working with creative media or forms of expression. An artist imparts his already cultivated taste to his work; he does not develop this taste merely by expressing himself. If, therefore, one aim of education is the development of taste in youth, the responsibility for executing this difficult task must be shared by teachers in all creative areas and all disciplines: it is as much the concern of teachers of literature, music, or dance as of the art teacher. Since it can only be achieved by all branches of learning acting in concert, it would be unfair to throw the whole responsibility on the art teacher. Being aware of his limitations, he should resent carrying such an undivided burden.

Misunderstandings in regard to taste and art education are not the only ones with which art teachers are often faced. There is also the popular belief that anyone actively engaged in producing creative works will by virtue of this activity almost automatically become a more "self-integrated" person. "Self-integration" thus used implies both emotional stability and a good social adjustment. Such a belief implies that any creative activity is per se a beneficial mental health agent. But can this be supported by facts?

A study of the lives of men who have spent years in pursuit of creative achievements might be expected to yield some answers to this weighty question. But one soon discovers that many creative artists were neither well balanced emotionally, nor well adjusted socially. Even if one disregards such great creators as the novelist Virginia Woolf, the painter Van Gogh, or the sculptor Lehmbruck, who in spite of their constant artistic productivity lacked stability and tragically ended their lives voluntarily, one still discovers many others who could not find peace of mind by expressing themselves creatively. The composer Rachmaninoff and the painter Munch, for example, experienced serious emotional breakdowns, and for a period of time were unable to create. The breakdowns occurred at a time when these artists were constantly creative and highly successful. One could make up an impressive list of great men who were artistically prolific, knew recognition and fame, and produced lasting works, but still could not balance their emotional lives or adjust themselves to their environments.

Basic studies on the relation between creativity and mental or emotional difficulties distinguish between three possible alternatives: 1) emotional difficulties *destroy* creativity; 2) emotional difficulties *exist independent* of creativity and neither hamper productivity nor interfere with creative work; 3) these difficulties *heighten* productivity and play a part during the creative process and in the outcome of the work.[76]

All these alternatives can be identified in corresponding living counterparts in many art rooms. It is not uncommon to find an unruly student who shows ability and aptitude for creative work during brief intervals, but who—for psychological reasons—has extreme difficulty in concentrating on his work. He cannot find satisfaction in his meager achievements, remains aloof and unapproachable, and finally drops the art class. Here the emotional difficulty appears to destroy a potential creative ability.

---

[75] Santayana, *The Life of Reason,* pp. 371–372.
[76] This statement is based on *Genie, Irrsinn und Ruhm* by Wilhelm Lange-Eichbaum (Munich: Ernst Reinhardt Verlag, 1956), 4th ed., pp. 236–238.

Even more commonly found is the student who shows sincere interest and ability in art, who begins to work as soon as he enters the art room, and whose achievements and behavior are most acceptable. Then the art teacher discovers, often accidentally, that the student has great difficulties in other classes, where his performance is poor and his behavior objectionable to teachers and to his peers. In spite of the student's progress and accomplishments in art, his attitude outside the art room does not change. Although he is eager to improve his art work and accepts criticism well, he resents any well-meaning advice the art teacher may offer to help him amend his relationships with other teachers and his fellow students. This form of student behavior corresponds to the second alternative: the alleged beneficial qualities of the creative activity remain independent of any other action or manner of conduct and are not transferred into other situations.

The third alternative, that creativity is heightened by emotional difficulties, can also be correlated with the behavior of some students in the art room. It is not too unusual to have a student who works with conspicuous intensity on a project most of the time. He is quiet, undemanding, and self-sufficient. His behavior does not indicate trouble or strain. As long as the subject, medium, and technique appeal to him he works with great fervor—otherwise he may show considerable reluctance, often alternating between these two extremes. Despite his interest in his work, he is most uncooperative and reticent, and is disinterested in, or even rejects, personal contact with his teachers and his peers. His behavior may not be offensive, yet he may create a disagreeable impression because of his indifference to everything except his creative work. His artistic achievements matter to him but his social behavior and his sometimes erratic conduct remain unaffected, although he often finds satisfaction through the creative outlet. He does not adjust to his environment despite the fact that he can give expression to his thoughts and feelings.

None of these alternatives considers the creative activity as a catalytic agent which helps to produce a stable and healthy emotional life. The reason is that there is as yet no way to determine what would happen to the emotional life of an artist if he were forcibly prevented from creating. Artists are known to have persisted in creating under the most adverse conditions, even endangering their physical welfare and safety. For instance, the painter Franz Marc still worked creatively when he served as a soldier in the front lines of World War I; artists like Heckel, Schmidt-Rottluff, and Barlach pursued their work secretly, in defiance of official interdicts and threats. Others continued to create in spite of very serious physical handicaps. Renoir and Dufy kept on painting even after their hands became severely crippled; the blind Milton created immortal poetry, and Beethoven continued to compose, defying deafness.

It is a reasonable supposition that the inner need to create exists independent of material comfort, security, or physical well-being. In other words, even dismal external circumstances may not hamper the will to create. Yet it would be wrong to conclude that because the artist possesses means to express himself creatively, he can endure hardships better than other mortals. Who knows how many potentially gifted individuals may have died unknown because of struggle and pain? Lacking the physical or emotional strength to overcome difficulties, they perished without having achieved anything of worth. No one can say whether their creative ability, their aesthetic sensitivity and flexibility of mind helped, hampered, or possibly destroyed them.

One thing is certain, however: the act of creating is a very strenuous process for many artists. Their diaries, letters, and poems bear witness to the pain, frustration, and struggle undergone during the formulation of visions and thoughts. Chopin wrote: "I have to go through terrible toil and worry, many tears and sleepless nights. You feel just as weak after giving birth to a child as I feel after finishing a composition."[77] Hardly anyone does serious creative work in a nonchalant manner, unperturbed, in a tranquil frame of mind.

Unquestionably the process of creating has, to varying degrees, profound emotional effects on the creator, be he artist, amateur, or student, which are often felt during the act of creating and/or soon after the work is completed (see pp. 32–34). In some cases the strain or struggle which is experienced causes animation; in others it often has the opposite effect. Inner excitement also frequently acts as a stimulus. The will to succeed, the desire to overcome inadequacies, has an agitating effect on the emotions of the creator, and sometimes may help him to overcome some of his limitations. Then again it may result in a disturbed state of mind. In other words, the act of creating, as well as the immediate aftereffects of a work, have emotional repercussions; although the creative act may relieve some inner tensions, it may simultaneously induce new ones.

The notion that the creative activity has a self-healing effect on a disturbed mind has not been proved—at least not to this date. In the realm of psychiatry, working with art media and visual forms of self-expression has been found beneficial but in no way a cure for mental illness. In psychiatry the creative activity has been explored from two points of view—as occupational therapy and as a diagnostic aid. Yet, particularly as occupational therapy, visual art expression has not been found superior to music, play-acting, or writing: any one of these media for self-expression can be of some help in restoring order to the mind.

It is significant that most books on the subject of art and therapy strongly emphasize particular conditions which must always be met if the disturbed person is to benefit from creative self-expression. Aside from some mild encouragement in regard to the utilization of art materials, all creative work must be produced *without* any influence or interference, praise or reward. It must never be displayed, or shown to relatives, friends, or other patients.

It is precisely on these last points that the decisive difference between the therapeutic and educational approaches to art is demonstrated. Art education is a process of learning, acquiring knowledge and skills, and cultivating aesthetic sensitivity and useful habits, none of which can be achieved without a teacher's influence and interference. Evaluation of creative works, praise, reproof, and challenges are the customary techniques of art teaching and guidance. These forms of interference are designed to help students progress, develop their innate potentialities, understand their problems, and appreciate their achievements.

The art teacher is trained to give this instruction and guidance, but he is not equipped to play the role either of a psychiatrist or of a psychologist, nor are his students patients in need of psychiatric treatment. With rare exceptions, the high school student is well able to handle his more or less minor emotional difficulties. Throughout the school day he has many opportunities to give vent to his thoughts and feelings, for he is offered a variety of constructive emotional outlets. These include participation in sports, dramatic arts, music, creative writing, and discussions of current events. Obviously art is only one among the many areas which can provide the high school student with a conduit for his emotions, and can sometimes act as a catalyst for inner tensions or difficulties. But art should never be singled out as the only activity which can perform such a function. It would be unfair to claim that this branch of education is mainly a laxative for the soul, and the art teacher nothing but a nursemaid for students who cannot take care of their emotional difficulties.

An equally dangerous assertion is that a preoccupation with art media and self-expression produces a well-balanced person, able to adapt himself to his environment

---

[77] Jan Holcman, *The Legacy of Chopin* (New York: Philosophical Library, 1954), p. 79.

without friction. To begin with, the task of creating is altogether private; an individual is very much alone, unconcerned with any thoughts other than his own.[78] It is a self-directed activity consisting of attempts to state something new or different. But "new" means leaving accepted premises; it is outside any conformity. All too often has creating been synonymous with producing a work which was resented at first and won acceptance only very gradually. The history of the arts is filled with examples of works which were publicly attacked and banned, and of artists who were isolated, ridiculed, or even persecuted because their achievements or their thoughts did not conform to the mode or beliefs of the day. How, then, can we claim that creating is an aid for better adjustment? Adjustment to what? To that which is already in existence and well established? But this would mean the opposite of creating! In our time when there is such pressure on the individual to conform, when he is constantly tempted to accept uncritically what is offered, when conformity can substitute for responsibility—particularly today art education has a serious obligation to strengthen the student's individuality, to help him develop the means to resist this pressure to conform, to force him to think independently and creatively, and to assist him in finding satisfaction in making independent decisions.

None of these qualities need have any direct bearing on the ability to balance one's emotions and adjust to life. If this ability is incidentally fostered in the art class, so much the better; but it would be misleading to claim that art education's major justification and primary contribution is to help develop more well-adjusted young people.

Because of the very nature of the creative activity, many students express hitherto unrevealed thoughts and feelings, not only in their work but in conversations with the art teacher. Their relationship with this teacher, therefore, is often quite different from that which they have with other high school instructors. From the art teacher's point of view, the guiding principle in this relationship resembles the one between a patient and his physician, or between a client and his attorney; it is based on a student's trust and confidence in his teacher, who must treat his communications with the utmost care. On the other hand, the teacher, like the doctor or lawyer, should never unburden himself to his students; his private life and his relations with his superiors or colleagues are personal matters which he must never discuss with his students. It is equally inadvisable for the art teacher to display his own creative achievements in the classroom and try to impress the pupils with his skill and creative ability. Inevitably these works will be regarded as examples which students mistakenly suppose they must follow if they are to achieve what is most acceptable to their teacher. If he for some reason cannot find a suitable example outside his own work with which to clarify a technique or a particular point, he should avoid mentioning that the work came from his hand. Also, whenever the teacher has to give a visual demonstration, he should do so with restraint, avoiding a conspicuous display of his skill.

Some teachers, insecure in their rapport with their students, believe that by being overly kind they are most effective and appreciated. This approach may take the form of indiscriminate spreading of praise, reiterating sweet phrases, and abstaining from enforcing discipline. Yet this strategy usually has a contrary effect on the students, rather than the desired one. They become disrespectful, produce only superficial work, and finally leave the art class with little regard for art. High school students expect their teacher to know his field well and, like a mountain guide, to

---

[78] "In the creative process a man is able to 'let go,' to let his imagination sail out, conscious of being alone though with a sort of second self for company. This feeling of being on a lone adventure I think forms a very distinctive part of the characteristic mental state in which all creative work is done." Elizabeth Schneider, *Aesthetic Motive* (New York: The Macmillan Co., 1939), p. 60.

lead them safely through difficulties, proceeding with kindness but determination. He should radiate confidence and invite trust in his ability to show the way; he should earn respect by purposeful action rather than by sugary words; he should first and foremost be concerned with carrying out his professional task well, and if necessary he should use harsh measures for the sake of those who trust him. His students will be grateful for his good deeds, though some perhaps only at a much later date.

Most important of all, every teacher must learn to trust himself. So long as he truly tries to be of service to his students, keeps their interests at heart, is impartial, unbiased, and tolerant of their differences and weaknesses, he should not be overly concerned with how much he is liked or disliked. Most students are very sensitive and almost instinctively know whether a teacher is genuinely interested in them or only pretending to be. The teacher who exerts himself on his student's behalf, who has the courage to tell them the truth and to insist on sincere work, and who exercises discipline even at the risk of losing his popularity, in the end is often the most appreciated and respected.

Still, there are difficult moments in every teacher's life, moments when he is plagued by uncertainties, when he wonders if he is doing the right thing for his students, and if what he is teaching is worth the time they must spend learning it. In such moments he may begin to doubt that art teaching can be justified in the light of our present uncertainties and that it can truly aid students in overcoming the many difficulties ahead of them. He may ask himself if it is really true that art can help them deal with the uncertainties of life in our time. In these moments of despair, when a teacher may begin to lose faith in his task or feel that his efforts are of no importance, he should remind himself that he is working in the field in which the most creative and sensitive minds in history found their life's fulfillment, a field so important that the world's greatest intellects and most of its philosophers gave it hours on end of their most profound attention. It is a field which has produced neither conquerors nor destroyers, but rather builders and creators. Few of these men earned the riches of the world; many died as paupers, unhonored and unsung. Yet later their achievements were recognized and they became celebrated as famous sons of their country, their works noble symbols of their time or culture. Their lasting contributions fill their compatriots with pride, and their masterpieces have become the common, great heritage, exemplifying what works of genius are possible to man's creative spirit.

Helping young people to become intimately acquainted with the act of creating does not really need justification, any more than art needs vindication. Experiencing the formulation of creative thoughts or visions, and learning from or about great artistic accomplishments of the past or present, are a part of education as important as anything taught today. Future generations may apply the same value measure to our culture that we use for those of the past: evaluation based on the quality of the arts produced. Surely, therefore, we should be most seriously concerned with the education of the gifted student. Since we do not know which among our students may make genuine or lasting contributions, we should try to teach, inspire, and encourage all whom we can reach. Only time will tell how much they have profited by our teaching. It is bound to be significant to some, perhaps to many, and possibly to more than we dare hope.

The teaching of art is linked directly to man's finest achievements; the history of art is a glorious history without destruction and without malice. It provides the best extant evidence that man is more than a temporarily tamed wild beast, that he is not merely a destroyer but a spiritual being who can create.

PART TWO

THE SCHOOL

The supreme misfortune
is when theory outstrips
performance.
Leonardo da Vinci

Any consideration of the teaching of art on the secondary school level would remain fragmentary without a detailed analysis of the character of what are commonly referred to as high schools. A thorough familiarity with the current aims and practices of junior and senior high schools is a prerequisite to a full understanding of the function of art education within these institutions.

To gain the proper perspective, it is necessary to begin with a review of the scope of art education at the elementary school level. This review should make the reader aware of the essential difference between the two divisions in our public schools, and of the influence of art instruction that is carried on from the lower to the higher grades. It also should help to give him a clearer insight into the problem of teaching art in the secondary school.

I Art in the Elementary Grades

The teaching of art in elementary schools is today an accepted part of the curriculum. It ceased to be a controversial issue more than a generation ago.[1] In fact,

[1] "The last decade has seen an intensified interest in the art program in elementary schools. College courses in public school art have increased rapidly; opportunities for in-service growth of teachers have been provided in the form of workshops and consultant services; and art in the elementary school, once regarded as a 'frill,' is now regarded as an integral part of every good elementary-school program." William B. Ragan, *Modern Elementary Curriculum* (New York: The Dryden Press, Inc., 1953), p. 454.

all teachers' training institutions now demand at least some work in art education for candidates for a degree in elementary education. Also, every state in the Union has certification requirements in public school art for elementary teachers.

The term "public school art" has little in common with the broad concept of art. It is a narrow, specialized subject which deals with children's art, with the development of children's creativity, and with the techniques and classroom methods useful in elementary schools. The teaching of "public school art" is mostly in the hands of elementary teachers. Their methods and standards vary greatly from classroom to classroom, from system to system. Hardly any elementary schools have a fixed place or a set goal for the teaching of art, and the approach to the subject depends on the individual teacher's background, training, and preference. Many elementary teachers see in the teaching of art only the playful manipulation of materials—a pleasant and to some degree harmless time-killer. Others see it merely as an area in which the less gifted child can compete successfully with the brighter youngster. Because of a lack of fixed standards, an illusion of success may boost every pupil's ego.

Unfortunately, there are teachers who make use of the art area to impress administrators and parents with their pedagogical skill. Their emphasis is on the finished product, and its success is judged according to adult tastes and standards. The medal or the ribbon presented to the child is transferred, figuratively speaking, to the teacher's chest.

Fortunately, there are also many teachers in the elementary schools who possess a deeper understanding of the function of art education. They regard the art session as a period during which a child can find an outlet for his emotions in a constructive manner: when he may explore materials and techniques freely, give vent to his innate curiosity, or exercise his inventiveness. And though he may be for the most part unaware of it, the child often will acquire a great assortment of new information.

The desire to create, which fundamentally sets man apart from animal, will receive its first encouragement and satisfaction during these early art sessions. Well-trained elementary teachers understand why children draw, paint, or model so differently from adults. They know that what a pupil portrays is not derived from visual impressions, but stems from the desire to state facts based on knowledge and/or emotional experience. These teachers understand that children pass through a number of recognizable stages in their creative growth, and that these stages have their own marked characteristics.[2] They accept the responsibility to motivate and stimulate this growth so that each child will pass from one stage to another without disturbance or retardations.

Understanding of the individual pupil is a prerequisite for any good teacher, and is of particular importance during the art session. Since children's creative works are often intimate revelations, many young pupils have to be stimulated and encouraged in a very personal manner. Without a deep understanding of the whole child, such encouragement may well be haphazard or ineffective. Therefore an experienced and/or well-trained elementary school teacher, with her familiarity with each pupil, is the most desirable educator for conducting the art session. It should be noted that a reciprocal relationship exists between the particular knowledge a teacher brings to the art period and the knowledge she will gain during these periods, provided that she does not superimpose her images or her preconceived ideas on the children. Through the art medium the youngsters often reveal feelings and thoughts about themselves which otherwise would remain hidden. These personal revelations give the classroom teacher added insight into each child and will, if intelligently

---

[2] See Viktor Lowenfeld, *Creative and Mental Growth,* revised edition (New York: The Macmillan Co., 1952).

utilized, affect her work throughout the school day. Because of her special insights a close understanding between teacher and young pupil can result from the relationship which is easily established during the art period. This understanding constitutes a significant contribution of art education to the total education of young children.

The Role of the Elementary Art Teacher

The opportunity to make this valuable contribution is often lost when a specially trained art teacher rushes into a class of elementary children once a week for a harassed twenty to forty-five minutes. In many school systems the elementary art teacher must work with 450 to 500 pupils per week, and in some situations with an even greater number. The brevity of her contact with so many children, often in large groups, rarely permits her to establish a personal relationship with each pupil. As indicated before, it is this personal relationship between pupil and teacher which is of the greatest significance on the elementary school level; through visual and verbal means the child often allows the teacher to gain a deeper insight into his personality during an art session than during any other activity. This intimate knowledge, a precious by-product of the art activity and of great value to the regular classroom teacher, is wasted whenever a specialized art teacher takes over a class of elementary pupils. It is therefore very doubtful whether an art instructor, specialized in teaching young children, will ever be more than a fair substitute for a good elementary teacher who is well trained in art education.

There is still another reason for doubting the desirability of an art specialist in the primary grades. An art session conducted by such a teacher must inevitably be focused on techniques and the production of finished works. But the uninfluenced grade school child is not concerned with the finished product; what matter to him are the enjoyment he derives from the activity, and, to some degree, the satisfaction he obtains from giving expression to his ideas. The freedom to give vent to his thoughts and feelings is a major source of fascination; techniques and materials play only a minor role.

"Techniques," in this context, implies the many different ways in which a material or tool can be exploited, ways which are not immediately obvious and are only the result of discovery and experience. For instance, covering an area on paper with a broad brush full of poster paint is an obvious utilization of a brush and cannot be considered a "technique." But if the wooden handle of the brush is then used to scrape lines into the wet area, we can call this a technique since it is no longer a self-evident exploitation of a tool. But this type of technique should never be taught; the child must be given an opportunity to discover it alone. Art techniques for their own sake, dealing solely with form, are a concept which is totally foreign to young children. Their only interest in techniques is based on finding a more satisfactory way of expression, if the familiar one proves inadequate. Here the teacher's obligation is to recognize the child's newly discovered technique, to make the pupil aware of it, to praise him for his accomplishment, and to encourage him to continue his search for other novel ways of expression.

Art Materials in Elementary Grades

It is highly questionable whether a great variety of art materials needs to be introduced to stimulate or satisfy young children's creative drives. A teacher's complete faith in the stimulating qualities of materials is frequently based on ignorance of the creative process in youngsters. Too many new materials are confusing, and each one also constitutes a new technical problem independent of creative thought; indeed, the introduction of this new problem often has a frustrating effect.[3] Therefore no new material should be introduced until children have fully exploited the familiar one and feel that it no longer has anything to offer them. An essential part of the creative process is the enjoyment derived from complete familiarity with materials and tools. Since this enjoyment often acts as a stimulant, it must be recognized and treated with the utmost care or its most valuable property, inspiring new achievements, will be lost.

There is an even more significant reason for advocating economy in the use of an already limited variety of art materials, tools, and techniques in the elementary grades: the relatively small choice must answer all needs for a period of twelve long school years! Under properly stimulating instruction the elementary school child will create freely. The art media will serve only as the means for giving form to expression, and will act as a creative stimulus in only a very limited manner. However, the child will enter a phase when he begins to become critical of his own work and to feel insecure in his own expression. It is then that he needs a stimulus which holds a new fascination and is different from any he has previously experienced. Such a stimulus is often found in a material or a technique. The child's preoccupation with handling a medium, attempting to master it and discovering new and surprising effects, will help him to disregard for the moment his own critical attitude, thereby perpetuating his desire to create.

Manifestations of the self-critical attitude appear most frequently in the junior high school youngster. During this phase the preadolescent is also most sensitive to the slightest implication that he is still considered a younger or grade school child, and he often associates those media and techniques which he has extensively handled in elementary school with "kid stuff." This association frequently acts as a retarding factor, whereas new materials and new manipulation processes usually have the opposite effect. Accordingly, the teaching of techniques and the distribution of art materials and tools should be carefully planned so that they appear novel at a time when this quality is most needed.

The responsibility for over-all planning, timing, and presenting of art media should rest with an art education specialist. As well as being trained and experienced in the limited field of elementary art education, the art education specialist also should thoroughly understand the function of art within a twelve-year program. He (or she) should act as a consultant to the elementary teachers, and as a coordinator of an art program for a total school system.[4] In this capacity the art educator should become a unifying force between the two existing rigid divisions in our public schools. All too frequently educators are so engrossed in either elementary or high school art that they lose sight of the entire function of art education.[5]

The Art Room in Elementary Schools

If elementary schools were provided with a special art room, the teaching of art

---

[3] "The art teacher should develop economy in the use of techniques. In most books on art education we find that most materials are introduced and used from the very beginning of childhood. At a time when the child is overwhelmed by his own creativity, when he is full of intuitive power, too many different media would not only be wasteful, but would often prove distracting as well." *Ibid.,* p. 140.

[4] "The writer is convinced that art education should receive more emphasis in the preparation of all elementary-school teachers and that the services of an art specialist should be available to all teachers in the elementary school." Ragan, *Modern Elementary Curriculum,* p. 456.

[5] "We must desist from the common habit of regarding the elementary and the secondary school child as two different animals, for whom different cages and different keepers must be provided. It is the same child, from birth to maturity, and its education should be a single undivided process." Read, *Education through Art,* p. 232.

to children would be greatly facilitated and the art supervisor's task more effective. Special rooms for music and physical education have been found essential and are an accepted part of many new elementary school buildings. Similarly, a large, well-lighted art room, furnished with simple but specially designed equipment adapted to flexible arrangement, should be provided. Such a workshoplike room would strengthen art in the elementary school, and would also help grade school children develop a greater enthusiasm for art which they would carry over into the high school.

It has been observed that children lose interest in the creative process soon after they have entered the fifth or sixth grade. A significant reason for this change is that only a very limited variety of offerings are possible in an ordinary classroom, and that many art activities therefore become repetitious and uninspiring. Elementary school students could be better prepared for high school art in a special art room where, for example, mural painting, pottery, and other large three-dimensional works could be carried out without difficulty. Many of these activities are often neglected or mishandled because of the physical limitations in an ordinary classroom. It is surprising that administrators do not insist on special elementary school art rooms simply for economic and organizational reasons: art materials and equipment could be utilized more efficiently, the planning of art periods would be much simplified, and the art supervisor could be of much greater service to the school.

Art Appreciation in Elementary Schools

Although numerous publications on teaching and curriculum planning for the elementary schools suggest or demand that time be devoted to art appreciation, it is the least fruitful phase of elementary art education. To begin with, the term "art appreciation" has no precise meaning. Most often it refers to a kind of amalgam consisting of various aspects of art history, components of applied principles of composition, and an analysis of the subject matter found in a work of art. As a rule, the last approach dominates the lesson on art appreciation in the elementary grades. Unfortunately, it appears that little or no thought is given either to what should be accomplished during this activity or how the undefined goal should be attained. Out of this nebulous thinking, the practise has developed of showing children a mediocre reproduction of a painting and then having them isolate the subject matter by verbalizing on this very limited aspect of a piece of art. It is indeed questionable whether such an approach could arouse in any spectator, regardless of age, an emotional response or desire to become more deeply involved with a work of art.

An important negative result of the sterile practice described above must be considered in this context: the spectator's age, experience, intellectual development, and capacity to react to emotional responses play a major part in his relationship to a work of art. For instance, the *Guernica* painting by Picasso will appear very strange and confusing to a person who has seen very few contemporary works of art. Without some notion of the historic background and some previous acquaintance with symbolism in art, this painting can hardly be effective.[6] In contrast, Pieter Brueghel's

---

[6] "This impressively large painting with its severely limited black-grey-white palette symbolizes the suffering of Picasso's countrymen at that moment: the screaming woman at the right; the dismembered man in the foreground; the agonized and cubistically viewed horse in the center (the Spanish people); and the brutal triumphant bull at the left (the invader), standing calmly over a mother who holds a dead child. It also foretells World War II, for which this struggle was one of the early tryouts. A naked electric light bulb casts its harsh glare over the scene into which an outraged figure (Justice) with an oil lamp thrusts its demanding arm. The great impact of this picture at the time of its creation, and its pervasive influence since then, cannot be computed mathematically, but it has surely provided a strong and fruitful source of ideas." Bernard S. Myers, *Art and Civilization* (New York: McGraw-Hill Book Co., 1957), pp. 643–45.

expressive painting *Children's Games* can be easily understood and enjoyed by any spectator. It requires no knowledge of the historic background of the work, nor previous experience with paintings.

Trying to comply with the demands of a lesson in art appreciation, youngsters will cling to isolated minor details in a work of art which correspond to their limited experiences. These isolated fragments are usually aspects of the story-telling element in a painting, drawing, or sculpture. They often acquire exaggerated importance because the child distorts them to fit into his experiences and cannot establish a meaningful contact with the whole work. One consequence of this premature and forced contact with great or mature art is the overemphasis on the story-telling element within a visual representation which is so often encountered in both high school students and adults. Another frequent outcome often carried over into maturity is fear of and resentment towards the entire field of visual art. The whole area of art appreciation should not be approached by children until they are sufficiently mature so that important art *can stimulate and support* their own creative activity. Children rarely reach this stage of development in the elementary grades.[7]

II The Basic Differences between Elementary and Secondary School Art Education

The previous review of some of the problems and practices most frequently encountered in primary school art education cannot fulfill its purpose without a short summary of the main characteristics which set elementary apart from secondary schools. First of all, the collective term "high school" designates schools within a school, while "grade school" refers to a unified type of school. Probably the most marked difference is that primary school education is unified in scope, whereas secondary school education consists of many distinctly different aspects of learning, each with its own limited goal. In grade schools all pupils participate in an identical curriculum and are commonly taught by only one teacher each year. They learn to

---

[7] "In many elementary schools 'art appreciation lessons' have often involved showing the children one or several pictures by an old master like Leonardo da Vinci, Titian, Goya, Rembrandt, or Gainsborough. The teacher indicates that these are great paintings and he gives evidence of their greatness by reiterating comments from an art book concerning the artist's use of color, his rendering of fabrics, or his subject matter. Too often pupils are required to memorize the name of the artist and the name of one or two of his famous paintings. The accuracy with which the child can later reproduce such information on an objective-type test determines his mark in art appreciation.

"Whether this formal type of lesson promotes real liking for such pictures and an understanding of what the artist was trying to do is extremely doubtful. It is likely that such lessons, which are almost invariably beyond the comprehension of the children, tend to stifle rather than stimulate a liking for and understanding of art of past centuries.

"Probably the soundest way to help children like art and understand it is to have them create their own paintings and clay models. In this way they learn intimately the problems faced by the artist and the skills involved in solving these problems. . . . Discussion of the old masters can, in most cases, wait until children are considerably older." R. Murray Thomas, *Ways of Teaching in Elementary Schools* (New York: Longmans, Green & Co., 1955), p. 458.

adjust to this one teacher, just as the teacher becomes attuned to only one group of twenty-five to thirty-five pupils.

Now let us compare this situation with the situation in the high school. The average high school student is exposed to at least six, generally to nine, different teachers, and must adjust to this number of personalities throughout the school year; the high school teacher is in daily contact with from one hundred to one hundred and sixty students. Obviously the teacher-pupil relationship in primary grades is entirely different from the one on the secondary school level. This is of considerable significance in regard to art teaching in the high school, as we shall see.

Of equal importance is the fact that it is one of the basic aims of grade school education to prepare the pupil for the next division of the educational system. This is in sharp contrast to the educational aim of secondary schools which defines at least five distinctly different categories, each with its own set of goals. These categories can be described broadly and are specified in the following terms:

1. College preparatory curricula with their numerous subdivisions
2. Preparatory courses for business careers or commercial education
3. Curricula designed for future skilled workers in industry or agriculture or industrial vocational education
4. Preparatory courses for future homemakers or home economists
5. General education programs for students without particular vocational interests or aptitudes

To some degree, art education enters into each of these categories. All provide opportunities and challenges to the art teacher, but each has a different optimum approach, varying with the vocational or avocational interest of each student.

From an art educator's point of view, the need for several approaches to the subject of art constitutes the chief difference between primary and secondary school art instruction.

In grade schools, art is a part of the daily or weekly curriculum in which all pupils participate. In most high schools, art is one of the subjects which are not required but may be elected, and which unfortunately only a small minority of students choose.[8] In summary, *art in the elementary grades is accepted as a general subject contributing to the development of all children, but on the high school level it changes into a special subject considered of value only for those who voice an interest in this form of creative expression.*

Comparison of the Time Element in Elementary and Secondary School Art Teaching

The time allotted for art in elementary schools varies from grade to grade. Art sessions in the lower grades may last from ten to twenty minutes, and in the upper elementary grades may be increased to thirty-five or forty-five minutes. Their occurrence varies from twice a day to three times a week. The hours, the frequency, and the length of each period is usually at the discretion of the elementary teacher. This flexibility enables the teacher to time the art sessions so that they will most benefit the majority of children. It also permits her to preserve an educationally sound continuity throughout the school day.

All this is quite different on the high school level. Subjects are arranged in inflexible schedules. The problem of developing such schedules is extremely difficult from a purely mechanical point of view, and rarely permits an administrator to give

[8] "In 1948–49, about 48% of all junior high school pupils, and about 10% of senior and regular high school pupils, were enrolled in art courses." *Biennial Survey of Education, 1948–50,* U.S. Office of Education, 1951, Chapter V, p. 24.

pedagogical cohesion to a program. For this reason we find students rushing into an art class between two difficult academic subjects, their minds tired and anxiety-ridden, unable to find any satisfaction in their own creative work.[9] This problem would be less acute if the art period were to last from ninety to one hundred and ten minutes, so that students could become deeply involved in the creative process and forget the cares of the school day. But art periods in most high schools last only from forty-five to fifty-five minutes—a time so short that a student has no sooner become completely immersed in his work than the bell rings and he has to leave. Many types of art work suffer severely from these interruptions. Some very desirable activities cannot be carried out successfully in this brief span; others suffer because the working process has to be prolonged over so many class periods that students lose interest.

These sessions of forty-five or fifty-five minutes may be perfectly satisfactory to a teacher of academic subjects. His work can commence immediately after the bell rings, and the period can be utilized up to the last second. In an art class, however, the situation is different. The students must spend considerable time in preparing materials and securing their tools and unfinished projects. This time-loss cannot be avoided in even the most efficiently organized art class. Toward the end of a period, more precious time is lost since unfinished works must be stored, tools cleaned and collected, and the room put in order if the next class is to perform smoothly. To my knowledge no study has ever been made of this double time-loss, but from observation I estimate that it averages ten to fifteen minutes, or 20–25% of each session. Obviously this unavoidable waste could be halved by introducing a double period for art two or three times a week, instead of continuing the present customary schedule of forty-five to fifty-five minutes daily.[10]

There is yet another reason for pleading for longer art sessions, assuming that one of the obligations of high school education is to prepare young men and women for the adult world. A prerequisite for vocational or academic success is the ability to perform a given task without interruption for a considerable length of time. Unquestionably, longer art sessions would help students develop this kind of work habit.

Isolation versus Integration of Art Education

Returning to the discussion of the major differences between the instruction of art on the elementary and secondary school levels: there is one more difference which, although not obvious, has an important bearing on the teaching of art in the high school. This difference is not immediately perceived because it is based on attitudes

---

[9] "I learned how rewarding but how rigorous it could be to inspire reluctant young boys and girls to drop their mundane perspective at 9:50 in the morning when they walk into an art class, become inspired and creative people for forty-four minutes, and then resume their normal mundane attitude at the sound of the 10:40 bell. . . . I could not help but think that teachers of art must be something in the nature of magicians, who at the touch of a celestial signal, are able to charm students into shedding their concern with 'How do I rate?' 'Who thinks well of me?' 'Who loves whom?' 'Who will ask me to what dance?' and such other disastrously important matters and become converted, by that celestial ring of the bell, into truly inspired people. But if teachers of art are akin to magicians, then surely there must also be something definitely magical about art itself, something which makes it possible, as good magic should, for ordinary mortals to leap up and out of their ordinary confinements of their daily lives to become, if only for forty-five minutes a day, different, new, fuller and richer human beings." Melvin Tumin, "Art Education and Creative Social Life," *Art Education: A Frontier for Freedom,* NAEA Sixth Yearbook, 1955.

[10] "Teachers in other subject fields have also discovered a need for longer blocks of time as they have tried to introduce their students to real experiences. Such activities as building, drawing, painting, or dramatizing require time—not only for the activity itself but for the preparation of materials and the cleaning up of the room afterwards." Roland C. Faunce, *Secondary School Administration* (New York: Harper & Brothers, 1955), pp. 298–99.

rather than on easily distinguishable facts. Yet it becomes quite apparent when one compares the position art occupies on the two levels of public school education. On the elementary school level, art is an integrated part of the whole educational program, and the classroom teacher is the major integrating force. Her understanding and constant contact with at least one form of art expression—children's art—helps her to develop an appreciation of this form of universal communication. Furthermore, most elementary school teachers have been exposed to a variety of creative art experiences during their training, and have become familiar to some degree with several aspects of the visual arts.

It is on this very point that the elementary school teacher differs from most of his colleagues in the high school. One rarely encounters a teacher in secondary schools who has had or maintains much contact with the visual arts in his mature life. It is even more unusual to find a high school teacher who is able to incorporate the visual arts in or relate them to his special field. Even subjects such as history or literature are often taught without any significant reference to the fine arts, although an affinity is self-evident.[11] There are many reasons for this lack of integration. One is that a great number of high school administrators and teachers were unable to keep in contact with the visual arts after they themselves left the elementary grades. Another is that on the college level insufficient efforts are made to point out existing affinities between various disciplines and the arts, particularly the visual arts. And unfortunately art is not a required course for high school students wishing to enter a teachers college. Teachers colleges have only very recently incorporated the art area into their secondary school teachers' preparatory programs; it is hoped that the effect of this will be to help liberate the fine arts from their present isolation in the high school.

As soon as secondary school educators become more aware of the importance of art as an *equal* part of the whole educational program for high school students, many misconceptions will disappear. One of the most current false concepts has led to the belief that the art activity is void of any intellectual challenge, hence contributes little to the acquisition of knowledge. But Santayana said: "The man who would emancipate art from discipline and reason is trying to elude rationality, not merely in art, but in all existence."[12] Another common erroneous belief is that occupation with the visual arts is profitable only for the so-called "talented" student, or for one with an acute emotional need for the therapeutic qualities which art education may possibly provide.[13] Of no less importance is the fact that many high school educators at present feel confused about the visual arts, particularly in regard to contemporary expression. Their confusion is often based on a lack of information and personal experience with the creative process: many teachers cannot distinguish between a copy, a tracing, and an impersonal imitation of a natural form. Since the ability to imitate mechanically or impersonally is often regarded as synonymous with

---

[11] "Integration of art with other subject fields, particularly with English, history, foreign language, and less frequently with the sciences, was done in several schools. The success of this kind of integration depended entirely on whether or not art faculty members were assigned some class time for cooperation with scheduled art teachers on a roving basis for a part or whole schedule. They were thus available to be called upon by the French teacher to show slides and to conduct a discussion on the characteristics of the Gothic cathedral, or by the chemistry teacher to explain the aesthetic aim and qualities of the scientifically interesting technique of fresco painting on a wet plaster wall." Frederich M. Logan, *Growth of Art in American Schools* (New York: Harper & Brothers, 1955), p. 196.

[12] George Santayana, *The Life of Reason,* p. 363.

[13] "Everywhere nowadays a decided accent upon art as an individually creative experience is evident, and in many places the need for art as mental and emotional therapy is definitely overstated; overstated not because art is not legitimately helpful therapeutically, but because the emphasis on art's therapeutic values is likely to reduce its quality as a creative experience, and, at the same time, effectively reduce its value as a mental or emotional corrective." Logan, *Growth of Art in American Schools,* p. 189.

talent, high school teachers are frequently unable to appreciate or understand forceful, creative, visual expressions which are subjective in character. The inability to appreciate creative efforts is probably the main reason why the visual arts find themselves in their present isolated position in the high school. As soon as the fine arts are given a more prominent place in the curriculum, teachers of science, mathematics, literature, history, and languages will find many new stimulating approaches to their own subjects.[14] Above all, they will be better able to understand those students whose creative originality needs recognition and encouragement *outside* of the art room.

In summary, we may note that although art has become an accepted, integrated part of elementary education, it is still an isolated appendage of secondary education. One of the undesirable outcomes of this condition is a kind of competitive attitude between the two major school divisions. On the face of it, it appears that elementary art education has outdistanced secondary art education. One need only compare the impressive amount of literature pertaining to elementary art education with the meager collection available for the secondary schools. Also, recent books on the subject of curriculum and teaching in the elementary schools give art the same status as any other discipline; similar books written for secondary schools hardly mention art education. Public exhibitions, television, and other mass-communication media are placing their emphasis on the art of the elementary child, giving little attention to the art expression of older students. It seems certain that these factors have largely contributed to instilling the belief in many educators, and to some degree in the public at large, that art education is an excellent medium for helping educate *small* children, but that it is of very limited importance for older ones. Lest there be any misunderstanding, this is not to say that it is advisable to slacken efforts in continuing to raise the level of elementary art education or to minimize its importance. Rather this is a plea for *equal* efforts to be exerted in clarifying goals of secondary art education to high school administrators and educators, and for equal prominence to be given to works of older students.

III Art in the Junior High School

From an objective point of view, the junior high school is a hybrid.[15] In some ways it is akin to the elementary schools; in others it employs the methods and practices

[14] "Since the material of science is itself often taught in our institutions of learning with little regard to science *as the method of observation and of interpretation of what is observed,* there is small cause for wonder that the scientific method has as yet found little recognition in other phases of human experience, and especially in art. . . . To learn to see anything well is a difficult undertaking. It requires the activity of the whole personality. Learning to perceive demands the interaction of the whole personality with things about it. This is true whether one is seeing a picture or painting it, mastering golf, building a new type of bridge, or reading the poetry of Keats." John Dewey *et al., Art and Education* (Merion, Penn.: The Barnes Foundation Press, 1954), pp. 5–6, 7.

[15] "The junior high school is at no point wholly like either the elementary school or the senior high school; it serves as a transition period. It has elements in common with both the upper and the lower division and also has some features and functions peculiar to it alone." Rudyard K. Bent and Henry H. Kronenberg, *Principles of Secondary Education* (New York: McGraw-Hill Book Co., 1955), p. 121.

of the senior high school. The junior high school has still a single aim, similar to the elementary school, but it gradually introduces electives which allow the student a limited choice of subject matter. A many-teachers plan is used, and there is a gradual change from closely supervised instruction to that which permits pupils more independent work, similar to the practices in the senior high school. As in the elementary grades, art is still largely a required subject in which all students participate, but it is taught by a specialized art instructor, generally in a special room equipped solely for this activity, and devoted only to it. The range of activities is restricted mainly to basic two- and three-dimensional work. Emphasis is placed on group unit teaching and group work.[16] In this sort of group unit teaching, every pupil in the class receives and carries out more or less the same assignment during any given period. Group work, on the other hand, denotes an art activity in which many students work together on one large project. The two approaches to junior high school art teaching should emphatically not be interpreted from a narrow or dogmatic point of view, and allowances for individual deviations should be made as a matter of course.

Approaches to Art Stimulation for Junior High School Students

Most students in the junior high school are entering one of the most critical phases of their development because it is during this period that the individual attempts to shed his dependency on his elders. During this process the young person often transfers his dependency temporarily from adults to his peers. Since the junior high school does not constitute a homogeneous group, but comprises different stages of pubescence, the teaching of art needs an approach which differs from that in either the elementary or the senior high school.

The individual student in the heterogeneous junior high school group is more critical towards his own creative effort than at any other time during his twelve years of schooling. In spite of the fact that he is frequently in a kind of emotional turmoil, he is often reluctant to give visual expression to his emotions. This reluctance is at times misinterpreted as a lack of interest in art activities. To overcome this pretense of disinterest, the art teacher should place the emphasis of his instruction on more advanced and diverse manipulation processes. The handling of different tools, the preoccupation with materials, the shaping, forming, carving, and experimenting should be of so fascinating a nature that the junior high school student for the time being forgets his self-critical tendencies and becomes wholly absorbed in the manipulation process. For example, if these youngsters produce a blockprint, it is not its design or the story-telling aspects which matter most to them, but the cutting and printing of the block. Therefore it is a major obligation of the junior high school art teacher to plan a program which will provide many opportunities for experiments with materials and tools and will make the doing more important than the telling.

The junior high school art teacher should be deeply concerned with the psychological growth and development reflected in students' creative works.[17] During this period of development it can be discovered with some degree of certainty how an

---

[16] "Group units are developed in the same manner as any laboratory experience. A common problem is developed; it is analyzed into its various parts; individual assignments are made, and the students proceed to fulfill their individual art assignments. Because of common student interests, students may work on the same phase of an activity, but each product will be an individual interpretation of the problem. Each interpretation will reflect the individual nature of the student. Each student will have an individual experience in a social group situation and will learn from the shared experiences of others a richer and broader approach to a particular problem which he faces." Laurence S. Flau, *The Activity High School* (New York: Harper & Brothers, 1955), p. 216.

[17] "An art teacher should not try to be a psychologist and deal with individual cases, but he should expect these sudden changes in individuals' behavior. He needs to be understanding

individual responds to visual stimuli and how he will formulate these reactions in visual terms. There are two possible modes in which these reactions or impressions manifest themselves, each depending on the individual student's disposition. One is the predominantly objective point of view, which is not emotional but *intellectual* in character. The narrative qualities in a visual representation are portrayed corresponding to an objective reality. Principles of composition, design, and color theory are generally used in a highly rational, controlled manner, irrespective of whether the work is abstract or representational in nature. The other mode is predominantly subjective, *emotional,* and expressive in character, mainly externalizing feelings. This subjective approach presupposes an emotional involvement which may be expressed by distortions, omissions, and/or exaggerations, but still in a representational manner. Or if expressed in an abstract manner, it may exploit the sensuous qualities of media. Their emotional impact, not rules or laws, becomes the principal force.[18]

However, the foregoing observations of the two different modes of response to visual stimuli and the possible visualized reactions to them should be understood only as a division in principle, because no allowances are made for individual reactions toward a particular situation. No person is constant in his reactions; he may respond more strongly on one day than on another, and the intensity of his reaction depends greatly on the particular experience which causes it. Not every happening produces the same emotional effect even on the same individual. A person who is easily emotionally involved, for instance, may suddenly become cool, calculating, and very controlled during an important event, while another who is usually quite detached, sensible, and rational in his actions may unexpectedly become impulsive, impassioned, and overwhelmed by his emotions. Similarly, a student may react differently toward one topic or task than to another. During one assignment he may become strongly involved emotionally with his work, externalize his feelings powerfully, and disregard the objective reality; yet during a different assignment he may remain detached and work quite rationally in a very objective and controlled manner.[19]

In spite of the possible deviations in the two modes of expression, the art teacher should conduct his sessions so that both the subjective-minded and the objective-minded student are stimulated in accordance with their natural bent. The problem of stimulating and motivating students is most acute for the junior high school art teacher. Whereas the elementary pupil can be aroused to express himself creatively with relatively little stimulation, the junior high school student requires

---

and reassuring as they seek to retain self-confidence while struggling with emotional problems and trying their wings at self-reliance. The tendency to be condemning of the unpredictable junior high school pupils is doubly difficult on them as they try to break away from dependence on parents, yet seek some adult support for their self-realization efforts. The teacher is in a position to provide some of this." Stanley A. Czurles, *Aims and Objectives of Junior High School Art Activities* (New York: The Related Arts Service, 1956), Volume XIV, No. 1, p. 4.

[18] Viktor Lowenfeld, in his book *Creative and Mental Growth,* Chapter IV, gives a detailed analysis of type development, similar to the one briefly described above.

[19] "A child may, during a given period of time, produce various pieces of work, some of which have haptic characteristics and others visual. The difference arises largely from his varying responses to unlike experiences. If he feels personally involved with a subject so that his emotions and intellect are noticeably aroused, he may sometimes give expression to his subject in a seemingly haptic manner. If the subject does not excite him, and certainly not every subject is equal in its appeal, the work may appear more visual in character. However, as many of the children gain facility with the media and tools of expression, as they mature through adolescence, as they become more selective in the choice of subject, they apparently tend to feel their way into the expressive acts engaging them. Hence, controlling their materials and developing their insight, they can give greater attention to the inner nature and meaning of their subject matter. Perhaps for this reason, some of their work seems to swing towards the type of expression associated with Lowenfeld's haptic category." Charles D. Gaitskell, *Children and Their Art* (New York: Harcourt, Brace & Co., 1958), pp. 151–52.

powerful stimulation and constant prodding, animation, and reassurance. Such reassurance means careful and deliberate criticism: praise for even the smallest achievement (or any other positive quality of the work), as well as explanations of shortcomings and suggestions for overcoming weaknesses. General, indiscriminate, all-embracing praise or disapproval is ineffective because such empty utterances are without any tangible direction and should under no circumstances be used in any art room. Neither praise nor disapproval should ever be an emotional reaction of the teacher. This form of appraisal should always consist of carefully selected points of encouragement or discouragement, and an explanation of the thoughts which led to the evaluation. But most of all, it should give the student facts which he can remember, *re-apply in,* or *transfer to* a new work situation.

The task of stimulating and motivating junior high school students is an important one. It consists of arousing their imagination and visual memory, and of creating the desire to give form to observation or reflection. It is unrealistic to assume that simply providing tools and materials is sufficient to incite and inspire junior high school students. It is equally unrealistic to hope that a demonstration and an explanation of a technique will inspire them to the point that they will unhesitatingly embark on new, creative adventures without further stimulation. The notion that stimulation and motivation are forms of interference with the individual's "creative spirit," leading to dependent thinking and hampering his freedom of expression, is an unjustifiable one. John Dewey stated:

> There is a present tendency in so-called advanced schools of educational thought . . . to say, in effect, let us surround pupils with certain materials, tools, appliances, etc., and then let pupils respond to these things according to their own desires. Above all let us not suggest any end or plan to the students; let us not suggest to them what they shall do, for that is an unwarranted trespass upon their sacred intellectual individuality since the essence of such individuality is to set up ends and aims.
>
> Now such a method is really stupid. For it attempts the impossible which is always stupid; and it misconceives the conditions of independent thinking. There are a multitude of ways of reacting to surrounding conditions, and without some guidance from experience these reactions are almost sure to be casual, sporadic and ultimately fatiguing, accompanied by nervous strain. . . . Moreover, the theory literally carried out would be obliged to banish all artificial materials, tools and appliances. Being the product of the skill, thought and matured experience of others, they would also, by the theory, "interfere" with personal freedom.
>
> Moreover, when the child proposes or suggests what to do, some consequence to be attained, whence is the suggestion supposed to spring? There is no spontaneous germination in the mental life. If he does not get the suggestion from the teacher, he gets it from somebody or something in the home or the street or from what some more vigorous fellow pupil is doing. Hence the chances are great of its being a passing and superficial suggestion, without much depth and range—in other words, not specially conducive to the developing of freedom. If the teacher is really a teacher, and not just a master of "authority," he should know enough about his pupils, their needs, experience, degrees of skill and knowledge, etc. to be able (not to dictate aims and plans) to share in a discussion regarding what is to be done and be as free to make suggestions as anyone else. (The implication that the teacher is the one and only person who has no "individuality" or "freedom" to "express" would be funny if it were not often so sad in its outworkings.)[20]

Art Experimentation on the Junior High School Level

Misunderstanding of the adolescent character and ignorance of the full meaning of the term "experiment" have led to the practice of urging students to indulge

[20] Dewey, *Art and Education,* pp. 36–38.

in experimentation for its own sake in the hope that these experiments will act as a self-perpetuating force leading to further creative endeavors. But experimentation suggests action whose outcome is undetermined; as soon as results are predetermined, we speak of production. The most obvious reason for any art experiment is a search for the solution of an unexplored problem, or for the improvement of an already existing solution. Genuine experiments in art derive from dissatisfaction with known forms of expression which do not convey what the artist wants to communicate, or with existing media and techniques which do not lead to the desired results. In each instance the discontent is based on an awareness of and experience with existing media, techniques, and forms of expression. Any justification for urging a student to experiment presupposes that he has reached a point of dissatisfaction which would frustrate him unless he tried to seek novel ways as a continued stimulus for his desire to create. Whenever a teacher suggests any experimentation, she also should point out that a single experiment rarely yields satisfactory results and that the student need not become discouraged if his first attempt fails to produce the desired result. As indicated, effective experimentation in art can only be carried out with a concrete aim in mind. Without this aim, an individual is unable to distinguish between a mere happening and a new, significant solution.[21]

Experimentation in art deals with the execution of an idea, not with creativity itself. Not until an idea or vision is established in the mind of an individual can the search for a new, more exciting and satisfactory form of expression be instituted. During experimentation in the art class the function of the teacher is, first, to establish a reason for this endeavor; second, to give reassurance when immediate success is lacking; and third, to help evaluate results in relation to previously established aims. The last is of special importance since a student may easily be unaware that he has discovered a new presentation of his idea, or a novel way of handling a material, and is therefore unable to profit by his experiment. Helping a student to become cognizant of his achievements does not mean interference with his originality. "Originality and independence of thinking are . . . connected with the intervening process of execution rather than with the source of the initial suggestion. Indeed, genuinely fruitful and original suggestions are themselves usually the results of experience in the carrying out of undertakings. The 'end' is not, in other words, an end or finality in the literal sense, but is in turn the starting point of new desires, aims and plans."[22]

Owing to natural insecurity, the preadolescent searches for certainty and is reluctant to do anything which may not yield a predetermined result. He strives to produce creative works which will not only help him prove a degree of mastery but will also conform to adult visual standards. Experimentation will be effective only if the junior high school student is confronted with a problem for which he has no satisfactory solution, and if he is reassured by the teacher that one can be found through this experiment.

Students' Creative Development from the Junior to the Senior High School

Comparing the preadolescent with the elementary school child, one soon discovers a change of attitude towards creative work. In the junior high school the finished product takes on more importance, and the working process begins to lose

---

[21] "A learner must be personally aware of a problem before its solution can have any real meaning for him so that the teacher may be forced to take time to help pupils clarify their problems before proceeding to other matters." Charles D. Gaitskell and Margaret R. Gaitskell, *Art Education during Adolescence* (Toronto: The Ryerson Press, 1954), p. 29.
[22] Dewey, *Art as Experience,* p. 39.

some significance. A sudden awareness by the preadolescent of a discrepancy between the world as it is conceived or known to exist and the world which is actually seen or perceived results in a conflict which has a restrictive influence. Since the small child, for example, *knows* that a table has four legs, he tries to depict the table with its four legs and is perfectly satisfied if he succeeds in giving visual expression to his knowledge or concept. The preadolescent, on the other hand, has become aware that although there are four table legs, not more than two or three can usually be seen simultaneously from any one position. He will attempt to portray the table in accordance with this visual impression or percept. This approach to visual representation borders on one frequently encountered in adults: a preference for representation of the world as it appears, with little or no allowances for deliberate distortions, magnifications and/or exclusions. Even students who by their natural bent find satisfaction only in expressing themselves in a subjective manner attempt to portray the world rather objectively during this period of their development. They often fight their natural way of expression, for they labor under the impression that they must express themselves in a conventional or realistic manner in order to produce work which looks as if it might have been done by an adult. Here the junior high school art teacher can be of the greatest service to students. Not only can she dispel their misconceptions regarding adult art, but she must also assist them in learning to accept their natural response to and expression of what they see or feel.

In pictorial works of preadolescents and adolescents, one can discover three distinctly different phases of interest reflected in their creative work. The first can be termed the "narration phase," the second the "sentimental attraction phase," and the third the "technical obsession phase." Usually students pass through these phases in this rigid sequence. They start in junior high school with the "narration phase" and reach the "technical obsession phase" during senior high school.

The "narration phase" is characterized by rather strong emphasis on the story-telling elements in visual expression. These story-telling components may be based on observation and experience, or they may be the result of emotional experiences and imagination. Color, form, or design are given a subordinate position and the literal message takes on major importance.[23] The junior high school student gains satisfaction from his work when he feels that he has clearly conveyed his story, because to him the content and not the form matters most. This approach to the content can be subdivided into two interdependent elements: the significance of the story itself, and the manner in which the story is expressed in pictorial terms. Therefore it is of considerable importance that the student can identify himself with the story, or that it hold real interest for him. It is immaterial whether the narration is an outcome of a significant emotional experience or whether it is based on observation of an occurrence which has left an impression on the student.

Clearly, the "narration phase" has a bearing on the teaching of art in the junior high school. Pupils will perform with greater enthusiasm if the teacher is able to incorporate some of their preferences into their work. This, however, does not mean that the class assignment should consist only of having students illustrate one story-telling event after another; rather, their interest should be employed as a kind of motivational lever. This can be carried out in two ways. The teacher may point out recurring shortcomings in previous works, and then motivate students by presenting other assignments and emphasizing strongly that these will help overcome their deficiencies. Or she may introduce assignments of a sort which are bound to lead to story-telling representations.

---

[23] "In early adolescence they tend to neglect design in the interest of realistic statements, but with approaching maturity comes an interest in this work often of an intellectual nature." Gaitskell and Gaitskell, *Art Education during Adolescence,* p. 67.

The "sentimental attraction phase" is characterized by oft-repeated subjects and forms which have little or no direct connection with the individual adolescent's own experience. As the name suggests, a predilection for these subjects or forms is often based on sentimentalized affections. Generally the work does not relate to a direct experience nor stem from genuine feeling for what is expressed, but is created because of a subject's superficial fascination. Interest in this kind of subject matter differs considerably between boys and girls.[24] For example, girls frequently portray

SIDE VIEW OF A HORSE
eighth grade girl
watercolor

SIDE VIEW OF A HORSE
WITH 2 FIGURES
twelfth grade girl
colored woodcut

SIDE VIEW OF A HORSE WITH RIDER
tenth grade girl woodcut

ballerinas, landscapes with palm trees, or side views of horses, whereas boys depict automobiles, airplanes, pirates, seascapes with ships, or panthers. Very often the subject is idealized and romanticized. Youngsters' attraction to these themes is based on vague association and has little connection with reality. There are almost

[24] "Many boys tend to keep aloof from any topic of feminine interest. A few girls, on the other hand, may select subject matter having interest for both sexes." *Ibid.*, p. 90.

certainly psychological reasons for the predilection for these recurring subjects which so often appear symbolic in character, but the analysis of their deeper meaning should by all means be left to the professional psychologist and should be of no concern to the art teacher beyond his having knowledge of them and recognizing their existence.

During this phase of development students begin to become aware of composition. The placement of forms or subjects is no longer left to chance and becomes a matter of definite concern. Most of the time, colors are chosen deliberately, and ready-made shades in boxes or jars are no longer satisfactory. The finished product takes on greater importance than at any previous time, and most students exert special efforts to give their work a polished appearance.

The "sentimental attraction phase" becomes most apparent whenever students are asked to represent their favorite topic. In many cases an individual will repeat the same theme in a similar manner again and again. Without stimulation by the teacher, these works show little variation. In fact, it is characteristic of this phase of development that students transfer very little of what they are learning into their sentimentalized works. However, under the guidance of a teacher who knows how to capture their interest and imagination, many repetitious themes will lose their fascination for the students within a relatively short time. The small minority who somehow cling to the "sentimental attraction phase" must be approached in a different manner: the students' sentimental interest in certain topics should be not only temporarily accepted but utilized. For example, the girl who loves to paint side views of horses should be made familiar with many great art works in which this subject has been treated, from Leonardo da Vinci's horse sketches and his bronze horse to Franz Marc's famous animal paintings. In this instance the apparent interest of the student is used both to acquaint her with important art and to stimulate her imagination in the hope that she will break away from her quasi-stereotyped concept and begin to search for different interpretations of her favorite subject. Variants of this method will be suitable for other students who cannot respond to more common stimulation and who hold fast to the "sentimental attraction phase" for an unnecessarily long time.

The "technical obsession" phase is characterized by an overemphasis on the skill needed for the execution of a work of art. The degree to which adolescents are interested in a project depends mostly on the opportunities it provides for the display of skill. An exhibition of isolated skill for its own sake is often mistaken for adult achievement. During this phase high school students are not overly concerned with manipulation processes for their own sake, but rather look to them as a means to an end. The end is a product which they hope will closely resemble the work of a mature artist.[25] Proportion, perspective, anatomy, and elements of composition become matters of conscious concern. Students are susceptible to any suggestion which they believe will help them increase their skill or improve their projects. A sketch or any other spontaneous statement rarely provides the satisfaction for which senior high school students are searching. From their point of view, these direct, "unlabored" representations are merely aids to a work, but are not in themselves significant or final products. They will often spend considerable time perfecting their undertakings, but will be reluctant to leap from one short-term activity to another. At the outset they will also resist any activity which is outside their previous experience because

---

[25] "Skill continues to develop in connection with technique, draughtsmanship and composition. Increasing confidence in his own powers as well as a developing vision assist the pupil in the development of these skills. During later adolescence many pupils will work for long periods with concentrated effort, not only upon new themes and techniques, but also upon those which are familiar to them. They do so apparently to achieve greater perfection—an attitude which is characteristic of the artist." *Ibid.*, p. 90.

new ventures rarely, at first attempt, result in skillful, professional-appearing works.

These three phases of adolescent development which are based on attitudes and revealed in art expression are somewhat analogous to qualities described in Mildred Landis' definition of "non-aesthetic elements" in the visual arts.[26] Landis defines five independent nonaesthetic qualities of which the first three—the "story-telling quality," the "sentimental association," and "isolated skill"—correspond to some extent to the development phases just described. The other two qualities, "monetary value," and "the label," may also be paralleled with certain aspects of art-teaching in the high school. The "monetary value" placed on a work of art can be equated with the grade a student receives for a single piece of work, regardless of his attitudes, work habits, and progress measured by previous achievements. A grade which is given independently of sound educational considerations, and the monetary value placed on a work of art (based only on commercial motives, independent of aesthetic virtues), are equally unreliable as manifestations of merit. The "label" put on a piece of art regardless of whether or not it is a significant achievement strongly resembles the certificate or ribbon which is presented to a student for his art project. A work of art may be "labeled" because it has come from the hands of a famous artist, or because it has been popularized by reproductions. One tends to forget that many a discarded scrap of paper, bearing a few spots or lines made by a renowned artist, has been retrieved from the rubbish bin and framed. The unwarranted prestige of these scraps of paper depends solely on the label fastened to the frame. Then again, mediocre works, which are inevitably produced even by prominent artists, have been mass-reproduced, and because they are well known are labeled "great." It is not common knowledge that the decision to reproduce a work is frequently based on other than aesthetic considerations.

A spectator who is impressed by a label blindly accepts someone else's judgment and automatically develops a biased attitude towards the work. Such a spectator will seldom be able to appreciate or reject a work on its own merit. Similarly, a teacher is likely to acquire the same sort of bias if he accepts, as a symbol of his own educational achievements, the recognition won by a student in a public competition, for he too is blindly accepting another's judgment.

Stages or phases of development as evidenced in students' art work are defined here as a convenience for teaching and guidance. The origin of these stage-concepts is observation; their characteristic is frequency. The whole concept of stage-development is superimposed on students' creative growth as seen in art expression. Similarly, grammar is superimposed on language. No living language was developed according to grammatical rules; rather, certain recurring principles in a language were discovered through observation. These principles were then formulated and are now known as grammar.

The stage-concept in art education has been developed from a similar point of view and, just as in grammar, many deviations from the rule exist. These deviations are variations within the norm and should not be looked upon as oddities. One of the commoner variations occurs when a student stays in one phase for a rather long interval, then, almost imperceptibly, passes quickly through the next phase, and again remains for some time in the succeeding one. Or a student may pendulate between two stages for a considerable length of time instead of following the more usual pattern of progression from one phase to the next.[27] Recognition and under-

---

[26] See Mildred M. Landis, *Meaningful Art Education* (Peoria, Ill.: Charles A. Bennett Co., Inc., 1951).

[27] "At certain stages, the young person's behaviour may fluctuate between that of childhood and adulthood. The art produced during one week may show signs of some maturity of expression, while during the next it may exhibit many of the characteristics of children's work." Gaitskell and Gaitskell, *Art Education during Adolescence*, p. 5.

standing of these deviàtions within the norm is important for any teacher; otherwise misconceptions can develop which may jeopardize the educational values of the stage-development concept in art education.

IV Art in the High School

The specific problem of teaching art in the high school has not been treated fully up to this point. The material reviewed and analyzed has dealt mainly with the aims and practices of elementary art education so far as they have bearing on art teaching on the secondary level. High school students' attitudes towards creative work and their stage development as revealed in their art works also have been scrutinized. There are, however, a number of issues unique in teaching art on the senior high school level which have not yet been discussed.

Several of these factors at first appear inconsequential since they do not deal directly with students' art expression and education nor with art itself. Nonetheless, they become very significant as soon as one leaves the theoretical approaches to art education and enters the classroom. The physical plant, equipment, materials, and the budget—seemingly extraneous matters—exercise a major influence on the teaching of art independent of any educational thought or goal. The success of an art program depends to a considerable degree on how much consideration is given to it, and how much money is made available for it. The ultimate responsibility for these issues is rarely in the hands of the art educator. Decisions concerning the budget for art materials, equipment, and similar matters are generally made by the school administrators.

The Art Room

Upon studying the external problems of art teaching in the high school, three critical areas relating to the art room become apparent:

1. Equipment
2. Work and storage space
3. Display space

The special equipment which art teaching requires does not in itself constitute a problem. Excellent functional furniture and fixtures which have been designed by art educators for this purpose are manufactured commercially and are easily available. Manufacturers of these special furnishings are equipped to give competent advice to any architect or art teacher regarding layout, arrangement, and similar problems. Since an art teacher rarely will carry the sole responsibility for planning an art room, a detailed discussion of this point seems unnecessary. Still, there are a number of facts which should be known to every art teacher so that he can give competent advice when necessary.

It is desirable that art rooms have a studiolike atmosphere, an appearance quite different from the ordinary classroom.[28] The size of the room will depend on the

[28] "The art room should be planned as an informal working laboratory rather than a conventional classroom." National Council on Schoolhouse Construction, "Guide for Planning School Plants" (Nashville, Tenn.: Peabody College, 1949), p. 64.

maximum number of students who will be receiving instruction in it at one time.[29] A reliable gauge of room size is that "about 30 to 35 square feet of net floor space per student is needed exclusive of storage."[30] It is advisable to have at least one large unbroken wall area covered with soft, durable material, such as cork panelling. This covering should extend from the ceiling to the floor so that large, murallike projects can be executed with a minimum of physical difficulty. Another basic necessity is provision for projections of slides and films, including a permanently installed, large, movable wall-ceiling screen.

Two seemingly unimportant items, often missing in an art room, are spotlights and a large mirror; both can be of considerable help in many teaching situations. The importance of the mirror as a means for evaluating one's own work has long been known. As early as 1436 Alberti in his "Treatise on Painting" wrote: "A mirror will greatly help you to judge of relief-effect. . . . Any defect in a painting shows its ugliness in the looking glass. Therefore, things drawn after the life are to be amended with a mirror."[31] It is often advisable to ask students to study their finished or nearly completed works in a mirror because the reflected image presents a totally different view. This "new" image may enable them to see clearly any weakness in their works and perhaps will help them find ways to make improvements without the teacher's assistance.

A mirror can serve still another function. A student may model in front of it to study difficult movements, poses, or details which he wishes to incorporate in his work; in the mirror he may well find the exact visual information he needs. The principal function of a large wall mirror in an art room is to provide students with the means to evaluate their own work, and with a constant source of visual information. Both factors should lead to less dependence on the teacher's help.

In an art room spotlights are probably of less importance than a mirror, but moods can be created with them, situations dramatized, and the volume of forms emphasized. (See also page 123.) The characteristic attributes of spotlights are brilliant highlights and harsh shadows; both give greater plasticity to three-dimensional objects than ordinary light. Powerful shadows amplify moods, and vivid highlights increase interest. These effects can easily be achieved with safe and inexpensive reflector spotlight bulbs in flexible fixtures. The fixtures should not be mounted permanently but should be movable so that they can easily be carried to wherever they are needed and attached to any stationary object.

Other furnishings should permit flexibility in arrangement; yet in planning an art room one should keep in mind that a teacher rarely has the time to rearrange furniture between the dismissal of one class and the beginning of the next. The sink —an important item in any art room—should be accessible from more than one side. The best location for it is halfway between the space designated for three-dimensional work and the area for flat or two-dimensional projects. It is important to know that during most art sessions one sink will serve only ten to fifteen students adequately. These sinks should be equipped with running hot and cold water, and also with sediment traps. As already indicated, a subtle division within the room is most desirable because groups of students working in two dimensions should not be hampered or distracted by those working in three dimensions.

---

[29] "Art rooms, because of the more active nature of the learning process and the need for use of model stands, easels and displays, will require more room . . . per pupil than is provided in the average classroom. This ratio of size may well be in the nature of one and one half or two to one . . . . The tendency today is to provide general classrooms of 800 square feet or more." John Herrick *et al., From School Program to School Plant* (New York: Henry Holt & Co., 1956), pp. 292, 263.

[30] National Council on Schoolhouse Construction, "Guide for Planning School Plants," p. 64.

[31] Robert Goldwater and Marco Treves (eds.), *Artists on Art* (New York: Pantheon Books, 1954), p. 36.

Any plan for the art room should also include a library area where art books and magazines are readily available to teachers and students. The current practice of having all books located in the general school library is unsuitable for the teaching of art. Books and illustrative materials should be within close reach at any given moment during art sessions. Frequently questions which arise during a lesson can be answered most effectively by consulting materials in the library, but because of the time and effort involved in locating, checking out, and transporting books from there to the classroom these valuable aids are very often neglected.

Some problems regarding equipment need further comment. There is many an art room which at first glance appears entirely adequate. For example, it may be equipped with one kiln, one potter's wheel, a small jeweler's bench, one or two sculpture stands, and other paraphernalia needed to conduct a diversified art program. Unfortunately, one soon discovers that the kiln is too small to fire large three-dimensional objects, and only very small, insignificant pieces can be produced. Since the single wheel permits only one student per week to practice throwing a pot, quite a number of students are deprived of this experience altogether during the semester. These limitations arising from a lack of sufficient equipment are serious educational drawbacks: they constantly force the teacher to make decisions based not on sound educational reasoning but on physical shortcomings over which he has no control. Obviously, *sufficient* equipment for a *few* activities is preferable to a great variety of facilities which can serve only a handful of students.

The most crucial area in any art room is the storage space. Many school administrators and architects regard the storage area as only wasted space where junk is accumulated. They rarely realize that there is a close connection between the amount of storage facility and the efficiency and smooth functioning of an art program. It is possible to enumerate at least six separate storage areas, each with its own function:

1. Bulk supplies of materials and expensive tools
2. Everyday tools and limited supplies
3. Students' flat works
4. Unfinished projects (especially wet paintings and prints)
5. Three-dimensional works, including works in progress
6. Students' works which are preserved as visual records

The amount of space necessary for the first five areas depends on the number of students participating in the art program during a semester. Since high school students tend to be wasteful with materials, it is best to keep only limited supplies within their sight and immediate reach. A separate storage room for expensive, sharp, or fragile tools and for materials purchased in quantity simplifies the supply problem and also permits greater economy of materials. This storage room should adjoin the art room but be off-limits for students. Thus the teacher can easily keep track of the reserve supplies and may also be saved the embarrassment of suddenly finding insufficient supplies on hand for a planned activity.

The storage space for ordinary tools and limited supplies should be spacious and centrally located in the art room. It should be easily accessible to students and so arranged that the teacher can keep watch over tools and carry out orderly housekeeping of materials without unnecessary loss of time. This can be achieved only if all tools and materials have their permanently assigned places and are clearly visible at all times.

The storage space for students' work should be arranged successively according to class periods, and should contain an assigned, separate section for each student, which should be large enough to store a portfolio and a drawing board without damage to the student's work. This is important because the senior high school student derives impetus and satisfaction from having produced a finished piece, and nothing is more disheartening to him than finding his work spoiled or damaged through no fault of his own.

Temporary storage for wet projects is one of the most difficult problems in any art room. This condition is aggravated by the extremely short time between one class and the next, and by the number of moist paintings or prints which have to be safely stored within minutes. Unless there has been provision for such a situation, orderly housekeeping may at times be impossible. Moreover, without a special storage area many works are in danger of becoming spoiled. The printing industry, which must cope with a similar problem, employs practices and makes use of special fixtures which can easily be adapted to an art room. A short visit to a printing plant or study of a catalog listing equipment for the printing trade should prove helpful in finding a suitable solution for this vexing problem.

Many three-dimensional projects suffer because of insufficient storage space. Three different types of storage facilities are needed for a smoothly functioning art program for three-dimensional projects: one storage area for finished pieces, one for unfinished sculpture, including clay models, and one—preferably a damp cabinet—for unfinished, moist clay work and objects in the process of being cast. There is hardly anything more discouraging to a high school student than finding his pot or clay model cracked because it dried too rapidly. Since moist clay pieces are extremely vulnerable, the damp closet should be sufficiently large for works to stand freely without being crowded. Storage for objects of harder materials should also be roomy enough so that each piece is easily accessible. As high school students are often clumsy, these storage facilities should be planned so that accidents are kept at a minimum.

Students frequently have to take home their three-dimensional pieces as soon as they are completed because of insufficient storage space. This is rather undesirable because the finished piece cannot be compared with an earlier or later one, and progress cannot be clearly demonstrated and specified. Moreover, successful accomplishments radiate confidence among students and often act as an inspiration for further achievements. Since this silent encouragement is lost as soon as a finished work leaves the room, it is desirable that the piece remain accessible until the teacher decides that it has fulfilled this purpose.

It is strongly recommended that storage facilities for accumulated records of students' works be in every art room. (The amount of space depends on the maximum number of students enrolled during a period of four years.) Some of the most characteristic works of each student should be kept every year as an artistic record, serving the same purpose as the students' records maintained by the guidance office. Personal files of creative works provide the teacher with an excellent guide for the understanding and evaluation of students' ability, development, and art experience. Moreover, such a collection is of particular value for an art teacher who is new to the school system.

A discussion of the physical requirements of an art room would remain incomplete if it failed to consider the question of how many students can be given effective instruction simultaneously. The length of each session, the age level of the different groups, their need for individual attention and/or critical commentary, and the types of programs must be considered in order to arrive at a meaningful answer.

By way of preface it may be asserted that the teaching of art on any school level is highly individualized, and consists to a great extent of personal communication between the teacher and a single student. While these personal contacts vary from age level to age level, still it is probably valid to say that on the junior high school level they are more frequent but of shorter duration than in the senior high school where they may not occur as regularly but often last much longer. No matter on what level a teacher instructs, one thing is certain: he must have sufficient time to give to each student whenever the need for individual counsel arises. This factor is of such importance that it alone can serve as the basis for determining the size of a class.

In our present high schools most art classes last from fifty to fifty-five minutes. Regardless of the particular activity and the efficiency of the teacher, a dual time loss inevitably occurs, leaving a net working time of about forty minutes. Commonly some general announcements or explanations of the assignment, topic, or technique consume additional minutes, and the actual time left for the teacher to work with individual students is often less than thirty-five minutes. Assuming that the teacher spends an average of not more than one minute (an extremely short time) with each student, he will be able to give individual attention to only about thirty pupils, since the remaining five minutes will be spent moving from student to student. This time schedule presumes that every student is able to work without much assistance, behaves perfectly, and presents no disciplinary problem. Moreover, in a class of thirty pupils usually only quite uniform activities can be carried out. There is rarely sufficient time to arrange poses and give adequate correction during life drawing or painting from models, to set up still lifes, or to supervise effectively more complex technical processes. As soon as a more diverse program is used during one class period, where small groups or individual students work on different problems—some in three dimensions, others in graphic media, and still others with colors—the distribution of instructional time becomes even more difficult for the teacher. One group alone may require anywhere from fifteen to twenty minutes, or a single student five to ten minutes, of advice, direction, or guidance. The older and more advanced the students are, the more individual instruction time they require; their work must be analyzed slowly and carefully, their critical questions answered fully, and their problems and technical difficulties clarified in detail. All of this is very time-consuming and cannot be hastened.

It therefore appears reasonable to state that in the junior high school no more than thirty students should ever be assigned to one class. Otherwise the offering must become so limited, the teacher's individual attention spread so thin, and his effectiveness so restricted that the art room becomes more a supervised parking lot or playground than a place for learning and creating. On the senior high school level the number of students in any class should never exceed twenty-five, and this should be decreased to about fifteen for the most advanced students. In a larger group the teacher will not be able to give the very personal encouragement, challenge, and stimulation which older adolescents often require to produce works in which they find the inner satisfaction without which their desire to create, to learn, and to advance cannot be sustained.

Unfortunately our present school systems are often compelled to enlarge classes beyond the teacher's capacity to instruct effectively. Yet whenever an art class becomes too unwieldy in size, the teacher's effectiveness does not simply become proportionally less; it is lost altogether. As soon as he has to repeat or restrict his offerings and can no longer give undivided personal attention to each student, the sound educational values of art teaching are lost; the students' interest in art is turned into discontent. Instead of finding satisfaction in art, they leave discouraged, their desire to create and their readiness to appreciate art all but extinguished.

The Exhibition Space

It is most desirable that every new high school building be planned with an exhibition area. "An adequate exhibition space . . . should be an integral part of

SCHOOL ART GALLERY
as seen from hallway
Senior high school
Beatrice, Nebraska

the building's design; a distinct room or large alcove; open to classes and casual visitors."[32] In an already established school, some centrally located area should, if possible, be adapted for display purposes. This type of exhibition area is not to be confused with the cabinet or wall space commonly used in the art room for the display of students' work. Usually these displays are seen only by the participants in the art program, and a large majority of students and faculty often are unaware of what is being accomplished in art classes. Thus the students in art are rarely accorded the recognition which they not only deserve but emphatically need.

A public exhibition area should serve several purposes. Obviously it should not be used only for the display of art works by the school's own students, but for exhibitions of original creative achievements by professional artists, for students' works loaned by other schools, and for faithful reproductions. This gallery space also can be employed to display many other forms of visual expressions such as posters and functional industrial and textile designs. During each exhibition a definite approach should be emphasized, stressing skills, techniques, the uses and properties of materials, or interpretations of subject matter by different artists. The aim of such exhibitions should always be to awaken and stimulate an interest in art in students and faculty alike. Exhibitions can easily be arranged from many other points of view and integrated with a variety of subjects. For example, for history: "Art during the French Revolution," or "Art in Early America"; for languages: "The Art of Spain" (or any other foreign country whose language is being taught); for home economics: "Clothing during the Centuries."

The material for such exhibitions is available, often at negligible cost, at major

[32] Lydia Powel and Thomas Munro, *The Art Museum Comes to the School* (New York: Harper & Brothers, 1944), p. 141.

museums, university extension divisions, art galleries, and art departments. Many large industrial and commercial enterprises supply well-organized displays to high schools, sometimes merely for the asking. Posters of superior design can be obtained from international tourist offices, and contemporary functional designs can often be borrowed from local sources. In addition, high school art departments will find the exchange of students' works with other high schools a valuable and stimulating adventure.

The incentive for a gallery program must come from the art teacher. School administrators have embraced the idea of using audio-visual aids, and should therefore be pleased to have an exhibition program which offers a variety of visual experiences to *all* students as well as to the faculty. Setting up exhibitions should be in the hands of students who participate in the art program, under the supervision of the art teacher. The very act of installing an exhibition can provide spontaneous learning experiences for these students. In performing their task they become familiar with the displayed works and also with the problems of arranging objects most effectively. Moreover, a school gallery would eliminate the need for large, once-a-year art exhibitions because small amounts of students' work could be on display throughout the school year. Annual exhibitions, displaying an enormous number of art works simultaneously, have two very undesirable features: one is the presence of overwhelming quantities which give an appearance of mass production and frequently overshadow individuality and uniqueness. The other is the great diversity of age levels, subject matters, and techniques which is often confusing and exhausting to the casual spectator. These large exhibitions generally fail in their aim to elicit admiration for the students' work and to foster an understanding and genuine sympathy for the aims of art education.

The Budget

No less than the space problem, fiscal matters decidely influence any art program. The amount spent for art materials and equipment, however, is not a reliable yardstick for measuring the quality or success of art sessions. Not only do the teacher's resourcefulness and initiative play a most important role; there is also the fact that a great variety of materials are obtainable without cost. Still, "it is undeniable that much can be accomplished in the area of the arts with limited financial resources, but it is nonetheless true that greater opportunity for varied educational activities is possible when adequate materials are available. In many cases, only money will provide these materials."[33]

The complex of a budget entails more than just financial matters; school policy and legal questions enter in. Budget provisions for an art program make up but a fraction of the total expenditure for instructional materials in a public school, and "these expenditures for materials in schools represent a relatively small per cent of total outlays as compared with expenditures for personnel."[34] The 1952 survey of a committee of the National Art Education Association showed that from 0.6% to 1.5% of educational budgets was allocated for art supplies. The specific amounts spent for these materials in 1952 ranged from 47¢ to $1.09 per student.[35] It cannot

---

[33] Helen Copley Gordon, *et al.*, "Comparative Expenditures for Art Supplies in Typical School Systems," *NAEA 5th Yearbook* (Kutztown, Penn.: State Teachers College at Kutztown, 1954), p. 13.
[34] Arvid J. Burke, *Financing Public Schools in the United States* (New York: Harper & Brothers, 1951), p. 506.
[35] "While attempts are made at running an art program on a very small budget, the most effective and successful programs in the larger junior high schools in this country provide a minimum amount of $6.00 per pupil for art supplies." Carl Reed, *Early Adolescent Art Education* (Peoria, Ill.: Chas. A. Bennett Co., Inc., 1957), p. 169.

be specified how much of these amounts, on a per-student basis, was allocated to the senior high school, since the figures represent averages for twelve-year programs. However, it may be of interest to note that budget allocations for senior high school art supplies averaged from 16% to 23% of the total budget for art supplies in a public school system.

As indicated before, many different materials which can be utilized during various art activities are obtainable without cost and therefore remain outside any statistical or budget considerations. Materials such as wood scraps for block printing and armatures, scrap materials for collages and mosaics, wrapping paper, newspapers, wire, tin, burlap, and many other items are commonly contributed by students. Nevertheless, this custom is not without educational as well as legal repercussions. Courts have ruled, for instance, that it is unreasonable to require a student to bring wood to the school.[36] Therefore a teacher cannot discriminate in any way against a student if he does not volunteer to supply such material.

Up to this point it has been taken for granted that schools supply all materials needed for an art program. This, however, is an assumption based neither on legal grounds nor on nationwide practice. In some states tax-supported schools must supply *all* textbooks and instructional materials, whereas in other states the schools must furnish only the educational books for the elementary grades.[37] The practice of a great number of schools lies between these two extremes; some materials are furnished by the schools, others are supplied by the student. This somewhat resembles the practice common in industrial arts where most students purchase the basic materials and the finished product becomes their property. This practice, however, is not without conflict in principle and raises a question as to what degree it offers equal educational opportunities. It certainly appears unreasonable, for instance, to expect a tax-supported school to furnish the silver for a jewelry project, and for the finished piece then to become the property of the student. But on the other hand, if jewelry making is part of the art program, each student should have an opportunity to learn this craft. Similar situations arise in oil painting, stone carving, or any other activity in which relatively expensive materials are needed. Unfortunately it is impossible to suggest a solution here which would be applicable to all situations. A teacher should be cognizant of the problem and try to find a tactful, sensible solution, based on educational considerations.

The mechanics of setting up a budget often *appear* more difficult than they prove to be in practice. To begin with, it is always advisable to study the budget and order forms of the previous year or years. By keeping in mind past and anticipated student enrollment, one can arrive at a rough estimate of the needs for the coming year. Two additional factors have to be considered before an exact budgetary plan can be drawn up. One is the total number of students enrolled in art, and the number of periods per week attended by each student. The other factor is the overall plan for activities and the duration of each activity. Both considerations should be figured on the basis of a whole school year. A breakdown in terms of days and number of students and the required materials per day per student should produce a fairly accurate estimate for the needed materials. It is advisable to add an extra ten per cent for an unexpected increase in students and as a margin for possible errors.

The budgetary discussion up to this point has dealt mainly with problems involving expendable materials; the complex of financing equipment has not yet been considered. It is difficult to decide which items belong to the group of expendable

---

[36] Lee C. Garber, *Handbook of School Law* (New London, Conn.: Arthur C. Croft, 1954), p. 149.

[37] Madaline Kinter Remmlein, *School Law* (New York: McGraw-Hill Book Co., 1950), p. 304.

materials and which should be regarded as equipment. A number of authorities on budget planning for and financing of public schools seem to agree on the following formula: items which will serve for more than three years and which cost more than $5.00 should be considered equipment. In many schools, budget allowances for equipment are separated from expendable materials. Art teachers are often required to separate these two groups of items in their yearly budget request. Special art equipment will be discussed later in connection with the various art activities requiring special implements and tools.

Obviously physical settings as well as material means are very important to any art program, but even the most careful planning, the most earnest consideration, and the most generous funds will not insure its success. Here the art teacher is the prime factor. The less time, thought, and effort he need devote to overcoming physical limitations and difficulties, the more time he will have to concentrate on his real task: teaching.

Discipline and Related Problems

Before considering those elements which are intimate parts of teaching, such as curriculum planning or grading, it seems necessary to focus attention on an aspect of teaching which is only too often considered disagreeable and therefore neglected in many discussions: the problem of discipline. It is a sad truth that not all high school students who enter the art room actually elected this subject, or enrolled quite voluntarily. The fact is that in many high schools it has become a common practice to send to art sessions those students who are either incapable of more exacting academic work, or who have personality problems which make their presence undesirable in many classes. Conversely, there are definite restrictions as to the number of art credit units a student is permitted to accumulate. In many high schools he is limited to two semesters of art, particularly if he is a very capable student and is enrolled in college preparatory courses.

These practices—which explain, at least partially, why one finds such a small art enrollment in so many high schools—have their roots in a lack of understanding on the part of many educators and administrators concerning the goals and educational contributions of art education. They accept the very limited therapeutic value of high school art and its possible benefit to emotionally disturbed students as the main reason for offering art in our public schools today. The potential therapeutic values of the creative area have been so overemphasized and so relentlessly propagandized during the past twenty-five years that it is no wonder that many educators have come to consider art a kind of patent medicine, good for any adolescent with alleged emotional or disciplinary problems.

The sad result of this misunderstanding of the true function of art education is that art classes are often degraded to the status of a sort of parking lot where students are watched over and may also be allowed to work off some of their alleged frustrations or aggressions. As one consequence, many young teachers become very disheartened and lose faith in their professional calling. This lack of faith frequently reveals itself in one of two ways: either the art teacher turns into a sergeantlike disciplinarian and forgets his real obligation—to teach art—or he becomes halfhearted, cares only for a few seemingly promising students, and permits the rest of the group to relapse into their often chronic state of laziness. Moreover, this misunderstanding has brought serious disrepute to the art area. Many fine students have come to regard art classes as snap courses where the loafers or the dull ones sit around and earn some easy credits without doing an hour of solid work.

There does not seem to be any simple remedy for this unsatisfactory condition; the misconceptions about art education can be dispelled only by the concentrated effort of all persons concerned with art teaching. This means that every single art instructor, whether he teaches in a large college or in a small high school, has an obligation to specify and to explain repeatedly to administrators and other educators art education's goals, possible contributions, *and limitations.*[38] Only then can art educators hope that the art area will be accorded its deserved and proper place in the high school, that the restrictions on high school art credits will be lifted, and that students will be permitted to choose art courses freely throughout their public school training.

On the other hand, the art teacher must cease to tolerate poor performance based on plain laziness. He must have the courage to demand unremitting effort from his students. He should never permit them to waste time or tax money. Every teacher has the obligation not only to train his students in his subject, but also to prepare them for the years when they no longer attend school. In any remunerative work outside of the classroom, poor performance based on habitual laziness is most decidedly not tolerated. If the teacher is unable to overcome a student's previously acquired negative attitude towards work, he must face up to the difficult duty of asking him to leave the class permanently. Otherwise the student's bad example may be imitated by some of his classmates.

"Discipline" has become a forbidden word in some circles of modern education, a word which terrifies many teachers and is omitted in numerous textbooks. As it is used in this context, "discipline" does not refer to restraint, but to control by the will through habit, and acceptance of the laws of society. The existence of disciplinary problems has been construed to mean that a teacher is incompetent. Supposedly the only teacher who encounters such difficulties is one who is unable to make his offerings captivating and his personality fascinating, and who sadly lacks understanding of his students. Such a concept is extremely unrealistic and has confused many beginning teachers.

The truth is that one routinely finds disciplinary problems in every high school and therefore in many art rooms. Neither the public schools nor the art teachers select their students, and even if they could, problems would not simply disappear. Often ignorance and misinformation are the decisive factors in students' choosing art: they have the idea that in art class they will earn good grades without any effort. Frequently they believe that art and the learning of art are so very personal that no one can grade it, hence they assume that covering a piece of paper with charcoal or paint within minutes means they have "expressed" themselves and deserve a good grade, even though they waste the remaining three-fourths of each class period. As soon as such a student's bluff is called, and his work unmasked as pretentious and insincere, he becomes indignant and difficult to handle.

Other students learn early—often in the lower grades—that the art session is a kind of play period in which they are supposed to relax. They have learned this particular lesson so well that they can no longer do anything else; they become resentful and often turn into disciplinary problems as soon as the teacher demands real effort and conscientious work. Still others cannot find any satisfaction in their visual creative work because the visual aspects of the world have little meaning for them. The media which provide these students with the means for expression and enjoyment are music, writing, dramatics, or even industrial arts. Their natural inability to find an affinity for the visual arts is a constant source of dissatisfaction which sometimes finds expression in some form of revolt or misbehavior. Not in-

---

[38] "Administrators are busy with the general problems of education. They do not have time to seek out current articles or reports on specific areas. When art teachers find significant information which will help to develop an understanding of art education, they should underline this, or make a short résumé of it, and forward it to the administration. Easily read reports concerning the activities and plans of the art department should be regularly prepared and sent to the administration." Reed, *Early Adolescent Art Education,* p. 180.

frequently they will exclaim that painting is good for girls but lacks any masculine attributes, or that art is child's work and that they have now grown up and no longer have any use for it.

Any and all of these misled, misinformed, misplaced, lazy, or erratic students can be found in an art room. Each constitutes a particular problem which at one time or another may require disciplinary measures. Unquestionably the difficulties of many students disappear if the teacher makes his teaching exciting and keeps in mind that "unless the pupils are continually sustained by the evocation of interest, the acquirement of technique, and the excitement of success, they can never make progress, and will certainly lose heart."[39]

But even under the guidance of a highly competent art teacher who can balance freedom and discipline, stimulate and evoke initiative, understand the workings of the adolescent mind, provide necessary encouragement, inspire confidence, teach competence in handling media, and plan each activity most deliberately—even under such exemplary guidance disciplinary problems are sometimes unavoidable. How then should such problems be handled and are any guiding principles known?

The prevention of disciplinary problems is of major importance. Many unpleasant disciplinary situations can be avoided by planning each art session with care and foresight so that even an unexpected situation does not find the teacher at a loss. Disciplinary problems are rare in a well-organized class, with the exception of a possible troublesome student. "An active class rarely has serious or persistent problems of discipline. On the other hand, when students find nothing useful or interesting to do, when dull routines of the same meaningless activity day after day bring boredom and frustration, problems of disturbance are almost sure to appear. If the whole class, however, is involved in varied activities—some working on individual assignments, . . . some engaged in an instructive creative project . . . what reason is there for disturbances of a disciplinary nature? But when only part of the class is involved, or some individuals, through poor planning of activities, are left with nothing useful to do, discipline is once again a problem of first magnitude."[40]

Probably patience is the most important single requirement in securing discipline. As the whole process of learning is slow, improvements in attitudes and behavior also take place slowly. Even if a student tries hard to improve, he rarely succeeds rapidly—wrong habits or confused ideas cannot be tossed aside like a soiled rag. Commonly, a student vacillates for some time between poor habits and improvement. What will help him most is a patient teacher who recognizes and appreciates even his smallest effort towards improvement, does not expect rapid changes, but still insists on definite standards of behavior and performance.

This brings to mind one other axiom: a teacher must be well able to distinguish between minor misbehavior and a more serious offense. Every misconduct should be evaluated in terms of its immediate effect on the group, its long-range consequences on class conduct, and the individual student's usual performance and behavior. Like any other human being, a student too may have a "bad day," a day when nothing seems to go right, when the slightest difficulty appears to be a major disaster, and when he does not feel like working.[41] As a result of such a momentary

---

[39] Whitehead, *The Aims of Education,* p. 60.

[40] Kenneth H. Hansen, *High School Teaching* (Englewood Cliffs, N. Y.: Prentice-Hall, Inc., 1957), p. 361.

[41] "Inconsistent and seemingly inexplicable behavior not only toward people but toward the work of the school itself often characterizes the high school student. . . . Part of this behavior may be explained as reflecting the unsureness that the student often feels about his own personal position with respect to himself, his family, his group, or his school. This unsureness is often translated into direct reactions to the curriculum, to the specific assignment, to the unit of work, or to the methods of attacking a problem. . . . Some days the student *feels* like working; other days he doesn't. This is a normal part of the normal changeableness of the adolescent." *Ibid.,* pp. 39–40.

mood he may flare up, accept or follow instructions poorly, or produce hardly a line during the art session. In these instances the teacher should be most tolerant in an unobtrusive way and try to avoid any situation which might require disciplinary action. Generally these moods disappear after a day or two, but if they do persist, the teacher should have a serious talk with the student. The result of such a talk should determine further action.

What disciplinary measures can an art teacher take? To some degree the answer to this question is dependent on school policies in regard to disciplinary matters and standards of behavior. In many schools a teacher must follow prescribed steps. For instance, in some schools every offender must be referred to the guidance counselor or the principal. In others only serious wrongdoers are handled by an authority other than the classroom teacher. In still others the sole responsibility for handling and correcting misbehavior is carried by the teacher.

As already indicated, the teacher should first of all evaluate the offense. He should never act in haste or become emotionally involved. He must be constantly alert to the happenings in his room. He must guard himself from becoming so occupied with one student that he loses contact with the rest of the class, thereby inviting disciplinary problems. It is much wiser to *prevent* misbehavior than to apply the best corrective measures. If some minor infringement does occur, a brief comment, a well-meaning humorous remark, or a kind word often will settle a situation without further action.

Sooner or later, however, every teacher is confronted by a more serious disciplinary problem, one which forces him to make a rather difficult decision. Undoubtedly the theory is correct that most unmanageable or ill-tempered adolescents can eventually be rehabilitated. The question is, can every one of these misguided, mischievous, or indolent youngsters be helped and set right in an ordinary public school situation? More important still, are high school teachers trained to handle pupils with serious emotional or personality problems? Also, is it possible for a public school teacher to deal adequately with such complex and time-consuming problems when he has to teach five or six hours a day, instructing between 120 and 160 students?

Here theory and practice seem to be poles apart. The fact is that high school teachers are trained for one *very* important job: to work with students who are essentially, and to varying degrees, willing, eager, and able to learn. Knowledge, preparation, and experience generally equip teachers to deal with minor personality or emotional difficulties, but rarely to handle students with major adjustment problems. Even assuming that a teacher did acquire the knowledge, skill, and psychological insight for remedying such intimate personal problems, he still would hardly be able to help these unruly youngsters in an ordinary school situation. Such a task can only be accomplished in small classes where the teacher can devote constant attention to one pupil for a long time—an obvious impossibility in an art room filled with successive classes of twenty to thirty students who spend only forty-five to fifty minutes a day there. In addition, the average well-trained art teacher is usually not prepared for work in the field of special education. His limited knowledge of psychology does not equip him with the skills needed to guide and instruct other than the ordinary, sensible students. Among these he should distribute his time, interest, and attention impartially; every student has an equal right to the teacher's instruction, regard, and even affection.

Consequently, when a student misbehaves and interferes in an unfair manner with the rights of his peers he must be treated as an offender. If the customary expeditious ways of dealing with such cases prove ineffective, and if the corrective measures deprive other students of valuable teaching time, or interfere with the orderly conduct of the class, the offender must be asked to leave. This has to be done not so much as a punishment as for the protection of the rights of all those who devote their time to their work and are genuinely interested in it. Democratic considerations based on individual versus group rights are the only fair and objective guide to handling disciplinary problems.

It is appropriate at this point to caution teachers against some practices which prevail in many art rooms. One is the typical first-day lecture in which a teacher establishes a series of rules and sets forth standards of conduct which every student is supposed to follow implicitly. As the teacher rarely knows his students when he makes such pronouncements, these rules are often very dogmatically conceived and presented in a manner which invites a negative attitude in some students. Quite often these opening speeches are boring; much worse, they force the teacher to adhere to rules which he may later find most inappropriate but cannot revoke without losing face with his class. It is much wiser to outline briefly and broadly the contents of the course at the beginning of a semester and to wait for a suitable occasion to establish a few basic and enforceable rules of class conduct.

Another detriment to effective teaching and handling of students is to make empty threats of punishment. It is so very easy for a teacher to announce that this or that behavior will not be tolerated in his class and will be punished forthwith. But when the specified offense is committed, the teacher ignores his own warning and is unwilling or afraid to implement his threats. If this develops into a pattern, students will soon realize that he is only bluffing, and he will have great difficulty in conducting his class effectively. Consequently, an art teacher should be chary of or, better still, abstain from threatening students. If this is unavoidable, he must have the courage to be consistent and carry out the proposed corrective measures.

Finally, every young teacher should be aware that he will have to live through a rather trying time for a brief period at the beginning of each new teaching situation. It is quite common that students start misbehaving after a few days in a class with a new teacher. This usually happens either at the end of the first week or some time during the second. The new teacher should not be alarmed; it is neither a sign of his ineffectiveness or incapability, nor of malicious student opposition, but a crude attempt at diagnosis on the students' part. It is their way of finding out about this stranger in front of them—a way of measuring his teaching skills, his sense of humor, and his understanding of young people. If the teacher remains unperturbed throughout this brief test, if he keeps his temper and his sense of humor, if he can anticipate some of the actions, if he has the courage, if necessary, to administer some mild punishment, and above all, if he can remain enthusiastic about his work—then he will have nothing to fear. This trying time will pass quickly and will result in a better understanding between him and his students.

Obviously there is a reciprocal relationship between a student's class conduct and his performance and work; his behavior is closely related to his achievements and, as a result, to his grades. Many schools record behavior and achievements separately on the report cards. It is often very difficult to decide how far to segregate performance and attitude, but the decision should always be determined by these aims: to help a student produce a more positive attitude towards his work, to improve his conduct, and to develop his potentialities. In some instances, grading down will help to achieve one or all of these purposes; a word to parents may suffice; or perhaps a private talk between student and teacher will prove most effective.

This aspect of handling disciplinary problems cannot be understood without a detailed analysis of the whole problem of grading, marking, and testing.[42]

---

[42] "It is necessary at this point to make a distinction, perhaps somewhat arbitrary, between 'marks' and 'grades.' *Marks* are basically a measuring device: a score based on performance. *Grades* are an *evaluation* device: a subjective judgment which takes into account not only marks, but a number of less tangible factors as well." *Ibid.*, p. 255.

Testing of Art Ability

Different means have been developed to discover creative ability in students, independent of their performance in the art class. Testing devices have been designed to estimate students' creative potentialities, and to measure, with some degree of accuracy, any active or latent creative abilities.[43] Usually these groups of tests are known as "talent tests." However, the term "talent" lacks precise meaning. "We know almost nothing about the psychological structure of special talent. Also, our ideas in regard to its hereditary determination are of the vaguest, for it is always quite possible that even the greatest genius owes much to his home environment as well as to his parents' chromosomes."[44] In actuality, "talent tests" are aptitude tests with a slightly different name.

The history of these tests goes back more than half a century; one of the earliest was devised in 1910 by Bullough. But the majority of tests for measuring art ability were developed during the thirties. Most of them single out one particular aspect or area related to visual responses or experiences and can be grouped as follows: art appreciation, preference for pictures, response to line or color, ability to draw, ability to compose, basic art ability, and intelligence in relation to art expression. Most of these tests are designed to measure one of these different abilities or responses in grade school children. Many tests assure degrees of accuracy only if the tested child has had little or no previous art instruction.[45] None appears to be designed especially for the high school student with art experience. Even tests in the area of art appreciation seem more or less geared to the young child, not to an older student who has been exposed to numerous creative experiences and important visual works. Since many tests use pictorial representations which are dated and/or have little universal significance, they can be effective as testing devices only for a limited period of time at best. Most educational psychologists and art educators agree that no reliable tests have been developed up to now.[46] "Reliability and validities of tests are far too low to permit final judgment of talent from test scores."[47]

In order to understand the whole issue of art tests, one should give at least some thought to this search for educational certainties. It appears that the very character of the creative force makes its measurement impossible, unlike any physical force which *can* be measured. The creative force is not tangible. What *are* tangible are the results or documentations of the creative energy, and only these can possibly be gauged or evaluated in regard to future accomplishments. In art tests measurements are based solely on documentation or results, and the genuine creative potentialities in an individual are left to speculation. Moreover, permanently valid criteria would have to be predetermined in order to yield meaningful results, or a definite set of art values would have to be established; aesthetic values have never been clearly defined, or universally agreed upon, including those of the visual arts.

---

[43] A test to discover color blindness in students should be known to every art teacher. One of the easiest to administer and most frequently used is the *Test for Color Blindness* by Shinobu Ishihara (10th ed.; Rutland, Vt.: Charles E. Tuttle, 1955).

[44] James L. Mursell, *Psychological Testing* (New York: Longmans, Green & Co., 1949), p. 246.

[45] "Tests of artistic aptitude . . . must not depend on special training, since this would give an untrue picture of a person with little talent who had begun artistic training." Lee J. Cronbach, *Essentials of Psychological Testing* (New York: Harper & Brothers, 1949), p. 227.

[46] "Attempts have been made from time to time to develop tests to measure the abilities of pupils both to appreciate and to produce art. None of these tests, including the *Art Judgment Test* by Meier and Seashore, the *McAdory Art Test,* and the *Tests in Fundamental Abilities of Visual Art* by A. F. Lauranz, have lived up to the expectations of their makers. All well-known tests of this kind have proved in time to be largely invalid and unreliable." Gaitskell and Gaitskell, *Art Education during Adolescence,* p. 32.

[47] Cronbach, *Essentials of Psychological Testing,* p. 228.

There is another significant factor which bears on ability-testing in art. Generally these tests are designed for use in the schools, but genuine creativity seems to manifest itself relatively late and slowly in painters and sculptors. There are, for instance, almost no known child prodigies in the visual arts[48]—"child prodigy" meaning a very young person performing expertly on the level of a mature artist. Indeed, it seems permissible to claim that the majority of great artists produced their most important works during the later part of their lives. If many of these artists had died before reaching their thirtieth year, their names and accomplishments would have sunk into oblivion. This is not true in the field of music, for example, where child prodigies are not uncommon, or in poetry or the sciences, where significant works have been written by fairly young men. Interestingly enough, the visual arts have produced many important painters who did not become absorbed in the creative process before having reached maturity, and showed no marked interest or ability in creative visual expression in their youth.

Finally, a very important question still remains to be answered: To what extent should any testing results of creative ability influence the teaching of art? For example, if students, according to tests, do not show ability in the visual arts but have developed an interest in them, should they be discouraged from taking further instruction? Or should a student be forced to take art merely because a test shows some ability? Since actual exposure to visual art and experience with the creative process appear to change students' attitudes towards art, it may be wise to continue permitting all who wish to express themselves in visual terms to participate in the art program, regardless of whether or not—according to tests—they show ability.

Grading and Marking

Grading or marking students' creative achievements constitutes a real problem. As a first step in attempting to find a satisfactory solution, it is necessary to determine the function of a grade. Basically, a grade gives pupils "the information they need for progressing in their school work; parents have facts they can use in guiding their children; and teachers are helped to give effective instruction and guidance."[49] That is, a grade should be meaningful to three different individuals: the student, the parent, and the teacher. The individual's interest in a grade varies with the age level. Most parents of small children are extremely concerned with each single achievement of their offspring, but this concern lessens markedly when the youngsters reach the senior high school. What usually matters most to the parents at this point is whether the student will be promoted. His performance in a given subject and his grade become less and less important; what finally counts is, "Will he graduate?"

In the art area on the senior high school level one frequently finds that it is the *student* who is most concerned with the rating of his achievements. Since each student's creative works differ considerably from those of his classmates and do not permit simple comparisons as in many academic subjects, a pupil is frequently unable to rate his own achievements. Moreover, a good art teacher does not base his grading on a comparative basis of different individuals' creative accomplishments.[50] There-

---

48 "No young child or his products has ever been so recognized, and it would be remarkable if any should be. There are many child prodigies in *artistic performance,* especially in music and acting, but few in art production or composition." Munro, *Art Education, Its Philosophy and Psychology,* p. 79.

49 Ruth Strang, *Reporting to Parents* (New York: Teachers College, Columbia University, 1952), p. 39.

50 "Obviously the school should not engage in making insidious comparisons of the individuals of widely diversified talents. Its concern should be that the student who has certain abilities should actually utilize those abilities." William L. Wrinkle, *Improving Marking and Reporting Practices in Elementary and Secondary Schools* (New York: Rinehart & Co., Inc., 1953), p. 47.

fore the need for personal rating of success or failure is often greater in the art area than, for instance, in academic subjects where objective grading as a result of tests and according to set standards permits each student to rate his progress and achievement fairly independently of the teacher.

The rating of a student takes on even more importance when the teacher is aware that report cards "influence a pupil's idea of himself—they often determine whether he regards himself as a failure or as a success. Moreover, they influence the parents' attitude toward the child and the school. Whether the school intends it or not, the items on the report card serve as goals for the pupils and influence the parents' idea of the relative importance of different kinds of school achievements."[51] An art teacher should realize that a grade not only influences the parents' attitude toward the child, but also their attitude toward the whole field of art. Frequently parents are unable to appraise the creative potentialities of their children, and are tempted to compare their efforts either with slick, popular works of art or with selected superior achievements of other young people. Recognition as expressed in a grade often helps youngsters to receive needed parental encouragement. On the other hand, parents usually rely on the grade in art if they have little experience in or understanding of this subject, and in such cases rating in art takes on more significance than grades in fields where parents feel that they have sufficient knowledge to recognize abilities, achievements, or weaknesses.

No less important than achievement as a basis for grading is the attitude of the student toward his work. The components of this attitude are sincere interest, attempts to leave trite ways in search of new and independent expression, initiative, work habits, and utilization of time. This attitude is reflected in every student's art work and can be observed most easily during any art period. Yet to evaluate a student's attitude solely on the basis of his art work would require studying a great number of his creative products. Such a burdensome task is unnecessary so long as the teacher remains alert and keeps a record of students' attitudes as well as of their achievements. Thus every student's grade should be based not only on achievement and progress but also on attitude.

Finally, every teacher should realize that the grade expressed in a number or letter represents no more than a symbol whose exact meaning often remains unknown to the recipient. Since such a symbol does not specify the reason for the grade nor convey the desired effect, it is advisable that shortly before a grade is given the art teacher devote some class time to each student, discussing his attitude, studying with him the work he has produced, and pointing out carefully any progress or lack of it. The aim of these individual review sessions should be to give future direction to each student and help him understand clearly why he will receive a particular grade.[52]

Many attempts have been made recently to improve the customary method of reporting grades. The two most frequently advocated suggestions are parent-teacher conferences, or regular, informally written, brief reports to parents. Both these proposals have more merit from a purely theoretical than from a practical point of view. In our present school systems it is hardly possible for a teacher to find the time to speak to approximately 150 parents, or to send them brief, personal communications every six weeks. An attempt at such an undertaking probably would result in a stereotyped form of reporting and might be even less satisfactory than the current practice. Nevertheless, occasional personal notes to and interviews with

---

[51] Strang, *Reporting to Parents,* p. 1.

[52] "In both junior and senior high school specific analysis of the pupil's progress and difficulties in each subject and suggestions for his improvement are necessary for the purpose of individual guidance. Much of this detailed help can be given to pupils during class period." *Ibid.,* p. 38.

a student's parents are advisable, particularly in the case of students who seem to possess a marked aptitude for visual creative work. Often such students need more encouragement than a good grade. The teacher can render an important service by giving the parents competent advice concerning their child's future vocational or professional preparations and opportunities. This assumes that the art teacher will remain well informed about the necessary preparations and opportunities for vocational or professional pursuits, and the ever-changing entrance requirements of training institutions.

Obviously, at times grading and counseling overlap: the line that can be drawn between guidance and grading on the high school level is often so fine that in practice they are almost indistinguishable. They also converge when high school students evaluate their own achievements and behavior.

Self-Evaluation in Art

On the senior high school level guided self-evaluation is often effective; it can help raise standards for attitude and achievement. Questionnaires which every student should answer at specified intervals have proved practicable. The following is an example:

Do I start my work as soon as the period begins? (always—most of the time—sometimes—very rarely)
Do I help to maintain a good working atmosphere?
Do I attempt to take good care of materials and tools?
Do I keep to a minimum those discussions which have little value for my work?
Do I try to find original and/or intelligent solutions for my art projects?
Do I strive for good craftsmanship?
Do I improve my skill in drawing, painting, pottery, etc.?
Do I spend time (in or outside of class) reading about art or artists?
Do I use a sketch book in or outside of class?
Do I spend time looking at art work reproduced in books or magazines or at original works at public exhibitions?

A questionnaire is only one of many devices for self-evaluation. It has the advantage of requiring a minimum of time and does not handicap those students who have difficulties in expressing themselves in written form. "With more mature pupils, the writing of the major part of their record for the purposes of college admission or applying for a job is a most interesting and realistic form of self-appraisal. For best results they should be given an outline or guide, and, when they have finished writing the appraisal, they should submit it to the teacher, who will then validate, approve, and supplement it."[53] Such an outline could cover points like these:

In which type of art activity are you most successful?
Which form of art appeals most to you? (Drawing, painting—oil, water color, etc.—graphics, sculpture, pottery, illustration, commercial art, etc.)
Have you found works of art or artists which you prefer over others? What are their names and what is it that fascinates you?
In which area of art do you feel that you are in need of more instruction or information?
Have you ever considered art as a vocation? If so, in which of the many fields are you particularly interested? (Fine arts, art teaching, commercial art, etc.)
If you were asked, "Why are you interested in the visual arts?" what would you answer?

The foregoing examples are without reference to a particular school situation or student body. In order to obtain results meaningful to student and teacher alike, it

---

[53] *Ibid.*, p. 88.

is best that the senior high school art teacher develop his own form of appraisal. When the teacher reviews his students' self-evaluation he will at the same time be faced with an appraisal of his own efforts: to what degree has he been successful in developing his students' ability to think creatively and independently, to acquire acuter sensitivity, keener perception, and, finally, greater inquisitiveness and interest in the visual arts?

The Art Curriculum

An art teacher's work is intrinsically linked with the framework in which he must carry out his task. This framework is the curriculum—the over-all plan in which certain courses are arranged in a progressive sequence. The progression may begin with the broad or general aspect of a subject and advance to the specific; or it may start with simple skills and proceed to more complex ones. But above all, a curriculum is the tangible expression of a conviction. In it are synthesized many subjects, approaches, and techniques. It is an over-all plan for reaching definite goals. Without goals a curriculum is bound to be nothing but an enumeration of various items, and cannot fulfill one of its major purposes: giving guidance to teachers in planning their art sessions.

Along with denoting the order in which subject matter should be arranged, the word "curriculum" also refers to the kind and character of the various high school art subjects. In all our thousands of high schools, it would be difficult to find two curricula which are identical in scope or character. Some courses of study concentrate on only a few art activities, techniques, or media; others focus on some techniques to be taught at a specific grade level; still others include almost indiscriminately all known forms of visual art.

The present range of art offerings comprises about twelve different techniques and media for drawing and painting, and a minimum of five graphic techniques; it also includes modeling and sculpturing, which may utilize as many as ten different materials. Many schools offer opportunities to learn pottery, jewelry making, and enameling. Some have separate courses in design, and units for color theory, perspective, and composition. Others offer specialized courses in commercial art which may include fashion and industrial design and lettering. Still others have separate units for architectural design or interior decoration. Craft classes, often a kind of catchall, are frequently included in a curriculum, and usually consist of weaving, leather tooling, silversmithing, textile painting, and sometimes pottery making. Stagecraft is occasionally taught as a separate course, and at other times as a section of a drawing and painting class. In some curricula one even finds photography as part of an art program. Finally, a course called "art appreciation," or in some cases "art history," is often included in the art curriculum.

This impressive array of offerings brings to mind some very pertinent questions: Is it desirable to incorporate all these different subjects and techniques into a high school curriculum, and if so, can it be done? Assuming that time, money, equipment, and trained personnel were available for such an art program, would this indiscriminate curriculum be more effective than one which has limitations and offers fewer choices? More important—since few, if any, high schools could offer such a vast art program—on what basis should the different subjects and techniques be selected or given priority over others? Which subjects and techniques should be considered of primary importance, which of secondary importance, and which of none? Can guiding principles be stated which will be meaningful in many different school situations? Moreover, and this is most important, is it possible to narrow down the art curriculum without superimposing an individual point of view?

A search for direction among the many existing curricula is more often confusing than helpful. The present vast range of art curricula includes about twenty different subject areas, some of which are a genuine part of the visual arts and many closely associated with them, while others are barely related. Most of the many different courses of study in art are designed for only a particular school situation, hence were developed from a limited point of view, if for no other reason than lack of time and/or equipment. Moreover, few of these art curricula seem to be based on concrete aims, or built on a logical progression. Previous experience with and instruction in art are seldom considered prerequisites even for more complex or specialized subjects or techniques. On the high school level, drawing, design, or composition, for instance, are not deemed prerequisites for painting or commercial art, nor is modeling regarded as a prerequisite for sculpturing. These areas are often freely interchanged and taught simultaneously. It appears that there has never been agreement among art educators as to how art experiences should follow each other. Even in such narrow fields as commerical art, the sequence in which skills should be taught is left undefined.

Yet that certain logical sequences exist is quite apparent to anyone who has ever been seriously engaged in the creation of a work of art. In many instances the effective handling and utilization of a variety of different techniques presuppose creative and manual experiences. Obviously these must be taught in a certain order. The need for this order is more noticeable in older students than in very young pupils whose enthusiasm and lack of experience frequently carry them over difficulties. On the high school level, drawing, for instance, should be considered a prerequisite for most graphic techniques, and modeling a prerequisite for sculpture.

It seems evident that at least one basic art course should be a requirement for students wishing to work either in more complex techniques or in more specialized areas. A curriculum should consist of three essential groups of courses: a broad general art course, advanced courses, and courses in specialized fields. The last two types of courses should be open only to students who have had a general art course for not less than a year. But of what should such a course consist? On the high school level, it should be composed of three sections, each of which should be given equal time and importance: drawing and graphics, work with colors, and work in three dimensions. On the junior high school level the same principle appears valid, but here the emphasis should be placed on numerous manipulation processes rather than on the learning of skills. In advanced courses students should concentrate less on variety and more on larger, time-consuming, and moderately difficult technical projects. Commercial arts, stagecraft, and possibly industrial or fashion design are commonly best taught in separate art courses.

This approach to curriculum planning brings to mind another aspect of curriculum development which directly concerns the purpose of art education, and only indirectly the problem of curriculum planning, for every curriculum is essentially a long-range plan which should enable students to reach certain goals. But what are these goals? More concretely, to what degree should art experiences be considered part of a general education, and to what degree should they be part of a vocational training? General education, as it is used here, implies a broad foundation in visual art which should eventually enable a student to choose between a vocation and an avocation. By contrast, vocational training refers to a form of instruction which should enable a student to earn a livelihood through the skills he has acquired in his high school training.

It is questionable whether our high schools can be considered—even in part—institutions for special vocational training. Decidedly, their major concern is with the broad concepts of a general education, culminating in the development of each student's capabilities, and equipping him to make intelligent choices for his future in accordance with his ability, knowledge, and preference. Students probably will be best prepared for these decisions by concentrating on several basic art areas rather than on a great many, learning to command these few well, and finding affinities for some particular form of art expression. This approach to curriculum planning—offering only limited choices—may be the least confusing to students and may give them a foundation for further artistic and intellectual growth. Any art course, whether it is specialized or not, should first of all contribute to reaching this goal.

Frequently during the art sessions individual students discover their marked aptitude for and interest in the visual arts. One can therefore ask: Should specialized art courses be offered for students who show a pronounced ability in visual art? Actually, with rare exceptions, few high schools have a sufficient number of outstanding students in art to justify such a course. (The exception is the specialized high school in a metropolitan area which provides specialized education for students with outstanding ability in visual art. However, such schools are uncommon and accessible only to a selected few.) Moreover, since the nature of art instruction on the high school level is flexible enough to permit making individual allowances without producing a detrimental effect on the group, a separate class for the possible few exceptional students appears unnecessary in most instances.

There remain two important points to consider regarding a curriculum; the first pertains to individual subjects, techniques, and media, and their place or places in the curriculum. Drawing, for instance, can be approached from various points of view, exploiting many media and techniques, and serving different purposes. Consequently, an analysis of each area, technique, and corresponding media is necessary if one wishes to develop a more detailed curriculum which will fit a particular school system, and will also treat each subject's many variations and specify its proper place. Material for such a detailed study follows this section.

The other point in regard to curriculum development deals with the question of who should be responsible for setting up the art curriculum. Is it desirable to have an authoritative art curriculum for the high school? Or would it be better to maintain a flexible plan? A mandatory kind of curriculum, written by an authoritative body of art educators, may easily lead to a standardization of art education. On the other hand, a flexible curriculum leaves most of the responsibility to the art teacher, permitting him to select and present his course material in accordance with his personal ability, command of skills, conviction, and particular school situation. The school situation not only includes the art room and its equipment, but also takes into account the students, their abilities, previous art experiences, and individual personalities.

When the development of an individual curriculum is in the hands of practicing art teachers, it is vital that these teachers have strong convictions in regard to their mission. Since curricula are only devices to help reach certain goals, the teacher must keep these goals clearly in mind, and must understand the basic ideals and principles of art education; otherwise a curriculum will foster only confusion and amount to no more than a casual enumeration of courses.

Finally, it can be taken for granted that an art teacher who has acquired a clear conviction of the value of what he is teaching, what his teaching should contribute, and how art offerings function in this frame of reference will find little difficulty in developing the curriculum which will serve his students best.

PART THREE

THE MEDIUM

Art is the most sublime mission of man, since it is the expression of thought seeking to understand the world and to make it understood.

Auguste Rodin

Art education's underlying concepts and aims, and the environment in which it is taught, should not be considered more significant than the means which make its teaching possible. These means are the many different art media and techniques which help to transform thoughts into tangible objects, theory into practice. Obviously the aims of art education are tightly interwoven with the teaching of techniques and the handling of media, including the clarification of the underlying principles of visual art. Much of this understanding consists of a thorough awareness of the unique qualities of each medium and each technique. These unique qualities must be considered from two different points of view: in terms of artistic expression (from the standpoint of the artist), and in terms of educational value (from the standpoint of the educator). For instance, from the artist's point of view, sculpture in stone is an expression in three-dimensional forms in which thoughts and visions are given plasticity and monumentality. The solidity of the material forces the artist to think in the round, of all sides and angles. His goal is to achieve a unified form in space which will convey his creative idea. In order to reach this goal he must accept the innate limitations of this very form of expression. Actual movement, for example, cannot be re-created in stone, and therefore he must strive for and be content with suggested movement. In addition, the sculptor must be sensitive to his material: he cannot ignore the stone's particular quality, its texture, its hardness or softness. He must combine these and several other considerations with his creative intent if he wishes to succeed in his task.

From an educational point of view, carving a stone is a creative activity with certain valuable pedagogical qualities. What matters most is not the finished product, which is the final aim of the professional sculptor, but the highly disciplined and rational manner in which the material forces students to work. It is of educational significance that the students, while carving, must first think and then act, whereas in modeling with pliable materials, for example, they may first act and then evaluate their action critically. It is also of particular merit that sculpture is a slow process, demanding considerable patience which at times may make severe demands on the students' span of interest. Sculpture in the high school could be called an exercise in self-discipline; during the working process students may not concentrate solely on one detail which momentarily appeals to their fancy, but are required to think constantly of the entire stone. Thus the activity may help accustom them to envision a whole project and to concentrate on an entirety rather than on details. These examples should illustrate very briefly two different approaches to the same activity.

Every art activity, every medium and technique can be approached from an artist's as well as from an educator's point of view. These approaches should be of equal significance to the art teacher. Yet media and techniques are not the only means which an art teacher must exploit in order to translate art education's goals and aims into tangible results. He must find ways to fuse media and techniques with concepts and ideas, ideas which are meaningful to his students and correspond to a particular material and technique, lending themselves to certain modes of expression. After all, "every mode of expression, no matter how mechanical, no matter how fantastic, no matter how impressionistic, has these two sides—idea and technique."[1]

The art teacher must know how to stimulate students to develop ideas suited to a medium or a technique, and to help them become so sensitive to the material's unique qualities that they can fuse their creative idea with it. He must also be able to present a material or technique in such a way that it can act as an additional motivating force. Moreover, in order to guide his students, a teacher must know which materials they consider easy and which difficult to handle. He must know which techniques require previous experience and which can be utilized effectively with little or no prior skill—in other words, which media or techniques should be considered prerequisites for other more complex ones.

None of the foregoing can be clarified by broad generalizations. Only by careful analysis of each form of art expression, each material, each method of procedure, each medium and tool is it possible to discover its innate characteristics, its individual strength and limitation, and—most important—its educational value. Every form of visual expression, be it drawing, painting, modeling, or jewelry making, can be approached from many points of view entailing many diverse techniques, materials, and tools. To determine their usefulness in the high school classroom, one should first pinpoint each technical variation of a given medium, specify each possible approach, and clarify each particular pedagogical merit in the hope of finding the optimum educational value.

As a first step in discovering the various educational values of media and techniques, the whole field of visual art is here divided into four basic areas: expression in monochromes (drawing and graphics); expression in color (the different media and techniques of painting); expression in three dimensions (modeling, sculpture, and ceramics); and finally, expression in art forms which originally were meant to render some utilitarian service (for example, commercial art, jewelry making or stage design).

As already stated, this material has been developed to help the reader gain an understanding of the contribution of each art subject to education. The treatment of the different procedures or techniques related to a given subject is aimed at making readily available to teachers precise information which is often needed to explain to and/or motivate students. To this end, there have been included brief historical backgrounds of the different art areas, in so far as they have bearing on the teaching of art, and also, whenever possible, variations of subjects. The latter too is intended to help teachers recall the many existing choices in techniques or approaches. It is hoped that teachers will thus be able to develop a diversified art program

---

[1] John Dewey, *Three Articles,* Teachers College Bulletin, 10th Series, No. 10 (New York: Columbia University, March 1, 1919), p. 6.

adapted to the aptitude, experience, and background of their students.

The material, however, is not designed to give detailed technical information which a teacher could immediately utilize in an art room. It is assumed that he has had previous knowledge and experience in many fields of art, and knows that he should never attempt to teach a technique, use a procedure, or present a problem with which he is not well acquainted. There are many excellent books dealing with every phase of art and its techniques. Whenever a teacher finds himself unfamiliar with a technique, he should consult relevant printed material or, preferably, a person experienced in this area. Not before he himself has worked with the technique and feels that he understands it and its related problems should he be willing to introduce it to his students. It is hoped that additional information, explanations, and possible means of stimulation presented in this book will truly be of help to him, and through him to his students.

In the pages which follow, the field of drawing has been divided into separate elements. Actually such a division is artificial and has been made only for the purpose of clarifying understanding of the various modes of drawing. Elements such as contour drawing and drawing in light and shade or in volume are not mutually exclusive and have often been successfully used in the same drawing. Yet treating these elements separately here is necessary from a pedagogical point of view; its purpose is to introduce students to various and distinctly different ways of translating impressions, observations, and concepts into graphic expression.

I Expression in Monochrome

Drawing

Probably the oldest form of visual art expression is drawing. Early man scratched sharp lines into the surface of stones and bones in order to transmit and preserve his thoughts and visions graphically. These prehistoric drawings are among the few authentic documents which reveal that early man not only was endowed with an intellect but that he was capable of creating. The verb "to draw" means "to drag a pen or other instrument over a surface which leaves a mark behind it. To draw is to outline; to delineate; to present a form or shape by lines or by means of light and shade alone or within a simple outline:—in short, to make a picture by such means. An artist's line has fundamental significance when it reveals form or design."[2]

It is almost impossible to decide exactly where drawing ends and where painting begins. The border between these two-dimensional forms of visual expression is so indistinct that it is futile to attempt to determine the exact line of division. Drawing is an expression in simplifications; the impression of a totality is achieved mostly through lineal abbreviations. One of drawing's major characteristics is mere suggestion of visual reality, and color plays only a very subordinate or negligible part in it. Moreover, width or depth, the third dimension of form or space, can be conveyed merely as an illusion or symbol. The true value of drawing is based on its

[2] Paul J. Sachs, *The Pocket Book of Great Drawings* (New York: Pocket Books, Inc., 1951), p. 1.

limitations and on an emphasis of its innate characteristics; the more fragmentary its statements of form and ideas, the more sketchy and fluent its portrayal of thoughts and visions, the more highly it is admired. By contrast, a drawing which is void of suggestion and is too detailed and tight is often boring, if not displeasing. In a drawing we long to find surprises, we expect to discover unique simplifications, and we are pleased when we are confronted with austere statements and rudiments which convey an idea or a vision.

Drawing permits an artist the same poetic license as any other form of creative expression. Even a drawing based on a direct study from nature should always be regarded as a creation, or possibly a re-creation, but never as an objective or

STUDY OF ELEPHANTS
Rembrandt van Rijn

Reproduced by courtesy of the Albertina Collection, Vienna

mechanical record of what has been observed.[3] Another significant characteristic of the drawing medium is that it permits considerable freedom of choice and expression and also the permanent capture of direct responses, or an immediate recording of sensations. Moods, expression, and movement can easily be retained because the medium is most sensitive and registers minute reactions of the artist, often without his conscious desire. With rare exceptions the actual mechanical skill needed to utilize drawing tools and materials successfully is quite small, yet at the same time a drawing from the hands of an accomplished master can exemplify a most superior skill.

The field of drawing may be divided into two broad segments. One concerns immediate studies of what is being perceived in nature or reality. The other encom-

---

[3] "One and the same subject in nature, rendered by various artists under identical conditions, and with the sharpest observation of nature, will result in a different picture every time. One will emphasize something that the other neglects or completely overlooks. The lines will have a different verve each time, once more squarish, once more rounded; also the size relationship of the individual parts will vary." H. Leporini, *Die Stilentwicklung der Handzeichnung* (Wien-Leipzig: Manz Verlag, 1925), p. 25.—(*Author's translation*)

passes works which spring from images or visions of the mind and have unquestionably originated in retained perceptions (see also pp. 24–26). Memorized impressions, however, are often so freely reassembled and distorted that their original source is frequently not retraceable.

With the beginning of the Renaissance, drawing from nature became the most accepted means of recording visual information and of training in the visual arts. Many drawings from nature were studies made either for the sake of learning how to draw natural forms, or as preliminaries for a particular composition. Quite early it was discovered that continued drawing strengthens the memory for forms and the understanding of the possibilities or limitations of visual representation on a flat surface. It was also recognized that a comprehension of the significance of the line or mass, the importance of dark and light, or the problem of representing space on a two-dimensional plane could best be gained through the actual practice of drawing. Often these drawings were studies of human figures, or parts of them, in a variety of motions; others depicted details of inanimate objects. Yet drawings from nature as self-containing final products are relatively new in the history of art and have only recently become widely accepted as independent artistic expressions. (Possible exceptions are portraits in monochromes.)

Drawing from memory or from the imagination, primarily in a more or less sketchy form, is the most common means of clarifying compositional problems or ideas. "The original idea," wrote Delacroix, "the sketch, which is so to speak the egg or embryo of the idea, is usually far from being complete; it contains everything, which is simply a mixing together of all parts. Just the thing that makes of this sketch the essential expression of the idea is not the suppression of details, but their complete subordination to the big lines which are, before all else, to create the impression."[4] Sketches depicting basic ideas, expressing the essentials of a composition, were produced by countless artists and were developed as basic plans for paintings, murals, tapestries, and many other artistic works. First sketching an outline for a major work is a practice still used today, though perhaps less frequently. Still, in teaching art, the sketchy outline or composition should be considered an important intermediate step between concept and finished product.[5]

Drawing from memory is probably the oldest form of visual expression. Early sketches were made with chalk and similar transient materials on cave walls, rocks, and wooden boards. In ancient times, a stylus and wax or clay tablets were also commonly used for simple outlines. Unfortunately hardly any of them have survived. Until the Renaissance, most finished drawings were contour or line drawings and were used in connection with decorations or manuscript illustrations. For hundreds of years drawings from memory were considered merely preliminary sketches and not finished independent artistic statements; only lately have drawings of this type been elevated as equals of painting, sculpture, or any other form of artistic expression.

In drawing one must distinguish between a finished work and a sketch. The English equivalent of the word from which "sketch" is derived is "improvisation." Commonly, any rough, incomplete, or vague drawing is called a sketch. Until recently

---

[4] *The Journal of Eugene Delacroix,* Walter Pach, trans. (New York: Crown Publishers, 1948), p. 375.

[5] "When drawing is consciously a part of an artist's preparation for a given major work, the plan in his mind must have achieved a certain maturity or at least distinctness. Then there is no relaxation to the little beckonings of reality around him, or to visual instinct and manual dexterity as they may happen to prompt him. He has decided what he wants, he knows his way. By deliberate experiment, variation, or exercise,—by rehearsing some difficult or crucial detail, or his pattern as a whole, over and over until it is perfect—he approaches the day of final execution in his chosen medium." Monroe Wheeler, ed., *Modern Drawings* (New York: The Museum of Modern Art, 1944), p. 9.

STUDY FOR A COMPOSITION
Salvator Rosa

Reproduced by courtesy of the Albertina Collection, Vienna

the term also implied that such a work was not meant to be shown in public and was considered an unfinished private statement by the artist. However, this concept has changed. The term "sketch" now often designates a comprehensive improvisation which is accepted as a meaningful representation not to be augmented, revised, or translated into a more complex work. By contrast, the finished drawing is complete and clear in meaning and appearance, precise in form or line and void of ambiguities and obscurities. Yet at first glance a finished drawing may also give the impression of an improvised or spontaneous work. Generally such drawings are achieved only through many years' arduous practice. Outstanding examples can easily be found among the works of the eighteenth- and nineteenth-century Japanese artists. Also many Ingres drawings, noticeably his pencil portraits, exemplify and display a sketchy quality despite the fact that they are carefully finished works. Doubtless the art of drawing reaches its highest form of attainment if the completed product contains an extemporaneous, unlabored, sketchlike quality.

Drawing can be divided into three basic structural elements: the line, the tone, and the texture. The term "line," as it is most frequently used in this context, is a slender continuous mark which is applied to outline objects or to define boundaries of voluminous forms or shapes within a form. Lines are most frequently used to represent the silhouette, contour, or edge of a given form, space, or configuration. Although they are easily understood and represent the most unassuming manner of visual expression, used even by very small children, lines are synoptic simplifications to the point of being abstractions. Line drawings are so prevalent because they incorporate and reflect simultaneously two important forms of perception: vision and touch. A drawn outline not only represents the total impression of a form gained by sight, but at the same time reflects the outer edge of shapes, perceived through tactile sensations. Because line drawing incorporates these two major sensations, it has been accepted universally as the most spontaneous and instinctive way to draw.

Reproduced by courtesy of the Albertina Collection, Vienna

VIEW OF THE HARBOR OF ANTWERP:
Albrecht Dürer: line drawing with silver point

CHRIST ON THE CROSS
Jacopo Palma il Giovine
brush drawing

Reproduced by courtesy of the Albertina Collection, Vienna

Yet "in considering lines as a means of drawing, it is well to remember that the *line* practically does not exist in nature. It is a convention we use."[6]

Tone in relation to drawing is the opposite of line. Tone is a means for visualizing planes, shapes, and most of all solidity, on a flat surface. Here drawing is

---

[6] Robert Henri, *The Art Spirit* (Philadelphia: J. B. Lippincott Co., 1923), p. 110.

FIGURE PAINTING
FROM MEMORY
eighth grade girl
poster paint
on wrapping paper

achieved primarily by covering areas with a monochrome, opaque medium; it is not the outline which is used to convey a pictorial idea, but dark and light distinctions, variations of gradation, or contrasts of light and shadow. Moreover, in this form of drawing, prime attention is given to the volume, and not the edge, of a form. Tone also permits the artist to state clearly the weight or solidity, the opaqueness or translucency of an object or shape. It allows him to model a form in a manner similar to modeling in clay.

This approach to drawing came into wide use when underpainting in monochromes was generally practiced by painters. The majority of drawings produced during the Renaissance and until the late Baroque were executed in light and dark areas, often on colored paper. Obviously this technique is a kind of bridge between painting and drawing; it does not require such distinct and sharp decision as is needed

LIFE DRAWING
WITH EMPHASIS ON TEXTURE
eleventh grade boy
conté crayon on newsprint

for a line, yet it forces a person to translate his visions or thoughts into monochrome areas, omitting all references to color. This is a task which many high school students find quite difficult. Still, exercises in drawing in tones are probably one of the best preparations for painting. A number of problems which are common in work with colors also occur in tonal drawings, but their solution is much simpler. Here only the relation of light to dark needs to be considered, whereas in painting an additional concern is that of colors and their relationship to one another.

Texture in relation to drawing refers primarily to a surface character deliberately produced with drawing materials on paper. Smears, scratches, clusters of dots, or fading, broken parallel lines of the dry brush are typical drawing textures. Their major function is to help convey a particular mood, or to add interest to the total appearance of a drawing. A totally different approach to texture in drawing consists of a conscious imitation of the surface characteristics of a form or material. Here the depicted texture serves as a means for a clearer understanding of what is represented. In this instance neither the line nor the tone is the sole transmitter of the pictorial idea. Yet texture as such is a dependent drawing element; it can function only in combination with lines or tones.

Few beginning high school students will use textural accents in their drawings for the single purpose of adding freshness, immediacy, or interest. Commonly, the conscious utilization of these drawing elements indicates experience and freedom of expression. As long as an individual struggles with the problem of how to draw a form adequately and convincingly, or as long as he experiences difficulties in rendering his ideas comprehensively, he is usually insensitive to texture as a characteristic drawing element.

On the other hand, attempts to simulate textures corresponding to those seen on the surface of objects are often found in the drawings of beginners. They may spend considerable time and effort imitating existing textures, feeling that the line or the tone does not adequately convey the visual thought. The result of such attempts is often a stiff, overworked drawing, conveying not only the sweat of labor but also the struggle and insecurity of the student. Yet deliberate studies of various surface qualities and of the many possible ways to represent them convincingly should be part of every drawing program. By discovering different means of utilizing the many possibilities for depicting textures in drawing, a student may become more sensitive to the aesthetic qualities of drawings, as well as to the great varieties of surfaces he encounters throughout the day.

Unquestionably, drawing is one of the most significant areas in the teaching of art. The earliest known writings on art training emphasize the cultivation of the drawing skill as a basis for further artistic development. Cennini wrote in 1437, "Do not fail, as you go on, to draw something every day, for no matter how little it is it will be well worth while, and will do you a world of good."[7] Cennini's statement is still valid. No other area in the training of visual art will help a student more in gaining creative freedom or will so rapidly give him the feeling of self-improvement. But progress in drawing can only be accomplished through *frequent,* carefully guided exercises. Many times drawing has been compared to grammar, because just as grammar must be studied for command of a language, so drawing must be practiced if students are to gain some freedom or competence in the language of visual expression.

It is not unusual to hear a high school student maintain that a fellow classmate can draw very well. Generally such a statement omits the most important fact—just what it is that this admired student can draw so well. The missing information, which

---

[7] Cennino d'Andrea Cennini, *The Craftsman's Handbook* (New York: Dover Publications, 1933), p. 15.

is mostly taken for granted, usually pertains to the human figure. The ability to represent graphically the human figure with force, conviction, and skill is commonly considered one of the highest marks of artistic accomplishment. It can be observed in museums and art galleries that the infrequent visitor admires most those works in which the human figure is depicted. One reason for this is that many people feel that art attains its highest form of accomplishment when it presents the human body re-created in convincing terms; another is that a casual spectator can and often will effortlessly identify himself with a creative work because it is focused on the human figure.

Most high school students take a similar position. To them the ability to draw a human figure, or parts of it, convincingly and freely, is art. In their view, this matchless level of art can never be attained by any portrayal of an inanimate object or abstract composition, regardless of how forcefully, meaningfully, or skillfully it may have been executed. They largely associate learning in art with acquiring the skill to portray people credibly and compellingly. It therefore follows that the more a teacher can help his students improve their ability to draw the human figure, the more he will be of genuine service to them. Much as the students desire to acquire this ability, they often resent the drawing exercises because these so mercilessly reveal their ineptness. This attitude presents a true challenge to the teacher; it becomes his responsibility, then, not merely to instruct, but to keep the interest of the students stimulated by presenting a variety of procedures, utilizing different tools and materials, so that these class sessions remain novel and exciting.

Before separating the field of drawing into different individual activities, it may be wise to discuss briefly the question of how much time should be devoted to it during a semester. Drawing is or should be considered a constituent part of any high school art class, regardless of the age level on which it is taught, or how general or specialized the course may be. In a general art course on either the junior or senior high school level, approximately one-third of the total time should be given to drawing. Yet this does not mean that for roughly six consecutive weeks, day in and day out, drawing should be the only subject taught. Such an approach to this field on the high school level could easily become monotonous, and would fail to accomplish its aims of broadening and intensifying students' visual perception and strengthening their visual memory and skill. A sound and realistic approach to the teaching of drawing is to distribute the sessions over a whole semester so that at times one or two weeks will be devoted solely to drawing, and at others only a day or two during a week. But if possible not a single week should pass without at least one drawing session. Even in advanced or more specialized art courses many sessions should be spent with drawing, for drawing is a basic skill which must be practiced constantly, or competence already gained will be lost. There is simply no short cut or special method which can act as a substitute for practice, concentrated effort, and trial and error. While there are many ways to draw, none is "the correct" or "the easiest" one, as sometimes claimed in "how to" books. Such patent or slick methods can easily become crutches, hampering the development of sensitivity and the process of perceiving, inhibiting freedom of expression, and retarding creativity. It is a teacher's obligation to expose his students to the various approaches to drawing so that each ultimately will discover the particular way through which he is best able to express himself.

Drawing in Contours

Probably the commonest form of drawing is in lines, and it is this method of visual presentation with which every student is most familiar long before he enters high school. Line drawing may be divided into three broad categories: contour, blind

CONTOUR DRAWING FROM MODEL
eleventh grade boy
marking crayon on newsprint

contour, and gesture drawing. During the act of drawing, the perceived form, figure, or shape is often involuntarily, in an almost unconscious manner, divided into two separate entities: the outer edge or boundary line, and the solid shape or mass. In contour drawing the edge or outline which confines the form or shape is of primary importance. The line is not only seen: it is a result of kinesthetic and touch perception as well. In fact, the knowledge gained through tactile perception is mostly lineal. For instance, when an object is touched, the entire hand moves, but usually the tips of the fingers feel the form only in lineal motion and not in its entirety. Angular, round, oval, or sharply pointed surfaces are sense data which are perceived by touch as well as sight and are fused in the line of contour drawing. This combination of the two kinds of perception translated into one medium of expression (the line) is of particular merit from the teacher's point of view.

The teaching of drawing in contours is not limited to a particular age level. As soon as a youngster begins to portray the world from a perceptional point of view (as he *sees* it), he should be exposed to drawing instructions and encouraged to draw in contours. This type of drawing is meaningful and helpful to the beginner as well as to the more advanced student. The teaching of contour drawing is like any other instruction based on drawing from nature, which is the opposite of drawing from imagination or memory. Drawing from nature implies that students are exposed to objects, figures, shapes, or forms, and are asked to depict them adequately and convincingly. However, this statement should not be given a narrow or dogmatic application which would require students to draw from nature in a manner so objective that it is devoid of any personal feelings or subjective interpretations. Regardless of the type of model used—a figure, a still life, or an outdoor scene—during sessions of contour drawing students should *constantly* be reminded to concentrate so intensely on the model that they have a feeling of almost touching the object or figure with their drawing tool.

A slightly different way of conducting the session is to ask students, just before they begin to draw, to move their hands as if they were actually feeling the objects. When this approach is used, it should be extended, whenever possible, to giving students the opportunity actually to touch the form they want to portray. If they are working from a living model, they should be encouraged both to imitate the model's pose and to feel on their own bodies the distribution of weight and the movement of joints and muscles.

Another equally important aspect of teaching drawing from a model is the pose. Here the emphasis is placed on kinesthetic rather than tactile perception. High school students usually produce more satisfactory work, draw with greater enthusiasm, and learn more rapidly if the pose they are asked to sketch shows varied arrested movements, is dramatic in expression, and permits the pupil to project himself into the posed situation. This presupposes that every pose contains a subject-matter aspect, regardless of vagueness or distinction.

By way of example, let us consider a simple pose—a boy walking. His feet are spread apart like an inverted V, one arm dangles forward, overlapping part of his body, and the hand of his other arm is in his trouser pocket, forming another triangle. These facts and the movement of his slightly bent head, shoulders, and hip line are pointed out to the students at the start of the assignment. However, for a great number of students this factual information is too objective and too limiting to inspire and stimulate them to the point that they can become truly involved with their project. To them the pose has to have a definite meaning which can be expressed dramatically. It will be a great help to these students if the pose is interpreted as a boy walking and trying to solve a personal problem, or—more specifically—as walking home with a report card, or in search of some lost money.

Most poses almost automatically become more interesting, more meaningful, and easier to draw if the model is given something to carry or handle. The "something" can be any ordinary object—a newspaper, a simple wooden stick, a piece of cloth, or an umbrella. Larger objects usually encourage more expressive or original poses which permit a greater variety of interpretations. Depending on the pose, a boy with an umbrella, for instance, may suggest a juggler, a tightrope walker, a man walking against the storm, or a child playing house. Some students will attempt to draw the model from a visual point of view. In this case the umbrella will help them to portray more correctly proportions, movements, and other visual factors. On the other hand, students who have to project themselves into a situation in order to portray what they see will find comfort in interpreting the implications and expressions of the pose. To them the challenge of the assignment lies in conveying the meaning rather than the facts.

The need to feel personally involved in a drawing assignment is not restricted to sketching from a live model; it is important too in drawing from a still life. Teachers often do not recognize the fact that a still life and its component parts must not only be interestingly arranged but must also possess an emotional appeal for students. For example, a grouping of a string of freshly caught fish with rod and reel and landing net, or of fowl and hunting paraphernalia, is much more meaningful to most adolescents than an assortment of attractive bowls and bottles, because it permits several different approaches and emotional reactions. Some students may interpret such still lifes as joyful scenes, reminiscent of happy fishing or hunting episodes while others may react strongly in the opposite way: a still life with dead animals may evoke a feeling of compassion or anger. Still others may see only a great variety of forms, movements, and textures, challenging their drawing skill.

Whenever feasible, any drawing assignment should thus include possibilities for approaches from many different emotional and visual points of view. Not only should the objects for a still life be interesting in form and texture: it is most important that they also produce emotional reactions in adolescents. Materials for interesting still life arrangements can often be borrowed from local sources or found within the school itself. Shop, physical education and music departments, physics and biology classes can supply many items, and even more exciting materials can be gathered from medical equipment and supply houses, antique and secondhand stores, taxidermists, sporting goods stores, and many other sources.

Furthermore, still life drawing need not consist only in sketching a group of items interestingly arranged by the teacher. To keep students interested in learning to draw, and to help them see keenly relationships between one form and another, the following method may at times be quite effective: place one large object in front of students and then ask them to make a careful contour drawing of this item in the center of their paper. After three or four minutes, or shortly *before* they have finished this assignment, another object should be set next to the one already on display. At like intervals other items should then be added until the whole still life is assembled. Naturally such an arrangement must be carefully worked out in advance, so that deliberate overlappings, size relationships, and design elements become obvious to the students.

In another approach to still life drawing, students are exposed to an arrangement for a brief period; then it is covered with a large piece of cloth and they are asked to draw from memory what they saw. A short time later the still life may again be uncovered, and the students asked to draw, with a different drawing tool, the changes and/or additions which they feel necessary for an adequate rendering. However, they should be given the option either of drawing accurately what they observe, or of interpreting their reaction to what they see. In the latter case, the drawing may be executed in an expressive manner, disregarding the objective reality. The educational aim of this type of assignment is to help strengthen students' ability to memorize shapes, and to force them to see totalities or unities rather than details or individual parts.

Another way to make still life drawing an interesting learning experience is to display many different items on a flat surface. These items should be scattered about in no particular order or arrangement. The students are asked to draw these objects in such a way as to fuse them, that is, to arrange them into an interesting composition. This fusion is, in fact, the essence of every composition. Every accomplished pictorial representation consists of an array of different forms, objects, colors, textures, movements, and thoughts, fused into one new unit. But when unity is missing, when the spectator sees only separate parts or individual items, then the artist did not succeed in one of his basic tasks, to create a unified statement. The aim of this type of assignment is to help accustom students to choosing among many possibilities. At the same time, the displayed objects should provide them with a degree of visual certainty, making it unnecessary to rely on their visual memory and permitting concentration on one problem only: how to fuse different forms into a unit without having to recall sharply details of lines and textures.

Obviously, contour drawing is not restricted to still life or figures. The world outside the classroom offers many fascinating motives for drawing. Busy streets, alleys, bus and railroad stations, freight yards, and hundreds of other city locales are excellent places for drawing sessions. In the spring, when youngsters become restless, outdoor drawing activities are particularly timely. Yet interesting places do not automatically produce stimulating art sessions. The success or failure of this type of assignment often depends on the teacher's preparation for the excursion. Having studied in advance the place where students are to work, he will know the different compositional possibilities so well that he can quickly advise his students on the subjects to choose and on the angle from which to draw them. The basic problem of this type of assignment is selection. Any interesting sight is filled with innumerable details, but it would be impossible to incorporate them all in a quick contour drawing. Therefore the problem concerns what to include and what to omit.

Another problem is how to arrange the selected forms on paper in such a manner that a semblance of what is seen and experienced is adequately rendered. Asking students to concentrate on only one common element, the contour line, should simplify their task considerably. Even so, many students encounter difficulties which are most pronounced when they first start to organize their work. Quite often, a few simple maxims should prevent their making the most characteristic beginners' mistakes. Students should be reminded to start their drawing with the largest object which is closest to their eyes, and to continue by placing other major objects around it, thus organizing their drawing so that every part of the paper is meaningfully used from the outset. They should be warned not to finish any part of the drawing before the whole composition is completely laid out. They should try to work on each segment for only a brief time and then move on to another so that all parts grow almost simultaneously and all areas are finished at about the same time.

There exists an intimate relationship between medium, technique, and expression; certain tools and materials have been found particularly suitable for drawing in contours (none of them limiting the user in his personal freedom of expression). Any tool which produces a sharp, distinct line and permits continuous work with little or no interruption is obviously most appropriate for this type of drawing; some tools are better suited for beginners, others more effective for advanced students. Simplest to handle is probably the heavy layout pencil, or the thick black marking crayon.[8] The more slender, conventional colored crayons also are excellent drawing tools. The latter, in combination with darker papers, often produce very satisfactory drawings. (Colored poster, bogus, or ordinary wrapping paper is most suitable for this purpose.) Since students on the junior high school level need a variety of materials, different kinds of paper and drawing tools sometimes act as an additional stimulus. For slightly more advanced work, the reed,[9] or stick and ink, and the carpenter's pencil with a chisellike point are particularly suitable. Of equal or possibly greater importance than the tool *with* which to draw, is the paper *on* which to draw. Redon's personal reaction to nice, clean, efficient, white drawing paper is also experienced by many high school students. He wrote: "I have a horror of a white sheet of paper. It creates such a disagreeable impression that it makes me sterile, even ridding me of my taste for work (except, of course, when I propose to represent something real, such as a study for a portrait, for example). A sheet of paper so shocks me that as soon as it is on the easel I am forced to scrawl on it with charcoal or pencil, or anything else, and this process gives it life."[10] In short, the costly, spot-

---

[8] "Generally, within the area of drawing, crayons are most serviceable for linear works. Their tendency to resist smudging and their lack of friability limit their usefulness in producing broad, tonal shading of subtle gradations—effects which are so easily obtained with soft fabricated chalks. Their fatty characteristics provide both a richer body to the strokes and a deeper chromatic intensity than do their counterparts in chalks, both being effects caused by the fatty binders which envelop the particles of pigments in semi-transparent encasements or films.

"Today, crayons of various viscosities and colors are obtainable commercially, or may be prepared in the artist's workshop. Whether the black lithographic crayons or the many colored types are preferred, the contemporary artist has a wide range of hardness and softness, texture, and pigmentation in the crayons at his disposal. Although they are not selected as often as graphite and pen and ink by our contemporaries, they provide additional diversity in the media of many modern artists, among them distinguished draughtsmen such as Henry Moore and Picasso." James Watrous, *The Craft of Old-Master Drawings* (Madison: University of Wisconsin Press, 1957), p. 122.

[9] "It has been mentioned that native reeds may be obtained throughout the temperate climate of the world and that they are very common in the U.S. Once a source is located along the bank of a neighboring lake or stream, enough reeds may be harvested within a few minutes to last for a year or more. Japanese reeds, which are imported for florists or garden supply firms, for supporting plants to which they are tied, make good reed pens." *Ibid.,* p. 64.

[10] Goldwater and Treves, *Artists on Art,* p. 360.

less white paper often has an intimidating effect on sensitive students. This is most evident shortly after the very first few lines have been set on paper. These fragments of thoughts or visions frequently appear so harsh, amateurish, and unsatisfactory that they immediately cause considerable apprehension, braking creative impulse and spoiling all the joy of drawing.

Probably the most suitable types of paper for contour drawing exercises are tough brown and off-white wrapping paper. They can easily be cut to specific sizes and, more important, they also have the least frustrating effect on students. The dull side of these two kinds of paper, with their slightly rough texture, works very well with soft pencils, crayons, and inks. Not as good but still very satisfactory is inexpensive newsprint and Manila paper. Only those students who are more advanced and express a desire to execute a finished contour drawing should be given the more expensive white drawing paper. This paper is particularly effective in combination with reeds, quills, sticks, or pen and ink.

Blind Contour Drawing

A separate category of contour drawing is blind contour drawing. Students drawing "blind" work from models without watching either their hands or their paper. They are asked to draw *solely* by looking at and concentrating on what has been placed in front of them without even so much as glancing down.

The best drawing media for blind contour drawing are those which, without the exertion of any particular effort, leave clear marks. Wax crayons and pressed charcoal sticks in combination with slightly rough-surfaced papers such as Manila paper meet this requirement. Moreover, these materials prevent students from making the drawings too small and help them to record sensitively what they are able to perceive through their fingertips.

Blind contour drawing is a means for helping students learn to see more intensively and sensitively. It should never be considered a method for achieving significant finished artistic statements. This type of drawing exercise has been devised because students frequently see only superficially, and then translate their hasty glances into insensitive generalizations. During many drawing sessions their minds are occupied simultaneously with two interrelated problems: perceiving what is in front of their eyes, and portraying it effectively. Often, after the initial drawing attempts have been made, the latter is given more and more attention, until finally students are concerned solely with their drawings, completely forgetting to study the objects or model. Blind contour drawing is aimed at helping them overcome this weakness by compelling them temporarily to ignore the work itself and to concentrate exclusively on the model.

During blind contour drawing sessions students often feel that they are not really responsible for the results since their critical judgment is not called on during the act of drawing. They therefore draw with less restraint but still show surprisingly sensitive lines and sharp observations. When this is pointed out, it strengthens their confidence in their drawing ability. Moreover, the experience of perceiving keenly and then immediately recording sensitively what is seen is often transferred into other drawing situations. That this transference has occurred is evident if a student begins his work by studying the model intently and immediately putting down a few expressive lines; then again viewing the figure attentively and adding a few more lines; and repeating this procedure until the work is completed.

The success or failure of blind contour exercises depends largely on the students' ability to concentrate *intensively* for periods of from five to ten minutes. It is an extremely demanding activity and should be pursued only for a short time during any given art session. Young students work well for about fifteen minutes if they are exposed to about three different poses, each lasting five minutes. With older and more advanced students these exercises can be extended successfully to four or five poses, some lasting up to eight minutes. A life model (a posing student) is commonly used for this form of drawing. For beginners the poses should be relatively easy to draw and show few or no foreshortenings.

Usually a few simple instructions enable students to understand what they are expected to do, but the teacher must insist that these directions be followed to the letter. During each individual pose students must remain absolutely silent; otherwise many will not be able to concentrate fully on their task. Noise will destroy the necessary working atmosphere. As soon as the model has taken his position, students should focus their concentration on the model until they feel they are actually touching him with their drawing tool. Only then should they begin to move their tools very, very slowly over the paper, leaving a continuous line, which should record exactly and sensitively the most minute lineament of the model. One of the best ways to begin blind contour drawing is to focus the attention on the top of the model's head and then move the eyes and the drawing hand simultaneously very slowly down to the feet and up again. The hand which is not holding the drawing tool should feel the edge of the paper so that contact with the work area is not lost. It is most important to ask students not even to glance at their drawing before it is finished.

Aside from the difficulty of concentrating, students frequently find it very hard to move their eyes and hands at the same rate of speed. At first glance their initial attempts often bear little resemblance to the model. Only by careful examination of these sketches can the teacher discover how well a student is able to coordinate vision and motion, and how intensively he has concentrated on this rather difficult task. After a number of blind contour drawing sessions, students frequently show marked improvement and are able to give extremely sensitive renderings of what they see. Nevertheless, with this type of exercise it is not the finished product which matters but the exercise as such.

Several variations of blind contour drawing can be used during such drawing sessions. One is to ask right-handed students to draw with their left hands, and left-handed ones to work with their right hands. This change often produces surprisingly good results. Lack of dexterity of the hand unused to drawing probably causes students to move more slowly, and therefore a noticeable coordination between eyes and hand is often achieved.

Another approach to blind contour drawing consists of having students draw more or less simultaneously with both hands. In this case the student holds a different colored crayon in each hand. Symmetrical objects (like pots or vases) are unsuitable for this type of assignment because such forms almost automatically force students to move their hands in an identical, mechanical manner. Since this assignment is strenuous and exhausting, it should be used sparingly, perhaps towards the end of a drawing session. It has great merit because it is very challenging and demands intense concentration; consequently a number of students improve rather rapidly.

Still another variation of blind contour drawing begins with asking students to close their eyes and then giving each an object to touch and to hold. The objects should be rich in texture and manifold in form, such as a piece of driftwood or a sea shell. When the students have investigated the object with their fingertips, and while they are still passing their fingers over it, they should begin to draw. All the time they are working they should keep their eyes closed and rely solely on their tactile sense. In most youngsters this sense is strongly developed, but during many drawing activities it is given little opportunity to play an active part. Therefore this exercise will most noticeably benefit those students who are accustomed to gathering many visual facts through touch. But almost all students will become more consciously aware of the significance of texture as an important part of any form.

Gesture Drawing

A form of drawing which bears some relation to contour drawing is known as gesture drawing. Its principle aim is to capture graphically a movement, a motion, or an action. In most gesture drawings, man's fleeting emotional expressions or physical actions are arrested by lineal suggestion, but such drawings are not restricted to the portrayal of man. The movements of an animal, the motions of a plant in the wind, the waves on a beach, or the turning of a machine, all can be recorded and expressed effectively in gesture drawing. Among the sketches by im-

Reproduced by courtesy of the Albertina Collection, Vienna

SIX MADONNA STUDIES
(Gesture Drawing)
Raphael

HORSE AND
TWO ACROBATS
Marino Marini
gesture sketch,
ink on paper

F. M. Hall Collection, University of Nebraska

portant artists, from Rembrandt to Goya, and from Delacroix to Degas to contemporary artists, one can find many exquisite examples of gesture drawings.

The main purpose of having students draw in this concise and suggestive manner is to help them see the major characteristics of an entirety. Like many visually untrained people, most students rarely see a whole. Their eyes wander from detail to detail, slowly forming an aggregate consisting of many minute particulars, but remaining unaware of the inherent unity within their field of vision. In this process many details may easily assume false importance, resulting in a drawing which not only lacks unity but also fails to show the characteristics of what is actually there.

GESTURE DRAWING FROM MODEL
eleventh grade girl
marking crayon on newsprint

Gesture drawing forces students to concentrate on whatever is most characteristic, and to portray this in a most simple and direct manner. By omitting what is superfluous and setting down economically only the essentials, students slowly become accustomed to seeing totalities rather than a continuous chain of details.

Students must be given frequent opportunities to do gesture drawing. Little progress can be expected in a few sessions, and, as with other drawing assignments, improvement depends largely on frequent practice. The basic rule for this method of drawing is to forget what is there and to anticipate and observe carefully what is happening. In other words, not the pose but the movement is important.

In an art room, gesture drawing is usually carried out by having students pose in a variety of motions. Two types of poses are definable; one is relatively slow in motion, similar to the slow-motion camera, and the other is the flash pose which consists of a rather rapid change of positions, lasting from thirty seconds to one minute. The slow-motion poses, extending from two to three minutes, are usually more effective at the beginning of a lesson, and the flash poses more effective towards the end. Since the former are not very strenuous and serve well for getting students into the necessary swing, they should be used before the more demanding flash poses are introduced. In the beginning the slow-motion pose is most effective if only the upper part of the body executes the movement. For instance, the model should stand on his spread-apart legs, moving only his torso, arms, and hands, bending down slowly as if he wanted to pick up a lost penny. Before students commence to draw, they should first observe the different phases of the entire movement. Then when the model goes through the motions for a second time, they should begin to draw at great speed. Their drawing should depict, in a rough, sketchy manner, the standing figure and then, superimposed on the same drawing, several phases of the bending action. While they are drawing, students should frequently be reminded that there is no time to portray details and that they must work swiftly. Their main objective should be to capture the movements with broad, simple strokes, not to produce skillful representations of a figure.

As a session in gesture drawing progresses, the movement of the model should become faster and the pose shorter. Poses such as a boy attempting to hit a baseball with a bat, dribbling a basketball, or standing on a wooden box imitating the motions and expressions of an orator are all meaningful to students and lend themselves well to this type of drawing. Naturally girls may pose as well, perhaps impersonating Joan of Arc pleading for mercy, or a girl playing a musical instrument or jumping rope. Flash poses can be especially fascinating when two people are used, as in wrestling or boxing, or one person assisting another as if he were hurt or were lifting something heavy. Any form of gymnastics or creative dancing also produces excellent and interesting gesture movements. However, gesture drawing in an art room need not be restricted to human models only. Pets serve equally well for this purpose, but since their movements cannot be demonstrated beforehand or readily anticipated, it is not advisable to use them with beginning students. On the other hand, short documentary films showing people or animals in motion lend themselves well to gesture drawing on all age levels. Even machines used to demonstrate principles of mechanics—often to be found in physics classes—can be employed for the study and drawing of motion. To make these drawing sessions really meaningful, the teacher must be enthusiastic, constantly spur on his students, be quick to invent many different exciting poses, and radiate confidence so that the youngsters forget their fears and inadequacies and become totally absorbed in their task.

Gesture drawing consumes a great deal of paper. The least expensive kinds, such as newsprint, serve this purpose well. Chalk, pressed charcoal, or conté or marking crayons are most suitable instruments for this type of drawing. They prevent students from becoming too absorbed in detail and permit them to cover large areas quickly with broad strokes which register their spontaneous impressions effortlessly and clearly.

Drawing in Volume

The contour line is only one vehicle for graphically conveying thoughts or visions. A totally different approach to the same activity stresses mass or volume rather than the edge of a form. This method of drawing can be termed modeling in two dimensions because both the solidity of a subject and its weight or massiveness are given expression. As in modeling with clay, forms are brought forward or moved back by the varying degrees of pressure exerted by the hand on the soft drawing medium. The underlying concept of drawing in volume has some relation to gesture drawing since the two are basically representations in broad simplifications. In both approaches the dominating quality is the whole rather than the detail. However, in volume drawing the massiveness conveys a static quality and rarely one of motion, since movement is of secondary importance.

Volume drawing is also used to register rather swiftly the bulkiness or solidity of an object.[11] The object can be anything which is not transparent (a water glass), or predominantly lineal in character (a net or a scaffold). Drawing in solids is another way to help students become acutely aware of a whole subject and how it relates to its surrounding space. In addition, foreshortenings which most beginners find difficult to draw often become easier for them when portrayed as a mass rather than as lines. Frequently those students who seem to have a natural affinity for modeling find this drawing approach more satisfactory and less difficult to handle than the line.

Drawing in which solidity of form is emphasized is effective with still life, live models, or landscapes. A good way to acquaint students with this method of draw-

TOWN SQUARE
Edward Hopper
charcoal drawing on paper

F. M. Hall Collection, University of Nebraska

ing is to arrange a simple still life against a window so that the different objects appear more like dark masses than detailed forms. After a few such exercises a model may be used, posing against either a window or a very light background. The major objective is to make students strongly aware of the massiveness of the figure. They should be asked to block out with simple and broad strokes what is in front of their eyes, and to draw in areas, possibly without using lines. They should begin by blocking out the inside of the form and then work towards the outside.

For beginners, poses should be rather compact with few foreshortenings, as for instance a person squatting on the floor, crouching on a stool, or standing upright in a toga-like costume. After students have become familiar with this manner of drawing, they may be confronted with more lively poses, such as a ballet dancer

---

[11] "By solidity I mean the employment of bulk as a factor of expression. Forms interacting with forms. The weight and density of the sea. The bulk and hard resistance of rock. The cavern of the sky. A blouse with a body in it. A head with a back to it. Bulk is only one of the factors of expression, but it is a mighty force." Henri, *The Art Spirit,* p. 163.

tightening her slippers, or a boy carrying a flag or throwing a discus. The duration of the pose depends not only on its difficulties but also on the medium used and the experience of the students. Simple, compact poses done with marking crayons or charcoal need not last more than five to six minutes. More intricate ones drawn with a heavy, blunt pen and ink may last up to ten minutes. If students are working with a blunt pen or a stick, they should be asked to keep the tool moving in all directions without lifting it, so that a dense net of lines slowly develops and gradually takes on the shape of the depicted subject. The temptation is great to draw with these tools by first setting down an outline; students must be reminded to start from the inside and work towards the outside, like a plant which, growing from a fixed, almost lineal core, slowly spreads its branches and leaves.

Another technique which is also effective with more advanced students is to work with a fairly thick hair brush (between #10 and #14) and a single dark watercolor. One first paints the whole shape of a figure quickly in a medium light shade, and then deliberately places over this a darker tone to emphasize weight and solidity. A different approach is to darken those forms which recede, leaving the parts which protrude in a lighter shade.

Outdoor drawing in solid areas also has great merit. Setting down in simple basic shapes the many different forms within a given scene, students will be less confused, will give attention only to the significant, and will spend little time on insignificant details. Unity is more easily achieved, since the individual is forced to portray what he sees in rather broad sweeps without becoming petty or trivial. This type of drawing exercise can be considered an excellent preparation for outdoor painting—in fact, for any form of creative painting.

Finally, drawing in volume is a particularly meaningful activity if it is employed in connection with modeling. It may be used as a transition from two-dimensional to three-dimensional work, or as a drawing exercise during a more time-consuming modeling project.

Drawing in Light and Shade

With the exception of contour drawing, probably the most widely accepted form of drawing, from a historic point of view, is in light and shade. Beginning with the Renaissance, western artists spent many hours studying the effect of light on forms, and drawing it accurately. Later on, the first books on public school art teaching covered this drawing technique at great length, and students were forced to practice skillful shading endlessly so that any form rendered had a three-dimensional appearance. This approach was based on the notion that concentrating on and representing the plastic properties of a subject is tantamount to achieving the greatest illusion of depth and the most realistic rendering.

Today this point of view has changed noticeably. Realistic drawing is considered one of numerous approaches and is no longer deemed the only acceptable or important one. Representing a form by emphasizing its light and shadow primarily conveys one of its characteristics: a surface quality which, depending on style and intent, can be very meaningful and satisfactory. Light and shadow can also be considered significant in giving form to a shape. They are helpful elements in identifying what protrudes or recedes, what is convex or concave. They can be very important in giving powerful expression to a subject, and this point should always be the foremost reason for incorporating light and shadow in a drawing.

Another inherent quality of light is its consequent cast shadow. Commonly whenever an opaque object receives light from one or several sources, some parts of the object and some of its surrounding area remain in darkness; this darkness is called "cast shadow." The degree of contrast between the lighted area and the

Reproduced by courtesy of the Albertina Collection, Vienna

THE PHILOSOPHER
Rembrandt van Rijn
brush and ink

shadow depends on the intensity of the light. Diffused light softens this contrast considerably, and brilliant light magnifies it. The relationship of a light and its shadow is determined by the position of the light and that of the object. While in nature the position of the sun or moon in relation to a subject defines the shape and size of a shadow, in the man-made world the source of light can be altered, moved, and freely arranged to fit a given situation. With artificial light, moods can be created, and scenes or objects can be dramatized. Caravaggio's and Rembrandt's paintings demonstrate excellently how light and shadow are used artistically to produce lyrical moods or dramatic effects.

In the teaching of drawing, the study of light and shadow has a definite place, not in the sense of bygone days, when it was considered the most important step in learning how to draw, but simply as one of numerous drawing approaches. In particular with older students, who often have a longing for realistic drawings, working with light and shadow, with its ever-changing effects on a subject or surface, should not be neglected. A modern and extremely effective method—effective because fascinating effects can be so easily achieved—employs one or more spotlights with which contrasts and dramatic shadows can be produced almost effortlessly. Moving a spotlight into different positions around one subject will demonstrate, without lengthy explanations, the importance of light and shade, and the role of the shadow and its expressive quality. For instance, if a spotlight is placed directly in front of a round object and on the same level with it, the object will appear rather two-dimensional or flat, like a shape cut out of cardboard. If the light is then moved towards one side, the object's depth or three-dimensional quality will reappear. Moving the spotlight below the object will produce a very dramatic effect. Elongated shadows, an unusual position of the highlights, and the artificial atmosphere created by the spotlight can give even a simple object an almost spectacular appearance.

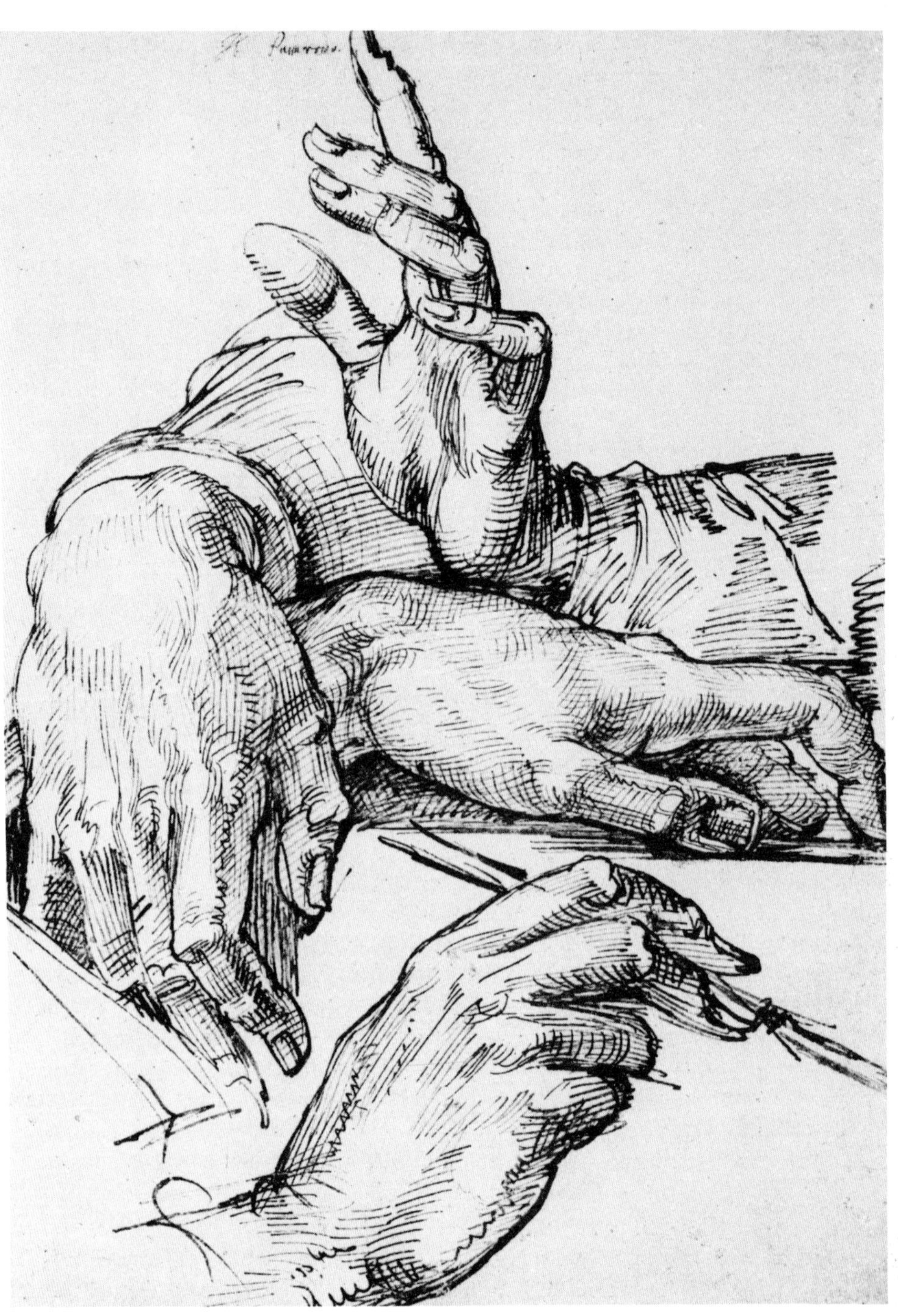

STUDY OF HANDS
Bartolommeo Passerotty
quill drawing

Reproduced by courtesy of the Albertina Collection, Vienna

Working with light, shade, and shadows is as effective with figure drawing as it is with still life. There are two distinctly different ways to represent shade in a drawing: with lines, and with mass or volume. In the lineal approach the shadow is composed of numerous fine lines laboriously drawn with a sharp pencil or a fine pen. The lines may either be crosshatched or paralleled with the shape of the subject. Both of these forms of line drawing are rather intellectual since every line must be carefully thought out and weighed before it is set down. The methods are usually effective either as preparatory studies for more advanced graphic techniques, or with older students wishing to produce more finished drawings. They also have considerable merit in studies of details, such as a hand, a flower, or a piece of cloth, because they require slow and deliberate work and expose any attempt at superficiality.

Drawing light and shade in volume, employing a soft medium such as charcoal, conté crayon, chalk, or a very soft pencil, is a natural and simple way to learn to understand the significance of the modeled form and the role of the shadow in visual art. The softer media permit a student to respond immediately to the dramatic effects of light on forms, and with little effort or skill he can achieve the gradations of shade and the darkness of shadows. A light, rough-textured paper presents the highlights or the brightest areas in a drawing, and the images are then produced simply by covering parts of this paper with different shades and shapes of darkness. In this drawing approach the contour line frequently is contrasted with a solid, dark area or shadow. A student may begin by outlining quickly the major parts of his drawing and then setting down quite deliberately the most important dark areas which he sees on the subject and its surroundings. Only after he has done this should he add the lighter shades which he still deems necessary. This method often prevents a student from becoming involved with minor details and from losing the feeling for his whole project.

The basic principle of drawing in light and shade (using a dark drawing medium on light-colored paper) can easily be reversed. Instead of representing shadows and dark outlines, the artist concentrates on highlights and light-colored contours. Again the spotlight can be of great help. Light-colored objects and materials, or models dressed in light-colored clothes, should be exposed to bright lights, so that the extreme contrast between highlights and shadows is brought out. Using very dark paper and white crayon or chalk, students should build up their drawings by focusing their attention on the light, instead of the dark, areas, and heavily emphasizing light instead of shade.

Three other tools which are often used for this type of drawing are the stick, the reed, and the brush. The strong line made by the stick or reed can be handled easily by high school students. The powerful lines, freely applied on a large piece of white wrapping paper, lend freshness to shades and shadows. These tools force students to decide and draw rather quickly, keeping them from overworking their drawings. By contrast the brush is one of the most difficult drawing tools to control and handle effectively. The slightest pressure of the hand will immediately change the width and character of the line or stroke. To produce numerous similar lines or strokes requires skill of an order which one rarely finds among high school students; it seems advisable to exclude this form of brush drawing from the average art curriculum and to suggest it only to exceptional, advanced students.

Chiaroscuro

Closely related to drawing in light and shade is chiaroscuro. The term "chiaroscuro" is used to identify "a manner of creating figures by light values over a dark halftone or to suggest the partial emergence of figures from a deeply shadowed background into atmospheric light. Consequently, chiaroscuro drawing is usually associated with those studies which have similar relationships of dark tonal backgrounds and figures largely defined by prominent, applied, lights."[12] The major difference between chiaroscuro and drawing in light and shade is that in the former *both* light and shade must be deliberately set down, whereas in the latter (depending on the color of the paper), only the contrasting lines and areas must be drawn. The background in a chiaroscuro drawing is always neutral, neither light nor dark. Highlights, light-colored areas, and contour lines as well as shadows, dark shades, and outlines must be most deliberately drawn. Every part in a chiaroscuro drawing is the concrete consequence of a decision.

[12] Watrous, *The Craft of Old-Master Drawings,* p. 34.

STUDY OF THE HEAD
OF AN APOSTLE
(from the Heller Altarpiece)
Albrecht Dürer
brush drawing heightened
with white on green-
grounded paper

Reproduced by courtesy of the Albertina Collection, Vienna

This form is a very exacting, intellectual, and controlled form of drawing, and probably demands more decisions than any other kind. Since it requires a considerable degree of self-discipline, it should be practiced in high schools. In order to prevent any misunderstanding it should be pointed out that chiaroscuro permits the same degree of freedom of expression as any other form of drawing. Any simplification, stylization, omission, or exaggeration can be convincingly achieved. As a matter of fact, this approach to drawing does not easily yield conventional realistic work.

Two different methods have been employed for chiaroscuro. One makes use of neutral-colored paper, and the other of white paper which is covered with thin,

Reproduced by courtesy of the Art Museum, Princeton University

SKETCH FOR TWO FIGURES
IN "TRIUMPH OF ST. GEORGE"
V. Carpaccio

neutral-colored washes. Until very recently, bistre was used for these washes.[13] However, bistre is not available commercially; adequate substitutes for it are watercolors or a mixture of India ink with denatured alcohol.[14] The merit of both types of translucent washes is that they make the quality of a drawing more pleasing, and that students draw on them with greater care than on a colored paper. Like a pen and black or white ink, poster paints and fine hair brushes work extremely well on this

---

[13] "Pen-and-ink drawings were frequently heightened with a brown wash, laid on with the brush. This wash, often of a fine warm colour, was made of *bistre,* a substance made out of the soot of wood fires, . . . and dissolved in water. . . . The artist frequently made use of two or more shades of bistre and so attained a very rich *chiaroscuro* effect." Henry Scipio Reitlinger, *Old Master Drawings* (London: Constable & Co., Ltd., 1922), p. 83.

[14] The proportions of this mixture consist of approximately one drop of India ink to one fluid ounce of alcohol. The advantage of this mixture over watercolor is that it will dry rapidly without forming puddles or causing the paper to buckle.

treated drawing paper, whereas the colored poster or construction paper is limited to use with poster paints or chalk. However, a beginner who has never drawn in chiaroscuro will work more easily on neutral colored poster or construction paper with chalk or crayons. A more advanced student should have no difficulty in drawing with two colors of ink or poster paints on washes. The teaching approach to chiaroscuro drawing is the same as working with light and shade, and no *special* type of subject appears necessary for students to learn or enjoy this method of drawing.

Drawing from Memory

The different approaches to learning to draw and to handling a variety of media and techniques have so far been focused on working from nature. However, drawing from memory or from imagination is an equally significant aspect of drawing as well as of learning. In fact, most learning takes place when an individual attempts to employ his newly acquired knowledge and skill. The more frequently he does this, the more they will become an active part of him. A casual acquaintance with knowledge or skill is passive; it cannot be recalled nor employed at will. The only way to attain and retain new knowledge and skill is to use them in a meaningful context, a context which is the antithesis of rote learning and drill lessons, neither of which has any place in a modern art program. These forms of mechanical learning cause animosities and unpleasant associations; they have frustrating effects, are unconsciously rejected, and defeat the aims of art education.

A steady interplay between drawing from nature and drawing from memory should take place in every art room. This can consist of such simple assignments as drawing a particular pose from memory immediately after the model has left, or drawing the unexposed side of an object or figure, as for instance a model standing with his back to the class, facing a wall. Students should then be asked to draw the side which they *cannot* see, that is, the model's front. This principle can be applied to many objects and to other poses.

In another approach to drawing from memory a student first describes verbally a pose which has been previously used or has just been invented by him. For example, in the pose of a beggar a man sits on the floor on his knees, his hands held out in front of him, his head turned slightly up and towards one side, and the upper part of his body bent forward. After verbalization, the students begin to draw. They should be urged to give expression not only to the figure but also to the background. The verbal description should help students clarify a memorized or imagined pose in their minds and learn to recall visual facts.

These types of drawing assignments can be varied even more. After students have had a number of lessons in figure drawing, they may be asked to compose a scene incorporating several persons. The expressions and/or movements of these persons should resemble those which were drawn previously. A teacher may deliberately plan drawing sessions leading towards such an assignment, relating all individual poses to one central theme. A subject may be conceived in as broad terms as a group of people witnessing an amusing episode, or excited shoppers at a sale in a department store; or it may be as restricted as a worried mother holding her sick child. It should be left to the students' discretion to interpret the theme, to present the atmosphere, to arrange the figures, and to treat the subject matter. It is important, however, that students incorporate poses of figures with which they have become familiar during previous art lessons. These examples can be varied in innumerable ways, depending on the students' maturity, interest, and progress, but most of all on the ingenuity of the art teacher.

Obviously, drawing from imagination is not directly connected with drawing from nature. The major problem here is one of motivation and stimulation. When students are inspired and encouraged, they transfer some of the knowledge they have gained by drawing from nature into their more imaginative works. On the other hand, an alert teacher who examines his students' works carefully, notices the kind of difficulties they encounter while they are drawing, and listens attentively to their questions will be strongly aware of their needs and shortcomings and able to adjust his teaching accordingly. In this way he will also discover in which areas they need further work and which drawing activities are most effective with a particular group of students. There is a reciprocal relationship between teaching drawing from nature and/or from memory or imagination. The two methods of expression must be given equal attention if students are to learn the skill of drawing, gain freedom of expression, and grow creatively.

Subjects Related to Drawing

Three subjects which are closely allied to drawing and often taught in connection with it are anatomy, perspective, and proportion. Yet as far as teaching art is concerned, it is questionable whether these three areas should be considered *independent* subjects, to be studied as separate entities, divorced from any creative activity. This approach was common practice until recently and might still be valid on an advanced level of art instruction, but it can no longer be advocated in teaching art to high school students. A thorough study of the three areas belongs in the realm of professional or vocational training, not in a high school art program. There is no evident necessity for such specialized instruction in these subjects, nor can the time for them be spared without curtailing areas more important for high school students. On the high school level these subjects should be treated as integral parts of the art curriculum and taught whenever the need arises—for instance, during a drawing session, a painting project, or a lesson in modeling. Also there are many isolated situations in which an individual student may show a definite need for information in any of these fields. In such cases the teacher should not hesitate to give the student some individual instruction, demonstrate the point visually, or provide him with appropriate printed material.

Plainly a teacher should have reasonable understanding and command of anatomy, proportion, and perspective, yet sufficient judgment to use his knowledge carefully and sparingly. Knowing these subjects well should enable him to explain a point clearly and concisely without confusing students or giving them the impression that to know these subjects is synonymous with possessing fixed formulae for the creation of art.

It is not known when artists first began to take a serious interest in anatomy. In ancient times the artist, like the physician, had access only to the anatomy of animals, and probably transposed his findings to that of the human body; or else he derived his knowledge from observation of athletes and nudes. With the beginning of the Renaissance artists began to study closely the anatomy of man and beast. They dissected bodies, often in secrecy, in order to understand the internal structure of the exterior form. Artists like Vesalius, Leonardo da Vinci, Michelangelo, and Dürer left a wealth of drawings in which their findings and observations are recorded. These drawings can hardly be distinguished from medical and scientific drawings, since the dividing line between art and science scarcely existed in this period. This material is still worthy of study and should be available to high school students. The modern approach to anatomy, from an artist's point of view, is considerably different from that of a scientist. Today the artist's interest in anatomy is restricted to practical knowledge regarding form and function of bone structure, tendons, and muscles, without precise medical particulars.

In high school art, teaching anatomy is meaningful to students only to the extent to which it has immediate practical implications. After becoming aware of certain difficulties in portraying a human or animal form, more advanced students may be greatly helped by information about bone structure and the position and function of muscles. One of the simplest but most effective methods of illustrating a point in regard to anatomy is to draw outlines on a living model with a grease pencil. In this way students can see how a moving muscle changes its shape, where bones are located, or how they take on a different appearance, depending on the viewer's position. In addition, an elementary anatomical atlas with clear, simplified illustrations should be considered part of the standard equipment in every art room, and students should be at liberty to consult it freely. Equally helpful is a plastic skeleton which is available in various sizes.

In many anatomy books for artists a section is devoted to a system of proportions in man or animal. Artists like Leonardo da Vinci, Dürer, and Schadow devised charts to clarify the basically different proportions in men, women, and children. These charts were in part the result of a search for an absolute in beauty as related to the human figure. However, the chart's main function was to demonstrate the different size relationships in human beings depending on sex and age levels. The head is the basic unit used to determine size relationships; the height of an erect figure is divided into sections, the length of the head determining the size of each section. In this instance the distance from the highest point of the cranium to the lowest part of the chin is called the head. Today an "average" man is seven and a half heads in height. This is divided into one "head" for the head, two and three-quarters for the neck and trunk, and three and three-quarters for the lower extremities. Other parts are similarly divided; the arm, for instance, from the fingertips to the elbow, usually equals two "heads" in length.

Any *formal* study of proportion should be discouraged on the high school level. Such a study can become a bad substitute for actual seeing. Instead of making a careful observation of a model, students may easily become absorbed in measuring parts and giving attention only to accurate proportions, thereby losing all feeling for genuine expression.

On the other hand, every art teacher should know the system of proportions well. In an art room, there are many situations in which a point arises relating to proportions. This can happen during a verbal clarification of a pose or during an individual critique. Occasionally a simple device consisting of a plain, netlike background filled with straight vertical and horizontal lines a foot apart placed directly behind a model will act as a silent reminder and help students look for related points and parts in a figure. Lastly, it should be mentioned that anatomy and proportion, taught in an unobtrusive manner, are of particular value when students are working from imagination or memory.

A *broad* knowledge of anatomy and perspective should be considered part of any sound education. The responsibility for the instruction of anatomy in the high school is commonly shared to some degree by biology and art. In the teaching of perspective, however, the major responsibility rests with the art field, because perspective is rarely taught in any other area in the high school. The word "perspective," as it is usually referred to in connection with visual art, means the method of creating the illusion of the third dimension on a two-dimensional plane. The fictitious third dimension is depth. The underlying principle of perspective is geometry, yet scientific mathematical perspective, with its complex calculations and measurements, is usually not employed in painting or drawing. Only such simplifications as have immediate practical value are used.

This kind of perspective is often referred to as linear perspective and is only one way to produce the illusion of depth on a flat surface. The feeling of depth

detail from
FISHING IN A
MOUNTAIN STREAM
attributed to
Hsu Tao-ning (ca. 1000)
ink on silk

Reproduced by courtesy of the William Rockhill Nelson Gallery of Art, Kansas City, Mo.

also can be convincingly created by the careful and deliberate use of shades, by employing different intensities, exploiting the contrasts of lights and darks, and utilizing vagueness and soft atmospheric hazes. This method is often referred to as aerial perspective, and can best be explained to students by showing and analyzing faithful reproductions. (Superior examples are found among predominantly monochrome Japanese and Chinese wash drawings.) However, this method of creating depth in a drawing (or a painting) should be taken up only after students have had considerable painting experience, and have developed sensitivity to shades and gained a basic understanding of the more conventional forms of perspective. Without these prerequisites they will be unable to profit by this knowledge and will become confused, because aerial perspective is rarely consciously perceived in reality and rather infrequently encountered in western art.

The illusion of depth is often created in a still different manner: by careful overlapping of shapes. (Giotto's murals are good examples.) This method has frequently been used independently as well as in conjunction with other forms of perspective. Overlapping is usually discovered accidentally and is rarely taught in a formal manner. Many times when junior high school students first begin to express themselves realistically, they use overlapping as the major means of conveying their awareness of depth. They do so long before they become acquainted with linear perspective.

Approaches to linear perspective methods can be divided into two groups. One consists of advanced technical methods which are rarely used in creative art; the other comprises more elementary applications which are frequently employed in painting or drawing. One of the more advanced methods is called isometric (literally meaning "equally measured") perspective. In isometric perspective an object is drawn either in exact scale, or to actual measurements and objectively correct proportions. In such representations no part of the object diminishes in size, but remains in accurate proportion even when receding into the distance. Isometric perspective is used mainly in mechanical drawing where height, width, and depth should not be distorted in any way.

Another advanced technical application of perspective is used to project accurately a ground plan into an elevation—that is, to transpose a floor plan and the plan view of objects into a perspective drawing. These two methods are of limited importance to high school students. Both may be introduced in connection with advanced stage or interior design, but otherwise are of little significance in less specialized subjects.

The most important and generally applied aspect of linear perspective is used to give a three-dimensional feeling to a drawing or painting by establishing the position from which a spectator sees the depicted objects or scene. Every form or sight can be observed from many different points of view, from above, below, straight on, or from the ground level. Depending on the artist's intent or eye level, a subject will change its visual appearance and must be represented accordingly. The point of observation is established by fixing a definite focal point (called the vanishing point) on the surface or plane of a picture. This corresponds to the point on which an artist focuses his eyes by looking straight into the real or imagined distance at an object, a background, or the horizon. By elongating this point horizontally in both directions, an imaginary line is established which is commonly referred to as the horizon line. The foremost function of both the vanishing point and the horizon line is to determine explicitly from which point of observation the spectator is supposed to see the depicted subject.

Most students encounter their greatest difficulty on this very point. Without having developed an understanding of perspective, they often use several different positions or focal points in one picture plan. Within a single representation they may show one section as seen from above and another as seen from a totally different eye level. Therefore, before students are introduced to the mechanics of linear perspective they should be made strongly aware of the necessity for having only one focal point in a drawing or painting. If this need is not felt, however, the teaching of perspective can easily become a crutch on which they will depend for all their creative efforts, thereby losing their freedom of expression.

A characteristic way in which students indicate their readiness to learn perspective is by announcing that their own work no longer pleases them, but that they do not know either what it is, exactly, that makes it so dissatisfying, or how to improve it. "Something looks wrong" is a typical phrase used to express their dissatisfaction. Sometimes, too, their wish to take up the subject can be expedited if the teacher deliberately exposes them to situations or places in which a knowledge of perspective would be very helpful. Drawing a room, a hallway in the school, an interesting alley, or a busy street corner may hasten their desire to learn perspective.

The teaching of perspective should, if at all possible, never be treated purely theoretically, nor divorced from visual experiences. On the high school level demonstrations are much more effective than lengthy verbalizations. Demonstrations can be given with chalk drawings on the blackboard, or with charts prepared by the teacher. Such prepared material should take up a single problem or item at a time. One may illustrate a detail such as the importance and effect of an observer's position or point of station in relation to a representation, and the change if this point is moved in any direction. Another may clarify the function and relationship between the point of station, the horizon line, and the vanishing points, and still another may cover the role of the one, two, or possibly three vanishing points and their usage.

Many students learn the principles and mechanics of perspective quite easily, but often find it difficult to know when and how to apply them in their own creative work. Here a teacher's patience and tolerant persistence is of major importance. Yet he must be able to realize when perspective is of help to students and their work, and when they should be at liberty to disregard it. In every instance he must study each student's bent and then either guide him away from the mechanics of perspective, or towards using them more correctly and extensively. Certainly perspective is one device which helps to convey a creative idea visually, but, as in the case of anatomy or proportion, it should never be considered more than one of several equally convincing or significant methods.

Printmaking

Like drawing, printmaking is predominantly a visual expression in monochromes; in fact, graphics (or printmaking) are extensions of drawing. Originally the use of these techniques was motivated by the desire to make multiple, faithful reproductions of a drawing. Today, however, this concept is no longer valid; printmaking has become an independent art form, equal in importance to painting or sculpture. Prints "have an intrinsic appeal entirely apart from the question as to whether they were made in the fifteenth or the twentieth century. They possess uniqueness, magic, a spiritual impress, the stamp of vivid personality, a singing quality of line or mass, some telling economy of expression that satisfies in a flash of immediate comprehension."[15]

Printmaking is divided into four broad groups. One is the relief process which consists of wood and linoleum cuts and wood engraving. Another is intaglio, comprised of etching and engraving. A third group is the planographic process whose major representative is lithography, and the last is a newcomer to the graphic arts, serigraphy or the stencil processes.

Wood-Block Printing

As a printing process woodcutting is probably the oldest in the western world. Although coptic textile prints made with wood blocks still exist which date back approximately to the year 600, the history of block printing is most closely tied to the history of paper. As far as we know, printmaking came into existence nearly two hundred years after the western world had learned the secret of making paper from China (roughly during the middle of the twelfth century). The earliest known block prints on paper were transposed from simple line drawings quite similar to the hand-drawn illuminations and illustrations of the period. The blocks for these printed illustrations, in all probability, were cut not by the artist, but by a specialized craftsman who prepared the wood plates for incunabula which were used in book printing before 1500, prior to Gutenberg's invention of movable type. In addition to serving as book illustrations, early woodcuts were often employed for calendars and playing cards. Slowly, over a period of at least two generations, the character of woodcuts changed from imitations of line drawings to a more individual form of expression. As early as the end of the sixteenth century, block prints were rich in fine and heavy lines which often followed the contour of a form, and dramatically brought into play contrasts between dark and light areas.

This approach to block printing became even more pronounced with the innova-

---

[15] Carl Zigrosser, *Six Centuries of Fine Prints* (New York: Garden City Publishing Co., 1939), pp. 10–11.

Reproduced by courtesy of the National Gallery of Art, Washington (Rosenwald Collection)

ADORATION OF THE MAGI: Anonymous, German XV century

tion of wood engraving which came about shortly after the widely accepted use of woodcutting as a printing method. To be sure, both are techniques of relief printing. This means that all parts which should *not* leave an impression on the paper or fabric are deepened in, or taken out of, a wood plank with a cutting instrument. The uncut, smooth wood surface is then covered with printer's ink which, under pressure, leaves an impression on a material: "the image to be printed stands in relief on the block of wood."[16]

There are several major differences between wood engraving and woodcutting. Woodcuts are made in wooden planks in which the grain runs parallel to the length of the board. In wood engravings, on the other hand, the grain of the hard wood runs vertically to the plank; it is an end-grain block, usually made from pieces which are cut horizontally from the trunk of the tree. In the print of a woodcut even the finest white lines in dark areas have been made by cutting into the wooden board and lifting out a sliver, while in a wood engraving these same fine lines are made by pressing in and forcing the grain to the sides. Finally, the end-grained hard wood for engraving permits more delicate lines, textures, and details than the slightly softer and long-grained woodcut planks.

Most blockprints dating from the high Renaissance to the last part of the nineteenth century were wood engravings. Then Japanese woodcuts suddenly became known to western artists and immediately had a strong impact on graphic expression. Our present renewed appreciation for and approach to woodcuts have their roots in the early prints made in Europe, as well as in the works of Japanese and Chinese masters. "The Chinese and Japanese were the first to use the woodcut to print images. One of the earliest dated woodcuts appeared in the *Diamond Sutra,* a Buddhist scripture, with the date 868."[17]

Japanese prints made during the last part of the eighteenth and the beginning of the nineteenth century probably exerted the greatest influence on western artists. Sharaku, Utamaro, and Hokusai became the most widely recognized masters of this art form. By far the largest part of Japanese woodcuts were in color. The blocks,

---

[16] Jules Heller, *Printmaking Today* (New York: Henry Holt & Co., 1958), p. xvii.
[17] Zigrosser, *Six Centuries of Fine Prints,* p. 180.

however, were cut not by the artist, who only supplied a brush drawing, but by a specialized craftsman. The colored prints were then made by a professional printer who chose colors according to the wishes of a publisher, who had usually bought the drawing for reproduction purposes. In spite of this apparently unnatural separation within the whole graphic process, the end result, the print, maintained a high degree of technical integration and unity of feeling. This division between the artist's drawing and the finished print did not exist only in the Orient. For example, many of the early European woodcuts were made by gluing a drawing on a wood block which was then cut and printed by someone other than the artist.

In the modern approach to printmaking, however, it is taken for granted that the artist not only designs but also cuts and prints the block. This contemporary concept derives from two generally held beliefs: that the greatest degree of artistic unity can be achieved only when the artist himself carries out the graphic process from his first vaguely conceived idea to the finished print; and that printmaking is not merely a technique or a mechanical means for reproducing a composition, but is a continuous creative process whose different working phases are intrinsic parts of the unfolding of a creative thought, ending only when the final image is printed.

THE SEVENTH DAY
Ernst Barlach
woodcut

This recent concept should also be considered the major reason for including printmaking in the high school art curriculum. Every printing project should always be regarded as a deliberate, slow, creative process in which students learn to fuse workmanship with visions or thoughts. Woodcutting "is a technique," wrote the sculptor Ernst Barlach, "which challenges one to self-expression, to the unmistakable revelation of one's real and ultimate meaning. It forces a certain universality of expression and represses the insignificant effects of soft and undisciplined techniques."[18]

Woodcutting, probably more than any other technique within reach of high school students, forces them to think. Very little can be left to chance; every step in the process, every cut, even the smallest, is a tangible result of a decision, literally a decision in black and white. Yet woodcutting does not require either a high degree of slowly acquired skill, or the considerable technical knowledge and expensive equipment which are needed for wood engraving. Of all printing processes woodcutting is perhaps the least costly, requiring no high-priced presses, tools, or materials to produce effective and skillful prints.

One of the best methods of teaching woodcutting is to have beginning students work first with linoleum, gaining experience with the procedures and artistic problems of this printing process without having to spend as much time on the cutting of a block as would be necessary for wood. Another advantage of this method is that cutting the softer linoleum requires almost no skill; it needs only sharp penlike knives and inexpensive battleship linoleum. The disadvantages are that the material is rather bleak and without a character of its own, that unlike wood it does not permit very fine details, and that it does not impose the same degree of discipline which is demanded when working with a harder block. Furthermore, only rather harsh and rigid black and white effects are possible in a linoleum cut, since isolated, fine relief lines break off fairly easily. Wood, on the other hand, permits various textures and gradations of lines and dots made either by cutting or by pounding coarse metal materials into the block.[19] None of this is possible with a linoleum block.

After students have had some experience with linoleum cutting, they may begin to work in wood. The blocks made from either material should, if at all possible, be fairly large. Small sizes (less than 4″ x 6″) force students to spend too much time cutting details which are technically hard for them to control. Also, working in very limited areas may hamper freedom of expression and the execution of an idea. This implies that creating a woodcut entails two separable entities: one is the creative idea, the other a sequence of technical processes. Yet almost every pictorial image or observation can be adapted to and expressed in a blockprint, from realism to abstraction, and from man to all aspects of his environment.

However, this does not mean that the idea for a woodcut should first be worked out in detail in a separate drawing, independent from cutting and printing. Certainly before actually beginning a woodcut a student should have not only a clear idea in mind but also a rough sketch of it. Such an improvised drawing should contain major space divisions, explicit details pertaining to subject matter, and clear indications of which areas should remain dark and which should be light. Still, such a sketch should never simulate a completed print or be a finished drawing. On the contrary, the whole working plan should be so loosely conceived that ideas and sudden inspirations can immediately and effortlessly be incorporated. To some degree every woodcutting process should retain opportunities for improvisations to the very end.

Yet blockprinting has educational merit only if students approach their work in a disciplined manner; they must learn to realize the importance of good workmanship. This includes respect for tools and materials, beginning with learning to sharpen the knives, and ending with neatly matting their prints. Finding a constant balance between freedom of expression and disciplined craftsmanship is the unending obligation of every teacher during any printing project.

---

[18] Ernst Barlach, *Aus Seinen Briefen* (Munich: Piper Verlag, 1947), p. 48.—(*author's translation*)

[19] "Cut pieces of wire screen to fit certain areas of your design and pound them into the woodblock surface. Remove and print.

"Nails of various sizes may puncture particularly dull areas to enliven them." Heller, *Printmaking Today*, p. 97.

One more characteristic of blockprinting is that it lends itself easily to color printing without expensive equipment or great skill; this can be carried out in two different ways. One is to apply a variety of colors on a single plate; the other to cut an individual block for each color. Printing in colors from a single block is the more difficult process because the whole design must be planned very carefully and in great detail before the first line is cut. In this method a few lines are incised; these are then printed with one color for as many times as finished prints are desired. Then more cuts are added to the cleaned block and printed with a different color on the same unfinished prints. This process is repeated until the design has been completely developed and printed in all predetermined colors. The method is so complex and exacting that a high school student rarely can handle it successfully. On the other hand, the Japanese method of color printing from a single block should not be too difficult for most advanced students. Here different areas on the carved block are immediately covered with various colored water-based inks, and then printed exactly

HEAD OF A MAN
Johannis Lievens
chiaroscuro woodcut

Reproduced by courtesy of the National Gallery of Art, Washington (Rosenwald Collection)

like any other woodcut. This method permits considerable experimentation with colors, and students can effortlessly and pragmatically learn the effects and interrelationships of colors.

The method of printing woodcuts in colors by cutting one block for each color is more adaptable to high school work than the methods just described. A very good way is to have students begin working with only two blocks, resulting in a three-color print. The three-color effect is achieved by utilizing the light color of the paper, and by designating one block for a very dark color (carrying the major part of the design), and the second block for a neutral color in which the light areas and highlights have been cut out. This approach is similar to chiaroscuro. Only after students have cut the major design and made a careful proof should they cut the second block. The problem of having the two blocks register accurately can be solved easily by pressing a very wet print of the major design (the first block) on the second, still uncut block, leaving a perfect impression. When this is finished it should be printed in a neutral color, and the first, dark-colored block with its major design pressed over it. Many old masters, like Lucas Cranach or Hans Baldung Grien, used this approach to blockprinting. After students have become familiar with this method of producing color woodcuts, they may be encouraged to try more complicated procedures, employing several colors and blocks.

One of the best ways to stimulate students before they begin a woodcut project is to show them the greatest possible variety of outstanding prints. Such a collection should include old as well as modern masters. In each instance, and this is of major importance, the teacher should not fail to point out and to explain the different approaches to subject matter and its treatment, the handling of black and white and color, and—most important of all—the effects of diverse techniques.

Woodcutting is unquestionably the relief printing process most suitable for high school students. Wood engraving is the most inappropriate because its special tools and blocks are quite costly, and—more important—it requires considerable skill, which can be gained only through many hours of arduous practice for which high school students rarely have the time, interest, or incentive. On the other hand, a few varieties of relief printing often hold some fascination. For instance, students can be asked to work out a printing project by creating a composition of pieces of cardboard, string, or various other materials which are to be glued to a board. After the finished composition has been coated with shellac it can be handled like a woodcut, covered with printer's ink, and printed. This technique is also known as collagraphy. The term is a combination of the French word "collage," meaning gluing or pasting on paper, and the Greek word "graphein," to write.

A still different reproduction technique which has some relation to relief printing, yet is not literally a printing process, is called "stone rubbing." "After the invention of paper the Chinese discovered that it was possible to take impressions of inscriptions and designs incised in flat slabs of rock. A dampened sheet of thin paper was laid on the stone and forced into all the incisions, whereupon black ink was applied with a flat pad to the surface of the paper (that side of the sheet which we would call the back) and the design appeared in white against a background of black. In this way was avoided that reversal of image which always takes place when ink is applied *between* the block or plate and the paper."[20]

This method of reproduction is easily imitated by students. They may begin by carving with linol block tools into a 2″–3″ moist block which is made out of plaster of Paris. Such a block is prepared by pouring wet plaster on a slightly greased glass plate which is enclosed on all four sides by strips of wood 2″–3″ high. As long as the block is kept moist, students should have no difficulties with their carvings. The

---

[20] Zigrosser, *Six Centuries of Fine Prints,* pp. 180–181.

DONOR ON HORSEBACK
Chinese stone rubbing
A.D. 528, Weil Dynasty

project can be used as a connecting link between two- and three-dimensional work. Technically it is simple enough for beginning students to handle without difficulties. More advanced students may find the project challenging and may discover untried ways of exploiting this ancient method.

Scratch Techniques

Several newly developed black-and-white techniques are based on wood engraving or on woodcuts and are commonly known as scratchboard techniques. Scratchboards, commercially manufactured white cardboards heavily coated with a gypsumlike substance, are used primarily as an effective substitute for a single wood engraving and are frequently used for mass reproduction by photographic means.

The technique is quite simple: after the coated board is evenly covered with black India ink, lines or areas are scratched into the surface; these then appear brilliantly white. The material permits endless contrasts of white lines, short white strokes, and dots against the black background, as well as the scratching out of white areas and leaving black lines. In short, the possibilities for black and white variations are almost unlimited.

The technique and material have merits within a high school art program. Students may use very fine details and must work with both sharp and precise lines and

CRAYON ETCHING
eleventh grade boy
wax crayon on shelf paper

areas, and severe short-stroked gradations from dark to light. It is obvious that the scratchboard technique demands rigid decisions, and herein lies its educational value. Scratchwork, if it is to fulfill its pedagogical purpose on the high school level, must be carried out slowly, and with considerable forethought, over several class periods. It should never be rushed, should be worked out on fairly large-sized boards (not less than 12″ x 18″), and should result in finished-appearing work. It is not limited by age level or previous experience; it can be effective with, and enjoyed by, junior high as well as more advanced senior high school students, and lends itself well to a classwide project. Special instruments (multiliner tools) are not absolutely necessary, and any sharp, pointed metal tool will serve; therefore few mechanical difficulties are to be expected.

Unfortunately, scratchboard is fairly expensive. However, there are two methods of preparing adequate substitutes. A white, preferably glossy, paper may be covered thoroughly with a heavy layer of dark-colored wax crayon which is then handled exactly like a scratchboard. This method can be varied by first covering the paper with a light-colored crayon over which a coat of black India ink is painted. A totally different (and, for high school students, better) substitute is made by pouring an inch or two of wet plaster of Paris on a sheet of glass, resulting in a thin slab of plaster. After the plaster has set and can be handled, the smooth side is covered thoroughly, with the help of a brayer, with a mixture of printer's ink and some linseed oil. When the ink is dry, the surface is ready for scratching. Both media work well for junior and senior high school students.

Intaglio Printing

The principles of printing in intaglio are exactly opposite to those of relief printing. Metals are used predominantly in intaglio printing; relief printing requires wood almost exclusively. Also, in intaglio the *incised* line or area is *filled* with ink which, under *considerable* pressure, will leave a sharp impression on damp paper. In relief printing the *raised* line or area is *covered* with ink, and only this elevated surface imparts an image (under *some* pressure) to the paper.

Two distinctly different techniques are used in intaglio printing; one is metal engraving, the other etching. Engraving is one of the most highly skilled methods of incising manually controlled lines into a hard surface. It is a technique which can only be mastered slowly through diligent practice over a long period of time. This is why engraving can hardly be taught successfully in a high school. However, certain forms of etching can be carried out to good purpose by high school students without undue difficulties. The basic procedure of etching is as follows: an image is scratched through an acid-resisting coat on a metal plate. The plate is then submerged in a shallow bath of acid and the acid slowly eats into the exposed lines and areas. After the plate is cleaned of the acid-resistant coat, it is covered with printer's ink and then wiped clean, so that the ink remains only in the incised lines. The plate is then ready for printing.

This technique is almost as old as woodcutting, but Rembrandt is the artist who perfected it. "He gave to etching the freedom and spontaneity and subtlety of drawing; and because his drawing was distinguished, dramatic, and noble, he proved that an etching could be as lofty a work of art as a painting or statue. Most prints before Rembrandt had been translations as it were from another medium; he composed directly in the language of etching itself. In him we see the beginning of the modern attitude."[21]

Etching, like other intaglio techniques, requires special equipment. Fortunately, relatively inexpensive presses and other necessary equipment are available, making it possible for many high schools to teach this printing process. Zinc and various other metal alloy plates (particularly aluminum alloys) are quite reasonably priced and have been effectively used with high school students.[22]

The merit of teaching this more advanced printing technique is that students learn to carry through a slow creative process consisting of many different phases, each demanding exactness, patience, and constant diligent attention. In etching, negligence or superficiality immediately lead to failure. On the other hand, it is an undertaking which many advanced students find very exciting. It often results in quite professional-appearing work, and each working phase is so different from every

---

[21] *Ibid.*, p. 87.
[22] "Zinc plates are adequate when the work is simple and without great delicacy of line or effect—especially when all the lines are of equal value or not too subtly different in value." Ralph Mayer, *The Artist's Handbook of Materials and Techniques* (New York: The Viking Press, 1946), p. 447.

other that students can almost literally experience the unfolding of a vague idea, from a slowly growing process to a convincing artistic statement—the final print.

Etching permits a richness of tonalities not attainable in a woodcut. The intensity of different lines and textures can be achieved in two principal ways: by covering the plate either with a *hard* or with a *soft* ground. (Both types of ground are manufactured commercially in a variety of mixtures.) Both methods have been used by high school students without difficulty. After the hard ground has dried, the design is scratched into the coated plate with pointed metal etching pencils. Different qualities of lines can be produced in two ways: by scratching with a number of different, pointed etching pencils or sharp, needle-shaped tools, or by using only one single tool. In the latter instance the depth and width of the line depend on the length of time the plate remains in the acid. By using stopping varnish at intervals, some lines are left exposed to the acid longer than others. Most artists combine the two principal methods. They use a number of tools as well as varying periods of acid baths for the etching of one plate. Areas can be created and textures achieved by using crosshatched or closely paralleled lines, or dots, and a combination of these three elements.

ETCHING
eleventh grade girl

In an equally effective etching process, which high school students can learn quite easily, a soft metal protective ground is used. (Commonly soft ground is a mixture consisting of equal parts of hard ground and tallow or vaseline, or other fats.) A piece of soft paper is placed over the soft ground-coated plate and an image is then drawn. The pencil pressure against the soft ground forces the paper to adhere temporarily to the plate. When the paper is raised, those parts of the ground on which pressure has been exerted remain on the back of the drawing, and the transferred lines and areas expose the metal. The plate is then ready to be submerged in the acid and is etched like any other; when printed it shows rather rough-textured lines not unlike lithography. This technique has the advantage that students can plan their project in great detail. On the other hand it has the disadvantage that it is rather difficult to control, that fewer varieties of lines and textures are possible, and that it can easily lead to a mechanical reproduction of a drawing.

A part of the intaglio process as important as etching is the printing of an etched plate. It begins with balancing and adjusting the press, cleaning, inking and wiping the plate, and selecting and dampening the paper, and ends with stretching and fastening the damp print on a board. Unfortunately the many different materials and tools involved in this process need not only good storage space, but also carefully planned arrangement. Wet paper, ink, wiping pads, felts and blotters, solvents, cleaning rags, cleaning table, all must have their places and all must be kept clean.

Without such precautions students will have so little success with their projects that they will not enjoy the art of printmaking, and its educational value will be lost. Since students will work with acids, printer's ink, and sharp tools, it is probably most advisable to permit only the more advanced, mature students to etch and print, and then only in small groups. Etching as a large class project can most easily end in failure.

Other techniques often employed in connection with etching, such as scraping, burnishing, engraving, and using aquatints or colors, are so specialized and require such a high degree of skill and experience that they can hardly be used even in an advanced high school art class.

Ready-prepared mordants (etching acids) are often used on the high school level. However, acids change their strength easily, varying with their freshness and the room temperature; the warmer the room, or the longer they are used, the more powerful they become.[23] It is therefore advisable to test the acids frequently to prevent serious damage to students' plates.

F. M. Hall Collection, University of Nebraska

RUDOLF RITTER
AS FLORIAN GEYER
Lovis Corinth
drypoint

Before students embark on an etching project it is wise to show them how various effects and expressions are achieved. If at all possible, they should at least become familiar with etchings by Rembrandt, Piranesi, Goya, Whistler, Rouault, and some of the modern printmakers like Lasansky. This should contribute to their understanding and appreciation of works by great artists, and should also act as an inspiration for their own work. The choice of themes suitable for expression in an etching is unlimited. Advanced students should not be restricted in their selection of topics, provided they attempt to imbue them with their own thoughts or feelings and stand clear of trite expressions and stereotyped forms. Etching is a time-consuming and exacting process and students should be particularly urged to produce ideas for prints in which effort and concentration correspond to the quality of the final result.

One more intaglio process which high school students should be able to carry out with little technical difficulty is called drypoint. In drypoint an image is scratched into a metal plate or a heavy plastic sheet which is then printed like any other intaglio plate. The technique seems simple at first, yet mistakes can hardly be corrected, and the freshly scratched lines look monotonous and expressionless, and convey poorly the actual quality of the image or design. Not before the plate is printed will the artist know to what degree he has succeeded in his task.

Drypoint is not a recent invention. "The technique was known in early times, Dürer and the Master of the Amsterdam Cabinet having both made dry-points, but Rembrandt was the first to use the medium with a full realization of its possibilities."[24] It is a medium which demands fairly spontaneous forms of expression whose execution consumes little time. Drypoint could also be called sketching in metal, except that it permits hardly any corrections. Since drypoint is a bridge between drawing and the more complex process of etching, it can be considered a good introductory technique leading to intaglio printing. A good way to acquaint students with it is to give them small plates, not larger than 3″ x 5″. After they have experimented on these and gained some experience with intaglio printing, they may undertake larger or more demanding projects. Plastic, zinc, and many other soft metal sheets work well with drypoint, so long as only small editions are printed. The

---

[23] For extensive information, consult S. W. Hayter, *New Ways of Gravure* (New York: Pantheon, 1949); Jules Heller, *Printmaking Today;* Ralph Mayer, *The Artist's Handbook* (New York: The Viking Press, 1957).
[24] Zigrosser, *Six Centuries of Fine Prints,* p. 17.

author has seen excellent works in drypoint, printed from plates made from metal covers of ammunition cases. Finding new materials for drypoint can be a challenge to students as well as teachers. The professional sharp drypoint needle can easily and effectively be replaced with many other metal tools which have been sharpened and pointed. Discarded dental instruments make particularly good drypoint and etching tools.

A variation of drypoint is glass scratching or cliché verre, which was quite popular for a short period among the French impressionists. The technique is simple: after a plate of clear glass has been covered with an *opaque* lacquer, an image is

THE LITTLE SHEPHERD
Jean Baptiste Corot
cliché verre

scratched through the dried, coated surface. The plate is then placed on a photographic contact printing paper for a few seconds, after which the paper is processed in the usual way. Commonly the result somewhat resembles a drypoint print since the black line against a white background is also the major means of expression. Still, despite the fact that glass scratching is a reproduction technique, it cannot be considered a genuine artistic printing process; the very act of printing is extremely mechanical and permits no variations, and the final product has a uniform, machine-made character.

Yet this technique is so easy that it can be handled without any difficulties by junior high school students. Since no press and few special implements are needed, it serves well as a substitute for drypoint if graphic equipment is lacking. Glass scratching also has the advantage that an error can be corrected simply by recoating an area and starting anew. Other advantages are that students learn rapidly to work with it, and need not spend much time in producing a finished product; also, it is rather inexpensive. On the other hand, it is an undemanding technique; it is very limited in its creative possibilities; and it has little to offer to more advanced students. It lacks the innate challenge of legitimate print media.

Lithography

The printing process in which Bavarian limestone is used was invented by Aloys Senefelder at the beginning of the last century. "The process is based on the well-known antipathy of grease and water. The artist draws with a greasy crayon on a slab of special limestone (found only in Bavaria) which has been grained to a requisite degree of fineness."[25] Lithography is probably the most direct printing process in which an artist's visualized ideas and feelings are graphically recorded and reproduced. The stone registers immediacies most minutely and accurately without requiring adaptations, transformations, or concessions, because the fat litho crayons or ink are handled exactly like any other drawing medium. Lithography is also a most sensitive printing medium, permitting the greatest freedom of expression, from the most lyrical to the most dramatic, from the softest tone to the severest black.

At present relatively few high schools are equipped to offer work in lithography, even though several types of printing presses are available which are neither bulky nor costly and are adaptable for lithography. These presses are sturdy enough to serve well in a high school over a long period of time. Except for the initial cost of the press, stones, brayers, etc., lithography is one of the most inexpensive printing processes. First preparing a stone, then drawing on, etching, and finally printing it are not too difficult for high school students, provided they follow instructions implicitly and give serious attention to details during each phase of the process.

Lithography is a natural connecting link between drawing and printing. It permits high school students to practice any freshly acquired drawing skill, and often gives new impetus to the desire to become more proficient in graphic representation. Frequently, from a student's point of view, a mere sketch is not worthy of much consideration, but if a drawing is put on a stone it is elevated to a significant artistic statement warranting one's best efforts. In fact, drawing on a stone is a unique experience which should be made available, if at all possible, to every serious advanced student. The relationship between the artist and the stone can hardly be described verbally; the stone responds very sensitively to the most minute pressure of the hand, records any suggestion, and stimulates the artist during the act of creation unlike any other graphic process or material. No doubt this is why artists like Daumier, Toulouse-Lautrec, and Kaethe Kollwitz seem to have preferred lithog-

---

[25] *Ibid.*, p. 17.

HELP RUSSIA
(design for a poster)
Kaethe Kollwitz
lithography

F. M. Hall Collection, University of Nebraska

raphy over other graphic media. Kollwitz said, "It's hardly a technique at all, it's so simple. In it only the essentials count."[26]

Yet lithography is a printing process which demands considerable time, and constant careful attention during each working phase. The cleaning of a used stone takes time; the drawing on the stone must be thoughtfully planned and cannot be rushed; errors are difficult to correct; and the stone must be kept immaculately clean throughout. On each use the etching and washing of the stone have to be carried out slowly and deliberately. This may include a waiting period of up to twenty-four hours, and haste can easily ruin the whole work. For the printing, the paper must be dampened, not too little and not too much. Subsequently the stone has to be moistened, inked, and proofed, and only then can the actual printing begin. It is clear that lithography can never be considered an effective project for a large class of students. A teacher is able to supervise and assist only a few students at a time, while the rest of the class may work on other projects. This, however, should never be considered a reason to omit teaching lithography. Unquestionably almost no other graphic process has so much to offer to advanced high school students.

Drawing directly on the stone is only one approach to lithography. In a different technique, a drawing is made on a transfer paper with lithographic crayons. The drawing is then transferred by moistening its back side and pressing its front against the stone. This transfer technique has very little meaning in terms of teaching, despite the fact that some great lithographic works have been executed by this method. Without drawing directly on the stone (a very important part of this graphic expression), lithography can degenerate into a merely mechanical method of reproduction. Moreover, certain techniques otherwise almost impossible to use can be exploited in working directly with stone. One of these is scraping: with the help of

[26] *The Diary and Letters of Kaethe Kollwitz,* Hans Kollwitz (ed.) (Chicago: Henry Regnery Co., 1955), p. 94.

sharp metal tools (knives, razor blades, or engraving tools), lines are lightly scratched into black areas already drawn on the stone. The technique is used as a means of expression as well as of correction. However, it is a difficult procedure requiring considerable skill; the scraping must be done with the utmost care, since the stone is easily damaged. Therefore only experienced students should be introduced to this technique. For rather similar reasons, color lithography is a method too advanced for high school students. Making the unavoidable color separations is a difficult and time-consuming task. Also, for color printing a different stone is needed for each color, and few schools have sufficient stones available for this technically advanced and complex printing process. Learning to work well with black and white lithography is enough of a challenge for any high school student.

Serigraphy

The only important new artistic printing process invented in our century is serigraphy (seri = silk, graph = to write), or silk screen.[27] However, it is questionable whether serigraphy can be considered a genuine part of the graphic arts since it is predominantly a medium for expression in colors rather than in monochromes. "The greatest virtue of the serigraph is color, and its greatest triumphs will come through the creative use of color, color in the rendering of form, color for emotive effects."[28]

Serigraphy is fundamentally a multicolor stencil process. A very fine silk mesh is stretched tightly over a simple wooden frame. The areas which are to print are left open, and the nonprinting areas are covered with an opaque substance—a piece of paper, a coat of glue, lacquer, shellac, or a commercially prepared film. Then paint is squeezed through the openings in the silk screen, leaving an exact, solid image of the openings on the surface below.

This part of serigraphy is quite simple and can be handled easily by most high school students. What makes this printing process rather difficult is that a separate screen must be prepared for each color. Each screen must register perfectly because if they do not overlap exactly, the finished print will be blurred and unintelligible. Many outstanding serigraphs are made of twelve or even eighteen different screens. To attempt such an ambitious project in the high school would be very time-consuming and could well end in failure. It appears more sensible for students to learn to work with not more than three or four stencils, the last one carrying the major design in a dark color.

A serigraph can be treated in several different ways, depending on how the screens are prepared. The choice is largely determined by how sharply and precisely an artist wishes to define each colored area or line, and on how spontaneously or slowly and deliberately he prefers to work. The purely planless and spontaneous method of creating presupposes considerable previous experience with serigraphy, hence is rarely suited to high school work. In the diametrically opposite approach, a commercially prepared lacquer stencil film is used. As the work and the working process can in this case quite easily become mechanical and dull, this stencil technique does not lend itself too well to creative high school work. The two methods best suited for high school students are known as tusche resist and paper stencils.

---

[27] "Silk-screen printing was first publicly sponsored as a fine-arts medium by the New York WPA Art Project, which organized a producing unit for silk-screen prints as a division of its graphic-arts department. The development of the process for artists' use is due largely to the work of Anthony Velonis, who has made considerable progress in establishing and standardizing techniques and in furthering their adoption by artists." Mayer, *The Artist's Handbook of Materials and Techniques,* p. 259.

[28] Carl Zigrosser, *The Book of Fine Prints* (New York: Crown Publishers, 1956), p. 195.

In tusche resist, tusche (grease dissolved in a black, inklike liquid) and soft lithographic crayons are used for drawing lines and covering areas which are to be printed. These materials are applied directly to the screen. After they have dried, the *whole* screen is covered twice with a mixture consisting of one part glue and one part cold water which seals all the remaining minute perforations in the silk screen. As soon as the glue mixture has dried, the screen is washed with a volatile fluid (gasoline or kerosene) which dissolves and removes the tusche or crayon without affecting the sealed and glued areas. After the porelike openings of the designed areas are clear and free of grease, oil-based paints can be squeezed through them and the printing can begin. Since the solid, glue-covered areas will not permit the paint to filter through, it can pass only between the sievelike openings in the screen, resulting in an exact facsimile of the unclogged lines and areas on the surface below. By using different screens for parts of the design, each in another color, a serigraph is slowly created.

This approach to serigraphy necessitates the designing of a master drawing which shows the whole project clearly and in detail. The colors are separated and their corresponding parts drawn on individual screens. This phase of creating a serigraph is extremely difficult. First of all, a master drawing must be precise but still sufficiently flexible and broadly conceived so that the innate characteristics of the medium can play a part in the creation. Such a master drawing should be a plan for action, not a finished work; otherwise the actual preparation of each screen is reduced to mere mechanical manipulation. Yet the drawing should be so clear that it can be placed under the screen and used as a guide or tracing for the design. This aspect is not easy for a beginner because rules have never been successfully developed which state how to proceed in separating colors or what should be on the first screen and what on the last. It may be wise for a beginning student to prepare the first screen with the broadest areas and the lightest colors, and the last screen with the most details and the darkest colors.

The same principle applies to the method of printing a serigraph with the aid of paper stencils. Here, too, a single stencil must be cut for each color. First the design is scored in the paper with the point of a knife. Only after the stencil has been fastened with a few drops of glue on the underside of the screen should the cut-out sections be removed. The necessary oil-based paint used for the printing will also act as an additional adhesive agent. This technique permits sharp outlines which are often quite difficult to achieve in tusche resist. But for this, the techniques permit a similar approach and are equally intricate. Unfortunately, both require mineral spirits or benzine-based solvents for the cleaning of the screen. Even when water-soluble paints are used for printing, the blocked-out solid areas on the screen must be made with a water-resistant liquid medium (lacquer or shellac) which again has to be washed or rinsed with a nonfireproof cleaning fluid.

Serigraphy's unique contribution to the art of printmaking is that it unites graphics and expression in color. It is a graphic process which requires considerable forethought since it turns into a rather intellectual activity as soon as the original creative idea has been captured on paper. The student must decide how to proceed, which colors to select, which part of the design to print first, which of the different drawing media to choose and how to use them, and finally how to change or incorporate ideas which occur during the working process. All of these are problems, and their solution requires thought and decision.

Serigraphy forces beginning students to accept limitations and to discover hitherto unnoticed possibilities. By exploiting a color's possible translucent quality instead of leaving it purely opaque, and by printing one color on top of another, they may find ways to create remarkable pieces of work with only a few screens. A teacher should encourage students to search for such possibilities, even hinting that they exist, but he should refrain from telling all he knows. Probably the best way to start a serigraph project is by having students experiment first with a simple design, using only a few small screens, trying the different methods of handling the medium and exploring the various means of exploiting colors. Only then should students be asked to undertake a more extensive project.

Monotype

A technique which also belongs vaguely to the sphere of printmaking is monotype (mono = one, type = impression). As in other printing techniques it is not the original work, the plate, block, or screen, which is the final product, but the impression made with any of these. So also in monotype the finished work is an impression taken from a painting created on a piece of glass. However, in this

Reproduced by courtesy of the National Gallery of Art, Washington (Rosenwald Collection)

AREAREA NO VARUA INO
Paul Gauguin
monotype

technique no more than one single impression can be made from one glass painting.

The technique of monotype is extremely simple and needs little time. After an image has been painted with slow-drying colors on a plate of glass or sheet of smooth polished metal, a piece of paper is placed over it and then pressed down. A wooden spoon, or something similar, is rubbed hard against the back of the paper, leaving a distinct and sharp painted impression on the paper. This single impression is the monotype.

Oil paints or oil-based printer's inks are probably the best media for this technique; both brayers and brushes can be used effectively with it. Monotype permits endless variations of handling the paint. For instance, after the glass is covered with paints, various wooden sticks with or without cotton points can be used to draw lines into the paint, which will appear as white lines on white paper. When different fabrics are pressed against the painted surface and then removed, they will leave textures on the painting and later on the print. Obviously monotype is an excellent medium to learn and an excellent way to discover what paints can do and how texture combined with color can become an important part of visual expression.

Since any student can try out several variations and create four to five monotypes in one hour, the process lends itself well to brief but intense studies of color and texture and their relationships. Monotype has still another aspect in its favor. Since it cannot be fully controlled it should help students to become flexible and to learn to accept accidental effects. This printing process is not limited to a particular age level and can be handled effectively by junior as well as senior high school students.

II Expression in Colors

It is possible to separate almost everything we see into two basic components: shapes and colors. One or the other usually leaves a stronger impression, depending on the individual's temperament as well as on the specific subject or scene. Some individuals react more strongly towards color than towards shapes, which is why many graphic artists and sculptors rarely if ever utilize colors as a means of expression in their work. Even people who show a predominant sensitivity towards color may react more intensely to one particular color than to others, and this color preference may dominate and possibly distort their impressions. Some people seem to perceive color almost independent of shape. Young children, for instance, often enjoy working with colors quite independent of forms or subject matter. The same one-sidedness is evident in the visual expression of prehistoric man. Monochrome clay forms and line drawings incised in bones or stones have been found next to elaborate and colorful paintings on cave walls. During art's long history there have been periods when shapes dominated colors; at other times—notably during the height of the French impressionistic movement—color governed the scene. This same split exists in many art rooms; some students seem to have a strong affinity for colors, while others, who apparently lack this sensitivity, may have strong feelings for shapes and textures and are thus well able to express themselves graphically or in three dimensions.

As soon as an artist begins to work with color he has three major elements, among several others, at his disposal through which he can give visual expression to his thoughts and feelings. Two, already mentioned, are shapes and colors; the third is texture. Texture, the structural quality or characteristic of a given surface, exists independent of color and is perceived through vision as well as through touch. Texture, in combination with color, is the principal means by which we identify what we see.

An important aspect of texture in relationship to painting pertains to the surface treatment of a work. The material, the paint media, and the specific tools used to achieve a particular expression play an intrinsic part both during the creative process and in the final appearance of the work. The surface characteristics of a Marin watercolor, of a Zerbe encaustic, or of a Van Gogh oil painting are an inseparable part of the entire artistic statement. Each paint medium has a particular and unique quality which strongly influences the effects of artistic expression regardless of its topic, style, or range of color. Yet the different surface characteristics are only one unique quality of paint media. Each expression in color—opaque, translucent, or transparent—has its own history, its own characteristics, its own merits and limitations, its advantages and peculiar difficulties. Finally, each medium has its specific place in the teaching of art in the high school.

The Opaque Media

Opaque colors, probably the oldest known paint media, are perhaps the easiest for high school students to work with. A major characteristic of opaque colors becomes apparent when one applies them on a flat surface: they at once change the original tone of the surface solidly and completely. Another characteristic is that these colors can be superimposed one on top of another without affecting the tonality of the color applied last.

Opaque paints have played a dominant role in the history of painting, from prehistoric times until today. Nowadays the best known and most widely used opaque colors are egg or casein tempera, poster paints, and, to some degree, oil colors. A reservation in regard to the last-named is based on the fact that oil colors possess the characteristics of all paint media; they are opaque, translucent, and transparent, depending on how they are employed. But because oil paints can be used in almost unlimited ways, they are hard to control and need time-consuming experience before their unique qualities can be effectively exploited. They can play only a very minor role in the teaching of art on the high school level. Moreover, the high cost of these colors in addition to other necessary materials makes them impractical for use in the classroom.

The most frequently used opaque colors which serve adequately as school materials are poster colors.[29] They are economical, inexpensive, available in great varieties of shades and tones, and, most important, can be handled easily without much technical instruction or previous experience. They also have two other advantages: they dry rapidly and can be worked in layers.[30] Although poster colors have some innate limitations, even these usually do not hamper freedom of expression. Probably their greatest drawback is that their tone quality changes in drying, and their brilliance diminishes. But the original intensity and tonality can easily

---

[29] "In America, poster or show-card colors sold in jars are sometimes labeled tempera. . . . Correctly, these colors, which are mostly of the simple gum-water, glue size, or distemper type, should be known as poster colors. The adoption of the term tempera by some makers in this country seems to have been prompted by the need for a name to distinguish the finer grades of poster colors from the inferior kinds. True tempera paints are never sold in jars, but in tubes." Mayer, *The Artist's Handbook,* p. 201.

[30] A fine coat of alcohol-thinned shellac or retouch varnish may prevent any possible bleeding through.

be restored by coating the finished work with a thin film of retouch varnish or shellac. Another minor difficulty is revealed when large areas are solidly coated with one color; these areas often turn out uneven or streaky. However, the streaking can be prevented if the colors are not used directly from a jar and immediately transferred to the paper, but are first thoroughly remixed in the brush on a palettelike surface.

The truly important problem of teaching painting with opaque colors lies not in the technical aspect but in the approach. One frequently finds that the majority of high school students in a class seem to have little understanding of the function of colors in terms of expression, or of their relationship to each other. Probably the best way to help develop this understanding is through guided experiences, designed to make students aware of the innate possibilities and characteristics of colors. These practical experiences should be supplemented occasionally by theoretical explanations. However, class-wide lessons or exercises in color theory are rarely effective because students are usually unable to transfer these forms of theory into practice. A more effective way of clarifying color problems is for the teacher either to employ color theory during the evaluation of work, or to incorporate aspects of it in different class assignments.

The key to the teaching of painting is careful planning motivated by educational considerations and observations of students. Such observations have resulted in the discovery of some of the most characteristic difficulties which students encounter while painting. The cause may be limited ability to respond sensitively to colors; lack of familiarity with and/or experience in mixing them; lack of knowledge of how to plan or begin a painting; and finally, inability to differentiate between light, shadow, and color. Each of these weaknesses calls for specific assignments aimed at helping students overcome their difficulties. The sequence, duration, and frequency of the assignments depend on the students' ability, experience, and progress.

It is quite characteristic of young children that they do not respond sensitively toward colors. Any red, for instance, from a reddish-orange to a warm purple, is red. Only the three primary and the three secondary colors, in addition to brown, black, and white, exist. Within this limited range children have no difficulty in expressing themselves most satisfactorily. As in their drawings, they portray in their paintings only essentials in broad generalizations, and it is purely by accident when their color simplifications resemble those colors encountered in reality. For example, a lawn painted by a small child is merely a large area in a rather brilliant green. Yet in actuality a lawn never consists of one single color, but of a multitude of different shades which—depending on the season, weather conditions, and time of day—may range from light yellow-green to dark green or blue. Most young children remain quite unaware of these variations of existing shades, and their unawareness often stays with them into late adolescence unless a sincere effort is exerted by a teacher to make them conscious of the rich interplay of colors.

There are several ways to help students become sensitive to and conscious of the fact that what is superficially seen as a single color often is many shades blended into one. One may, for instance, hand students a variety of rocks, large pebbles, driftwood, or odd-shaped pieces of different woods. They are then asked to study these items and compose a painting, emphasizing the subtle shades and gradations of colors discoverable in these objects. In a different approach students are shown reproductions of paintings by various masters who used a limited palette in their work, such as Picasso during his blue period, or Daumier and Rembrandt in their brown-scaled paintings. After viewing the paintings students are given a choice of a narrow range of colors, perhaps from brown to red or yellow, or from yellow to green and blue. Once they have made their choice and begun to paint, they should be reminded to break up large areas of one color into smaller sections by using a number of different but related shades, instead of covering the surface with a single color. Throughout the work students should be encouraged to incorporate great varieties of kindred tones, fusing them, as an orchestral composition blends the sounds of different instruments, into one harmonious whole. This type of assignment should be carried out in a spirit of experimentation rather than with the expectation of obtaining seemingly accomplished work.

Closely related to the problem of helping students become sensitive towards color is that of acquainting them with ways of combining colors so that they will be able to produce various shades and tones at will, and want to work with other than harsh or loud colors. No single, simple procedure is known to help students understand the intricate interactions of colors which they can apply immediately and meaningfully in their work. A means to help them develop a greater sensitivity toward color is to make available only a very limited choice of premixed colors. Rather than giving the original high-keyed paints to pupils, the colors may be subdued by adding small quantities of complementary colors, or slight amounts of black and white. After students have become accustomed to working with these slightly subdued shades and have been told how the various tones were made, they should then be allowed to mix their own tones, but with the understanding that they work very carefully, using brilliant colors only as accents for special emphasis. It also should be pointed out to them that the color in the jar is usually of maximum brilliance, and that for it to be most effective it must be surrounded by other, less brilliant, rather low-keyed tones. As a rule, students also should be reminded to begin painting with the more subdued shades, and to add the more brilliant ones later.

This introduces the vexing question of how to begin a painting. All rules regarding this procedure are quite arbitrary and are valid only in a very limited way. Yet many painters have stated, at one time or another, that they began most of their work by covering a surface rapidly with one or several low-keyed colors. This was often followed by painting the major areas of the theme in subdued shades, rather broadly and without many details. These large areas were then again subdivided into smaller segments, and finally the high-keyed or brilliant colors added to the work in a seemingly improvised manner.

This method is often effective with beginning students. Before they start working with opaque colors, however, they should be advised first to cover the entire paper with paints and to keep these in a low key. Only after the surface is fully coated should they begin to work in details. Since inexperienced students frequently have a tendency to concentrate on only a few parts of their work (those which are important to them) and thus lose a feeling for the whole, it is necessary for the teacher to insist that they follow these simple procedures. Painting is a disciplined activity consisting of careful planning, and the deliberate mixing and thoughtful application of colors. It is only at the beginning, when the idea for a painting is improvised on paper, and during the final minutes before a work is finished that the temperament and the emotions should be given free rein. Students who have not been taught that painting requires discipline and the ability to follow basic rules will be unable to carry out a planned project, control the medium, or find satisfaction in their work.

The problem of how to begin a painting starts with the question of the most commendable procedure for planning it. From a historic point of view the answer is rather simple: most artists began with various detailed, individual studies which they later combined carefully in a drawing which became their working plan and was often transferred mechanically to the actual painting surface. Other artists, like Rubens, began with a small sketch in colors containing the major idea, and space and color divisions. Constable first made detailed small watercolors from nature and then used these as guides for his larger or more important works; Van Gogh made black-and-white sketches from nature which he annotated with exact descriptions of the colors he later intended to use in the painting. Most French impressionists, on the other hand, began their work directly from nature without previous study. Many artists today start painting without any preconceived plan, expecting to see the work grow, hoping that the action will be a sustaining inspiration, and waiting for accidents which will quicken their imagination.

Historically this last approach is unique, but it has proved effective with artists who have acquired considerable skill and experience in painting. With high school students who are beginners, such an improvised and planless approach to painting rarely leads to meaningful and satisfying results. For them it is most advisable to explore all of the following forms of preparation for a painting:

(1) Composing a plan from numerous studies and using such a composition as an outline. (2) Drawing persons, a scene, or a still life from nature and utilizing such a drawing as the basis for the painting. (3) Utilizing a roughly colored sketch from nature as a guide. (4) Making a black-and-white drawing and writing the names of the intended colors in each area. (5) Painting directly from nature without a previously conceived plan, but studying carefully in advance what is to be portrayed before setting down the first brush stroke. (6) Beginning a painting in an improvised manner without any definite plan. This last approach, if it is to be successful, demands considerable stimulation by the teacher, since students must become strongly involved with their work emotionally; otherwise the results will be rather stereotyped and superficial.

A drawn outline for a painting should never simulate a finished work. The main reason for discouraging such a practice is that students may easily lose the inner need to use colors and unconsciously produce a colored drawing rather than a painting. In a colored drawing, color is secondary; the important means for conveying the visual idea or impression is the line and/or the contrast between light and dark. In a painting, however, the major vehicle is the color, even when some lineal structures are noticeably incorporated in a work. Dark areas or shadows as well as light areas are achieved with the use of distinct colors; dark is not simply black but consists of a variety of dark shades. (Rembrandt's paintings are superior examples of this.) A brief study of many impressionistic paintings, particularly of the works of Cézanne, will often help students understand the difference in concept between achieving light and shadow in a drawing, and portraying it with light and dark colors in a painting. Cézanne's famous blue shadows are a case in point. Many other artists exploited the contrast between light, warm-toned areas, and cold, dark-colored ones in their paintings, or played complementary colors against each other in different, rather extreme intensities.

Students should be made thoroughly aware of these different basic concepts in the approach to drawing and painting. It is often advisable to curtail the use of black during many of the painting sessions, since this should compel students to solve the problem of achieving darkness or shadows more sensitively and deliberately than by simply using black paint. At times assignments may be given which specify the color range or the contrasts with which they are to work. For instance, they may be asked to paint with light, warm colors and to contrast these with dark, cold shades, or to employ complementary colors in various intensities, using them so that they will oppose each other—for example, setting a light yellow against a dark shade of purple, or a soft orange against a dark-toned blue. Such occasional, limiting assignments often need definite suggestions in regard to subject matter. These suggestions should never be narrow in scope, but should permit many different approaches and/or interpretations. "City Lights at Night," "Hunger," "Joy," or "Summer Evening" are examples of subjects which permit endless interpretations in color and thought without forcing students into stereotyped patterns.

Obviously the materials for painting play an important part in creating a work. If the budget permits, tempera paints, which are obtainable in many more shades and tones than poster paints, should be made available because they are an excellent opaque medium for more advanced high school students. Tempera paints can be worked layer upon layer; they permit minute shadings and allow the incorporation of many textures and details. These opaque colors do not require expensive papers; large pieces of corrugated cardboard, heavy brown or white wrapping paper, or even pages from an ordinary newspaper are often more suitable for high school work than any costly white paper. These ordinary materials frequently put students at ease, and thereby encourage freedom of expression. Most junior high school students, in particular, work with greater ease and enthusiasm if permitted to paint with wide and thick-bristled brushes on large-sized wrapping paper about 24″ x 36″. Their grade school experiences, which usually consisted of painting on 9″ x 12″ or similar, small-sized paper, may have made them so timid that only a totally different approach will help them overcome their lack of confidence and regain their spontaneity.

There is still another approach to the problem of making students thoroughly aware of the differences between painting in light and dark colors, and drawing in black and white; this is to use medium dark, instead of white, papers on which to paint. Many famous painters preferred to work on dark backgrounds; Rembrandt, for instance, often used medium dark brown, and numerous other old masters worked on gray-green colored grounds. Both shades are sufficiently neutral to act as a foundation for light as well as dark tones. Frequently such middle-toned backgrounds force students to use the brush in a manner which brings out its most characteristic qualities: leaving distinct marks which give direction to the stroke and add textural interest, blending one color with another, or permitting solid-colored areas to flow into each other without forming harsh borders. The more students experience these innate and typical characteristics of paint, the less will their work be reminiscent of a colored drawing, and the closer they will come to understanding and appreciating the art of painting.

Another opaque medium which has been successfully used by high school students is a mixture of pigment and wax called encaustic paint. Encaustic paint is one of the oldest and most durable media; perfect examples have been found fully intact which had been made more than two thousand years before by Egyptian and Greek artists. During the last days of classical antiquity the use of this medium was most widespread. Its working process consisted of heating beeswax, a pigment, and small amounts of oil or resins which were blended when in liquid form and then, still in a heated stage, applied to a hard surface, usually wood. After the individual colors were placed on the board, they were fused, refined, and shaded with hot irons which resembled soldering irons. This method has been revived recently, and a number of contemporary artists, notably Karl Zerbe, are using it again.

A simplified way to utilize this ancient medium has been developed for high school students. First, ordinary wax crayons are melted in small metal containers standing in very hot or boiling water; next, very small amounts of turpentine are added to the waxy liquid, and for a brief time the mixture can then be handled like any other liquid paint.[31] Electric hot plates and pie pans filled with water serve well for heating and maintaining the paint in a fluid condition. Stiff bristle brushes and

---

[31] In a different method an equal amount of beeswax and crayon are melted. To about 1½ cups of this melted mixture two tablespoons of linseed oil and one tablespoon of turpentine are added. The linseed acts as a thinner, the turpentine as a drying agent. From Pauline Wright Kagan, *From Adventure to Experience through Art* (San Francisco: Howard Chandler Publ., 1959), p. 42.

PORTRAIT OF A LADY
unknown Egyptian artist
(4th-5th century)
encaustic on panel

Reproduced by courtesy of the William Rockhill Nelson Gallery of Art, Kansas City, Mo.

palette knives are used as tools, and any wood panels, hard boards, or corrugated cardboard can be utilized as a paint surface. But in order to achieve the jewel-like quality of encaustic paints, it is advisable first to coat this surface with any white paint or cover it with a sheet of white paper.

Encaustic painting requires concentration and speed. Herein lies its merit as well as its limitation. It demands constant action, quick decisions, and diligent attention. Without these, the activity can easily lead to failure. Once the student has chosen his topic, made his plans, and drawn a rough outline, he must begin to work with great rapidity; otherwise the applied paint is hard to control and also dries in the brush. In spite of these requirements encaustic painting has many potentialities which are not found in other media. With a hot palette knife, for instance, colors can be fused, textures made, lines incised, or areas ingrained. Students should be urged to exploit these innate qualities of the medium; it may help them to discover means and ways of painting which are more individual and less trite than those to which they so easily fall prey with more conventional media. In the beginning it is often advisable to suggest relatively simple themes—a portrait of an old peasant, a madonnalike face, or a happy young child. When students have developed a feeling for the medium, they may then be encouraged to paint more detailed, complex themes, to exploit the jewel-like quality of the color, or to concentrate on topics calling for the stained glass effect which can be achieved with this medium. Beginning students might become involved in and enjoy the different manipulative processes of encaustic, and produce very meaningful work. However, the medium has much more to offer to advanced students who may delight in its unusual qualities, its seemingly professional results, and, most of all, the unlimited possibilities for finding less familiar ways of treatment and expression.

One type of opaque medium in which significant expressions in color have been created is yet to be mentioned. This medium is made from crushed and powdered soft limestone (calcium carbonate), gum arabic, and pigments, which are combined into a paste and pressed together to form sticks; these are known as pastels or colored chalk. The difference between the two is that pastels are made with more permanent pigments and use more refined and fine-grained chalk powder. While chalk is a rather old drawing medium, pastels as an opaque, paintlike medium are relatively new, and have only come into wide use in the last two hundred years or so. The earliest literature to mention pastels comes from France, and it was probably

PORTRAIT OF
MAX BECKMAN
Karl Zerbe
encaustic on masonite

Collection of the Nebraska Art Association, University of Nebraska Art Galleries

there that this medium was most highly developed, culminating in the famous impressionistic pastels by Degas, Manet, Redon, and Renoir.[32]

> As far as the technique is concerned, one is free to handle the material to suit oneself. The color tones may be placed broadly and abruptly alongside of one another or laid one over another, for which purpose a dark ground will be very serviceable in the shadows and transition tones. The color tones may be applied and wiped off with the finger, with the brush, or with a chamois skin, and uncommonly soft, velvety tones [are] thus obtained, which, to be sure, often display a deceptive brilliance of execution rather than excellent draughtsmanship. The tones may be easily fused with the fingers or a brush; in this way they are softened and serve as a basis for the light and dark accents, which are set in very spontaneously and freshly, thus giving to pastel its typical charming and playful character.[33]

Colored chalk, the poor relation of pastels, can be treated in exactly the same manner. Its more limited range of colors and slightly coarser quality are insufficient reason to consider it unsuited for high school work. In addition to being inexpensive, colored chalk has certain other advantages: large surfaces can be covered rapidly and easily with the side of these long sticks; when they are dipped into water they become soft, their color brilliant, and their covering power as strong as any pastel. Any roughly textured paper will serve well as a working surface. On the high school level, Manila and the rough-textured side of brown wrapping paper, among other inexpensive papers, have been used successfully.

In the high school colored chalk has many advantages over numerous other color media. It is most excellently suited to sketching in broad colorful areas because it can be applied rapidly. This helps students concentrate on the most significant parts first, and prevents their spending time on trivial or minor details. Moreover, it is quite difficult to portray fine details with colored chalk because the sticks are rather clumsy and do not retain fine edges or points. One other important advantage of colored chalk is that colors can easily be placed over one another, and therefore a work can be developed from simple broad shapes, which are slowly subdivided into smaller areas of different colors. In addition, chalk can be worked from dark to light colors as well as from light to dark. The medium requires large sheets of paper which in turn force students to be less tight and more free, spontaneous, and direct.

Any subject which can be colorfully expressed and treated in broad generalizations or in a sketchy manner is suitable for chalk. Chalk's only severe disadvantage is that it cannot take the slightest abuse: it is easily damaged and the finished work is hard to preserve. Even fixatives are rarely satisfactory; they commonly blow some colored dust from the work, do not truly bind the chalk particles to the paper, and can easily discolor a work. Yet these shortcomings of chalk are overshadowed by its positive qualities. The medium has invaluable merits, particularly for high school students who often find it difficult to learn to express themselves in color directly, precisely, and plainly. Chalk is as satisfactory for sketching as for more finished work.

The Transparent Media

Next to poster paint, watercolor is the most widely used medium in our schools. It consists of *very finely* ground pigment combined with glycerin, gum arabic, or similar binders; its diluter is water. No other medium in visual art has a history as

---

[32] Two of the most prominent French artists who gave status to pastels were Maurice Quentin de La Tour, and Chardin.

[33] Max Doerner, *The Materials of the Artist, and Their Use in Painting,* Eugen Neuhaus, trans. (New York: Harcourt, Brace & Co., 1934), p. 248.

VIEW OF INNSBRUCK
Albrecht Dürer
watercolor

Reproduced by courtesy of the Albertina Collection, Vienna

unusual as watercolor. The practice of binding pigments with gum and diluting them with water was known even to the ancient Egyptians. During the Middle Ages watercolor was commonly used for coloring ink-drawn illuminations and illustrations. With the invention of printing its popularity as a colorant increased, but it remained a subservient medium until the late eighteenth century. Besides serving as a colorant, "the water-color medium was chiefly used by the 'limners' or portrait-painters in miniature, of whom that exquisite 'Little Master,' Nicholas Hilliard, was the chief."[34]

Dürer was probably the first western artist to use watercolors as a major means of artistic expression, but his exceptional landscape watercolors, which he painted in the late fifteenth century, did not influence other artists to use this medium. It was not until the end of the eighteenth century that English painters like Gainsborough, Constable, and especially Turner gave status to transparent watercolor and demonstrated that it could be an important medium in its own right, equal in power, significance, and expressiveness to tempera and oil paints. In spite of this, watercolor still remained a second-class medium in the eyes of the public and many artists. Often it was considered effective only for sketching and planning major works—later to be executed in oil or fresco—or for Sunday painters and little children. Here too it was employed as a coloring material rather than as a paint medium. Many had the idea that watercolor was inexpensive, easy to carry about or store, and neither messy nor hard to handle.

Yet the fact is that watercolor demands expensive equipment and is very exacting and difficult to manipulate. Its transparent quality is without any covering power, and its vividness and luminosity are solely dependent on the color of the background to which it is applied. It demands fast decisions, speedy execution, and skillful handling. It is hard to control; minute amounts of water will change its intensity, even the smallest particle of one color will immediately alter another, and inadvertent

[34] Laurence Binyon, *English Watercolours* (London: A. & C. Black, Ltd., 1933), p. 3.

errors are quite difficult to correct. Contrary to popular belief, few media require as much skill, experience, and speedy judgment as watercolor.

Some of watercolor's most typical features are the immediate brilliance of even the softest tones, the flowing washes of varying degrees of intensity, and the spontaneity which may leave areas either sharply defined or soft and fluid. But none of these innate effects of the medium can be achieved, none of its unique and characteristic qualities exploited, without rather expensive papers and brushes. More than any other paints, watercolor demands brilliantly white, heavy paper (not less than 72-pound stock) which is cold pressed, not absorbent, grained to various degrees, and made from linen rags. Sable brushes are undoubtedly to be most highly recommended, but ox hair brushes, round and pointed, also serve well, provided they are between ½″ and 1″ wide.

Despite the importance of superior equipment, one finds many art classes in which very inferior materials are used, not from lack of knowledge but from lack of funds. Poor equipment severely hampers the desire to do one's best, whereas the right material acts as an additional stimulator; it can lead toward the unfolding of beautiful colors, and toward the gradual materialization of a vision or an image.

Watercolor is a medium which demands spontaneity, courage, and intense concentration. Since it cannot be worked over, it must be handled in a manner similar to sketching, in bold, direct simplifications and subtle suggestions. It must be worked swiftly; otherwise its imperative immediacy and continuity cannot be sustained. Yet swift work demands courage, above all the courage to make mistakes in choice of color and design. Along with quick action, watercolor requires rapid decisions, and these can only be executed by full concentration on the task. All of these demands are extremely challenging, and it is just these challenges which make up watercolor's contribution to education.

The teaching of watercolor can be approached in several ways. Most methods advocate that students begin their work by first sketching a small-scale outline of the essentials of their pictorial idea on ordinary paper. In such an outline they should indicate roughly the contours of the major forms, their placement, other facts pertaining to space division, and possibly the tentative distribution of light and dark areas by shading. After students have finished the organization of their work, they should carefully transfer the essential elements of the outline to the larger watercolor paper, using only basic lineal simplifications void of details or value indications. However, they should preserve their more detailed, small sketches to serve as an occasional guide to and reminder of their original intentions.

The question remains: What should beginning students attempt to depict in their watercolors? Three distinctly different approaches may be used: painting directly from nature; basing the first painting studies on facts they have seen and previously drawn; or depicting visions of their imagination. The last has been found a more difficult way of learning to control and derive pleasure from working with watercolor, because students must rely solely on their memories. They need to recall forms, colors, and shades, and must divide their attention between remembering and the act of handling the watercolor. Therefore it seems more advisable for students to refrain from painting from the imagination or memory until they have become thoroughly familiar with the medium. Painting from nature, on the other hand, relieves them to a large degree of the difficult task of recalling, and permits them to concentrate fully on painting. Significantly, many great watercolor artists—Constable, Turner, Homer, Marin, Burchfield, and Kingman, to name just a few—did not execute watercolors from the imagination but began their paintings by working directly from nature, or by utilizing previously made nature sketches.

There are three basically different approaches to painting with watercolors. In one the various dark colors are placed on the paper first, followed by the lightest ones. Only after the two contrasting intensities have been permanently arranged are the remaining middle tones added. In a second approach, the work is begun with light colored washes. As long as these are still moist, areas may be taken out (with a sponge or brush) so that the paper reappears as brilliantly white. After the washes have dried, the darkest colors are set down broadly, and only then are the middle tones added. In a still different approach the most intense colors of the largest areas are painted first; these are then contrasted with the darkest shades, and the remaining middle tones are placed last.

From an educational point of view, no one of these methods of painting a watercolor can be preferred over the others, and each merits individual assignments. The three have an important common aspect: they prevent students from working only on portions of their project and completing one section of a painting before others have been begun. Frequently if students are left without guidance they will concentrate only on isolated parts of their work, or minor details, thereby losing a feeling for the whole and producing either poor, unbalanced, or overdone works. One of the most difficult problems in working with watercolors is knowing when to stop—knowledge which comes slowly and only through experience. Therefore, whenever students begin a watercolor they should be made to realize that a potentially good piece can easily be spoiled by too much working over. They should also be told that it is wiser to stop a bit before they think the watercolor is finished than to work two minutes too long. Students must learn to accept and find satisfaction in painted suggestions rather than fully completed and detailed representations. Helping them decide whether to go on painting or be satisfied with what they have already accomplished is one of the teacher's major functions during any watercolor session.

Another characteristic method of painting with watercolor is painting wet in wet. This technique can be handled in two ways: either the whole sheet of paper is wetted thoroughly with water before the work is started, or else individual areas are moistened before color is applied. Both techniques are difficult to control, shapes are hard to define, and images cannot easily be given precise meaning. These techniques are suited neither to beginners, nor to advanced students with little experience in watercolor. However, there is one exception: purely experimental work aimed at giving students opportunities to learn the handling of and develop a feeling for the watercolor medium. During such experiments the deliberate running together of colors and the ensuing effects, the intricate yet accidental movements resulting from moist colors on a wet surface, and the bizarre shapes which often appear as soon as watery colors are placed on moist paper should acquaint students with the unusual possibilities so characteristic of watercolor.

During such investigations of the less apparent qualities of watercolor, students should be urged to use not only various soft-hair brushes, but also wide bristle brushes for dry-brush effects, sponges and cloths for unusual washes and unexpected textures, sticks or brush handles for drawing lines in the wet pigment, and razor blades for subtle surface treatments. Experiments of this type should lead to a freer use of the medium, inspire students' imaginations, and enable them to gain new knowledge which they may transfer to their creative work. Still, such experimental work must be carried out under careful guidance during which students are informed of the aims of these experiments and are given criteria for evaluating their success or failure. Otherwise such activities can easily relapse into meaningless, demoralizing, and time-wasting play sessions.

In order to help students learn to use watercolor efficiently, and enjoy working with it, a few simple rules must be impressed upon them: (1) to keep plenty of moist color always in the brush, except when a dry-brush effect is deliberately intended; (2) to start painting with a large brush, and to use a smaller brush only towards the end of the work; (3) to change water frequently so that it is always

LANDSCAPE—MOUNTAIN
John Marin
watercolor

F. M. Hall Collection, University of Nebraska

clean and does not become muddy; (4) to rinse out the brush frequently while painting, as well as after the work is finished; (5) to use only clean, moist brushes or a sponge to correct errors; (6) to clean frequently the surface on which colors are mixed by wiping it with a damp cloth so that old paint deposits will not interfere with the blending of new tones; (7) to prepare washes in sufficient quantities and in separate containers.

Another medium in the family of transparent paints is colored inks. These inks possess some qualities which are similar to watercolor, yet differ from it because they can readily be used without a diluter, and because their colors are even more transparent, strikingly brilliant, extraordinarily powerful, and difficult to modulate or modify. Probably for these reasons colored inks have never come into as wide use as watercolor, but the inks have enough desirable qualities to make them worthy of recommendation for limited high school work. One pleasing feature is that they dry very rapidly, hence permit speedy work with almost no delaying interruptions for drying. Another feature is that their illuminative power is so strong that it will not break or greatly diminish even on very poor or dull paper. The inks also permit reworking, repainting, and glazing without noticeable effects on their brilliance or intensity. They can easily be diluted by being mixed with denatured alcohol, and used for washes which will not cause puddles or wrinkles even on very inexpensive papers. Colored inks therefore lend themselves extremely well to sketching in colors. Visual ideas can be set down speedily; objects, landscapes, and persons can be defined easily and effectively. In combination with black ink lines, colored inks are an excellent medium for drawing as well as for experimentation. In the latter case they may be combined with watercolor, permitting experiments in intensities.

Mixed Media

A widely accepted method used throughout the practice of art has been to combine different media in order to convey a particular mood, to produce a specific textural effect, or to give special expression to a form or idea. Purity in terms of media has never been regarded as important, nor have the technical means by which the work was accomplished; what has always counted has been the final accomplishment. Actually, many media which are today considered legitimate, originated from a fusion of two or more. One of the better-known examples is oil painting, which came into existence when water soluble paint was covered with protective varnishes to which small amounts of pigment had been added.

Most mixed media cannot be handled according to simple or inflexible formulae; their use therefore is certainly to be encouraged in the high schools. They provide students with additional opportunities to invent or become acquainted with less frequently encountered means of expression, and they often help students to rid themselves of trite mannerisms and to discover personal ways of presenting thoughts and feelings.

One of the best-known mixed media today is gouache. It is neither transparent nor opaque, but translucent, and combines certain characteristics of transparent watercolor with those of opaque waterpaints. The principal difference is that in gouache, opaque white paint, instead of water, is used to lighten a color. Commonly the major vehicle in gouache is watercolor, but because of the use of the white paint —which lessens the transparency of the colors—expensive papers are not required.

RECEPTION IN MIAMI
Jack Levine
gouache

F. M. Hall Collection, University of Nebraska

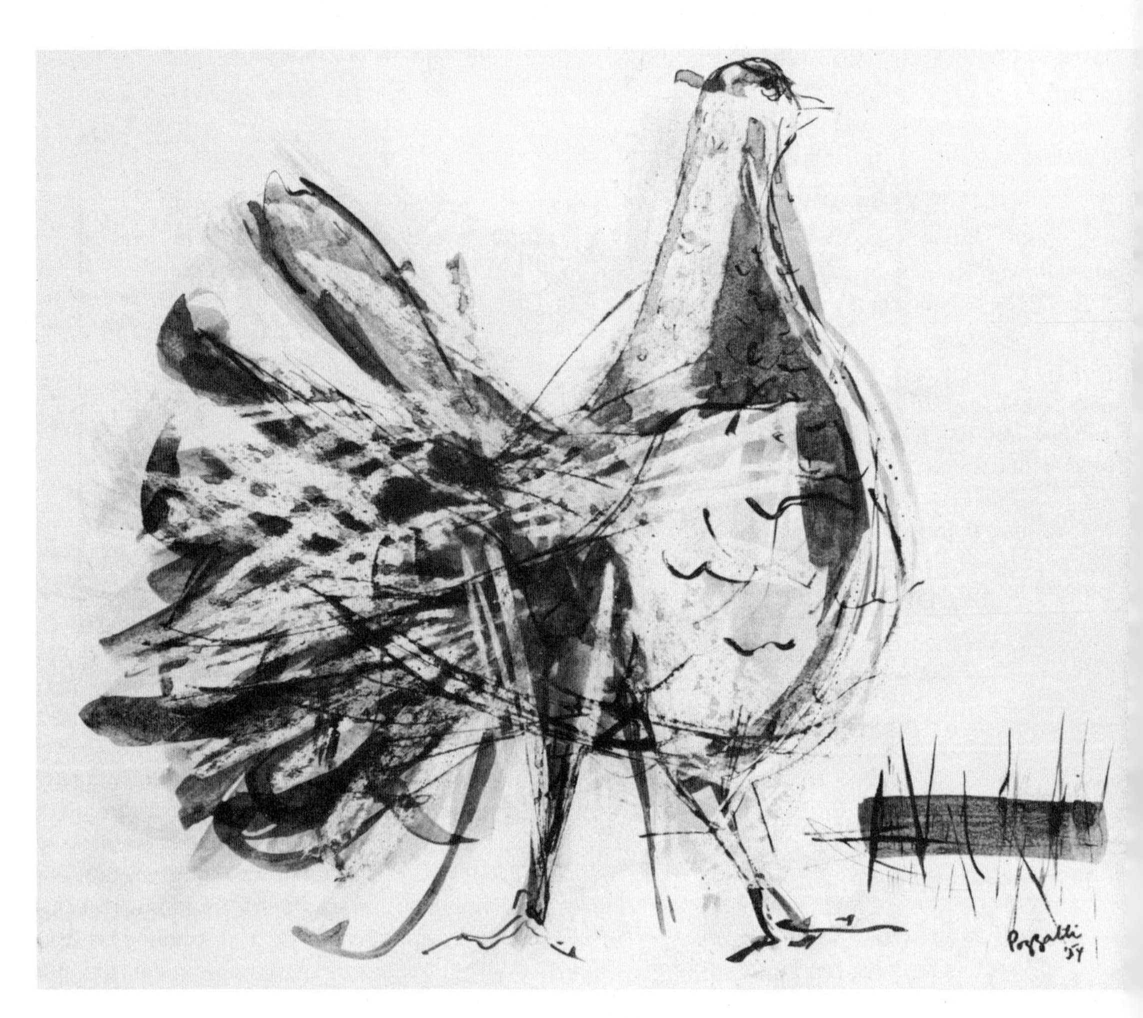

BIRD
Rudy Pozzatti
crayon, ink, and
watercolor on paper

Wrapping paper, newsprint, and similar papers all serve well. Inexperienced students often find painting with gouache much easier than with pure watercolor because they can clearly see and judge a mixed shade before it is placed on the paper—a certainty which does not always exist with watercolor—and because errors can be corrected more easily, shapes can be changed, and colors altered. The knowledge that changes can be made legitimately often helps students to be freer and more daring than they usually are with watercolor. Gouache is an excellent medium to bridge the gap between poster or tempera paints and watercolor. In many school situations it is desirable that students paint with gouache before they learn to work with pure watercolors.

Many noted artists used gouache with a very limited palette—for instance, a range of warm brown tones and one cold color (green or blue), or a series of cold colors and one warm color. Gouache was frequently painted on light brown or gray paper and contrasted strongly with opaque white paint. Students too should begin gouache painting with similar restrictions; it may help them learn to control and develop greater feeling toward translucent as well as transparent colors. After they have worked successfully with a preselected limited palette, their choice of colors should be widened, in the hope that the temporary restriction has helped them learn to use colors a little more effectively, and with understanding as well as with feeling.

Another combination of media which has a place in the teaching of art in the high school is wax crayon with watercolor or poster paint. In this mixed technique, the artist capitalizes on the familiar antipathy between water and grease. Lines or areas are drawn on paper with wax crayons, and watercolors are applied over them.

Since wax repels water, the watercolor can adhere only to the parts of the paper which are not covered by crayon, the crayon lines or wax-covered areas remaining unchanged and clearly visible. This technique, which is sometimes referred to as "crayon resist," was developed largely in art rooms and so far has been given relatively little attention by professional artists. But this does not mean that the combination of media is lacking in artistic merits or is so limiting that it hampers freedom of expression. On the contrary, in many instances high school students become more self-confident, hence freer, if they are permitted to concentrate first on the more lineal aspects of a representation instead of devoting themselves immediately and solely to painting. As indicated, in this technique drawing and painting are treated separately, each being used to supplement the other. It is here that crayon resist differs considerably from other methods of expression in color: commonly, drawing plays only a very subordinate role in painting, and is chiefly considered a guide which is to become invisible in the finished work. But in crayon resist drawing remains an equally important partner, even in the finished product.

The fusion of separate approaches and techniques is inherent in the very nature of mixed media, and this is why they are often excellent means for combining and/or utilizing characteristic dissimilarities of autonomous media. Mixed media also frequently help students to transfer gradually previously gained knowledge and experience into a new or different learning situation or creative activity. In the case of crayon resist, experience gained working with contour lines can, without any adaptation, be utilized at once in working with this mixed medium. This can occur in two different ways: in one, the line drawing is carried out in rather conventional manner with a dark crayon, and watercolor is then liberally painted over this and the unused areas. The dark lines remain a significant part of the whole work. A different and more unusual approach consists of making a careful drawing with *white* crayon on white paper over which watercolor is freely applied. Because the white crayon lines are scarcely visible when the actual painting is begun, they are not as confining or restricting as dark lines. The almost invisible contour drawing should serve mainly as a structural support, and during the painting phase should permit students to concentrate solely on color, giving only minor attention to the definition of shapes, lines, details, and subject matter. The freedom to work with color independent of other considerations often helps students to develop a genuine feeling for it, and to begin to realize the countless possibilities innate in color.

A different application of the same technique consists in starting not with a black or white line drawing, but with a colorful, more detailed and finished crayon drawing over which watercolors are freely painted. Here the watercolor should act both as a unifying agent and as a means to suggest the particular mood of a work. In this approach the watercolor is placed in a subordinate position since the major responsibility for the pictorial statement is carried by the drawn crayon representation. Such a method has but a limited merit because the watercolor, being reduced to a very minor role, must be considered an enhancement rather than an intrinsic part of the whole work. Watercolors can be applied haphazardly, without the exercise of forethought, care, or skill; and mood and unity often are produced quite by accident and without genuine effort to achieve such results. Mood and unity being significant parts of any artistic work, even a very mediocre drawing of this kind may superficially appear to be acceptable and effective, hence the technique must be used with the utmost care. This particular form of crayon resist, however, is quite justifiable with students who have extreme difficulty in expressing themselves, or who may have been conditioned to follow step-by-step procedures literally, and to produce very exacting and restricting work. In cases where there is an obvious need for work which immediately shows an expressive and finished appearance, this method is very satisfactory, but it should never be considered more than an intermediate step toward genuine, significant achievements. Otherwise it can rather easily lead to self-deceit, deluding students into believing they possess ability when actually such basic attributes as capability, competence, and proficiency are almost nonexistent.

Aside from the few examples just described, the possibilities for combining various media are manifold. Many of those extant were invented and effectively used by artists. For instance, there are combinations of pastels or colored chalk and poster paint, or ink and tempera. Yet most of these combinations are handled so individualistically and are used for such personal reasons that they can hardly be classified and perpetuated in a classroom as valid techniques. Most materials and media have a special characteristic of their own, a particular virtue. As Ruskin said: "Whatever materials we use, the virtues of that material are to be exhibited."[35] Becoming sensitive to these distinct virtues and learning to gain mastery over them is a serious challenge to anyone, be it a high school student or an artist. Combining several different materials is a permissible artistic freedom, and no law restricts the artist from using a variety of media or techniques in a single work. Yet this must be done with restraint and solely for the purpose of giving credibility and expressive verve to a work. Otherwise the mixing of media and/or techniques will deteriorate into an exhibition of technical facility or mechanical inventiveness, detracting from the total creative statement. Any combination of media, well known or uncommon, must always be used in an unobtrusive and convincing manner lest it convey the impression that it was contrived merely for the purpose of cloaking incompetence or lack of skill or imagination.

The art teacher, aware of the danger of pretense and deception, must constantly be wary of introducing shortcuts, even though they may at times be fashionable or seem convenient. While they may bring about apparently skillful accomplishments, they are the result neither of genuine exertion or understanding, nor of a search for proficiency. The teacher must always be alert to encourage any student who shows incentive and initiative while working. If a student professes a desire to experiment with media either because he hopes to find a particular, personal way of expression, or simply because he would like to try to discover an interesting and possibly new method of utilizing different materials, he should be granted every opportunity to do so. Even if the teacher believes that the intended experiment will lead to failure, the student should not be hindered. In an art room no serious student should ever be prevented from learning through his own experience, regardless of whether or not the result will be successful.

As in all other cases of experimental work, the basic duty of the teacher is to act as an analytical critic, separating success from failure and explaining the probable cause of each. In some instances a teacher may also have to encourage and console, but he should never fail to praise initiative, interest, courage, and perseverance whenever they appear.

The Mural

Probably the oldest branch of visual art is mural painting. From a historic point of view mural or wall painting is almost coeval with the first manifestations of man's ability to record and preserve what he saw or felt. Today the word "mural" implies a large, often decorative painting which is a permanent part of a wall, but also, and more importantly, it signifies a component of architectural design, imparting a particular character to a room or building. This character may be of either sacred

---

[35] *The Works of John Ruskin,* E. T. Cook and Alexander Wedderburn, eds. (London: Georg Allen, 1906), Vol. XIX, p. 135.

or secular nature, radiating an atmosphere consonant with the particular function of the place.

With the exception of cave wall paintings, whose function has not yet been determined with certainty, a strict division between secular and religious murals is easily made. The famous murals of Pompeii and Herculaneum are typical examples of early secular wall paintings. Later examples, dating from the Middle Ages and the Renaissance, have been found chiefly in the castles and estates of the nobility. "Walls worthy of decoration could belong only to gentlemen or better; and such people, being conscious of their station, would care chiefly for courtly stories in which the events moved with a certain deliberate consequence, for stateliness is known to imply leisure."[36] Today secular murals are mostly seen inside and outside of public buildings; they sometimes convey a message pertaining to the purpose of the building, but their major function is to add prestige and lend atmosphere.

Murals which create a particular mood in a sacred edifice probably pre-date those which lend prestige to a worldly building. In ancient temples both the walls and the floors were covered with decorative pictorial designs; as well as conveying a certain atmosphere, they also dramatized religious messages to the faithful. The murals in the catacombs and early churches were "there for anyone who cared to look, particularly in the churches where every man might enter freely; . . . the cathedrals were like great illuminated manuscripts in which the most illiterate could read. The Church had taken all knowledge to be its province and was setting properly selected portions of it before the eyes of the most ignorant of God's poor."[37]

Mural painting can be approached from two wholly different points of view, independent of purpose and media. In one approach the flat surface of the wall is visually retained, and the painting operates only in the two dimensions of height and length. Typical examples are the early Egyptian, the medieval Byzantine, and the Romanesque murals. In the opposite approach a space illusion is created on the wall. Here the wall is visually destroyed, so to speak; it no longer seems a solid partition, or a compact and massive support of a building but becomes a three-dimensional space, seemingly boundless in depth, and limited only by the artist who has created this visual deception. So far as we know, the Greeks and certainly the Romans employed mural paintings to overcome the physical space limitations of a room; they relied heavily on perspective and used it extensively. During the Renaissance, when this art or science was rediscovered, most mural painters again utilized the illusion of depth. Only very recently have artists returned to the earlier approaches of two-dimensional wall painting. For instance, the murals of Léger at the United Nations Building in New York, Matisse's wall paintings in the chapel at Vence, and Miro's murals in the Harvard Graduate School are without any formal perspective; they are flat in appearance and void of visual deception.

Mural painting occupies a category by itself, not only in approach and purpose but also in terms of media and technique. The two most significant media developed almost exclusively for this branch of visual art are fresco and mosaic. The Egyptians, for instance, "perfected *tempera,* a method of mural painting which is considered to be of even greater antiquity than that of painting in fresco. Their procedure was to mix with the pigment such glutinous products as honey, egg, size, glue, fig juice, animal blood, or any flexible gum; then to apply this mixture to the dry wall, usually to the thickness of about one eighth of an inch."[38] Aside from the tempera medium, the Egyptians also employed mosaics to add prestige to and create moods in their

---

[36] Elizabeth L. Harris, *The Mural as a Decorative Device in Mediaeval Literature* (Nashville: Vanderbilt University, 1935), p. 46.
[37] *Ibid.*, p. 24.
[38] *Ibid.*, p. 2.

temples and tombs.[39] They seem to have been ignorant of fresco painting, however; the earliest known works were discovered in the palace of Knossos on the island of Crete about 1500 B.C. The Greeks, and later the Romans, perfected fresco painting, and their technique was almost identical with that still being used today. As indicated, the term "fresco" designates a particular medium which requires a specific technique. Actually "the word fresco is constantly misused. Because of the clumsiness of the terms 'mural painting' or 'mural decoration' we have naturally come to speak of any wall painting as a fresco. But there is a more significant reason for this confusion: true fresco painting has been the principal and at times almost the only medium used for large scale wall decoration during the great art periods of the past.

"Technically fresco is the name of a medium, like oils or water color. It consists of painting on freshly laid plaster with colors ground in water only."[40] Fresco can be used in three different ways. One is buono fresco, or true fresco; a second is called fresco secco, or dry fresco, and the third is graffito, or incised fresco.

Buono, or true, fresco in many respects is quite different from any other paint medium. It does not require any binder; the water-diluted pigment is painted on a fresh and moist plaster wall, and during the drying process the color particles become quasi-cemented to it. The natural crystalline plaster surface forms a minute, glasslike layer which holds the coloring matter absolutely and permanently in place. In buono fresco the final layer of plaster is applied on the wall in very small sections as the painting progresses. Such areas may not be larger than the space an artist is able to utilize during any single painting session. Because fresco is the most permanent wall painting medium, and is never glossy so can be viewed from any angle without glare, it is well suited for mural painting.

Buono fresco painting is difficult; it requires laborious and careful preparation of the wall,[41] and a high degree of skill in painting. It is a very time-consuming technique which permits no errors. In true fresco, "there can be no hesitation, no mistakes, for the only correction possible is to destroy the day's piece and begin again the next morning."[42] It is quite obvious that this technique is not too well suited for high school work.

Fresco secco, which is akin to tempera painting, is not quite as demanding as true fresco, and can be executed quite easily on relatively small portable panels.[43] Advanced high school students can handle it without encountering great difficulties. Metal lath is tightly and carefully nailed into a strong wooden frame (made from 2″ x 2″ studs); the lath is then covered with at least two different coats of plaster. The first coat is rather coarse, made of about three parts sand and one part lime putty or Portland cement. After this has dried, a second, smooth, final coat is plastered over it. The last coat consists of equal parts of sand and lime putty.[44] The painting can now be started on the moist or remoistened panel. The colors used in fresco secco must either be pigments mixed with lime water (lime putty heavily

---

[39] "Decoration for the capitals of columns has been found at Tel el Yehudia in Lower Egypt. Here, bits of colored glass and earthenware have been inserted into sinkages to form lotus and other patterns. In a temple of Ramesis II, near Heliopolis, there are some wall reliefs with an inlay of glass paste." Edgar Waterman Anthony, *A History of Mosaics* (Boston: Porter Sargent, 1935), p. 29.

[40] Gardner Hale, *Fresco Painting* (New York: William Edwin Rudge, 1933), p. 3.

[41] "Formerly murals had to be prepared in six stages: (1) the wall was nicked so that the next layer would adhere; then there were added (2) a thin layer of chalk painted with ochre; (3) a layer of mortar composed of sand and chalk containing straw; (4) fine whitewash; (5) whitewash containing blue coloring; (6) a thin layer of chalk and sand to give a final smooth and polished surface to which the pigments could be applied." Anthony, *A History of Mosaics,* p. 64.

[42] Hale, *Fresco Painting,* p. 24.

[43] For detailed information see Olle Nordmark, *Fresco Painting* (New York: American Artists Group, Inc., 1947), and Ralph Mayer, *The Artist's Handbook of Materials and Techniques.*

[44] Metal lath, sand, and lime putty can usually be obtained from building supply dealers.

diluted with water), or pigments mixed with casein binder. The casein-bound colors remain brilliant even after they have dried, but the lime watercolors usually become lighter when dry, and as soft in character as pastels.

Graffito, or sgraffito, is a still different form of fresco, chiefly used for painting murals on the outside of buildings. Exterior murals were common during the Renaissance, and this form of painting is still frequently practised on houses in some European countries, notably in Switzerland, Austria, and Germany. In graffito fresco a dark colored coat of plaster is laid over a light colored or white one, but before the second, dark coat has set, the design (usually lineal in character) is incised. The design must be cut sufficiently deep for the light coat of plaster underneath to show through clearly.

Portable panels are constructed in exactly the same manner as those for fresco secco. After the two different coats of plaster have been placed on the metal lath, a third is placed over them. The latter may be coarse (again about three parts sand to one part lime putty), and is mixed with large amounts of dark pigment. As soon as the moist plaster is evenly spread, the student must begin to incise the design, because this can only be done during the brief period when the plaster is still soft and pliable. Therefore this last dark, coarse coat must be applied in sections; only as much of it should be placed on the panel as can be utilized by a student during one class session. The instruments best suited for incising the design are wire and hardwood sculpture tools.

Fresco painting has several unique educational values. Working with these mural media and techniques, the students have the opportunity to become acquainted at first hand with the problems which also confronted many of the great mural painters. If reproductions of their works are shown while students are working with fresco, they may learn to respect, understand, and perhaps admire these great achievements. Since fresco paintings were executed in almost all periods of art, students should be shown the magnificent murals created during the Renaissance, from Giotto to Leonardo da Vinci as well as those of our century by men like Orozco, Rivera, Siqueiros, Matisse, and Reginald Marsh.

Almost no other form of painting requires such careful and laborious preparation as fresco painting, or must be carried out with so much forethought and concentration. "The artist," said Orozco, "forced by strict discipline, must find out beforehand exactly what he wants to do and must prepare his designs and materials with thoroughness before the actual execution . . . ."[45] What is true for the experienced artist is, in this instance, equally correct for the beginner. In fresco the medium and technique force the student to adhere to strict discipline, and herein lies another educational merit. Finally, even if painted on movable panels, a fresco is a considerable project; it must be carried out in sizes much larger than anything that is commonly done on paper. Yet the panels are sturdy, relatively inexpensive, and not too difficult to store during the working process.

Next to fresco, mosaic is the most permanent and widely used medium for conveying images on walls or otherwise decorating them. "Mosaic in its broadest interpretation may be termed a method of placing small pieces of differently colored materials closely together so as to form a surface, usually with a pattern or a pictorial representation. These spots of pure color when viewed at a certain distance tend to fuse together upon the retina of the eye and produce a result which may be called 'impressionism'. The materials composing a mosaic must be fastened upon or set into a base or foundation which will hold them in place and thus the result may be defined as a kind of inlay."[46]

---

[45] José Clemente Orozco, "Foreword," in Hale, *Fresco Painting.*
[46] Anthony, *A History of Mosaics,* p. 27.

The technique of mosaic pertains neither to a definite style nor to a particular period of art. Throughout history mosaic has been used in secular as well as in religious buildings, in ancient temples and mosques, in eastern and western churches, and—in our time—on buildings and in ships. Before man was able to make large transparent glass windows, mosaics were the most favored medium for interior wall decorations. They were found "best suited to dimly lighted interiors and to constantly changing surfaces, such as the curves of an apse. As they reflect so much light themselves, the light which strikes them should never be too direct or intense. The great mosaic interiors like St. Mark's at Venice . . . and the Dome of the Rock at Jerusalem, are all dimly lighted."[47] During the Renaissance, when lofty buildings with large windows were erected, frescos gradually replaced mosaics in many parts of the western world. Thus mosaic slowly lost its importance as a medium for major creative works, and remained, until very recently, a technique employed mainly to decorate minor works of art and jewelry.

Today we are witnessing a kind of renaissance of mosaic. It is found on exterior and interior walls of modern buildings; it is set into framed, movable panels which are hung like paintings; and it is widely used for decorating useful objects. The reawakened interest in mosaic probably is a result of the search for media which are different, new, or have been largely neglected, media which will permit experimentation and give new expression to thoughts and feelings. The main difference between painting and working in mosaic is that the latter requires the artist (or the student) to adjust to the medium rather than to force the medium to obey him, as in painting. In mosaic the artist cannot create a texture as he is free to do in painting; he must adapt himself to mosaic's innate textural quality and utilize it as a significant, contributing element within the total design. He must find the colors among already existing shades instead of mixing his own; he must accept the maze of lineal divisions between colored stones, and shape every stone so that in the end these divisions will add to and not detract from the whole. He must laboriously compose the whole from countless little parts without being able to set large, solid areas against small, subdivided spaces—a technique commonly practised in painting. He must be able to achieve differences in textural feeling despite the fact that he works with an over-all pattern which permits only minor variations. All this is a challenge, and it is probably this challenge which has attracted artists once again to mosaic. The reasons for offering mosaic in a high school art program are similar to those which have made artists turn to it anew. Mosaic challenges high school students' mental flexibility and creative capability, and, more significantly, their ability to carry out a slow and rather laborious task in which good workmanship ranks equal in importance to praiseworthy designs.

Two basically different techniques are used in developing a mosaic, both of which first require a fairly detailed layout of the design on paper. In one technique this layout (correctly called cartoon) is mechanically transferred (usually pricked through or stenciled) to the surface on which the mosaic will be made. The surface is then covered in sections with an adhesive into which the stones are set one by one. The artist commits himself only gradually; though he must choose the size, shape, and shade of each stone, and decide on its placement every time, he can still alter the design as it develops under his hands. In sum, the "direct" method of developing a mosaic permits the artist to remain constantly creative, to control the most minute details, and to change the design throughout the entire working process.

The "indirect" method is somewhat more mechanical. Individual stones are first pasted face downward on the cartoon, which is then cut into sections. The sections are transported and permanently fastened to the final surface so that only the paper

---

[47] *Ibid.*, p. 36.

and not the stones shows on the outside. After the sections have adhered, the paper is removed, exposing the right side of the stones. The artist has less liberty to change the design than in the "direct" technique: he must follow his predetermined outline quite accurately because the down-turned stones convey the total impression of the mosaic very poorly. At this point the work can be seen only in reverse; the end result cannot be judged before all sections have been permanently attached to the final surface. Therefore the artist must trust his cartoon implicitly, work the actual mosaic in a more or less mechanical manner, and concentrate not on actual creating but only on matters pertaining to workmanship.

Of the two, the second approach is probably better suited to students who have never before worked with mosaic because they can first occupy themselves solely with the design and then, rather independently, with the more workmanlike aspects. More advanced students who have had some experience in creating a mosaic should be encouraged to try the "direct" method. Obviously beginners should first work on relatively small sizes, not larger than four square feet. When they have gained some experience, students should be encouraged to tackle larger projects. Mosaic has only a few basic limitations in regard to subjects and ideas. The design should be static rather than dynamic, sharp and distinct rather than vague or impressionistic. Figures should be depicted in repose rather than in movements, and the total design should be conceived in broad spaces rather than small details, and in areas rather than in lines.

Regardless of whether the "direct" or the "indirect" method is used, a small sketch should first be made for the cartoon. It should contain the basic idea, the major space divisions, the various directions for the stones, and the intended range of colors. While the cartoon should be identical in size with the finished work and should be a carefully worked out layout, it should never be an attempt to imitate the appearance of the projected work. The cartoon should permit the student to change, rearrange, or add color, form, and movement in the actual work with the mosaic.

The many types of materials which can be used in mosaics may be divided into three groups. One comprises different kinds of glass tessarae (the Latin word "tessara" means a die or a square piece); the second group consists of several types of small glazed or unglazed ceramic or porcelain tiles; and the third includes different colorful small pieces or scraps, such as stones, pebbles, and shells; broken bottles, dishes, and window glass; plastic; linoleum and floor tiles.

Most of the great mosaics of the past were made with various types of glass tessarae. These beautiful and colorful glass cubes may be either transparent or opaque; their surface may be uneven, as Byzantine tessarae, or smooth with beveled sides, as the Venetian kind. For hundreds of years mosaic cubes have been manufactured almost exclusively on the small island of Murano near Venice. Unfortunately they are quite expensive, and often too costly to justify their use in a high school art program even though they are not too difficult to handle. High school students wishing to execute a beautiful mosaic could easily learn to work with them effectively.

Small porcelain, marble, or glazed ceramic tiles for mosaics also are manufactured commercially. Most of them come from Italy, Japan, and Puerto Rico, and are not as expensive as glass tessarae; still they cannot be considered inexpensive. Glazed ceramic tiles can be handled and shaped like any other kind of mosaic material. One type of small ceramic tile is made in this country; it has a mat surface and comes almost entirely in subdued colors. These tiles are quite inexpensive, and are available in all stores which handle bathroom tiles. They are easy to cut and are well suited for various mosaic projects; their major limitations are their dull finish and their limited range of colors.

Probably the least costly type of tile which also has the widest range of colors and shapes can be made by the students themselves. These tiles are fashioned from clay which is first rolled out flat (about ½″ thick) and then cut into small pieces; these are bisque-fired, glazed, and fired again. The tiles can be produced easily in any school which has a kiln; they have many advantages and only one drawback—their manufacture is somewhat time-consuming. Yet this process can be organized so efficiently that it requires only two or three sessions—one for making and cutting the clay tiles (each student should be responsible for a certain number of tiles in one color), and a second, and possibly third, for glazing. The advantages of making tiles, aside from the economy, are that both the standard ¾″ x ¾″ squares and odd shapes are easily made; that they need not be smooth but can also be treated with unusual textures; and that their color range is practically unlimited. These additional opportunities for creativity may act as an added stimulus to the designing of mosaics.

MOSAIC
eighth grade girl
tiles, glazed by student

Mosaics can be made from many kinds of hard and more or less flat substances which are small, or can be broken or cut into small pieces. Perhaps the most challenging materials can be found on beaches or among discards. For instance, bits of colored glass from bottles, tinted window glass, and glazed earthenware are excellent for creating effective mosaics. Large pieces can be broken by wrapping them securely in layers of rags and pounding them with a mallet; then they can be shaped with a mosaic cutter and treated like any other mosaic pieces. Pebbles, small stones, and shells or shell fragments have also been successfuly used in mosaic although their limited range of color and their largely unalterable shapes are somewhat limiting for freedom of expression. Here the composition of the mosaic must be developed from the materials rather than from a preconceived idea; the artist cannot simply superimpose his creative thoughts on the material but must accept it as a partner with equal rights. Yet this interchange between creative imagination and existing and unbending forms and shapes may lead to unique and highly expressive works.

The forms and materials found in nature can be combined very easily with man-made objects; there is no law which forbids the artist to utilize various types of materials within one mosaic. In fact, the oldest known mosaics were made with combinations of stones, glass, bones, and even metal pieces. The only criteria valid for mixing different materials are that they be blended to form a unit, that every piece in the mosaic add to the total effect, and that no single material draw attention more than any other.

In recent years linoleum and the softer types of floor tiles have been used successfully for mosaic. These floor coverings exist in many slightly subdued colors and textured surfaces; they are rather inexpensive, can easily be cut into small pieces and are not difficult to fasten. Thus they are especially suited for mosaic projects to be carried out by younger students and beginners. Their particular drawback is that the finished work, regardless of how ingeniously it is executed, always remains somewhat reminiscent of an inlaid floor cover and never looks quite like a genuine mosaic.

All one needs to create a mosaic, in addition to the actual mosaic materials, are panels, adhesives, and a few tools. Plywood or masonite is most suitable for portable panels; wood panels should be shellacked before they are covered with an adhesive. Several types of commercially manufactured adhesives—most of them rubbery in character—are available and have been successfully used with mosaics. They are usually easy to obtain through building, tile, or floor covering supply houses. Such stores commonly also carry grout, which is often used to fill in the separations between the individual pieces. The only special tools needed for mosaic work are tile cut nippers, possibly simple glass cutters, and spreaders for the adhesive, all of which are relatively inexpensive.[48] Many mosaic projects can be carried

[48] For further technical information see Edwin A. Hendrickson, *Mosaics: Hobby and Art* (New York: Hill and Wang, 1957).

out quite economically in high schools and still retain a high degree of aesthetic merit and educational effectiveness.

Murals can of course be created with media other than fresco or mosaics. Casein, tempera, poster, and even oil paints have been successfully used on sized or canvas-covered walls. However, high school students rarely have an opportunity to work directly on walls; most of their mural projects are made on large portable panels, or on sizable sheets of paper such as wrapping paper. The chief media employed are water-soluble paints which in most cases serve the purpose well. Often these murals are made to serve a temporary purpose, such as a festivity, or a more permanent one, such as enhancing a particular place within the school building (for instance, the cafeteria, the library, or a hallway).

On the high school level, murals are usually made by individual students since group work is rarely satisfactory to older students. Frequently the total area for a mural or murals is divided into several sections or projects, and one or two students are made responsible for one particular segment. This practice has the advantages of pinpointing responsibilities and of permitting individual students to create while remaining part of a group without having to conform to it. The over-all planning of a mural project is the responsibility of the art teacher. Although he may solicit the cooperation of the group and listen to their wishes and suggestions, he should not discharge his obligations by simply signing over the whole project to them. In the final analysis it is he who decides who is responsible for what; who may work with whom; which design should be placed where.

Before any mural project is undertaken, it must be assumed that the students have had many opportunities to learn to paint and draw well, and to study numerous reproductions of great murals. It should also be taken for granted that the teacher knows his students well and is quite familiar with each individual's capacity, performance, and skill. For the teacher, conducting such a project is demanding; it requires constant vigilance, countless tactful decisions, and continuous unobtrusive supervision. Yet these demands should never discourage a teacher, nor prevent him from having his students carry out such an assignment, for a mural project can become a lasting and most significant experience for all participants.

Collage

An entirely different means of expression in color, which does not make use of pigments, binder, and diluter, is known as collage. The origin of the term is the French verb "collage," which means to glue or paste. It came into wide usage in the art world shortly after the First World War. Collage is a visual presentation in which various colored or textured papers and materials are pasted together and arranged to form a unit. Pasting papers and materials together in order to create a pleasing tableau, however, is not an invention of our century. During the early part of the nineteenth century it had become quite fashionable to assemble different materials, such as glossy, colored papers, foils, ribbons, and paper doilies for whimsical or sentimental mementos. Later, Froebel- and Montessori-type kindergartens used shiny, bright-colored, gummed papers which children first tore or cut into various shapes, and then assembled to form pictorial images.

The considerable interest, after World War I, in creating artistic presentations with flat pieces of different materials coincided with the peak of the cubistic movement.[49] This was the movement seeking a visual absolute, a common denominator

[49] "When the first tide of cubism broke on our shores . . . collages aroused more amazement than appreciation. The founders of cubism—Braque, Picasso and Gris—seized upon collage as one means to escape from realistic description of subject matter." Margaret Breuning, "Tracing History of the Collage," *The Art Digest,* Oct. 1, 1948, p. 16.

fitting all visible phenomena. It searched for a supreme principle void of human emotions and individual preferences, applicable to whatever the eye could see, the mind conceive, and the hand make visible. In this quest artists turned to simple geometric shapes. For a brief time they believed that by reducing everything to such simple shapes they would be able to reveal the most fundamental truths and work with unquestionable aesthetic laws and certainties.

Because of the longing for aesthetic certainty, which led to the preoccupation with basic geometric forms, nothing seemed more natural than for artists to paste together already existing plane shapes of various materials which they found in their immediate surroundings, or to produce such shapes by simply cutting them out. This was considerably less time-consuming and cumbersome than the more conventional and laborious method of painting them meticulously. Also, in creating a composition this device permitted the postponement of crucial decisions until the very last moment. Individual pieces of the design could easily be arranged and rearranged; objects, textures, and effects which would have been relatively difficult to represent convincingly with paint could effortlessly be incorporated. Because artists did not have to rely solely on their vocational skill, collages gave them considerable freedom and permitted them to concentrate almost exclusively on the task of shaping, arranging, and inventing.

Inventing, in particular, entered strongly into the creation of a collage: exploring the less obvious qualities of materials (by treating, twisting, or crumbling them), utilizing most incongruous and often useless or discarded matter, and taking advantage of it in an unprecedented manner. As a result, artistic statements were created which were unique, often bizarre, or lyrical. They demonstrated more than other forms of creative expression that beauty does not rely entirely on aesthetic forms, but can be the result of ingenuity, and can be achieved with even the common and the useless.

The first prominent attempts in collage were made shortly before World War I by artists like Picasso and Braque. Collage reached the height of its popularity during the first part of the 1920's, and the most typical examples for this period can probably be found among the works of Kurt Schwitters.[50] At that time form and texture in collages were predominant, and color played only a subordinate part; austerity and rigidness rather than gentleness and animation characterized these works.

A totally different approach to collage came into existence when the possibilities of arranging geometric shapes had been somewhat exhausted, and the results were often trite and repetitious. Possibly the most outstanding examples of this completely disparate approach are to be found among the last works of Matisse.[51]

---

[50] "Kurt Schwitters' collages were composed of such odds and ends as bus and theater tickets, scraps of colored paper, and other commonplace objects, and it is one of the mysteries of the artistic process that he was able to evolve so personal and convincing a statement from so humble a rhetoric. . . . Schwitters created with his pasted snippets an apotheosis of the discarded. His collages take form with a touching graciousness. They have an uncanny ability to focus mood." James T. Soby, "The Importance of Collage," *The Saturday Review of Literature,* Nov. 6, 1948, pp. 36–37.

[51] "Matisse's use of cut-and-pasted papers is in fact radically different from that of the cubists thirty years before. He is indifferent to the aesthetic and psychological conceits which involved both cubist and, subsequently, dadaist collages. . . . Matisse's papiers découpés are as pure in intention as they are in technique and they are completely controlled. Unlike the cubists who used scraps rescued from wastepaper baskets or the dadaists who cut up old mail-order catalogs, Matisse was not even satisfied with the best commercial colored papers: he had his own papers painted with gouaches of his own choosing and then proceeded with his scissors.

"Matisse said: 'To cut to the quick in color reminds me of direct cutting in sculpture.' " Alfred H. Barr, Jr., *Matisse, His Art and His Public* (New York: The Museum of Modern Art, 1951), p. 274.

Color and not texture is of major importance, and seemingly spontaneous, unconfined, and delicate forms rather than rigid geometric shapes dominate these works.

The two types of collage have one cardinal idea in common; they attempt to serve beauty rather than thought, and are decorations rather than conveyors of messages. Their foremost function is adornment; any possible representation of images, objects, or events is purely coincidental. Moods rather than facts find expression in collages.

These characteristics of collages become significant whenever high school students are asked to express themselves in this medium. They should immediately be introduced to the idea that their task is to produce a pleasing arrangement instead of a story-telling work. They also should be told that their ability to invent is being challenged, and that finding new ways of utilizing discarded or insignificant materials is rated more highly than designing naturalistic forms or employing mechanical skills effectively. Students' ingenuity must constantly be challenged during collage sessions. Their task is not simply to cut out squares or triangles and then to paste these, in a laissez-faire manner, next to each other, but to try to arrange the pieces tastefully in ways which are not immediately obvious. Bending, interlacing, and combining different forms and materials, cutting out shapes and overlapping or joining them, are a part of this challenge. Poor work is trite, lacks inventiveness, and shows only the most obvious possibilities of utilizing forms and materials; what is more, it frequently exhibits poor workmanship. Good collages, among other positive qualities, are carefully worked, are clean and precise without smudges, and have all parts fastened invisibly. The whole work has a pleasant, fresh over-all appearance.[52]

The field of collage, from a teaching point of view, can be divided into three areas, each of which can be taken up individually in the classroom. In one the major emphasis is placed on designing and arranging geometric shapes. Color and texture are treated as relatively unimportant, and the work is carried out in monochromes of different intensities rather than in various colors. This approach can be varied so that color still remains quite insignificant and greater emphasis is placed on texture. Here, however, students should *invent* textures rather than utilize those which they find ready-made. They should be asked to do so by using a variety of papers, and to create textures by such means as folding, pleating, creasing, notching, indenting, embossing, incising, and perforating.

In a quite different approach to collage, color is strongly emphasized. The main materials are glossy and dull colored papers. Students should be asked to create definite moods rather than interesting or pleasing arrangements. Subjects such as "Dusk over a City or a Lake," "Quietness before a Storm," "The Briskness of a Winter Morning," or "Fog in a Forest," are suggestive without forcing students to resort to purely representational forms of expression. With more advanced students, concepts may be taken from music; for instance they may be asked to visualize such terms as "crescendo," "staccato," or "legato," or such abstract expressions as joy, hatred, fear, gaiety, pessimism, optimism, buffoonery, or tranquillity. These abstract subjects are quite challenging since students must translate them into concrete forms in terms of colors, and simple or complex shapes. They are forced to

---

[52] "Collages are usually abstract rather than realistic, emphasizing good composition and strong, forceful, expressive shapes. The advantage in using this medium is that the designs tend naturally toward strong, architectural shapes and forms quite different from those obtained in other mediums.

"This medium . . . permits working with actual space composition. To be sure, the third dimension is limited to not more than half an inch at the most, but even this is sufficient to establish several planes occupying different positions in space. These arrangements are interesting not because they copy the external appearance of objects. They are designs in space." Ray Faulkner, "Creating a Collage," *Design,* Feb. 1952, p. 106.

invent, because little exists which can simply be borrowed from the world around them.

Finally, collages can be made without any restrictions by having students combine all sorts of materials to create a pleasing or expressive design. Aside from papers and fabrics, both natural materials such as leaves, twigs, bark, and straw, and man-made materials like plastics, colored cellophane, wire, and string can be used. Yet creating collages without any form of limitation or frame of reference is extremely difficult, because both students and teachers find them hard to evaluate. In theory, such criteria as balance, rhythm, equal distribution, or unity are relatively easy to state, but in practise they may be quite perplexing to analyze, clarify, and appraise. Very often it is hard for the teacher to conceal his personal taste and preference; to demonstrate that what has been done is only superficial; to explain tactfully to a student the weaknesses and limitations of his accomplishments; to challenge him to do better and to use more initiative, imagination, or inventiveness. Because of these difficulties it is better for a teacher to wait with unrestricted collage assignments until students have learned to use and arrange various materials, and have become well acquainted with the numerous but more limited possibilities of this form of expression. Otherwise students are apt to cover a sheet of paper aimlessly with all sorts of pieces of material, bewildered and dissatisfied, even though in the eyes of their teacher they have achieved the desired results.

An offspring of collage which must also be mentioned is photomontage. Actually a photomontage is a collage, but instead of colored and textured papers and other materials, fragments of various photographs are assembled and blended to form a novel photographlike representation. Photomontage is a kind of hybrid, half photography and half creative art. Probably the unwitting inventors of the technique were the futurists and Dadaists who were the first to use parts of photographs as an added feature in their collages. This innovation was later followed up and fully developed as a method of composing, used by commercial artists, muralists, and photographers. However, it never became an independent technique or means of expression in the realm of creative art.

Photomontage has little to offer within an art program. On a nonprofessional level it requires almost no skill: after the selections—possibly quite arbitrary—have been made, the work for the most part consists merely of cutting and pasting. Whatever else may be required to produce an effective collage—giving form to a visual idea, or applying principles of composition—can be learned more thoroughly in other areas of creative art and then transferred to the production of photomontage. Because it is so very simple to produce a superficially acceptable photomontage, the task is void of any true creative challenge. Sessions devoted to photomontage can easily deteriorate into time-wasting periods in which precious opportunities for instruction are lost. Time spent versus learning gained are poorly balanced; too much time must be allotted in exchange for too little learning or genuine creating.

Enamel

Enamel is one of the oldest media through which man has been able to enhance a metal surface with color, capture an image permanently, and produce objects on which the beauty of color is pre-eminent. Enamels are radiant, colorful glazes made of glass which is melted by heat and caused to adhere to a metal surface. Glass is basically a compound of silicates and alkalis; to make it suitable for enameling, 25% to 40% lead oxide is added. This type of glass, called crystal or flint glass, is first powdered, then augmented by very small amounts of various metals or oxides which serve as pigments, determining not only the color but also the transparency or opaqueness of the enamel. Finally this mixture is melted into lumps, and the now colored lumps of crystal are pulverized once more, resulting in a dustlike powder which is the material used in enameling.

Today enameling is regarded mainly as a means for decorating pieces of jewelry or knickknacks, and is only too rarely considered a unique and powerful medium with which magnificent works of art can be created. The history of enameling is very long, and it probably begins with the ancient Egyptians; it has played a prominent role in nearly all important periods of art, especially in religious art. For many centuries Byzantine enamels, originally created in Constantinople, exerted the greatest influence on this form of art expression. These enamels were a combination of European (classical) and eastern (Persian) art, and were strongly influenced by both. Byzantine enamels were a significant part of early Christian art, and the technique as well as the style spread rather rapidly throughout civilized Europe. Ravenna, Venice, and small towns along the Rhine were major centers in which this art form flourished. Artists fashioning Byzantine enamels had only a few colors with which to work, and their technique is known today as cloisonné[53] (a French word literally meaning "divided into compartments"). Narrow metal strips (mostly wire) are laid on a metal surface to form the contour lines of a design. The resulting spaces or compartments are filled with different colored enamels and then fired. This process is repeated until the enamel is level with the top of the metal strips. A characteristic of cloisonné is that the enameled surface appears inlaid and that each inlaid area is edged by metal.

Toward the end of the Middle Ages a different enamel technique, known as champlevé, came into wide usage. The term is a combination of two French words, "champ" meaning field or ground, and "levé" meaning to take out or to lift. In spite of the fact that many champlevé enamels bear a superficial resemblance to cloisonné, champlevé is a totally different technique. In both exposed metal carries a significant part of the design, but in champlevé the areas and lines are deeply *incised* into a metal plate, quite like in engraving and etching. These lines and areas are then solidly filled with enamel powder and the plate is fired. In champlevé one need not cover the whole plate, but may incise lines and areas only in some parts of the metal surface, leaving entire sections untouched. Thus these plain sections become an intrinsic part of the total design. The finished work is characterized by a shiny metal surface broken up by colorful enamel inlays.

A technique closely related to champlevé is basse-taille. (The French word "basse" means shallow or flat, "taille" means cutting.) Basse-taille, also sometimes referred to as enameled bas-relief, became quite popular during the Renaissance. Benvenuto Cellini in his extensive treatise on metal work and sculpture devoted considerable space to this technique. As in champlevé enamels, the design in basse-taille is incised into a metal plate. But whereas in champlevé the deepened design is filled with opaque enamels, in basse-taille an additional composition or texture is engraved or embossed into the bottom of the carved-out sections. These lowered areas are then filled with *transparent* enamels so that the details and textures remain evident and continue to play a significant part in the total visual statement. Today this technique is used in decorating jewelry; otherwise it has largely been lost. Yet basse-taille merits a revival (not necessarily in the high school, however) because it permits beautiful, delicate, and unique forms of expression.

There are two likely reasons why basse-taille enameling has become almost extinct. One is that it is a slow, time-consuming technique, requiring highly developed skills. The other is that a different enameling technique came into existence

---

[53] "The colors employed were two beautiful shades of green, opaque light blue, transparent dark blue, a brownish transparent red . . . and opaque white." Henry H. Cunynghame, *European Enamels* (London: Methuen & Co., 1906), p. 50.

towards the end of the Renaissance. This new technique, which received its name from the French town of Limoges, gave painters a greater opportunity to use their craft without first having to adopt the skills of engravers and jewelry makers. The technique was probably discovered in Venice, but since it was perfected by the glass painters of Limoges the name became attached to this form of enameling. Actually limoges enamels are simply paintings on metal in which enamels instead of other color media are used. As in painting, the ground is first primed, and the outline of the design is then drawn on it. In limoges enameling the metal surface is covered with a paste made from white enamel powder and small amounts of gum arabic, and outlines are painted on this with black enamel paste. This is then fired. The baked, solidified, permanently attached black and white design is again covered with enamel pastes, only this time in various colors, and is fired once more. This process may be repeated with additional colors and details until the enamel painting has attained the desired finished appearance.

Another technique often used in limoges enamel painting is known as grisaille. (The term is a derivation of the French word "gris" meaning gray.) In grisaille the metal plate is first covered not with white but with light gray enamel over which the composition is glazed with various transparent or translucent colors. Interestingly, many enamels executed in Limoges were copies made from works of artists who did not reside in this city. The main reason was that the techniques perfected in Limoges were kept secret there for more than two hundred years. Regrettably "during the seventeenth and eighteenth centuries the art of enamel slowly declined, until it was only used for the making of snuff-boxes and coat-buttons."[54] The art of enamel painting still has not fully recovered from this decline. Yet the various old enamel techniques merit studying once again. It is unfortunate that today's major emphasis in enameling is on decorating to the neglect of enameling as a genuine and unique paint medium. Nevertheless even this limited, renewed interest in enameling has helped to make a great variety of excellent enamel powders easily available, has caused the invention of efficient and inexpensive electric kilns, and has brought about the publication of numerous competent technical books on the subject.[55]

A technique somewhat similar to limoges enameling is sgraffito. The term is derived from the Italian word "graffio," meaning a scratch. In sgraffito, after an undercoating has been melted by firing, the metal plate is covered anew with enamel paste into which lines are deeply scratched; then the plate is fired again. This process may be repeated several times, with fresh lines added on each occasion. In a varied sgraffito technique the fired undercoat is again covered with enamel powder or paste, but this time instead of scratching lines into it, whole areas are carefully taken out so that finally only a net of raised lines remains on the undercoated surface. The plate is then fired again and the major part of the image or design is carried by the now elevated enamel lines. Both types of sgraffito permit endless variations in color; undercoats may be of one color and the upper enamel of a contrasting one. Or several colors may be applied to the undercoat and only one used on the upper layer.

A more recent method of using enamels merits mention. This technique, which has no name, consists of cutting the composition on a metal plate into numerous parts which are separately enameled. These various flat metal pieces of different sizes and shapes are then reassembled like a picture puzzle and fitted permanently together on a background. The whole composition is conceived in large, relatively

[54] *Ibid.*, p. 138.
[55] Some of the more recent books which contain useful information on enameling are D. Kenneth Winebrenner, *Jewelry Making* (Scranton: International Textbook Co., 1953), Thomas E. Thompson, *Enameling on Copper and Other Metals* (Highland Park, Ill.: Thomas C. Thompson Co., 1950).

simple shapes, similar to a stained glass window. An added effect can easily be produced by soldering fine wire to the outer edge of each shape before it is covered with enamel powder, so that every colored area will appear as an inlay. This enamel technique is rather simple and decorative, and permits the creation of sizable enamel works even in relatively small kilns.

None of the various enameling techniques, with the exception of basse-taille, are too difficult to be attempted successfully by high school students. Despite the fact that the students are forced to work slowly and attentively in a disciplined manner, many might enjoy enameling and the diverse manipulation processes belonging with each technique. The beautiful colors, the many and diverse possibilities of this medium, and the potentially attainable, fascinating results often motivate students to work to the utmost of their ability.

Nearly all of the materials for enameling, such as enamel powders, gum arabic, agar, and acids, and the tools for handling them, like spatulas, brushes, or instruments for cutting and engraving, are within the budgetary means of most schools.

STILL LIFE
art education junior
champlevé technique
using wood and melted
crayons

Many schools own or can afford to purchase electric kilns which can reach the maximum temperature (1700°) required to melt any enamel powder. The only serious monetary problems might be presented by the copper plates which are commonly used for this work; these are expensive. Some schools, however, are able to find inexpensive scraps of copper locally; others use discarded copper plates from obsolete photoengravings. There is certainly a great need for research aimed at discovering other suitable and inexpensive metals or alloys which can be used as a substitute for copper.

One enamel technique which can be adapted to other materials with relative ease is a variation of champlevé. A wooden board is used instead of the metal plate, and hot colored waxes take the place of enamel powders. As in woodcutting, a design is cut into the board, and the cut grooves and areas are then filled with encaustic colors. This technique is worthy of experimentation, for it gives students genuine opportunities to find new and very interesting ways of representing their creative ideas.

Subjects Related to Expression in Colors

Color Theory

The subject which has the most direct bearing on any expression in color is color theory. Covering an extremely broad area, it is a part not only of visual art, but also of three other disciplines: physics, physiology, and psychology. In everyday life color is commonly considered a significant property of anything perceived through the eyes. For instance, a bird appears to be blue, red, or yellow, but in fact its color is a sensation caused by the light of a particular wave length which stimulates a spectator's visual apparatus.[56] What is called color is nothing but light which is partially absorbed and partially reflected by a pigment; without light we see nothing but darkness. To say an object has a certain color means that particular rays, producing definite sensations, are reflected from its surface. Light, whether sunlight or artificial, is the source of all visual sensations, and surface colors are only secondary light sources.

The properties of primary and secondary light sources, their wave structure, behavior, and radiation belong, among many other significant factors, to the realm of physics. The relationship between man and light (as well as color), the whole complex of having color sensations and effectively differentiating between them, and man's intricate visual apparatus with its many variations, such as color blindness, pertain properly to the field of physiology. The relationships between color as a physical phenomenon, the manner in which color is perceived by the mind, and the reactions toward color consisting of such factors as attraction, attitude, and feelings, belong to the sphere of psychology.

In the field of color theory as related to visual art, the terminology is deceptively simple. Yet as soon as one attempts to work with and use these terms meaningfully, he is confronted by amazing confusion. For instance, the word "color," according to Webster, is the generic or general term, whereas "hue" is its poetic synonym. But "hue" may also suggest a modification of color, implying a less vivid tone. Then again, according to the 1949 Physical Society Report on Colour Ter-

---

[56] These light or color waves are "like radio waves but very much shorter. The longest wave lengths we can see are red, the shortest violet, with the other colors lying in between. White light is a mixture of many wave lengths, and most of the colors of nature consist of several wave lengths in different proportions. Our eyes respond differently to these different wave lengths and send different signals to the brain, and this results in the sensation of color." Dr. Brian O'Brien, from a series of broadcast talks, in Egbert Jacobson, *Basic Color* (Chicago: Paul Theobald, 1948), p. 114.

minology, "hue" is the subjective term for a dominant wave length which is applied to distinguish the intensity of one color from another. The term "shade" does not appear in this report, only "luminosity" or "brightness"; the obvious conclusion is that "shade" is nothing but a hue with reduced brightness. Yet shade, according to Webster, is not only a dark pigment or the opposite of brilliance, ranging from a medium or saturated color to black, but is also a relative term used to indicate minute differences between colors, such as "a shade lighter or darker." According to Rigway's Color Dictionary, any full or saturated color which is mixed with black is a shade; any hue which is free of white, gray, or black is a full or saturated color, and any saturated color which is mixed with white is a tint.

The problem of clarifying color theory becomes even more complex: in addition to the divisions in basic terminology, colors are divided into several groups. First of all, they are separated into chromatic and achromatic colors. Chromatic colors comprise the full range of hues; achromatic consist of a monochrome, ranging from white via the intermediate grays to black. Chromatic colors are again subdivided into primary (reds, yellows, blues), secondary (greens, purples, oranges), and tertiary (the various browns from yellow-brown to red-brown and purple-brown). Primary and secondary colors are again divided into complementary and analogous colors. Complementary colors are two hues which are radically different and oppose each other diametrically, as, for instance, red and green, or yellow and purple. Also, when combined in certain proportions, complementary colors will produce gray. Analogous colors are closely related hues, such as yellow-orange, orange, and red-orange, and always have one element in common; in these analogous oranges the common element is red.

The divisions between analogous and complementary colors can be refined even more if chromatic colors are arrayed in a circle. (This is known as a color wheel.) Here the analogous hues are placed next to each other in sections of equal size. Inevitably in such a circular arrangement the complementary colors will be diametrically opposite each other, and the two analogous colors, or those on either side of the complementary color, will be nearly opposite a complementary hue. In this combination the two analogous colors are called "split-complementary colors." For example, orange and blue are complementary colors; the analogous colors to blue are blue-green and blue-purple; therefore, blue-green and blue-purple are the split-complementary colors of orange.

Finally, colors are also divided into warm and cold tones. All colors which are red or have a reddish overtone are usually referred to as "warm," and all those which are blue or contain an element of blue are called "cold." This rule is also applied in relative color relationship and we may speak of a cold red or a warm blue: one blue compared to another blue, for instance, may appear slightly reddish, or warm, or a red, when set against another red, may seem slightly bluish, or cold. Therefore, the references to cold and warm colors are relative and do not constitute a genuine form of grouping.

It is certainly desirable for high school students to become conversant with basic color terminology as well as with the precise meanings and concepts of the terms in regard to the various color groupings. But this aspect of teaching should be considered a part of general education rather than of visual art because its primary purpose is to develop students' ability to communicate intelligently; only a minor function of it is to strengthen their ability to control colors. After all, one can create a superior painting without a knowledge of the exact differences between a hue, a color, a tint, and a shade, or without being able to name the two split-complementary colors of blue. From all indications it appears that a knowledge of color theory, particularly a study of the behavior of colors, although most significant and helpful in analyzing the merit or weaknesses of a work, does not contribute to creativity. Color theory can be compared "with the grammar and vocabulary of a language which makes speech possible but does not in the least guarantee that anything said will be worth listening to."[57]

Color terminology is probably best taught and learned in an informal way. Using the most precise terms deliberately, a teacher can familiarize his students with the correct expressions applicable to colors, or color theory. As the need arises, usage may be supplemented by occasional detailed explanations or brief demonstrations of more complex terms. On the high school level, however, class-wide exercises in pure color theory, such as the production of color charts or wheels, are of dubious educational merit. Such assignments are very mechanical and monotonous, quite time-consuming, and at best constitute a questionable method for learning or understanding color theory.

Nonetheless, a knowledge of color theory should be considered an integral part of every art teacher's intellectual equipment because his task, to a considerable degree, consists of analyzing students' works. He must understand how colors behave toward each other, when an arrangement of colors is harmonious, and when it conveys the impression of being confusing or disharmonious. Unfortunately no objective criteria or absolutes exist by which one can simply determine this, because in all color relationships two significant modifications must first be established: proportion and intensity. Whenever we speak of the behavior of different colors toward each other, we must determine not only the relative size of the area covered by each, but also the comparative brilliance of each hue. For example, it has often been stated that complementary colors, such as red and green, not only "vibrate" but may appear to clash or disharmonize. Yet this notion is incorrect without modification: red and green are displeasing *if* they are of equal intensity and proportions. They are not displeasing if, for instance, a small area of brilliant red is placed on a large area of slightly darkened green. In fact, "almost any two colors may be used together. Pairs that will not make satisfactory combinations are:

> Those between which there is not enough contrast of lightness or darkness to prevent confusion.
> Those between which there is an insufficient difference of hue to be clearly recognized.
> Those which strain the eyes, as in the case of 'vibration'.
> Those which arouse unwelcome associations."[58]

Since paintings are rarely restricted to only two colors, the question arises: How do colors behave if they are used in combinations of more than two? It is hard to give an answer because, first of all, every color is affected by those which surround it or are adjacent to it. "The effect may be one of additional lightness, or darkness, of more or less purity, of a change in hue, or of a combination of these."[59] Consequently it is impossible to establish valid rules in regard to the incalculable color combinations. Still, colors in a painting may affect us either as harmonious, or as shocking and unpleasant. They may seem harmonious if

> "they reflect properly balanced amounts and varieties of chromatic light (complementary colors);
> they satisfy a need of rhythm (repetition of interval);
> they suggest a sense of form, of direction, or of space;
> they please us with their similarities (recognizable relationships);
> they surprise or stir us by their opposition (contrast);
> they arouse welcome memories."[60]

---

[57] Albert C. Barnes, *The Art in Painting* (Merion, Penn.: The Barnes Foundation Press, 1925), pp. 77–78.
[58] Jacobson, *Basic Color,* p. 103.
[59] *Ibid.,* p. 138.
[60] *Ibid.,* p. 56.

It would be wrong to claim, however, that every artistic expression in color must be harmonious to be acceptable. "Unpleasant or shocking combinations are a legitimate tool of a designer or painter when they are intentionally and successfully used to produce displeasure or shock."[61]

Obviously the artist's intent plays a major role in the selection of colors, and this most significant factor again makes it impossible to establish meaningful criteria or basic principles. The few stated above—if taught as inflexible rules—cannot be of help to an artist or student during any creative undertaking. Even to learn established, effective color combinations from commercially manufactured color wheels is rarely meaningful since so many qualifying factors enter as soon as these combinations are used (the artist's intent, proportions, intensity, and adjacent colors). Such a study can hamper rather than facilitate creative freedom. Last but not least, hardly any known painter ever relied on his knowledge of color theory during the act of creation. Matisse might have been expressing the thoughts of many other painters when he said: "My choice of colors does not rest on any scientific theory; it is based on observation, on feeling, on the very nature of each experience. . . . I merely try to find a color that will fit my sensations. There is an impelling proportion of tones that can induce me to change the shape of a figure or to transform my composition. Until I have achieved this proportion in all the parts of the composition I strive towards it and keep on working. Then a moment comes when every part has found its definite relationship, and from then on it would be impossible for me to add a stroke to my picture without having to paint it all over again."[62]

Finally, it needs to be pointed out that our relationships with colors are subjective rather than objective. Colors are linked with moods; they cause certain feelings, and give rise to likes and dislikes. Blue may be associated with a sky, with a pleasant summer day, or with a feeling of depression, as in "feeling blue," or "having the blues." Yellow may be pleasing when it is unconsciously connected with wheat fields of the wide open spaces, or with sunflowers, but it may also be associated with something extremely unpleasant, as "being yellow" in the sense of being cowardly. These associations probably have their sources in the unconscious, and strongly influence individual reactions to and choices of color. They are extremely personal and are outside of any aesthetic considerations. "The aesthetic relation to colour is simply this: that we enter intuitively into the nature of the colour, appreciate its depth, or warmth, or tonality—that is to say, its objective qualities—and then proceed to identify these qualities with our emotions."[63]

Because of this intuitive rather than intellectual relation to color, it seems that little can be accomplished on the high school level by a lengthy study of color theory. Yet the different aspects of this theory can be of the greatest value to students if the teacher employs them in analyzing and evaluating their works. Here the teacher should use his special knowledge to make it clear to students why some of their paintings are effective or pleasing and why others are not.

Design and Composition

Design and composition are as important as color in organizing a work of art, and like color theory they are fields which cover an extremely broad area. They overlap in many respects, with resultant confusion as to exactly what belongs to composition and what belongs to design. The term "composition" (a derivation of the Latin word "compositio," meaning made up from parts) is commonly applied

---

[61] *Ibid.*, p. 56.
[62] *Ibid.*, p. 147.
[63] Read, *Education through Art*, pp. 22–23.

to the art of uniting or organizing different objects, shapes, textures, lines, areas, and colors so as to form a new unit or a harmonious whole. Yet "composition" also implies an action aimed at the creation of a work of art; its purpose is directly connected with the artistic intent and meaning. In sum, composition is "the manner in which inner experience is brought into being through a *technique,* artfully and skillfully, the result being a symbol of the creator's expression."[64]

The term "design" is synonymous in many aspects with composition. Its use appears more often in connection with servile than with free art. However, this connection is arbitrary and not inherent in the term; its first meaning is "plan."[65] The study of design commonly consists of an analysis of the elements used in a composition. In design the emphasis is placed on individual elements such as space or shapes and their possible function; in composition the emphasis is placed on the arrangement of the whole, and its relationship to the intended meaning of the work.

A listing of those elements of composition and design which are recognized and accepted is virtually impossible because to a greater degree than in any other subject related to art, a confusion of semantics exists in these two fields. In composition, for example, the word "balance" means "equilibrium" as well as "equal in volume, size, or proportion," hence some schools of thought maintain that balance should be treated as a part of proportion and not separated from it. Yet proportion is the relation of one part to another and, according to Webster, also means a symmetrical arrangement. Consequently some aspects of proportion belong to symmetry; symmetry again is a significant part of harmony and should not be treated as a separate entity. In brief, all of these terms lack precision in regard to composition and design; they represent arbitrary separations and depend on individual points of view and on the context in which they are used.

Yet a number of basic terms commonly used in connection with design can be defined with fair precision, their character described, and their functions indicated. The foremost and most obvious elements of design are line, shape, mass, and space; any of these can be isolated and analyzed. In reality, however, none of them exists independently; they always appear in combination with or in contrast to each other. Masses, lines, and shapes cannot exist without space, and can often be identified only in relation to each other.[66]

The word "line" can be defined as the visual connection between two points, as the boundary of a shape or shapes within a shape (usually referred to as "contour line"), as the visual indication which divides spaces and masses, or simply as a slender mark which conveys the illusion of being continuous, yet can be discontinued at will as long, short, or dotted. A line can have many characteristics; it may be described as weak, bold, powerful, stocky, slender, or spontaneous. A line can appear in many forms: straight, bent, decidedly curved, or angular; it may manifest itself in many configurations, such as meandrous, jagged, or tapered. A line can indicate different directions—horizontal, oblique, or vertical—and can be placed in space in these different positions. Lines may be arranged in rhythmical patterns, in parallels with equal space between them, or in intervals with increasingly large

---

[64] Martin L. Wolf, "Composition," *Dictionary of the Arts* (New York: Philosophical Library, 1951), p. 177.

[65] "Design is the arrangement of lines or forms which make up the plan of a work of art with especial regard to the proportions, structure, movement, and beauty of line of the whole. . . . Design in one sense is synonymous with composition, and has to do with all the arts, though more pronounced in the applied arts than in the fine arts." "Design," *Encyclopaedia Britannica* (Chicago: William Benton, 1956), Vol. 7, p. 259.

[66] "A line drawn on a piece of paper does not seem to lie *in* the plane but on top of it. The empty environment does not border the line—the way two floor tiles border each other—but continues underneath without interruption. The thicker the line, the more striking the phenomenon." Arnheim, *Art and Visual Perception,* p. 177.

or unequal space. Arrangements of lines can be repetitious, continual, irregular, or sporadic. Depending on the movement of the lines, they can suggest a static or dynamic, lyrical or dramatic quality; they can suggest repose or movement, quietness or tension. A straight line "represents the most concise form of the potentiality for endless movement."[67] The horizontal line conveys a feeling of repose and calm; a vertical one strength, firmness, and static support. The effect of a bold line or stroke is rather dramatic or striking, suggesting forceful or quick action. In contrast a fine line is lyrical, inferring tenderness, subtlety, and sensitivity. A curved line may imply tension,[68] a jagged line agitation, a meandrous line uncertainty or vagueness. Certainly the lines' character and the context in which they are used will influence the mood or the idea they help to convey: lines may oppose or support each other, cross, unite, or run parallel; they may be compatible or antagonistic. In short, lines can be used in countless ways; they can influence the total composition, and can play an active part in every visual design.

Like the line, the shape or plane is an important structural element of design. In spite of the fact that the terms "shape" and "plane" are not synonymous, they are often freely interchanged in connection with design. Both terms characterize a form which is predominantly flat, two-dimensional, hardly convex or concave, without volume, and with no or only very slight elevations. Three types of shapes can be identified: geometric, amorphous, and polymorphous. The most characteristic geometric shapes are the triangle, the square, and the circle. Kandinsky referred to these as "primary forms" and compared them to primary colors because all other geometric shapes are composites or variations of one of these three primary shapes. The oval, for instance, is a derivative of the circle; the rectangle and the rhombus are variations of the square, and all polygons are principally combinations of triangles and squares. Polymorphic and many amorphic shapes are characterized by an absence of distinct geometric features and are often oblique, ambiguous, intricate, and anomalous; they are sometimes referred to as cloud, kidney, or microbe shaped.

In design shapes can perform various functions, the most frequently encountered being to represent three-dimensional forms either as flat projections, front planes, or impersonal simplifications. Any form in nature can be reduced to its bare essentials in shape and thereby rendered most clearly and concisely. When an object is represented only as a shape, it often loses most of its descriptive and trivial qualities and becomes an element which can be placed in an arrangement freely and objectively. Such simplified shapes can play a most significant role during the development of a composition; they permit the artist to concentrate solely on his arrangement because the forms have temporarily lost their story-telling quality. In other words, objects can be more freely arranged when viewed as shapes rather than as particular items.

Neither in painting nor in nature do shapes exist independently; they are always in space or surrounded by it. They are rarely found in isolation and exist chiefly in connection with other shapes. As soon as two or more shapes are perceived, a relationship becomes apparent; through such a relationship the spectator or creator establishes proportions. One shape by itself is neither large nor small—such size concepts are always based on a comparison either with the given area, with a familiar fact, or with something more tangible, such as another shape. The most frequent and intimate shape relationship is called overlapping. Overlapping exists in two forms; either one shape *blocks out* part of another, visually altering its appearance and

---

[67] Vasili Kandinsky, *Kandinsky, Point and Line to Plane,* Hilla Rebay, ed. (New York: The Solomon R. Guggenheim Foundation, 1947), p. 57.
[68] " 'Tension' is the force living within the element and represents only one part of the creative 'movement'." *Ibid.,* p. 57.

thus forming an entirely new unit, or the two shapes *retain* all of their visible contours despite the fact that one is placed partially over or in front of the other. In such instances the illusion of transparency is created.

A different relationship between shapes is established when they are arranged in a particular order or sequence. Such a sequence may either regress or progress. In a regressive sequence the smallest shape is at the beginning and the largest at the end of the succession; in a progressive sequence the largest shape is in the foreground and the smallest in the background. A progressive sequence of shapes in combination with overlapping can easily create an illusion of depth even when formal perspective is not used.[69] Shapes can also be arranged in repeated or rhythmical patterns. However, this particular aspect of arrangement is an intimate part of composition and is not closely related to the characteristics and functions of individual shapes.

Shapes as such carry within themselves certain characteristics which add meaning or feeling to a work. Geometric shapes, for instance, are often equated with beauty, certainty, and clearness. In Plato's words: "Geometry will draw the soul toward truth."[70] Symbolically the square represents perfection, the triangle strength, confidence, and possibly faith; the circle unity, closeness, and universality. Yet these symbolic attributes are not derived from the geometric shapes themselves but depend largely on their position in space. For instance, the triangle may convey a notion of strength as long as it rests on its broad base, but it loses this quality when turned upside down; in this position it appears precariously balanced and top-heavy, and conveys the idea of uncertainty and suspense rather than strength and confidence. The same is true of the square; as soon as it is tilted 90° it becomes diamond-shaped and is associated with many concepts other than perfection.

The meanings connected with polymorphic shapes are even more complex. Their possible symbolic quality is dependent not only on the context in which they are used but also on common associations, and their placement in space. They may be floating in space or resting on the ground; they may radiate stability or buoyancy, constancy or movement, or permanence and certainty, instability and restlessness.

The movement of shapes or lines in a painting is probably one of the most difficult concepts to clarify. As soon as a shape is portrayed on a two-dimensional surface it is permanently affixed. How then can we speak of the movement of shapes in a composition? The terms "movement" or "motion" are very relative ones, intimately connected with time. Commonly we think of movement as a rapid succession of changes, a ball flying, a boy running, now here, now there. But movement need not be rapid. The four seasons are a constant movement in time; a flower's life cycle from the bud to full bloom to its final wilting is actually one uninterrupted motion. Yet if we look at a flower we are rarely aware of seeing only one phase of a constantly changing process, a movement which lasts over a considerable span of time. Inasmuch as we commonly cannot see the life span of a flower as a movement, we literally do not perceive *any* movement. When we claim we see a motion, we really perceive a succession of individual impressions which are assembled and fused in our minds, as movement is recorded on a motion picture film. When we believe we see a movement, we are actually exposed to a situation where our eyes are compelled to jump, so to speak, in rapid succession from one vision to the next.

This form of compulsion can be induced by a "stationary" painting. An artist

---

[69] "Overlapping is of particular value in creating a sequence of objects in the depth dimension when the space conception of the picture relies on contour rather than on volume or light. For some painters space is realized best through a continuous series of overlapping objects, which lead the eye like steppingstones from the front to the back." Arnheim, *Art and Visual Perception,* p. 201.

[70] *Plato's The Republic,* VII, B. Jowett, trans., p. 271.

can arrange shapes so as to force a spectator's eyes to "leap" from one part of the painting to another, assembling the painting in his mind and thereby having an experience which simulates actual movement in time and space. Whenever this is accomplished in a two-dimensional work we speak of the composition as having movement. Characteristically, such attempts fail when a movement is *intended* but the spectator's interest is caught by one shape which does not lead his eyes to another, thus breaking the continuity, or by a shape which directs them away from and not *into* the work. Movement, however, is not an integral part of *shapes* since they themselves do not possess motion but can be arranged to convey an idea either of stability or of movement.

Shapes can be used in a composition to transmit static as well as dynamic impressions; in contrast, mass or form can be employed to convey static effects only. Mass as such is not an actual component of design on a two-dimensional plane; it is three-dimensional and has volume. Properly it pertains to such areas as architecture, sculpture, and volume design. Yet a significant part of certain compositions is the created illusion of mass as a three-dimensional form, and it is this illusion which is a structural element of design. The illusion of the plastic quality of a form in relation to design is most often called mass, and is usually synonymous with bulk, volume, and solidity.

Mass has height, width, and length. Its sides may be clearly visible, as in dice, or quite vague, as in clouds. They may be straight, convex, or concave, partially protruding or receding. Mass can have elevations, cavities, and forms within forms. Mass exists in simple geometric forms as well as in complex forms. The primary geometric forms which have volume are the sphere, the cone, the cylinder, the pyramid, the prism, and the cube. Their shape equivalents are the circle, the triangle, and the square. Any mass can be either simplified and reduced to one of these primary forms, or shaped by combining several of them. In these simplified forms, mass, like shapes, can be worked with objectively and can be overlapped and easily arranged. Temporarily deprived of its story-telling quality, it permits the artist to see it as a part of the composition rather than as a visual element of a thought or feeling.

Mass is an aggregation of particles, things, or beings; as such it has hardly any character of its own. Its color, texture, illusion of weight, and placement in space, and the context in which it is used determine its expressiveness and meaning despite the fact that mass or solidity often conveys the notion of strength and gravity. But depending on its treatment, mass can also give the idea of flabbiness and weakness, or buoyancy and gaiety. Frequently mass in a composition will add to movement by establishing a point of rest against which motion becomes more obvious.

Yet mass, more than line or shape, cannot be meaningfully understood without being contrasted with space. Space is a most difficult element to clarify, despite its presence in every design or composition.[71] Depending on purpose and point of view, many different kinds of space can be identified, for example, etheric, infinite and finite, inner and outer, and absolute and relative. "A definition of space which may at least be taken as a point of departure is found in physics—'space is the relation between the position of bodies'."[72] Defining it another way: space exists wherever movement in any direction is possible. In this context the antonym of space is solid. Space may be encountered in two distinctly different forms; one can be called undefinable, or infinite, and the other definable or finite space. Undefined space is all

---

[71] "The purpose of composition is to organize all the physical elements which make up a work of art into a coherent pattern, pleasing to the senses. If the work of art involves an illusion of *space*, then all these properties must contribute to that illusion." Read, *Education through Art*, p. 23.

[72] L. Moholy-Nagy, *The New Vision* (New York: W. W. Norton & Co., 1938), p. 163.

around us; a monument or a chapel on the hill stands in undefinable space. By contrast definable space has discernible limits, as the space in a bottle or a ring.

The frequently encountered terms "negative" and "positive" space are very confusing, particularly to students. Space has no characteristics of its own, but the terms "positive" or "negative" do; they imply either a suggestion of certainty (positive) or denial (negative). "Negative" also indicates a lack of affirmation, and "positive" indicates the existence of an absolute, or of an affirmative quality. Yet space, defined or undefined, is free of any attributes. It is neither laudable nor illaudable, neither beautiful nor ugly, neither real nor unreal. There is one possible exception to the neutral quality of space and that is entailed in the terms "above" and "below." "The 'above,' " Kandinsky points out, "gives the impression of great looseness, a feeling of lightness, of emancipation and, finally, of freedom. [By contrast] the effect of 'below' is completely contrary: condensation, heaviness, constraint."[73] Yet none of these indirect attributes are genuine properties of space. They are sensations related to space, just as claustrophobia or exaltation are due to feelings either of being incarcerated or of being in the wide open spaces. These sensations are similar to empathy with space; they are extremely personal and cannot be considered an inherent quality of space.

Considerable difference exists between space as it is perceived, and as it is represented. The visually untrained person rarely pays any attention to space. The beginner in art seems to feel that only in solids can he capture interest, arrest expression, and visualize ideas. When he represents a figure or any other object, he concerns himself mainly with the mass or form, paying little heed to the undefinable, and almost entirely ignoring the definable space. He is unaware, for example, that the front view of a person standing, his feet spread apart, his arms akimbo, embraces three definable spaces; each of these spaces is triangular and just as important as the solid mass. Definable space, however, does not exist only *within* objects or persons, but also between them. The space seen between two trees in a forest is defined, although the topmost boundary may be missing. Definable space exists everywhere indoors and outdoors, in still life, in rooms, and between flowers. These spaces are just as significant to the whole as the solid parts, and must be given equal attention. Yet this is very difficult for beginners since their space concept is extremely limited and consists mainly of an "above" and a "below." As soon as they have established these two, the two remaining important parts of the space concept, front and back, take on secondary importance. They consider "front" synonymous with the picture plane, and they either ignore "back" or try to represent it with a perspective of sorts; in fact, to most beginners "back" is not a direction in space but an attribute of a three-dimensional form. Their world consists of solids or nothingness, and space is either an empty word, or an area through which an airplane or a rocket can travel. Because of their lack of awareness or their failure to comprehend, they pay little attention even to these spaces which they cannot help but perceive.

Their lack of space awareness is less acute when students express themselves in three-dimensional forms. Sculpture consists of solids and definable space, mostly placed in a void, and is achieved largely through an interplay of mass and definable space. The sculptor's task is to establish the distribution of solids and defined space, and to determine how the mass should be seen in an undefined space. In contrast to the painter he need not *represent* space; he works with it as much as he works with solid materials and does not have to create its illusion on a flat surface.

Creating the illusion of space on a flat surface is very difficult. Space, in this context, entails two distinctly different concepts. One could be described as atmosphere or distance; as such it is active and contributes directly to the meaning of a composition. The other could be termed pause, rest, or circumjacence, and as such

---

[73] Kandinsky, *Kandinsky, Point and Line to Plane,* p. 117.

is rather passive. In a painting, for instance, the sky, regardless of its color, is an active part of a composition and adds directly to the understanding of a work. By contrast, the circumjacent background against which forms are placed is seemingly passive; "seemingly" because it does not appear to contribute a tangible idea to the visual statement. Yet these "passive" spaces are of the greatest importance; their roles are similar to the pauses in a musical composition which make preceding and following rapid movements of sound become more pronounced. Like the pause, the "passive" spaces frequently function by making solids discernible, or by conveying movement. As sound in music is contrasted with a sudden silence or pause, so in design shapes or masses must be contrasted with "passive" spaces; otherwise they will be unrecognizable and have no meaning. Since shapes or masses are so dependent on the active or passive space which either surrounds them (undefined), or is between or within them (defined), there must be as much attention given to space as to any of the other structural elements of design. Helping students to become aware of the significance of space is one of the teacher's most time-consuming and difficult tasks. Apparently the only way for him to accomplish it is by referring constantly to space, by pointing out definable spaces unceasingly, and by discussing them whenever any student's work is reviewed.

This brings to mind the question: How should the other structural elements of design, such as line, shape, and mass, be taught? Should they be presented separately, independently, and out of context? On an advanced level this is the way they are usually studied. In professional art schools and university art departments, the study of color, texture, line, shape, mass, and space is offered in courses separated from such subjects as graphics, painting, and drawing. Advanced art students with considerable previous experience in working with media and various forms of art expression usually profit most from such specialized courses. But it is questionable whether students without this previous experience are able to incorporate this knowledge into their own work even if they obviously can be taught to carry out all the required exercises, and can also learn and comprehend the various aspects of design.

If the structural elements are taught too early, there is considerable danger that the facts pertaining to each area will be used as a crutch, hampering rather than furthering the development of creativity. The more immature student believes that learning the integral components of design will provide him with simple rules or even absolutes with which he can solve every design problem. With the exception of an occasional exercise in arranging shapes or textures, high school students should learn the structural elements of design in an informal rather than in a rigid and formalized manner. The teacher should constantly refer to the various design elements, explain their function, point out their characteristics, and make use of them to clarify the success or failure of a work. In drawing, the line with its different possibilities should be incorporated in various assignments; in painting, problems related to shapes, space, and mass should be emphasized in a similar manner; in sculpture, space and solids should be clarified.

The same approach should be used on the high school level in relation to composition; its components—balance, harmony, contrast, rhythm, movement, and unity—should not be treated as separate entities. Their significance should be conveyed to students informally, whenever the occasion arises, particularly since each of these concepts is complex and difficult to separate and clarify. They are very closely related to each other and in many respects overlap. Balance, for instance, has two aspects—formal and informal. Formal balance is practically the same as symmetry, which is a constituent of harmony. Harmony is in many aspects synonymous with unity, and "formal unity is the same as balance which is achieved when all single parts are counterbalanced."[74]

---

[74] Wolf, *Dictionary of the Arts,* p. 747.

In a composition balance is achieved when opposing visual attractions (for instance, color) or forces (movements, shapes, or masses) equilibrate. The two most significant factors which determine balance are weight and direction; in a formal balance each is symmetrically divided. The distance from the fulcrum (or imaginary point of equilibrium) to each of the identical weights is exactly the same. In an informal balance, weights of different sizes counterbalance each other. The lengths from the fulcrum to each weight are no longer identical; they are changed so that the distance to the heavy weight becomes shorter, and the distance to the light weight longer. Yet this relatively simple principle of distribution of weights in an informal balance becomes complex as soon as colors enter the picture. Squares of identical size but of different colors have different "weights." For instance, "red is heavier than blue, and bright colors are heavier than dark ones. A black area must be larger than a white one in order to counterbalance it. This is due in part to the irradiation effect, which makes a bright surface look relatively larger."[75]

In a composition the problem of balancing colors is even more complex, since a color is usually not seen in isolation but is surrounded by others, which in turn exert a strong influence on one another. For instance, a small rectangle in brilliant yellow is perfectly balanced with a large black square if both are set against a purple background. But if the same squares are placed against a *white* background in an identical manner, they will no longer balance each other; the large black square now obviously dominates the small yellow one. Informal balance in a composition depends on many factors which cannot easily be classified meaningfully or stated in simple, definite rules.

The balance of a composition also depends on the desired meaning imbued in a work. A composition may be perfectly balanced if its upper three fourths are covered with a light and soft color, and its lower fourth with a dark and heavy shade. Yet if this same composition is turned upside down, the balance will be disturbed; the dark area will no longer counterbalance the large, light one, and the work will appear ill-balanced, top-heavy, and possibly displeasing. The oft-stated rule, that "turning a work upside down will reveal whether it is properly balanced," is not always applicable; it usually works only if many different shapes and colors of various intensities are used.

The concept of balance in regard to composition pertains mainly to critical judgment, and much less to the factual production of a creative work. The proficient artist uses this judgment to evaluate his achievement shortly before its completion. Through experience he has learned that balance in a work is something extremely precarious, dependent on many factors, and destroyed or established by a single stroke of the brush. During its growth, a work pendulates almost constantly between balance and imbalance, and therefore the artist cannot be certain that he has achieved a balanced composition until he has actually finished his task.

Being able to know whether or not a work is balanced results from a combination of two factors: heightened sensitivity, and experience. Sensitivity is developed through guided exposure; experience is gained simply by working with media. Two forms of guided exposure are possible. One is the study of great achievements, during which the problems of composition are given special attention and such matters as balance and unity are pointed out and explained. The other is a careful analysis of students' works, during which pieces of paper are used to cover up or temporarily change lines, areas, and colors, thereby proving how easily balance can be achieved or destroyed. Such brief demonstrations not only should help students learn how to examine their own works critically, or find ways to create balance or unity when it seems to be lacking, but should also give them tangible evidence that these complex

---

[75] Arnheim, *Art and Visual Perception,* p. 12.

matters are not based on individual whims but can be proved concretely despite the absence of fixed principles.

As indicated, there are no exact rules concerning either balance or unity which can be mechanically applied in order to obtain coherence in a work. "Unity" and "oneness" mean that all parts of a composition are integrated, that it has coherence and consistency. Yet unity is not synonymous with uniformity or monotony; it can have accents and emphases. In fact, unity is achieved through an interplay of dominant lines and areas, and weak and strong colors. In other words, unity in a composition must be achieved *in spite* of a conflict and not by elimination of it. The more conflicting elements are portrayed (such as contrasting lines, directions, or colors), the more dramatic is the composition. Unity is a fusion of various pictorial elements, each of which must play a significant part similar to the blending of different instruments in an orchestra. Just as all the instruments do not always carry the melody or play the same theme, so the various elements in a pictorial composition—a color, a line, or a space—may counteract or heighten each other's visual effectiveness and expressiveness. In fact interest is created when opposing visual elements are formed into a unit which predominates over these conflicting parts.

However, not every form of unity needs to be dramatic or have conflicts or movement. Therefore we can speak of static as well as of dynamic unity. In a static composition the emphasis is placed on inert forms which do not suggest motion; they are arranged to capture the eye of the spectator within limited areas of the pictorial plane. These areas, in relation to others, have been made to appear as the climax, to carry within themselves the total visual expression, superficially making other parts of the composition seem insignificant. Yet as soon as any of these seemingly unimportant parts are minutely altered, the whole composition loses its unity and its precarious static quality. Rembrandt's painting "Man with the Golden Helmet" is a good example; it has static unity, but if any line, shape, or color were to be only slightly changed the composition would fall apart. We would no longer see a man *with* a helmet *against* a background, but a man, *and* a helmet, *and* a background.

The same principle applies in the case of dynamic unity; movement is utilized so that the eye is led from one color, shape, or line to another in an endless motion, always returning to the same elements of the composition. This unending movement is synonymous with unity. As soon as it is disturbed and the eye is no longer led to return to its starting point, the unity is destroyed. Like balance, unity in a composition is extremely fragile and cannot be captured or determined until the very moment a work is finished. Therefore before a student has actually completed a painting, neither he nor the teacher can know whether unity has been established. In a case where a student fails, the teacher should help him realize by slow and careful analysis why and where he is unsuccessful, and what possible alternatives there are which will unify his work. Finally, every teacher should remember that "composition implies unity; the words are synonymous. To say that a composition lacks unity is a contradiction of terms. If it does, it is not a composition. In the fine arts unity is axiomatic."[76]

[76] Maitland Graves, *The Art of Color and Design* (New York: McGraw-Hill Book Co., Inc.), p. 90.

III Expression in Three Dimensions

Throughout history, regardless of culture or geographic region, man has formed and carved images with as much fervor as he has painted and drawn them. No one can say which of these means for visual expression came into being first, or gave man deeper satisfaction or greater freedom to convey his ideas. During some periods of history it would appear that more consideration was given to three-dimensional expression than to other art forms; but this cannot be definitely asserted since most artistic works, except those of stone or bronze, deteriorate and ultimately disappear. Still, during certain eras and in some geographic regions three-dimensional expression did dominate (as evidenced in the wood or stone carvings of the Aztecs, Mayas, and certain African tribes); throughout most periods of art, however, painting and sculpture were considered of equal importance, enjoying the same esteem, recognition, and attention.

The field of three-dimensional expression has often been divided into four large groups. One comprises all small works (statuettes, amulets, and fetishes); a second group embraces monumental sculpture, free standing, massive, and impressive, a third includes all those forms of sculpture which are primarily part of or dependent on architecture, and the fourth encompasses all works which are primarily nonrepresentational, or extreme simplifications of natural forms.

The function of the earliest known sculpture was probably related to aspects of idolatry. These works, "amulets," as Herbert Read has called them, were mainly symbols of fertility, deity, might, or fear. Most of the few surviving prehistoric pieces are small, carved in limestone, soapstone, or ivory, or modeled in clay. Many of these statuettes represent female bodies;[77] others portray animals, or, less often, male bodies.

Almost all prehistoric and primitive sculpture was conceived "in the round," which means that as much work and thought were devoted to the back and sides as to the front. This approach to sculpture changed markedly with the development of civilization. With man's increasing desire for edifices and his progress in the art of building, sculpture became an ever more intrinsic part of architecture, and incised, bas, and high relief consequently developed. The Egyptians, Assyrians, Babylonians, Greeks, and Romans enhanced their temples, palaces, and mausoleums with sculpture. The ancient and classical approach was dominated by the frieze in sunken or high relief, by the murallike treatment of wall carvings with permanently fastened figures, and by the caryatids and atlantes. The same intimate relationship between architecture and sculpture can be found in India and China, and in Central and South America. The practice of enhancing edifices with sculpture continued in west-

---

[77] "Prehistoric sculptors paid no attention to faces; they were interested only in the characteristic features of the body. Female characteristics, such as breasts and thighs, are strongly accentuated. It is generally believed that these statuettes were idols—images of goddesses of motherhood or childbirth. But it is possible that primitive artists merely liked to portray a principal object of their appreciation, either sexual or aesthetic—probably both." Leonhard Adam, *Primitive Art* (Harmondsworth, Middlesex: Penguin Books, 1949), p. 84.

ern culture almost until modern times. Outstanding examples can be found on such great Romanesque or Gothic cathedrals as those at Chartres, Lincoln, and Bamberg, documenting the significance and major function of this form of sculpture: to exalt and give magnificence to places of worship.

In the main, these powerful expressions in stone were carved to be seen against a stationary background and from a fixed position, and were not conceived as works "in the round"; the parts which remained out of sight were neglected. As some confusion exists as to when a sculpture is considered "in the round," one must distinguish clearly between an artist's concept and execution of his work, and the manner in which it is displayed. If the sculptor gave equal attention to all sides, disregarding how the piece would be seen outside his studio, he created a work "in the round"; if he conceived and worked out only those parts and sides which he knew would be in view and ignored all others, the work was not carved "in the round." The ancient Greeks are commonly credited with first having achieved monumental sculpture which was conceived "in the round." At the beginning of the Renaissance, it was again advocated that all sides of a major three-dimensional work are of equal importance and must therefore be given equal attention.

This last criterion is still considered valid today, and the sculptor wishing to comply with it is confronted with several problems peculiar to this form of expression. The most obvious problem is that of determining and accepting the limitations which are so characteristic of the plastic arts. The sculptor must be thoroughly aware of what *can* be meaningfully expressed in three dimensions, and what *cannot.* Such a restriction hardly exists for the painter, whose range of topic, approach, and mood is nearly unlimited. The sculptor's limitations are largely defined by the fact that sculpture is an expression in concrete terms, nearly devoid of illusion and subtle suggestion; whatever is formed or carved can be examined by touch and sight, and is thereby verified by two senses.[78] Moreover, the sense of touch perceives only what is tangible and can rarely be deluded. Unlike the painter, the sculptor cannot be vague; he can give neither an *illusion* of depth nor the *suggestion* of shape and expression, but must represent them in solid, concrete form. Because of these limitations inherent in the plastic arts, the sculptor is confined to visual phenomena which possess emotion and movement, permitting him to present a new, significant interpretation and insight.

"The topmost aim of all plastic art," said Goethe, "is to render the dignity of man within the compass of the human form. To this aim every nonhuman element, in so far as it lends itself to treatment in this medium, must subordinate itself."[79] From prehistoric times to the present, nearly all representational three-dimensional works of art have belonged to one of three groups. The largest embraces all aspects of representations of man, and the other two all representations of man with animal, and animals only. With rare exceptions, man himself has been a subject of endless fascination for the sculptor: he has represented him young and old, nude and clothed, alone and in a group; has shaped his whole body and parts of it—head, torso, hands; has transformed him into god and devil, angel and satyr; into a symbol of wisdom, folly, might, meekness. Sculptured creations have evoked the gamut of human emotions from veneration to pity, from hatred to love, from admiration to rejection.

Next to portraying man alone, the sculptor seems to have found the subject of man with an animal most suitable for embodying thoughts and feelings. Although

---

[78] "Good sculpture develops the sense of touch. And it is not always necessary to touch it; it is sufficient to know that one can do so. A sculpture has no value if it does not awaken in us this longing." W. R. Valentiner, *Origins of Modern Sculpture* (New York: Wittenborn & Co., 1946), p. 11.
[79] Curtis, *Goethe, Wisdom and Experience,* p. 242.

HORSEMAN
Marino Marini
bronze

F. M. Hall Collection, University of Nebraska

hunting or fighting with animals was an ancient recurring theme, the mounted man was and still is a most favored subject, and has been executed in variations (man riding on a donkey, a horse, a buffalo, or a camel), in relief as well as in the round. The mounted man can be found in Assyrian and Persian reliefs, in Greek friezes, in tombs, on Gothic cathedrals, and as a major subject of Roman and Renaissance monuments. That the idea has never in more than two thousand years lost its attraction appears to derive from psychological and formalistic reasons. From a psychological point of view the rider symbolizes man's power over the beast, and the beast symbolizes nature; accordingly, the work can be interpreted to mean man's conquest of nature. It may also suggest man's superiority over all those who are below his elevated position, the movement of the horse emphasizing his strength and power. In the more modern approach, however, such sculptures often represent man's closeness to nature. The horse again symbolizes nature, but nature as it comprises man's terrestrial roots, his past, and his heritage. From a formalistic point of view, since the rider is passive (he sits and is carried) while the horse is active (it moves), the sculptor is relieved in part of the necessity to solve one of his most difficult problems—that of representing movement convincingly. Only the horse needs to convey the feeling of movement, which the sculptor may try to suggest by exaggerating taut muscles and tendons to contrast with flat and relaxed ones. Through such subtle means a sculptor may capture movement in an immobile form without seemingly freezing it or giving the impression of rigor mortis.

There is still another reason why the equestrian statue has always been considered a fascinating subject. Because they know that the work will be set high on a pedestal and thus not be viewed in an ordinary way, sculptors have felt free to exaggerate forms and take liberties, which they seldom dared do with other realistic subjects. Exaggerations of forms are even more pronounced in relief representations where the sculptor, not having the problem of balancing his forms, carved even more extreme movements, giving the theme profound drama and life.

Obviously not all equestrian statues show movement. Sometimes the subject is treated in repose, the horse standing quietly on three or four legs, the rider sitting calmly. In these cases, the interplay of forms and defined space becomes a matter of significance; the statue is no longer a solid form but a perforated mass, and space becomes an added vehicle through which motion, thoughts, and feelings are conveyed. Defined space becomes a particular matter of conscious concern—for instance, the space between the horse's legs, from its body to the ground, and the space within the pose of the rider himself. The equestrian statue gives the sculptor an opportunity to demonstrate his skill and his control over both the solid form and space.

In animal sculpture the same problems exist in representing suggested motion and establishing an interplay between solids and space. Most of the early statues of animals were conceived in a solid mass, conveying repose and quiescence. (Cats carved by the ancient Egyptians are probably the most famous examples.) Later, statues began to show animals in motion: prowling, attacking, jumping, or showing agitation. In fact, from prehistoric times until today all living creatures—birds, fish, insects, or reptiles—have been immortalized in three dimensions. There are numerous reasons for the interest in and predilection for this subject. In many early cultures certain animals were considered holy and represented deities (for example, the cat, the baboon, and the zebu); later others (such as the lamb, the fish, and the dove) were endowed with sacred symbolic meanings; still others became secular symbols, the lion representing courage and power, the eagle valor and pride, and the dog loyalty and dependability. Furthermore, from the beginning of recorded time, man has always been in close contact with animals; they have provided him with food, with services, and with companionship. The last, particularly, seems to have resulted in man's attributing to animals almost human qualities, projecting on them the thoughts and feelings which he possesses and for which he longs. To him an animal can be sad or happy, lonesome or companionable, hostile or friendly. Like him it can be hungry and thirsty, content and satisfied, cautious and afraid, spirited and fearless. Above all, it is alive, it moves, it acts, and it possesses a will to survive.

Man enjoys observing animals; the graceful movements of the deer or gazelle delight him, the antics of monkeys amuse him, the strength of the buffalo or elephant impresses him, the elegant motions of birds charm him, and the fluent movements of lizards and snakes fascinate him. The sculptor, enchanted with these movements and shapes, aware of the potentialities of revealing the beauty of forms and surfaces as well as emotions, has never tired of translating animals into works of art. He has formed them in clay, sculptured them in marble and granite, carved them in wood. He has portrayed them alone, in pairs, in groups, in repose, in action, and purely for their own sake, or for decorative purposes. Animal sculptures have adorned buildings; they have been found in temples, churches, and museums; they have been set high on pedestals, have been sculptured as free-standing monuments, and have been rendered in miniature. Today they are still a favorite subject and have engrossed such contemporary artists as Picasso, Brancusi, and Calder.

An important question remains: Why are the subjects which can be treated in representational sculpture confined largely to man and other living creatures, a limitation which is unknown in painting? One reason is that sculpture is more confining than painting; moods, illusive impressions, vagueness, and subtleties can hardly be expressed in three dimensions. Moreover, unlike a painting which lets the spectator project himself into the depicted situation, the statue allows him only to feel with or for whatever has been carved or modeled; form and mass are tangible and seldom permit the spectator to see or feel more than what is factually there. A painted subject is never represented in isolation; it is always set permanently against an unchanging background. The background surrounds the subject, adds meaning to it, and frequently lends a particular mood or atmosphere to the work. This atmosphere is created partially by the light and shadow which are irrevocably established by the painter. In contrast, the sculptor is much more restricted; he is limited to the isolated subject (the solid form) and must express his thoughts and feelings within these narrow confines. He can neither imbue the background with parts of his idea nor create a supporting atmosphere. The sculptor can never be certain how and under what conditions his work will be seen; it may be bathed in sunlight or enveloped in a soft haze; it may be illuminated from above, below, or from the side. Yet a good statue should be effective not only from all sides but in any light, indoors or outdoors.

As already indicated, one of the sculptor's most difficult problems is to find ways not to arrest movement but to suggest it convincingly. The captured motion is not isolated accidentally from a chain of actions, but is carefully weighted to suggest what has probably happened before and what may happen an instant later. "This single moment [the sculptor] makes as pregnant as possible, and endows it with all the illusions which art commands . . . in the representation of visible objects."[80] The better the sculptor is able to capture this single instant without conveying a feeling of static finality, permitting the spectator to anticipate what the next moment may bring, the more he has succeeded in endowing his figures with inevitability. "Even in those of my works in which action is less pronounced," said Rodin, "I have always sought to give some indication of movement. I have very rarely represented complete repose. I have always endeavoured to express the inner feeling by the mobility of the muscles."[81] It is exactly this "inner feeling," this "indication of movement," which sets a three-dimensional work of art so far apart from an imitation, a mechanically made cast, or a purely decorative carving.

A still different approach to creating the illusion of movement in static form is virtually the same as that employed by painters: first, attracting the attention of the spectator briefly to the whole, then inducing him to focus on a single part of the work, next guiding his vision to others, and finally compelling him to form an image of the whole in his mind. Lessing said: "Our senses perform these various operations with so astonishing a swiftness that they seem to us but one, and this swiftness is imperatively necessary if we are to arrive at a conception of the whole, which is nothing more than the result of the conceptions of the parts and their

---

[80] Gotthold Ephraim Lessing, *Laocoon,* William A. Steel, trans. (E. P. Dutton & Co., 1930), p. 71.
[81] Gsell, *Art by Auguste Rodin,* p. 66.

combination."[82] The sculptor gives direction to his forms; he simplifies, indents, or projects them so that the spectator's eyes will be caught somewhere for an instant, and then will continue to sweep the work, following the artist's intentions. Creating the illusion of movement is more difficult for the sculptor than for the painter since the sculptor must induce the desire in the spectator to see more than that side which he accidentally encounters first; the work must convey sufficient movement so that the onlooker, walking around it, will find life,[83] meaning, and interest from any position.

Finally, in attempting to answer the question of why the sculptor until very recently has restricted himself to subjects dealing with man and other living creatures, it must be kept in mind that his primary task is twofold: to synthesize and combine in a three-dimensional work aspects of reality containing feelings, thoughts, and movements, and also to transform an inert mass into an image. This image should be so fascinating or provocative, so suggestive and convincing as to make the spectator momentarily forget that he actually sees nothing but a stone, or a piece of wood or metal. If this is to be achieved, the image must be of such a nature that the spectator can effortlessly establish an inner relationship with it. Symbols or images which do not represent living beings can rarely be adapted to these basic criteria. Empathy seldom occurs when forms have been inspired by or represent inanimate objects. Yet a brief fusion between the spectator and the sculptured work must take place if the work is to be truly effective. This union occurs involuntarily, and takes place most readily when a plastic work is inspired by living creatures endowed with vitality, feelings, and meanings with which a spectator can identify himself.

One recent form of expression in three dimensions is outside of these criteria and belongs to a totally different category. This group is often incorrectly referred to as "abstract sculpture," thus combining two distinctly different approaches to modern sculpture. In one approach man or animal is portrayed in extreme simplifications but is still representational in concept. Everything an artist believes nonessential is excluded, and the quintessence is stressed or exaggerated. Such works are usually without reference to a particular time, occasion, or locale; they express broad generalizations, timeless in character and universal in meaning, but not truly nonobjective. Most works by Archipenko, Moore, and Lipshitz, for instance, are characterized by this approach.

In genuinely nonobjective or experimental sculpture, the artist attempts to give form to an aspect of reality which has previously existed only in his mind as a thought or notion. While this "new" reality has its roots in the known world, it has been altered and transposed to such an extent that it appears void of any reference to its basic origin. These three-dimensional forms are often claimed to represent aspects of the cosmos or the universe, and are referred to as archetypal or biological. At times they are given deep symbolic significance and are believed to represent symbols from man's unconscious. At other times they have been enjoyed as purely aesthetic creations void of reference to anything but form, texture, and space. Here "the form is made to please: there is a free play with the form that is independent of function."[84]

It is another characteristic of these nonobjective works that "not the representation of an object, or even of a feeling, is the real problem here, but the sovereign

---

[82] Lessing, *Laocoon,* p. 61.

[83] Rodin said: "Art cannot exist without life. If a sculptor wishes to interpret joy, sorrow, any passion whatsoever, he will not be able to move us unless he first knows how to make the beings live which he evokes. For how could the joy or the sorrow of an inert object—of a block of stone—affect us? Now, the illusion of life is obtained in our art by good modelling and by movement. These two qualities are like the blood and the breath of all good work." Gsell, *Art by Auguste Rodin,* p. 66.

[84] Herbert Read, *The Art of Sculpture* (New York: Pantheon Books, 1956), p. 35.

organization of relationships of volume, of material, of mass, of shape, direction, position and light."[85] Yet the organization of relationships of volume or materials are abstract concepts, and if these concepts are divorced from the obvious reality and treated independent of concrete references to life, they become obscure and difficult to comprehend.

Yet in terms of content, the vagueness of nonrepresentational sculpture is not without appeal for many sophisticated spectators; it permits them to project their own ideas into these works, to interpret them in individual ways, or fallaciously to discover meanings which are neither self-evident nor intentionally inferred by the artist. This form of attraction to a work of art, however, is of dubious merit; it has little bearing on the work as such since the spectator is fascinated by his own thoughts and reactions rather than by the thoughts of the creator, or by the creation itself. Yet it would be wrong to believe that nonrepresentational sculpture is nothing but a device carefully designed to animate the imagination of a casual spectator, or to provide him with configurations which he may interpret as a game. On the contrary, many of these works are significant interpretations of an aspect of reality which is relatively unique, and is characteristic of our century. The innumerable "firsts"—the countless new concepts, findings, and innovations in every field of human endeavor—which are representative of our time are often reflected in these works. The microcosm with its ever-growing significance has also become a constant source of inspiration for the modern sculptor. Here the epitome is not man but the living cell, and life is no longer related to emotions, thoughts, and feelings, but to motion, structure, and form. What matters is the impersonal and the fundamental, not the individual, the humane, or the subjective. In nonrepresentational sculpture, therefore, life is frequently interpreted without specific reference to man, his tribulations and felicities, and is understood as the essential which pertains to all forms of existence, be it a plant, a micrococcus, or any living force found in the macrocosm. This essential is the living cell, a composite of various geometric shapes and spheres; these basic elements are transposed into visual structures which consist of forms, lines, and patterns, and are arranged in rhythms which often have symmetry and balance.

But the fundamentals of living forms are not the only source of inspiration for the nonobjective sculptor. Sensitive to his environment, he is frequently influenced by machines, industrial structures, and modern edifices and their underlying scientific principles; he is inspired by new materials or, as a result of technological progress, finds new ways to exploit old ones. In consequence, totally new forms have been created which bear no semblance to any previously encountered in the world of art. Many others are images in space, either possessing actual movement—instead of merely giving the illusion of motion—or appearing dynamic in spite of being static. The source of inspiration for these particular images are the various forms of motion all around us: the graceful movements of leaves in the wind, the purposeful motion of machines, the artistic and flowing movements of a dance or a musical composition. These aspects of the world which previously were largely ignored have become major subjects for the contemporary sculptor.

Many nonobjective works are the result of a search for images which reveal or express order; they are an immediate consequence of our recent past with its horrible wars, of dramatic social changes, and of the almost frightening technological innovations which seem to have intensified man's longing for order. These new images exemplify order instead of feelings or emotions, and have aesthetic merit because they reflect the order which is innate in all substance—an organic order found in all living matter—rather than the order which is frequently associated with uniformity, classification, rules, or severe discipline.

---

[85] L. Moholy-Nagy, *The New Vision,* p. 155.

SMALL FORM RESTING
Barbara Hepworth
white marble

Collection of the Nebraska Art Association, University of Nebraska Art Galleries

Among the most prominent contemporary sculptors who have expressed themselves in nonobjective terms are Barbara Hepworth, Jean Arp, Alexander Calder, Naum Gabo, and Antoine Pevsner. As evidenced in their writings, the underlying concepts and thoughts in their works are very intricate, the result of years of preoccupation with purely artistic problems and a thorough awareness of the many problems and perplexities of our time. Although many of these works have their roots in simple observations, direct experiences, and universally accepted ideas, they are not simple manifestations but extremely complex visual statements.

Not surprisingly, young people have great difficulty in understanding or enjoying nonobjective sculpture. Their lack of experience in thinking in abstract concepts, their unfamiliarity with artistic expressions not obviously connected with their intimate environment, and their characteristic insecurity (most evident when confronted with something new) all hamper their ability to appreciate these works. Only slowly, through guided exposure and with increasing maturity, will they be able to understand and derive pleasure from these contemporary forms of expression. Appreciation of nonobjective sculpture is a question of time; it cannot be forced by having students imitate it.

For most adolescents a work of art must be expressive and reveal meaning, stimulate them, and permit them to identify themselves with it; otherwise it will antagonize them. When they are working with three dimensions, their own attitude toward creating resembles that of a primitive sculptor who "works with the knowledge that he is creating, not a lifeless object, but a living form. Emotion determines form, as it does in all expressionistic art, and once the form has been determined it *contains* the emotion."[86] It is exactly this emotion contained in a sculpture which

[86] Read, *The Art of Sculpture,* p. 43.

appeals to young people, and if a work does not immediately manifest this quality it often remains outside their understanding and interest.

The question arises: Why should sculpture be taught to adolescents? Why are opportunities to draw, print, or paint not sufficient to develop creativity and an understanding of art? Michelangelo supplied an answer when he wrote: "Painting and sculpture are equal; if this be so, every painter should not fail to practise sculpture as well as painting, and similarly every sculptor painting as well as sculpture."[87] Thus in order to strengthen and heighten the capability for expression in one form of visual art, the other form must be cultivated also. Michelangelo and Leonardo da Vinci demonstrated this, as well as many more recent painters like Thomas Eakins, Degas, Renoir, and Picasso, all of whom at times devoted themselves to three-dimensional works.

There is still another aspect to the question of why sculpture should be taught in high schools. Most young people, acquainted with only a few forms of artistic expression, do not know which of the many media and modes are best suited to their particular temperaments or aptitudes. Only exposure to various forms of expression and work with numerous basic materials will help them discover their own abilities and preferences. Through guided experiences they will be able to conquer their prejudices, overcome their ignorance, and uncover their capabilities. The last in particular is not easy; even outstanding artists often need a long time to discover in which media and modes of expression they can find most inner satisfaction, which one offers them the greatest opportunity to release their imagination, and which is best suited to their artistic temperament. Modigliani, for example, started as a sculptor but became famous as a painter; Maillol and Marini began as painters but are known today chiefly as sculptors.

Modeling

To understand fully the educational value and creative possibilities which sculpture provides for high school students, the whole field must be divided into its basic components: modeling, sculpturing, and working in relief. The oldest known three-dimensional work modeled in clay was found in a cave next to a large wall painting. Apparently man discovered very early in his history that moist clay could be formed, and that it would retain its shape after it had dried and hardened. The same discovery is made time and again by very young children playing with mud or sand. It seems that scratching lines into a soft surface and forming shapes with moist earth are natural human activities; proof of this can be found on every continent and in every period of history and culture. Giving distinct form to an amorphous mass appears to satisfy the almost instinctive desire to create. In brief, forming shapes from clay is one of the oldest activities known to man; it is timeless and has never lost its significance.

Clay is a natural product which consists mainly of kaolin, water, and possibly some quartz (or other silica), feldspar, alumina, or mica. Modeling with clay is essentially a growth process, a method consisting largely of adding to and developing a form slowly and by degrees. It is a characteristic of modeling that the action usually comes first and the critical judgment moments later. Possibly a more important characteristic is the fact that clay is chiefly a temporary medium, used primarily for preliminary work; the final statement is usually made in a different and more permanent medium. This factor, among others, sets modeling quite apart from sculpture. When carving in stone or wood the artist actually thinks and works constantly in the medium which becomes his final creation.

---

[87] Leonardo da Vinci, *Paragone,* Irma A. Richter, trans. (London: Oxford University Press, 1944), p. 91.

Modeling may be approached in two ways: by developing the form solely from clay, or by building it over a supporting wire skeleton (armature). In the first approach, mass is strongly emphasized; in the second, attention is divided equally between mass and space. The first approach has both advantages and disadvantages. Working in solids without first building an armature forces students to think in terms of a compact mass, and helps them to develop a genuine feeling for three dimensions. Also they can postpone final decisions regarding the movement, size, and shape of the piece for a considerable time during the beginning phases; they can still add to the form, they can bend, twist, dent, pull, and elongate it without difficulties. Probably the greatest disadvantage of this method is that the form must remain more or less solid and compact; perforations are difficult to achieve without the support of a wire skeleton.

The other approach, modeling over a wire armature, permits students to utilize freely an interplay of solid and space, and gives them considerable assurance that the work in progress will not accidentally change or collapse. The armature's disadvantage is that the sculptor must envision his project clearly in advance and shape the wire skeleton accordingly. Soon after he begins to work he cannot easily change what has been started and is more or less compelled to follow his original plan.

Before students begin to model a solid form with clay, they should be given a set of simple rules to help them avoid the failure and discouragement caused by a lack of technical knowledge or experience. Such basic rules should cover the following points:

1. Always build with relatively small pieces of clay, first determining the height of the masses and causing them to grow out into space.
2. Work three-dimensionally over the entire design, building the larger masses first.
3. Continue this building process, using progressively smaller pieces of clay until the design is complete.
4. Underbuild rather than overbuild.
5. Consider the consequences of a change or correction before making it. There are usually two or three ways of effecting a change—use judgment in deciding the best one.
6. Use modeling tools when the fingers are unsatisfactory.
7. Do not try to shape or change the form by pushing or squeezing. Use only sufficient pressure to make the pieces of clay adhere.
8. Do not work meaninglessly; the form should be touched only when you are consciously and deliberately building or cutting to make corrections.
9. Do not rub the clay. Rubbing will not make a smooth surface, but will deaden the form. Work for an evenness rather than slickness.
10. Do not try to model edges to knife-like sharpness; the nature of the material does not grant that. Relative sharpness is sufficient.[88]

Perhaps one of the best ways to acquaint students with modeling in solids is to have them form a human head—a massive form in which movement and expression can be included almost effortlessly. This subject can be approached in several ways but should never be carried out smaller than half life-size; otherwise students are apt to encounter difficulties when working with their hands directly on the form and are forced to rely solely on tools. Modeling with fingers is most desirable since students can not only see but literally feel their work progress. Modeling should be a tactile as much as a visual experience, and the utilization of touch sensations should be considered of major importance.

In one approach to modeling a human head, a basic or more or less cylindrical shape is made first for the neck, and next a partially oval or egglike (front view), partially circular form (back and top view) is shaped. These two shapes should be

---

[88] Jules Struppeck, *The Creation of Sculpture* (New York: Henry Holt & Co., 1952), pp. 29–30.

symmetrical and carefully balanced, so that one side is exactly like the other. The forehead is added to these impersonal forms; then places for the eyes are indented, the cheekbones heightened, the jawbones formed, and finally the nose superimposed. Only after all these parts of the head have been attended to conscientiously should the hair and ears be fashioned. This method is intended to prevent students from modeling aimlessly without control or understanding and running into difficulties which often are almost impossible to correct. As a rule, the greatest difficulty for beginners is to form and provide sufficient space for the upper and lower jawbones and the forehead and hair. The above method of systematically developing a head should help beginning students to understand the individual forms and their relation to each other, but is not so dictatorial as to hamper freedom of expression. In a different and slightly more advanced approach to modeling the human head, students should be asked first to form the simplified shape of a skull, and then to model the head by slowly adding small pieces of clay to the skull-like form. They may be encouraged to give a definite character to their work, such as a sleepy child, an angry young man, or a friendly old woman.

Many other subjects may also help students develop a feeling for a massive form, and for the beauty and impact which can be created with simple and compact shapes. A basic theme may evolve around the hunched, resting, or crouching figure (man or animal). In such an assignment, emphasis should be placed on simple, elementary forms and plain areas, devoid of detail and ornament. Expression and interest should be confined to the play of simple planes which may be curved or angular, protruding or receding. In modeling a crouched figure, students may pose briefly for each other, and should be reminded to study the front as well as the back and both sides. Moreover, they should be told that success or failure is often determined by the meaning and interest given to the back and sides as well as to the front. At times they should be encouraged to close their eyes and feel whether their incomplete works convey the intended meaning and form. In modeling an animal (dog or cat), the ideal situation is to have the pet in the room, but if this is impossible students should first briefly study animal forms in short documentary films, or in good photographs, and in an anatomical atlas. Even more important is the teacher's explanation emphasizing the characteristics of the different animals, their bone and muscle structure, and the size relationships of the various body parts.

Innumerable other themes exist for this type of modeling assignment: a reclining figure, a fallen angel, a beggar, a man sitting and whistling, a kneeling person praying, symbols for day and night, someone huddled against a storm, or a memorial. Subjects pertaining to animals may include a sleepy fawn or calf, a sitting frog, a watching owl, or a grazing bull. Such projects should not be less than six inches in height or width; otherwise the forms become too small and the work too fragile, losing its educational value. Other ideas can be gleaned from publications on sculptors and their works, which are treasure-troves of excellent suggestions well worthy of being introduced to high school students who, with their limited skill, can interpret them in their own way, often without much difficulty.

Before discussing the other approach to modeling (working with solids and defined space), it may be wise to give some attention to the old and still unresolved question of whether or not a three-dimensional work should first be sketched on paper, or improvised directly in wax or clay. Seen objectively, no one method is superior to the other; both have been used successfully by famous sculptors. (For instance, Rodin "sketched" mostly in clay, Barlach with charcoal on large pieces of paper.) The question remains: Which of the two ways should be given preference in the classroom, and why? Improvising directly in clay seems to help students most to come to grips with a three-dimensional idea. The reasons are, first, that because of lack of experience with three-dimensional work many students have great difficulty in envisioning more than one view of the projected sculpture; and second, that when they actually feel the clay, model forms, and see volume growing under their hands, they are often more strongly stimulated and their imagination is more aroused than by drawing. This is most noticeable when they are working in a *solid* form.

In the high school two methods for three-dimensional work should be used, some projects started with a solid lump of clay, others with a carefully built wire armature. Many beginners find it difficult to envision their contemplated projects in volume while building the armature. Working with wire is to them almost the same as drawing contour lines; their first attempts are usually rather lineal, often lacking movement and depth, or the wire skeleton becomes an end in itself instead of a means to an end. Because beginners frequently have little feeling for plastic expression, they rarely make allowances for the bulk which will be added to the wire skeleton. Obviously, therefore, students should have had several experiences with modeling in solids before starting to work with solids and space, and the required building and shaping of wire armatures.

When students are modeling a project requiring a wire armature, it is sometimes advisable to give them the option either to block out the intended idea on paper, simply and in heavy black areas, showing several different views, or else to begin immediately by building an armature. The armature, however, should be made with both the conventional heavy wire and with fine wire (stovepipe wire); the latter should be twisted around the heavier wire to simulate volume and indicate where mass will be built up. This may help students realize the plastic quality of the projected work, possibly forcing them to change, twist, and bend the wire forms before starting the actual modeling in clay. It can never be stressed too strongly that students should study carefully their completed wire armatures from *all* sides *before* any modeling on it is initiated. It is not easy for them to understand that these wires later dictate the action, and that once the actual modeling has begun they will be caught, hardly able to alter anything without destroying nearly all that was done before.

When working in solids and space on an armature, attention must be equally divided between the defined space and the solid form. Moreover, suggested movement becomes a more acute problem when space is an active partner of modeling. Forms move in and out, space attracts attention, drawing toward the work or detracting from it. When students model in this technique they must learn to think not only of the subject matter but also of form and space, and to realize that what matters in a work of art is not only *what* is said but *how* it is said.

This approach to modeling—visually destroying the mass, so to speak, cutting in and out—is not without its perils. "[It] tends not only to looseness and imprecision of form but also to a preoccupation with surface effects to the detriment of mass. Cutting tends to monolithic rigidity, to a fear of freedom."[89] Proof of the correctness of this observation can be found in any art room where beginning students learn to work with an armature. One of the few ways to help them shed some of their rigidity and gain more freedom is to have them form a human figure which expresses a distinct emotion and movement. It is only when students become emotionally involved in their work that they begin to lose that insecurity which frequently causes rigidity. The choice of subject and the stimulation and encouragement given during the working sessions do much to determine their interest and their willingness to overcome their natural inhibitions. The range of subjects is almost unlimited; every human emotion and activity can be translated into a three-dimensional expressive form, as for instance such simple happenings as a baby taking its first steps, a boy enthusiastically watching an event, a man dreamily gazing at the stars, or a thirsty

---

[89] Read, *The Art of Sculpture,* p. 77.

woman drinking. Other more general suggestions might be a prophet, a discoverer, a lawgiver, or a statue for a humanitarian (the unknown rescuer, a doctor, nurse, or donor). These few examples are broad enough to be interpreted in many ways, to be translated from various artistic points of view, and to be meaningfully expressed by many different types of young people.

Shortly after students have selected a subject and have bent the wires of their armatures, but before they begin to model with clay, they should be urged to study the structural features of the human body, perhaps by literally feeling their own. Such a study should help students to comprehend that the appearance of a form is not accidental but is based on a cause, and that what is seen is usually the effect of this cause. In the human figure every protrusion is caused either by the anatomical structure or the results of constrictions of muscles or compressed flesh, and the skin is only an exterior layer which follows the forms underneath.[90] The more clearly this is understood, the better the form can be controlled and given meaning. For this reason students should be asked to develop their projects by first modeling a semblance of the bone structure, then adding muscles, and finally shaping suggestions of clothes. At times it may be wise to encourage them to exaggerate individual forms: to elongate what is supposed to be long, shorten what is supposed to be compact, make heavier what is to be massive, and scale down what is to be thin. In addition students should be reminded frequently to keep the individual forms plain, simple, and devoid of details. Their desire to add details is often motivated by a vague awareness of shortcomings; not knowing how to overcome these defects they attempt either to detract from or hide them. Yet even when details are intrinsic parts of the total design they should be added sparingly, and incorporated only shortly before the work is finished. Examples of such details are folds, accessories, or textural differences in clothing and hair.

One aspect of modeling details is synonymous with surface treatment. In clay nearly any texture can be achieved: smooth or ragged, sleek or coarse, uniform or disparate. Any reason for emphasizing the surface must be based on the meaning of the work; in good sculpture the surface is fused with the form and contributes to its meaning. But the problem of surface treatment is still more complex: "Sculpture must be lovely to touch, [and] friendly to live with, not only well made," said Brancusi.[91] Yet not all sculpture is lovely to touch, even though it may be powerful and expressive in its appearance; then again it may be pleasing to the touch but displeasing to the eye. It may look too worked over and "fussed with," the surface consequently taking on exaggerated importance. Sometimes students labor under the impression that scraping and rubbing the surface and giving it an extremely smooth finish will enhance their work. Actually such an almost machine-made appearance often detracts from the piece instead of enhancing it. Students should be encouraged either to accept the rough qualities which are so typical of clay modeling, or to find a textural treatment which will add to the meaning of the work, and not merely to its appearance. At times it may be advisable to show reproductions of works which were originally modeled in clay and distinctly show different textures (Rodin, Rosso, Epstein, Degas, Marcks), or to give students an assignment simply to create five to ten different textures with clay. Both approaches may help them become aware of the various possibilities of treating the surface.

Modeling on an armature need not necessarily be carried out in clay only; a

---

[90] Rodin said, "instead of imagining the different parts of a body as surfaces more or less flat, I represented them as projectures of interior volumes. I forced myself to express in each swelling of the torso or of the limbs the efflorescence of a muscle or of a bone which lay deep beneath the skin. And so the truth of my figures, instead of being merely superficial, seems to blossom from within to the outside, like life itself." Gsell, *Art by Auguste Rodin,* p. 60.

[91] Malvina Hoffman, *Sculpture Inside and Out* (New York: W. W. Norton & Co., 1939), p. 53.

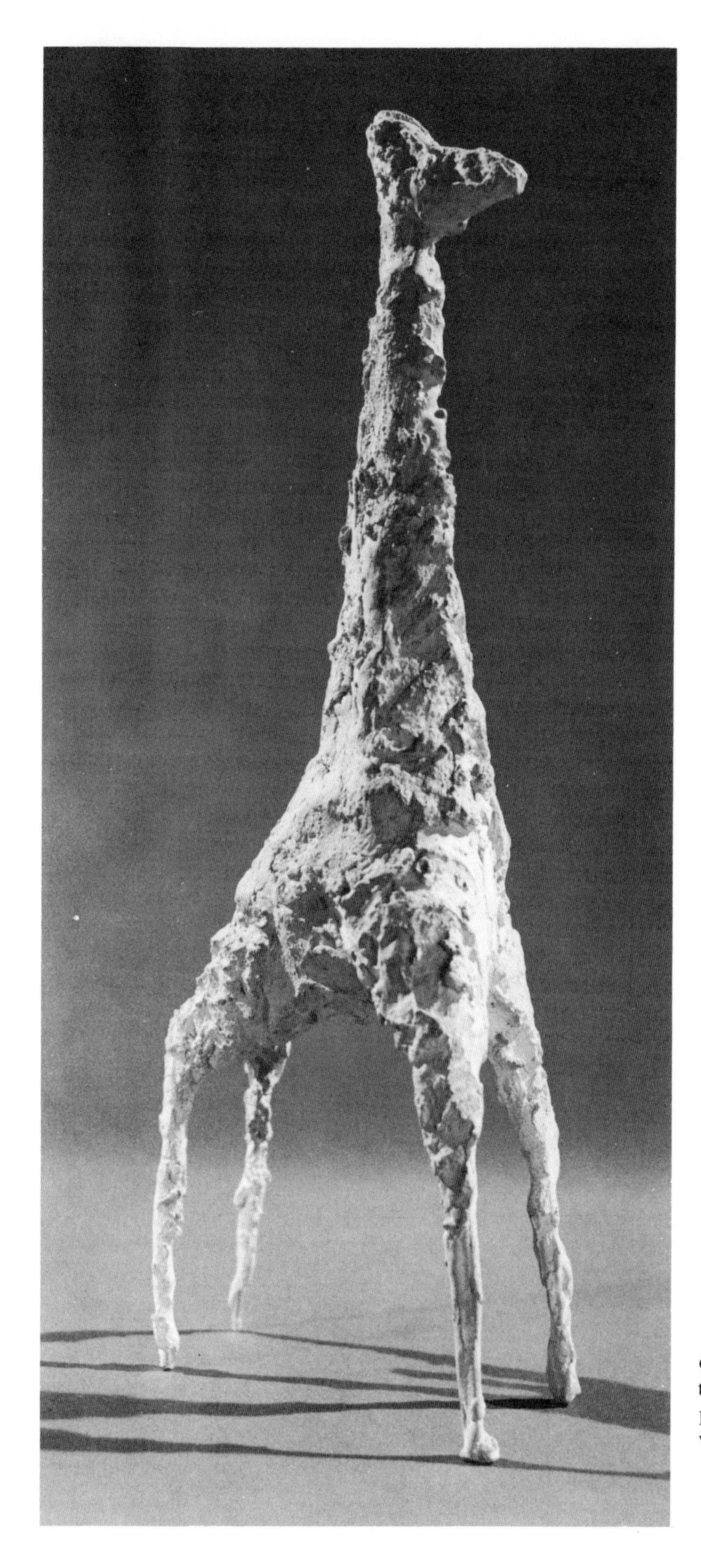

GIRAFFE
tenth grade boy
plaster of Paris on
wire armature

wholly different material which can also be effectively used in this combination is gypsum, better known as plaster of Paris. Modeling with wet plaster is similar in many respects to working with clay (for instance, the process also involves the gradual building up of a form by adding small lumps), yet in other respects it is quite different. Plaster of Paris forces students to work rather rapidly, and in the early stages leaves them little time to concentrate on anything but basic forms. Also the material is more permanent than soft clay, hardens rapidly, permits fewer corrections, and therefore conveys the feeling that what is being done is fairly final. As soon as the plaster begins to set, it becomes firm and cannot be changed accidentally, but parts can be added without any difficulty as long as it is kept moist or is remoistened. Even after it has hardened it can be scraped, sanded, or carved, provided it is moistened again. In plaster of Paris the many surface textures—except those which are a direct result of the working method—can be achieved only by careful and deliberate work. In addition to being very inexpensive, plaster of Paris is a material which has many merits and can be used on every high school level.

From a technical point of view, modeling with plaster of Paris is almost as simple as modeling with clay, one important difference being that plaster always requires an armature. Since plaster adheres very poorly to the smooth surface of the wire and often slips, making it very difficult to build up forms, the wires of the finished armature should first be wound tightly with string which has been soaked in shellac. The shellac acts as a binder between the wire and the string; the string serves to hold the wet plaster in place until it has set, and later to prevent its cracking and chipping. After the first coats of plaster have become firmly attached to the armature, the actual modeling over them is almost as simple as working with clay. Forms can be built up easily, details incorporated, and the surface shaped and coated. "The plaster surface can be made to look like stone or marble or any desired medium by cleverly working over the forms with the right tools and with the knowledge of just how the desired results can be achieved."[92]

Modeling with moist plaster can serve still another purpose: as a preparatory step for modeling in wax. Wax is a beautiful plastic material, easy to work with and regrettably neglected today. It is chiefly thought of as a medium for transposing a modeled piece into bronze, and rarely as possessing an aesthetic quality of its own. Many of the greatest sculptors used wax extensively: Michelangelo made many of his preliminary three-dimensional studies in it, and Rosso used it as a medium in its own right for some of his major works. Modeling in wax has considerable merit and is in several ways very different from working in clay or plaster of Paris. The form is developed over a dry plaster core by lamination, in thin layers, instead of being built up with clusters of small pellets or lumps. Moreover, modeling with wax over plaster gives students a degree of certainty which they can hardly find in other pliable materials. The reason is that they must first concentrate on fashioning broad or basic shapes in plaster, and then devote their attention to the wax, to individual parts, and the final appearance of the work. In sum, the total modeling process is rigidly divided into two creative operations, one consisting of forming the broad volume in plaster, and the other of modeling particulars in wax.

Wax can be most easily molded in a hot or warm stage; as soon as it is cold it becomes hard and retains any shape, but even when cold, parts can be added or taken away. Carving wax requires neither special or very sharp tools, nor highly developed skill; mistakes can most easily be corrected with the help of a warm spatula; shapes can be changed or cut with a knife. As a matter of fact, if the final result is unsatisfactory and major changes are desired, the wax layers can simply be scraped off the

---

[92] *Ibid.*, p. 106.

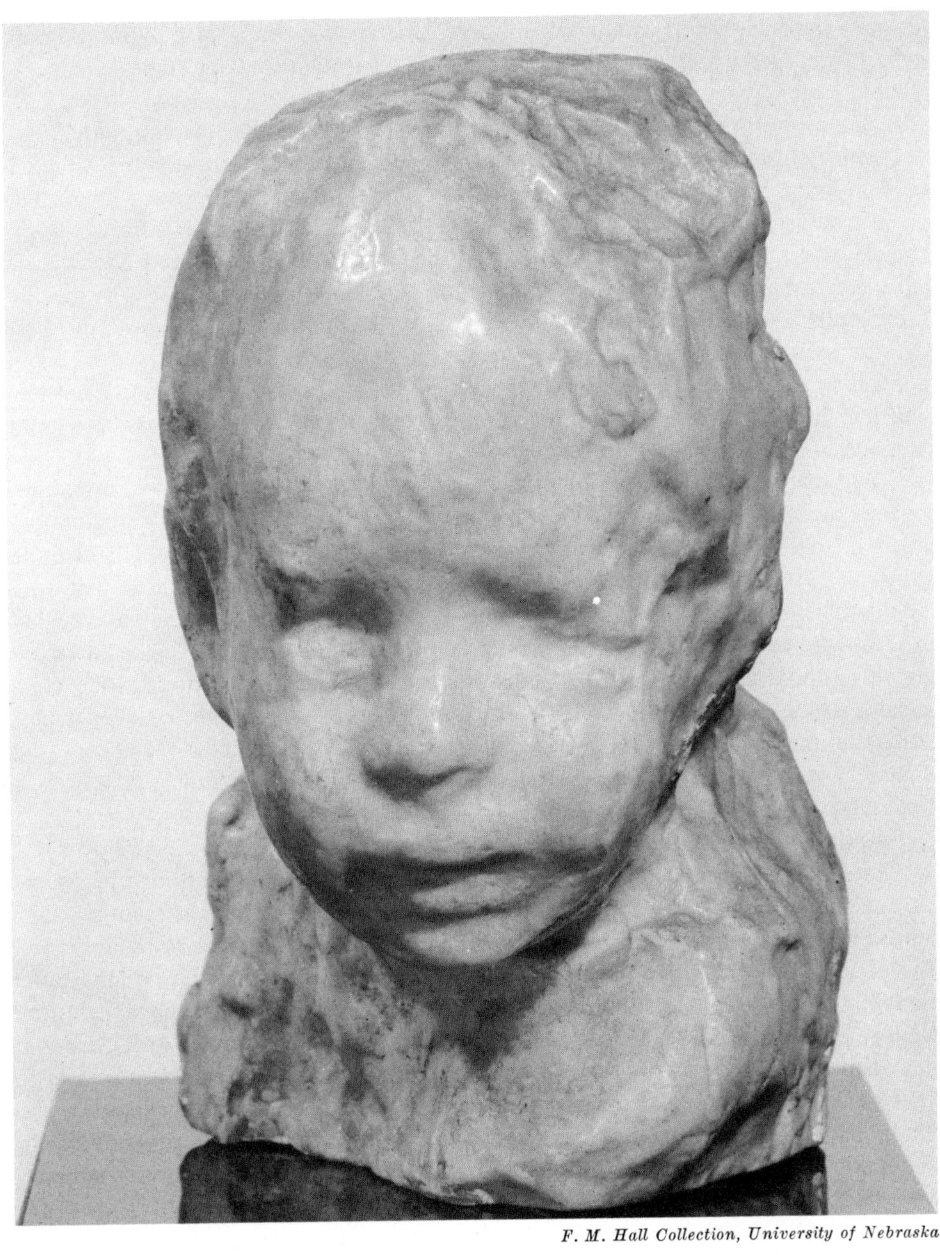

BIMBO EBREO
(JEWISH BOY)
Medardo Rosso
wax over plaster core

F. M. Hall Collection, University of Nebraska

hard plaster core and the work started anew. The plaster core permits the final shaping of the wax without fear of altering the form accidentally.

The technical requirements for modeling with wax are few: a double boiler and an electric hot plate for mixing and melting the wax mixture, and keeping it soft and pliable; a few ordinary kitchen knives and spoons, palette knives or metal spatulas; and some wire sculpture tools. Numerous formulae for mixing modeling wax can be found in professional literature on sculpture or dental techniques.[93] Here are two of the simplest mixtures: about eight parts beeswax and one part turpentine, or equal parts of beeswax and paraffin, and a very small amount of turpentine (just enough to prevent the mixture from hardening too fast). In preparing a wax mixture

[93] The following books contain valuable information pertaining to this material: Jack C. Rich, *The Materials and Methods of Sculpture* (New York: Oxford University Press, 1947); Carl Dame Clark, *Molding and Casting* (Baltimore, Md.: The Standard Press, 1946); Ralph Travers, *Professional Moulds and Castings* (Boston: Plastic Service Associates, 1952).

one rule must be strictly followed: *always add the turpentine last to the already melted wax to prevent overheating.* Very hot turpentine and its fumes are combustible!

Before any wax mixture is chosen for classroom work the teacher should experiment with it so that he will know whether the proportions are correct, whether the compound remains pliable for a sufficient length of time, and, more important, whether students must work fast or can model slowly with it. It is inadvisable to introduce wax modeling before students have become familiar with modeling in clay and plaster of Paris; without such experiences they will not be sensitive to or able to explore the different qualities and possibilities of this material. One of the best ways to acquaint them with the medium and its technique is to ask them to begin by forming a basic and very simplified shape of a human head with plaster (not less than half life-size). When it is thoroughly dry, the features and expression should be modeled with wax over the hardened plaster core.

Wax can also be effectively modeled directly over a simple wire armature. Various mixtures or ready-made dental wax are excellent media for three-dimensional sketches about three inches in height. Used in this manner wax is still quite economical, but for large, solid works it becomes rather costly. Sketching with wax should serve the same purpose as sketching on paper: capturing quickly and roughly an idea—the essence of a movement or an expression. Occasionally, more advanced students should try to improvise three or four such "sketches" during one class session; speedy work of this kind should force them to concentrate only on major forms and movements, and help them to develop a sense of what is significant and what is not. Their best results later may serve them as preliminary studies for larger and more complex projects.

Another medium for quick sketching in three dimensions is oil-based clay, also known as nonhardening clay or Permaclay. Again the most meaningful results are achieved if students first build three or four small, simple wire armatures; they can be made from thin but not too flexible wire, such as stovepipe or bailing wire. The nonhardening clay is easy to work with; it sticks to the wire and permits rapid modeling, and adding or taking away. Because of these virtues it is a valuable medium for sketching, but for larger works it is not quite suitable; it is expensive and clay shapes are easily damaged, and—more important—it often tempts students to work in minute details, as a result of which they frequently lose the feeling for the whole. Moreover, the surface of oil-based clay quickly becomes very smooth and shiny, giving the piece a lifeless and worked over appearance. For these reasons oil-based clay seems to have only a limited use on the high school level.

One other modeling material should be mentioned: a soft metal or plastic compound of pastelike consistency which becomes as hard as any other metal when exposed to the air. There are several such compounds which are known under various trade names: Sculp-Metal, Metal Mend, or Metal Putty. (The first can be obtained through art material supply houses; the two others are commonly sold in automobile body supply stores.) These metal compounds can be modeled most effectively, in a manner similar to wax. They work well over a dry plaster core and even over dry clay. To use them properly the surface of the core should be covered with a coat at least ¼" thick, so that it can be filed, engraved, or sanded when the modeling is finished and the metal surface has dried. Most compounds dry rather rapidly, but not too fast to hamper careful and deliberate work. Still the actual working time is somewhat limited, and projects should be planned and the voluminous hard core worked out with the utmost care as major corrections or changes are quite time-consuming. The metal compounds are relatively expensive, but if used over a hard core and only on the surface, to model features and expressions, they are quite economical and within reach of the budget of many schools.

The silvery color of metal compounds sometimes tarnishes and turns a dull gray, detracting from the beauty and expressiveness of a work, but otherwise these compounds have hardly any negative qualities. They easily take on and retain any form, and portions can be added even to an already dried surface; so long as they are still soft they can be scraped and scratched, and after they have dried, the surface can be sanded, burnished, or buffed. These many positive qualities make metal compounds particularly suited for more advanced work on the high school level. Students with some experience in modeling may well be able to exploit the various innate possibilities of these materials and combine them with their artistic intentions.

Papier-mâché is another modeling medium which has been used successfully in public schools for several generations; it was invented centuries ago in the Orient, probably in China, and was widely used in Persia and Japan long before it became known in the western world. The term "papier-mâché" is French, "papier" meaning paper, and "mâché," freely translated, to grind or to crush. The process is based on the fact that paper becomes strong and durable as soon as it is saturated with an adhesive and agglutinated in layers.

Papier-mâché can be prepared in two different ways: converting paper to pulp, then adding glue or paste, and using this mixture like clay; or cutting paper into narrow strips, covering each strip with paste, and building up a form in thin layers. Ordinary newspaper usually works well for modeling the major forms, and tissue paper is best for adding more delicate details and finishing the surface. No matter which technique is used, papier-mâché usually requires an armature which can be made in several ways and from several materials: wire, stiff cardboard, or tightly rolled paper.

The pulp method permits students to model in the customary manner by adding small pellets, but they must rely on tools rather than on their fingers. This technique is well suited for large projects, requiring more complex armatures built with woodstrips and chicken wire. The chicken wire is a very good surface over which modeling with pulp is not difficult. One of the best ways to make a pulp mixture is by shredding paper and soaking it in water for a day, then leaving it to dry. The now brittle paper is crushed into very small pieces and saturated in a mixture of carpenter's glue, paste, and a little water. This pulp is ready for modeling when it has the consistency of mush or soft clay. After the actual modeling, the dried pulp mixture can be sanded, or finished by being covered with tissue paper, depending on the desired surface.

Building up a form with thin layers of paper is the most frequently used method of modeling in papier-mâché. From a technical point of view it is so easy that even elementary school children rarely encounter difficulties. This technique also requires an armature which may be made with wire or with long rolls of tightly coiled paper.[94] Commonly the wire armatures lend themselves better to smaller and more delicate projects than the more voluminous paper construction. The actual modeling is very simple: layers of long, thin (about one-inch-wide) strips of ordinary newspaper are firmly fastened over the armature (usually with wallpaper paste) until the desired volume is achieved. The surface may be covered with tissue paper, permitting the modeling of fine details and the inclusion of various textures.

A problem common to the whole field of the plastic arts becomes very acute after the papier-mâché has been modeled—the difficult question of the role of color in sculpture. Reams have been written on this subject, but no one has as yet been able to state indisputable criteria which could be used as guides for solving the

[94] Edward L. Mattil in *The Meaning in Crafts* (Englewood Cliffs, N. J.: Prentice-Hall, Inc., 1959) has a thorough and informative chapter on papier-mâché.

problem.[95] Generally speaking, we find two diametrically opposed positions. One holds that all color, except that which is innate in a material, is superimposed, distracts from the form, and is foreign to three-dimensional art expression. It is claimed that the surface properties of a material, be it wood, stone, metal, or plaster of Paris, are an intrinsic part of any plastic expression and should never be altered or visually destroyed; therefore, no paint should ever be applied to any piece of sculpture. On the opposite side it is asserted that the deliberate avoidance of various colors in sculpture is unjustifiable and is largely the result of a misconception which originated during the Renaissance. This misinterpretation was a consequence of the rediscovery of and heightened interest in ancient and antique sculpture. The classical statues which had never been painted or which had lost their original colored surface with the passage of time became the models for most Renaissance sculptors,

HIPPOPOTAMUS
Egyptian
decorated glazed surface
(Faience)

Reproduced by courtesy of the City Art Museum, St. Louis, Mo.

who, in turn, stressed purity of materials. Slowly this concept became a fixed idea even though it is contrary to the principles of art, since art per se is an expression in illusion, and anything contributing to the illusion is justifiable. Color should therefore not be banned from sculpture so long as it contributes to the total artistic statement.

No matter which concept is favored, color is a necessity in papier-mâché because the material is an artificial compound whose dry surface is an unpleasant, spotty, dirty gray which detracts appreciably from the modeled work. Nonetheless, the question remains: When does color contribute to a plastic work and when does it detract? The answer seems to be that in sculpture color must always remain subservient; it should never be used as a substitute for form nor be permitted to become more significant than the form itself. In a modeled head, for example, the features

---

[95] "There are two methods of colouring sculpture, the one conventional, the other illusionistic. In the conventional mode we find colour used without regard for the local tones of nature, purely for the sake of enhancing the effectiveness of the piece, either to emphasize the main masses or to decorate the figure. . . . It is in the illusionistic use of colour that we have lost our innocence. There cannot be the slightest doubt, much as many scholars long to ignore it, that ancient custom sanctioned and encouraged a highly realistic use of colour. The process called ganosis with which the Greeks treated the marble surfaces of the nude, the study and particular attention we know Praxiteles to have given to the colouring of his statues can have had no other end and aim than heightening the realistic illusion." Agnes M. Rindge, *Sculpture* (New York: Payson & Clarke Ltd., 1929), pp. 124–125, 126.

THREE FIGURES
eighth grade students
wire, scrap materials,
and painted papier-mâché

must always be *formed;* they should never merely be *painted.* Once they have been modeled, however, it should be considered quite permissible to coat various parts of the face with different colors.

The rather complex question as to when colors are subservient to form and when are they not, needs further deliberation. The answer depends chiefly on the forms, on the combination of colors used, and, to some degree, on the subject. If a color appears to recede but is placed on a projecting form, this color conflicts with the sculptured intent and will interfere rather than remain subordinate. On the other hand, if the form recedes and the color appears to produce a similar effect, lending support to the movement of the form, it is acceptable.

The second problem regarding a painted surface on a modeled form deals with the question of a painted decoration, a superimposed adornment which is neither an essential nor an organic part of the modeled form. Simply to condemn such a supplementary embellishment as aesthetically unacceptable or improper is unreasonable. Beautiful works exist on which decorations are an enhancing element; some of the most successful examples can be found among the ancient Egyptian hippopotamus statuettes. Their glazed surfaces are richly decorated and the adornment is effective because it does not interfere with the form but adds to its meaning. So long as a painted decoration is used with restraint, is not employed as a substitution for form, and helps to convey a particular meaning, it may be quite acceptable. But the moment it obtrudes, detracts from the form and its movement, and attains major visual significance, it becomes most undesirable. While these criteria are relatively easy to state, they are more difficult to adhere to in practice. Hence it may be wise to encourage students not to rely on superimposed adornments, but to try working out their papier-mâché projects without decorations.

Up to now, only some form of painting has been considered a possible surface treatment of papier-mâché. However, textiles and other flat pliable materials have been successfully combined with paint in order to give a finished appearance to these works. The surface in such instances resembles a sort of collage which sometimes heightens the meaning of a piece and adds to its visual attractiveness. Here again the basic rule is the same as for other forms of surface treatments: The materials must never interfere with the form; they must remain inconspicuous and not draw attention to themselves. So long as such a surface treatment remains suggestive, contributes in an unobtrusive way to meaning, and adds to the total statement, it is in no way objectionable. As a matter of fact, asking students to treat their projects in this slightly unconventional manner may inspire them more than having them merely paint their papier-mâché works; it permits them to experiment and possibly to find novel ways which might otherwise never have occurred to them.

Relief

An aspect of modeling belonging to a quite different category is relief. Relief modeling is the opposite of modeling in the round; it is essentially flat and its forms, which are permanently set against a stationary background, are shallow to varying degrees and without much depth. From a historic point of view, reliefs have been linked predominantly with architecture; most frequently they were attached to buildings to enhance them and to impress the passerby with the secular or sacred significance of the edifice. "The subjects of the relief are always narrative—they explain to us, in factual or allegorical stories, the character and cause of [worldly or religious] power. In early Oriental art, the reliefs with battle or hunting scenes and processions tell us of the worldly power of the kings ruling in the palaces whose walls or staircases were so decorated. In Egyptian art, the reliefs in the tombs give us a vivid account of the life of the deceased. In Greek, Buddhist and Christian art, the reliefs show scenes from the life of the god or prophet to whom the temple or church was dedicated."[96]

Characteristics of relief are that its narrative quality is usually its focal point, and that a definite picture plane exists against which the subject is modeled. Since these facts relate relief modeling more closely to two-dimensional than to three-dimensional expression, it seems permissible to claim that it is a form of drawing with plastic means rather than modeling in three dimensions. For this reason, relief can be considered an excellent transitional medium from two-dimensional to three-dimensional work.

The field of relief is commonly divided into three basic groups: intaglio or inverse bas-relief, bas- or low relief, and alto or high relief. The basic differences between these groups derive from the relationship between the plane and the modeled forms. In intaglio relief the forms do not project as in bas-relief, but are incised into the plane. This technique was frequently used in ancient Egyptian murals and is still practised in a modified way. The principle of intaglio relief is that the surface of the relief remains flat and grooves are incised to outline the forms. Because the grooves can be cut in various degrees of depth and width, and volume can be suggested by a slight shaping of the edges of different forms, the possibilities of this relief technique are almost unlimited.

---

[96] Valentiner, *Origins of Modern Sculpture,* p. 79.

In bas- or low relief as in intaglio relief, the third dimension or depth is not actually present but is suggested in subtle ways. The contours of forms are sharply defined and their volume is raised above the background, but at no point are they separated from it or modeled in genuine three-dimensional shapes. The volume and the different planes of a form can be either slightly elevated, or built up to a considerable degree; yet regardless of the treatment, the forms must remain without undercuts. (An undercut is a section of a form which is partially attached and par-

Reproduced by courtesy of the William Rockhill Nelson Gallery of Art, Kansas City, Mo.

METHETHY WITH
HIS DAUGHTER AND A SON
Egyptian VI Dynasty,
ca. 2450 B.C.
polychromed limestone relief

tially extended into space.) Bas-relief, too, is more closely related to drawing than to modeling in the round.

The modeling of low relief can be approached in two different ways: by building up or by cutting away. In the building up process, forms are developed by placing layers of clay on a flat clay background. In this rather slow method a lineal design is sketched into the soft, flat surface. Next the total volume of each form is raised by adding clay, then individual portions are elevated slightly more, and finally those parts are heightened which are to protrude most. In this way and by indenting and overlapping the various forms, the illusion of a third dimension is gradually achieved.

The other method, cutting away, also begins with sketching the contours of the design into the flat clay surface. This is followed by taking away the areas surrounding the outlined forms so that they appear like raised silhouettes against the solid clay background. By varying the levels, lowering some more than others, and by modeling the individual parts of forms, the bas-relief is slowly created. In both methods, lines can be incised, textures modeled or embossed, and materials suggested. Assyrian, Greek, and early Romanesque reliefs, and those done by Donatello, Ghiberti, and Luca della Robbia exemplify beautifully the various possibilities of this medium.

A wholly different approach is used in high relief. Here the illusion of a third dimension is rarely encountered; instead one finds a rich interplay of three-dimensional forms protruding from their background. High relief is characterized by the fact that most major forms, although attached to a fixed background, have many undercuts and are nearly fully formed in the round. Of all forms of relief it is most closely related to actual three-dimensional expression. The most famous high relief adorns the metopes on the Parthenon; others can be seen on many cathedrals of the Gothic or later periods. It is probably the most difficult form of relief modeling (in fact, many sculptors maintain that it is the most difficult form of three-dimensional expression); assuredly it is not suitable for beginning students.

As already indicated, both intaglio and bas-relief are methods which link drawing with sculpture; they are certainly sufficiently challenging, different, and educationally valuable to be explored by high school students. When working in relief, students may be able to utilize former drawing experiences and to transfer some previously acquired skill to this form of modeling. Others may in time develop a feeling for three-dimensional work if they are given an opportunity to make the transition from drawing to sculpture gradually.

From a technical point of view, these two types of relief are neither difficult nor expensive. Unlike other methods of three-dimensional expression, working in relief *must* begin with a drawing. When a subject has been chosen, a few thumbnail sketches are made and the most suitable one is then selected. It is highly advisable that students enlarge the selected sketch and make a contour drawing on paper in the exact dimensions of their relief project. For beginners the most appropriate designs are relatively simple, have a rather plain background, and contain figures which have some movement and expression but few or no foreshortenings. These projects should never be less than 18″ x 20″, since smaller sizes are more difficult to execute. In large projects students need not be so dependent on tools. They can use their fingers and model more freely; also, they have a wider choice of textures and greater freedom to explore the various possibilities of this form of expression.

When the drawings are finished, students should begin to prepare the relief panel. This is usually done by nailing at least two, possibly four wooden strips along the edges of a board. The board should be somewhat larger than the contemplated work because it must also accommodate the width of the wooden strips. The height of the strips should correspond to the approximate depth of the relief. If the building-up method is used, one inch is usually sufficient height, but in the cutting-away method these strips should be not less than two inches high. Before the board is tightly packed with clay, all wood should be coated with shellac to prevent absorption of moisture, thereby counteracting any undue shrinkage and possible cracking.

After the clay has been firmly pressed on the board, the surface should be scraped with a straight-edged strip of wood until it is perfectly smooth and level with the raised edges. With the help of a simple, pointed wooden tool the previously drawn design should be transferred, by means of pressure, to the soft clay surface; then all is ready to begin the actual modeling. Students should be reminded to work slowly because mistakes are discouraging, and their correction time-consuming. They should be cautioned against cutting into the clay too deeply or raising areas too much, because very severe contrasts give the effect of dark holes and can destroy the unity of the work. Not until the relief is nearly finished should students begin to pay attention to surface details; the basic planes and forms should be fully developed before any lines are inserted, edges beveled, or textures incorporated.

Working in relief is not difficult for high school students provided they have been shown reproductions of superior examples to familiarize them with the various possibilities of this form of three-dimensional expression. Sometimes, to stimulate interest, the teacher should suggest a basic theme around which students may develop their ideas for a project. They may be told to create a relief befitting a monument, the facade of a particular building, or the interior of a hall. The choice of subjects is wide, and the students' maturity, background, and interest should be considered to arrive at an appropriate suggestion.

HAMBURG WAR MONUMENT
(major part)
Ernst Barlach

Casting

Modeling in clay is not an end in itself. Shapes in wet or dried clay are not only extremely vulnerable but are often quite displeasing in their appearance; a completed work in clay rarely satisfies students' longing for finished work. The two widely accepted methods of preserving such works and making them attractive are firing (terra cotta) and casting.

Casting is a process of reproducing an object identical in form and texture with the work from which the copy is made. This process consists of two phases: making a mold or negative cast, and producing the positive or actual cast. The mold is the relatively thin, hollow form preserving an impression of the *outside* of the *object,* and the cast is the solid impression taken from the *inside* of the *mold.* Many different materials are used for various mold and casting processes. Yet in terms of usefulness in the high school only one material—plaster of Paris—is of real importance, and only the casting process known as "waste molding." As the term implies, the mold is wasted; after it has been filled with plaster of Paris it must be destroyed in order to free the positive cast. Obviously the process permits only one copy of the original clay work, whereas most other mold processes—for instance, those using rubber or gelatin—permit countless reproductions.

There are three types of waste molds, all of which are commonly made from plaster of Paris: a one-piece mold which is most frequently used in the casting of bas-relief; a two-piece mold which usually suffices for casting objects with only a few undercuts; and a multi-piece mold which must be used for casting complex works with numerous space divisions and undercuts. The depth and type of the undercuts always determine the number of sections into which the mold must be divided. Another consideration in determining the number of individual mold pieces is the relative ease with which they can be removed from the clay model, avoiding excessive strain on the plaster mold. Regardless of how many sections a mold may require, the whole casting process always consists of many different operations. Each operation is of equal importance and all need the same careful attention to detail. Casting is time-consuming and cannot be rushed at any point, for a single mistake can easily spoil weeks of work.

Yet the real problem in casting comes not from students' possible carelessness or lack of interest, but from the fact that the usual fifty-minute class period makes it necessary for the process to be divided into many short steps. Unfortunately, many casting operations must be executed without interruption and are very difficult to carry out during a class session lasting only fifty minutes. In consequence, the activity needs to be planned with extreme care in terms of time. The different operations must be divided into blocks of time, each block equalling one class period. For instance, whenever a two- or multi-piece mold must be used, the surface of the clay model should first be divided into sections corresponding to the individual pieces of the mold. The division may be made either with clay or plasticine walls about two inches high, or with thin brass or aluminum shims. The making of the clay walls or cutting of the metal shims can be done during one class period, and their careful fastening to the model during the next. Then the actual mold-making can begin. Depending on the size of the work and the number of sections demanded, this operation may be stretched over more than one period, provided that at least one section of the mold is completed each time: the clay section is covered with a thin coat of plaster of Paris which has been colored with a small amount of blueing, and then a heavier white coat is immediately placed over it. This dual coating must always be done in one operation, without any time lapse, otherwise the two coats of the mold will not fuse. The colored coat should be about ⅛″ thick; its purpose is to tell students (when chiseling away the mold from the cast) where the mold ends and the cast begins.

The initial colored coat is usually made of a heavy mixture of wet plaster and a small amount of blueing, and is flipped on with the fingertips. Then the outer coat is placed over the colored coat before the latter has had a chance to set. This final coat is made from pure plaster and should be about ¾″ thick. Finally the outer surface of each mold section should be smoothed, and possibly strengthened with a piece of hemp fiber which has been dipped into wet plaster. Also, before the class period is over, the base of the model, tools, and other paraphernalia should be cleaned and the project covered airtight with a sheet of plastic or oilcloth. In this manner the mold can be made section by section during several class periods. Taking the mold apart will require one session, and cleaning and possible repairing, soaping, and putting it together will occupy one or two more. Mixing the plaster and pouring it into the mold must be done in a single operation, which often takes more than fifty minutes. Finally, chiseling away the mold may require several more class periods. All in all, the process may last from five to ten sessions.

The success of casting depends on several factors: on the proper and deliberate mixing of the plaster; on the slow pouring of the plaster into the mold; on the careful shellacking of the broadside of each section and the meticulous soaping of the inside of the entire mold. Obviously casting is in no way a creative activity, but although it is an exacting technical process, demanding adherence to established methods, it is still a distinct part of artistic expression in three dimensions. Casting teaches discipline, good work habits, and—above all—respect for workmanship.

One more problem related to casting should be mentioned: In many instances a white plaster cast does not enhance the appearance of a work, but gives it a dull, lifeless, and even actively unpleasant quality. There are several ways to overcome this disadvantage: adding sand, or pigment, or both to the liquid plaster before it is poured into the mold; treating the surface of the cast to give it the appearance of a material other than plaster; or using any of the cement-based mixtures (generally known as "cast stone"), such as hydrostone and Keene's cement, instead of plaster.

These artificial, stonelike mixtures, however, require a burlap-reinforced mold since they expand considerably during the setting period.

Adding pigment or sand to a plaster mixture does not constitute a problem; a few brief experiments should give high school students a clear idea of what can be accomplished, and which mixture will best serve their projects. The second method, treating the surface of a cast, is more complex. Many formulae exist for giving a convincing bronzelike appearance to the plaster. The selection of a particular recipe will depend on the availability of the various ingredients, the amount of time available for such an activity, and the precise effect desired. In addition, oil paints, waxes, and shellac have also been successfully used in lending an attractive quality to a plaster cast. Here again the student should not merely paint with the first thing within his reach, remaining ignorant of many other possible effects, but should be urged to experiment with different surface treatments so that he will be able to select the most desirable finish for his work.

Lastly, while casting with materials other than plaster is desirable on the high school level, it is often difficult if not impossible to execute for technical reasons. Casting of cement-based mixtures can be done only if the teacher has had practical experience with it, and has ample time to supervise the operation. Cement-based casts, unlike plaster of Paris casts, can be corrected only with great difficulty after the cement has hardened; any errors may spoil weeks of effort. Moreover, some mixtures must be packed into the mold rather than poured, a process which requires a degree of skill which can be gained only from experience. Casting with cement mixtures is often more time-consuming than with plaster, and time is at a premium on the high school level and must always be balanced between actual learning experiences and the production of work. As a rule, the learning of technical processes should be considered less important than that of experiencing genuine creative challenges, and in case of doubt should always remain subordinate.

Terra Cotta

The simplest way of giving permanence to a work modeled in clay is by exposing it for a brief time to considerable heat. Clay hardened by heat is called terra cotta, literally, "cooked earth." Heat changes the color of clay—baked, it usually turns a rather brilliant red or red-yellow—but does not affect its texture. The method of making terra cotta has been known for centuries: prehistoric man formed clay figures and baked them; the Greeks used this method of preservation or fabrication for many of their small statues; during the Renaissance it became a favorite of the sculptors, and today it is still widely used and appreciated.

The red color of terra cotta is caused by a small amount of iron oxide, occurring naturally in the clay, or added (up to five per cent by weight) to light-colored clay. (The simplest way of mixing the oxide with clay is to do so when both are still in dry, powdered form.) Pure clay, regardless of its color when moist, becomes whitish after it has been fired, but most of the clay easily available in this country turns pink or buff when baked. Before any clay is used for terra cotta, therefore, its color should be tested by firing a small amount. Should the color turn buff or be otherwise unattractive, it can easily be changed by adding some iron oxide; this will not interfere with the modeling, drying, or firing of the work.

Clay for terra cotta must be carefully prepared and should, if possible, be mixed with grog. Grog is made from bisque (fired clay) which has been pulverized into particles the size of fine sand or to dustlike powder. It is available commercially, sometimes under the trade name of "Brick Dust." Up to 30% of grog can be added without interfering with the actual modeling. Depending on its fineness or coarseness, grog not only adds interest to the textural quality of the clay surface, but, more important, it reduces shrinkage and warping of the clay. The most significant aspect of preparing clay for terra cotta, however, is wedging. Moist clay is first formed into a large lump which is then cut in two; these halves are banged hard against a board, then thrown together, cut again, and banged once more, and the procedure is repeated until all air pockets are removed and the clay has taken on a uniform consistency. Ample time should be allowed for this vital operation because during the firing even a single air pocket could cause an explosion which might break the piece into many parts. Consequently, students should be made fully aware of the reason why the clay must be wedged diligently, and why they must model most carefully, avoiding making or leaving any air pockets.

Creating a work in terra cotta consists of three phases: first the actual modeling, second a drying period, and third the firing. From a technical point of view, modeling can be approached in several ways, but regardless of which method is chosen, the final work must always be a hollow form. A solid mass of clay breaks, warps, and cracks very easily, and dries and fires poorly. To put it another way, every terra cotta work is a shell whose outer walls are shaped so as to convey the creative intent.

The most frequently employed method of modeling terra cotta is quite similar to that used in modeling works of clay for casting. A solid mass is slowly built up and shaped, but in terra cotta extra care must be taken to press the added clay parts or pellets tightly against the moist surface in order to prevent the formation of air pockets. Immediately after the project has been completed, the moist work is cut into several parts with the help of a thin wire, and each segment is carefully hollowed out, finally leaving a shell whose walls are uniformly ½″ to ¾″ thick. Then the sides of the walls are serrated, covered with slip (see page 220), and the work is reassembled by pressing its pieces firmly together. Next the seams are carefully examined to assure their tight fit and the absence of air pockets. Lastly, any noticeable seam scars are lightly retouched so that they blend into the surface and become invisible.

In a different method, the terra cotta project is begun with a hollow form. This form may be developed either by employing the coil method, as in pottery, or by using clay slabs. For beginning students the coil method is probably preferable to the slab method; usually it gives them greater freedom of expression because every step during the development of the project can be controlled. As in pottery, the work is started by making twenty to thirty thin, cablelike, narrow cylindrical shapes, about ½″ in diameter and not less than 12″ in length. These clay rolls are then arranged in a spiral and pressed tightly against each other until the basic form of the project has been established. The surface of the form is then smoothed, and details and texture are added.

The slab method begins with rolling out a lump of clay to form large sheets about ½″ thick. These sheets are then cut, bent, and formed into various shapes in accordance with the particular project. After the pieces have been assembled and the seams tightly united, the modeling of details and the incorporation of possible textures can begin. Both methods should be used principally in the high school; the slab method, however, should be considered more experimental since it differs considerably from the usual way of developing a plastic work.

In a still different method of modeling in terra cotta, a paper armature is used. It is built with newspapers which are tightly rolled into long, narrow cylinders, bent, and fastened together with thread. All large spaces between the rolls should be stuffed with crumpled paper, transforming the skeleton into a solid form. After the paper surface is thinly coated with shellac to prevent the absorption of moisture from the clay, the actual modeling can begin. Both thin coils and small pellets can be used for building up a clay layer which should not be more than ½″ thick. Again the wedged clay must be handled with utmost care to prevent air pockets. When the modeling has been completed and the clay has dried and hardened thoroughly, as much of the paper armature as possible should be removed from the inside without damaging the work. The piece is now ready to be fired. Small amounts of paper which remain inside the work will usually burn out without leaving blemishes on the outside.

Creating a work in terra cotta over an armature is most suited for junior high school students, since they can combine some of their previous experiences with papier-mâché and clay and transfer them to this method of modeling. Unfortunately this technique is more limiting than any of the others mentioned previously because the paper armature restricts the range of approaches and topics, which usually must be confined to ideas capable of expression in a more or less solid mass, such as a human head, a crouched figure, or a resting animal.

No matter which of the modeling methods is used, the success or failure of a terra cotta project often hinges on the final firing of the work. This in turn depends on the handling of the kiln as well as on how thoroughly a piece has been dried. During the drying period the modeled work should be turned frequently and placed in different positions so that air can circulate freely, and the inside as well as the outside become thoroughly hardened. The drying process should be very gradual and never hastened; too rapid drying can cause cracks. When the work is placed in the kiln for firing, the heat should be raised very slowly, permitting moisture to evaporate gradually without forming steam pressure which inevitably causes cracking, possibly even an explosion. Terra cotta clay commonly matures between 1830° and 1900° F., or cone 06. The length of the firing time depends on the particular clay, the size and nature of the work, and the thickness of its walls; the larger the piece and the stronger the walls, the more time is needed for the firing. Yet for all practical purposes if the firing is started very early in the morning, is kept low for the first two hours, then turned up gradually to reach the required degree of heat in the afternoon, and finally cut down slowly shortly before the end of the school day, the work should be ready the next morning. For safety reasons no kiln in a public school should ever be left turned on and unattended throughout the night.

After terra cotta has been fired, it should have a uniform red color which is pleasing and enhances the work. Yet terra cotta need not be an end in itself; it can be developed still further by glazing its surface. Glazed terra cottas are commonly referred to as ceramic sculpture. Covering a baked clay work with a coat of powdered silicates mixed with other chemicals or glazes is a very old process: Babylonians, Persians, Chinese, and Etruscans used this method extensively and were masters of it. The Greeks covered their terra cottas with a very thin coat of a translucent white glaze which not only enhanced them but also gave the surface more permanence and moisture resistance. Today ceramic sculpture is considered a part of the decorative arts rather than of purely artistic expression. Still, leading contemporary artists like Picasso and Leger, among many others, employed this method to create powerful, expressive works.

As in any three-dimensional expression, color in ceramic sculpture must always remain subordinate to form. For this reason many sculptors have been reluctant to use color with terra cotta. Also many artists feel that, with the exception of color which is innate in a material, sculpture should be limited to pure form. To them "terra cotta is . . . a humble medium and it should be used with simple directness."[97] Still, glaze and baked clay are a combination which is neither alien nor artificial; the materials are dependent on each other, and both must undergo the same process to become lastingly effective. Glaze and terra cotta are as intimately related as glaze and color; they legitimately belong together.

---

[97] Rindge, *Sculpture,* p. 129.

A permanent colored surface can be achieved on terra cotta in two ways, one by slip painting, and another by glazing. Slip for painting is a liquid consisting of a rather thick, creamlike mixture of clay, water, and metal oxides. The slip is painted on the work after it has dried thoroughly but before it is fired. The painting must be done quickly because the clay is thirsty and rapidly absorbs the moisture, making it rather difficult to distribute the slip over the surface. When the slip has been applied, details may be added by scratching areas and lines into the painted surface. This method of painting is not easy to control and should therefore be used mainly by students who have already had some experience with glazing which, demanding less dexterity and proficiency, can be considered a good preparation for working with slip.

Glazing is a method of covering a clay surface with colors which are suspended in a variety of chemicals; this compound is melted to form a glasslike surface. Glazes are liquids before they are applied to a bisque-fired work. They are made with a great number of different minerals and chemicals, and exist in many textures and colors. Competent ceramists and potters study thoroughly the various compositions and the behavior of glazes, and spend much time preparing them. Yet in the high school commercially prepared glazes are commonly used, because compounding glazes requires a large supply of many different oxides and other chemicals, equipment for exact measuring, considerable knowledge of chemistry, constant study of technical information, and—above all—time. Since few of these prerequisites can be met in the high school, it is advisable to use commercially prepared glazes which have been tested, are easy to handle, and serve their purpose well as long as the manufacturer's specifications are followed. Several types of glazes are available: underglazes and transparent overglazes, matt, semi-matt, cracked, and glossy majolica glazes.

Underglazes are opaque colors which may be applied either before or after firing. They are available in two forms, in crayon, or pencil-like sticks for lineal work, and in cake form (similar to watercolor) for working in areas with a brush. Regardless of which form is used, an underglaze must always be covered with a protective transparent glaze. If underglazes are applied on a bisque-fired work, it is most advisable to fire the piece once more at a low temperature (about cone 010) so that the colors fuse with the bisque-fired surface, and then apply the transparent glaze. If the underglazed color is not permanently attached to the surface of a work, the liquid, transparent glaze can easily injure or dissolve it. After firing, the transparent glaze forms a coat which protects the design and intensifies colors, and gives the work a finished, smooth appearance. The glaze should be applied rather thinly to prevent the formation of an overly glossy surface; frequently, light reflections on a shiny surface interfere with the visual impression of a work, and draw attention to even the smallest irregularity and surface indentation which would otherwise remain unnoticed. For the same reason, the glossy majolica glazes are not recommended for this type of high school work. On the other hand, matt glazes in subdued colors work extremely well; they have a stonelike quality, are easy to handle, and, when used sparingly, add considerably to the expressiveness of a beginner's work.[98]

Perhaps the best way to familiarize students with the many possibilities for using glazes is by temporarily separating the problems of form, texture, and color. The

---

[98] The following books have excellent information on terra cotta, tile-making, and glazes: F. H. Norton, *Ceramics for the Artist Potter* (Cambridge, Mass.: Addison-Wesley Publishing Co., 1956); Herbert H. Sanders, *Sunset Ceramics Book* (Menlo Park, Calif.: Lane Publishing Co., 1953); Carol Janeway, *Ceramics and Pottery Making for Everyone* (New York: Tudor Publishing Co., 1950); Ruth H. Randall, *Ceramic Sculpture* (New York: Watson-Guptill Publications, 1948).

ideal project for this purpose is tile-making, in which the student need fashion only a simple, flat shape, and then can concentrate all his efforts on treating its surface. In fact, tile-making can be considered an excellent way to bridge painting, ceramic sculpture, and some aspects of working in relief. The tile may be any thin, flat piece of fired clay which need not necessarily be square; it may be rectangular, polygonal, discoid, or reniform.

The making of tiles is very simple. A lump of moist, wedged clay is set on a board which is framed on two opposite sides by strips of wood, each about ¾″ high. The clay is pressed against the board with a rolling pin which rests on the two wooden strips. The flat clay sheet is then cut into the desired shape and is now ready for further treatment, which may consist of incising lines, embossing textures, or modeling a design in bas-relief. The design may be sketched first on paper or improvised directly on the clay; the latter is particularly recommended because the soft clay surface can be flattened almost effortlessly whenever an attempt proves unsuccessful. Moreover, feeling the clay and working directly with it may stimulate students to develop ideas which might never have occurred to them by working on a piece of paper. These ideas may require more than one tile for adequate expression. A project may take up several tiles which can be assembled into one unit after they have been modeled, fired, and glazed. Subjects for tile projects are unlimited, and the student's age level, previous experiences, and interest should determine the choice.

After the tiles have been modeled, they must dry slowly. To prevent warping it is best to have them dry on plaster slabs; after they begin to harden they should be turned over and if possible placed on another dry plaster slab. When the tiles have become leather hard they may be colored with underglazes and fired, or they may be bisque-fired and students then given the opportunity to work on them with different matt and transparent glazes. Students should be given as much freedom to experiment as is technically permissible. So long as they keep a record of the various kinds of glazes and how they were used, enabling them to duplicate any positive results of their experiments, the project should be considered meaningful regardless of its outward appearance. The experience gained through tile-making is valuable and useful in other ceramic work, be it pottery or ceramic sculpture. There is no age-level restriction to this type of project; beginning junior as well as advanced senior high school students may find the activity full of challenges, offering many different ways of creative expression.

Sculpture

As mentioned previously, there are two completely different approaches to three-dimensional expression: modeling and sculpture. Sculpture is a method of developing a three-dimensional artistic statement by taking fragments away from a hard, solid mass; its characteristic is that conscious thought and critical judgment precede action. Whereas modeling requires inexpensive, easily obtainable materials, few and very simple tools, little equipment, and almost no formally acquired skill, sculpture demands rather costly materials, many special tools and much equipment, and, above all, a considerable degree of skill which can only be attained slowly. "Sculpture is an exacting and difficult medium," said Jacob Epstein. "I cannot assert here too strongly that sculpture is a science needing many years of preparation and study, and requiring an exercise of the imagination equal to that needed in any form of creation, poetry, music, or great drama; the same effort and sacrifice and lifetime of devotion."[99]

---

[99] Epstein, *Let There Be Sculpture,* p. 197.

Studying the history of sculpture, one finds two different approaches which often have existed side by side. In one, sculpture is considered an appendage to modeling, so to speak, a medium for giving permanence to a fragile work which was conceived and executed in clay. Through mechanical means (a pointer or an enlarging machine), a clay model or its plaster cast is enlarged and transferred to stone or another hard material. Professional stonemasons or wood carvers usually handle most of the physical labor, and the artist only retouches the work or makes minor changes shortly before it is finished. In the other approach, the artist envisions and executes his idea directly in the final medium; having studied the material, he sketches his basic plan either on paper or in clay or wax. But the sketch is merely a rough visualization; while it may serve as a guide, it is never to be slavishly followed during the actual sculpturing.

Michelangelo, like many other sculptors, "considered stone-carving the only true sculpture. He described its progressive stages as follows: 'One must imagine the figure as if it were lying under a body of water which is allowed gradually to run off, thus permitting the figure to come little by little above the surface, until at length it lies completely exposed.' "[100] Today many sculptors feel that working directly with a material is the most inspiring and satisfying form of sculpture; they regard the material as their friend. José de Creeft said: "Materials have qualities which will speak to you if you listen."[101]

However, the significance of this intimate relationship between the sculptor and his material may easily be exaggerated, or dogmatically interpreted to mean that an artist is dependent on a stone or piece of wood as his source of inspiration—that the material dictates what he should shape, and how to shape it. This is not true. The accomplished sculptor, like artists in other fields, controls his medium through skill and experience while he remains sensitive to his material. The great modern sculptor Ernst Barlach said: "Why shall I make myself dependent on a piece of wood? I glue the material together until I obtain the basic shape. The *form* I carry within myself."[102]

Today the belief is not uncommon that materials are *more* than a means for creating and have inviolable rights of their own, and that the artist must kowtow to textures, veins in stones, or grains in wood instead of simply recognizing and utilizing them. The notion that a material is more than a means for giving outward form to an expression, that its character determines the form, that the beauty of a work is dependent on its material rather than on the profundity of feelings and thoughts and the vitality of the creator, is a shallow and indefensible concept. The greatness of a work is determined by the keen penetration and the creative, mental, and spiritual powers of a mind, not by a dead material or by the adroitness with which it is utilized. "Art needs to find a material relatively formless which its business is to shape; and this initial formlessness in matter is essential to art's existence."[103] But matter is never more than the means through which an idea is visualized; what truly transcends is the idea and *not* the medium.

Perhaps the simplest definition of sculpture is "to give form to an existing massive volume." There are only a very few massive materials which can be exploited without considerable skill, time, equipment, and proper work space. Michelangelo deplored the fact that sculpture causes "much perspiration which mingling with the grit turns into mud. [The sculptor's] face is pasted and smeared all over

---

[100] Leonardo da Vinci, *Paragone,* p. 84.
[101] José de Creeft, "Statement on Sculpture," *Seven Arts #2,* Fernando Puma, ed. (New York: Permabooks, 1954), p. 64.
[102] Paul Schurek, *Begegnungen mit Ernst Barlach* (Hamburg: Classen & Goveros, 1946), p. 52. —(*author's translation*)
[103] Santayana, *The Life of Reason,* p. 308.

with . . . powder . . . his dwelling is dirty and filled with dust and chips of stone."[104] Because of this dust and because sculpture is often a noisy procedure, very few types of sculpture projects can be carried out in an average high school art room. The physical plant and the materials as well often constitute a problem; even soft, easily carved stones such as alabaster, soapstone, freestone, limestone, or sandstone are not readily obtainable and are relatively expensive. The same applies to wood blocks. Woods such at butternut (or "white walnut"), Philippine mahogony, or sugar pine, which do not require great skill or patience to carve, can often be obtained locally in planks, but blocks of suitable size usually must be ordered from metropolitan suppliers, which considerably raises their initially high cost. Furthermore, working with any of these materials requires a variety of gouges, chisels, files, rasps, mallets, and sharpening stones, as well as tables with vises, and strong sculpture stands, possibly with turntables.

Unhappily, for these reasons and lack of time, sculpture must often remain a rather limited activity in the high school. Of all the possible and desirable art activities, sculpture is the most time-consuming; very little can be accomplished in fifty minutes, and even rather simple projects may well consume two to three weeks. Much of this time will be taken up by purely mechanical labor, particularly if proper tools are unavailable, and relatively little of such work can be considered genuinely creative. This need not be considered an adverse factor, because the capacity to remain interested in a slowly developing project often is a requirement for success in many areas other than art, and high school students are too seldom afforded opportunities to train themselves for tasks which demand long sustained power. Since time is always at a premium in an art room, one must choose projects which consume little time and sculpture materials which are simple to handle, or a large segment of a given art program must be devoted entirely to sculpture. The teacher must choose between these two possibilities, basing his decision on the maturity, aptitude, ability, and previous art experience of the particular group. Added considerations are the availability of materials and of sufficient and proper tools and equipment, and the accessibility of stimulating resources. More than in any other art activity, students should be exposed to numerous examples of sculpture, see many different approaches, and possibly feel various textures and surface treatments before embarking on a project, because they so rarely encounter sculptured works in everyday life. They may chance to see paintings or reproductions in school, in books, magazines, or stores, but sculpture is much less frequently encountered than other art forms in such a casual manner. Moreover, two-dimensional reproductions of paintings are much more satisfactory than their counterparts in sculpture; really to see a piece of sculpture one must walk around it and view it from all sides and from different angles. Visiting museums or viewing films dealing with sculpture should be a definite prerequisite for students beginning to work in this medium. Otherwise their ignorance of the many possibilities inherent in sculpture, their fear of an unfamiliar medium, and their lack of skill will result in the production of the tritest and most uninspired forms and, at best, an involvement only in the technical manipulative process. On the other hand, to a greater degree than drawing, painting, or modeling, creating a sculpture can turn into a genuine adventure; it can be an almost magical process during which students gradually bring to life forms which seem to have been hiding within a solid mass. This sense of adventure is the strongest motivating force for such an activity, and not until a teacher has been able to capture students' interest and arouse their imagination should they begin to work in this medium.

Of the few materials readily available for sculpture in the high school, plaster

---

[104] Leonardo da Vinci, *Paragone,* p. 95.

of Paris is probably the best. Students can make plaster blocks without difficulty; their production demands little time and hardly any equipment. By adding—singly or in combinations—sand, marble powder, brick dust, or dry pigments to liquid plaster, its color and texture can be modified, and made interesting and aesthetically pleasing without much effort. The simplest way to manufacture these blocks is to pour liquid plaster into cardboard boxes, preferably two feet square, whose interiors have been coated with shellac. The blocks can be carved easily so long as they are kept moist; whenever they become dry they should be thoroughly remoistened. The carving of plaster blocks does not require special tools; anything with a relatively sharp edge will serve well, from a screw driver to a kitchen knife, from a nail file to a wood rasp.

Before students begin to sculpture they should either roughly outline their project as seen from several sides, or use plasticine to make a quick small sketch of what they intend to shape. Such improvisations, however, should serve only as a clarification of intentions, and should never be followed explicitly. When students have a clear concept of what they want to carve, they should draw the contours of the projected work on the block in heavy lines, making outlines on the top and all four sides. Then the actual sculpturing may begin. Students must be reminded almost constantly to work all around, to attempt to develop all sides simultaneously, and to carve slowly, taking away only a small piece, even a particle, at one time. They should first eliminate those portions of the block which are not part of the representation, and only after the rough form has been brought out should they begin to think of the subject itself, and to define details.

There are several reasons for emphasizing these elementary rules. One of the most characteristic difficulties inherent in shaping the many sides and different images of the same subject and combining them into an organic unit arises from the fact that the sculptor at work can usually view only one side of the block at a time, and only one particular aspect of the image. He is therefore in constant danger of losing contact with the whole, of unwittingly chipping away too much on one side without possessing legitimate means for correcting such a mistake. The only safeguard is to prompt students to turn their blocks constantly while carving, to work in the round, and to stay only briefly with one side of the piece. Moreover, they must be reminded often to refrain from shaping details before the whole image has emerged. When the entire representation is at last exposed, minor details and refinements frequently become unnecessary if not undesirable. A work should be considered finished when everything intended has been made clearly visible; too detailed and overworked a piece produces a tired and lifeless impression, attracting attention to the sweat rather than to the work itself.

Before students begin to sculpture they should be informed that, mainly for mechanical reasons, carving always should be started at the top, slowly unveiling, so to speak, the upper part of the piece first, before work is started on its lower portion. It is not uncommon for a beginning student, unaware of this basic rule, to weaken the lower section of his block to such an extent that the whole piece suddenly breaks off its base when he resumes work on the upper part. Moreover, students often forget that they must give the same careful consideration to the base as to any other part of the sculpture; they do not seem to realize that the base of a three-dimensional work is an important part of the whole statement, and can in no way be compared with the frame of a painting. The latter is not an intrinsic part of the work; it can be changed without actually altering a painting. But the base of a sculpture, with rare exceptions, is a significant, unchangeable component of the entire visual statement, is part of the over-all design, and carved from the same material. However, the base should never be made in such a way that it draws attention to itself; it must remain a factor which adds to the total impression without ever becoming conspicuous.

HEAD OF A GIRL
twelfth grade girl
soft fire brick

As students, when they begin to carve, are seldom able to envision their project in its entirety, they often have great difficulty in relating the forms they develop on one side to those on the other. For this reason modeling should be a prerequisite for sculpture; it may give students some of the experiences necessary for visualizing a whole, not parts. It is common practice to draw very simple outlines of a project on the top and sides of the block before the carving is begun. But even this first step toward giving form to an image is difficult for a beginner and should be examined by the teacher. He should check whether the suggested forms will fuse later on, whether sufficient space has been provided for the volume of the different shapes, and whether allowances have been made for minor changes which often become necessary during the execution of a work. It is wise to ask students to choose a subject which can be represented in simple shapes and can be sculptured in compact form, with very few extreme cavities or extensions into space. Good sculpture is solid in appearance, rich in different planes, and varied in texture. Students should attempt to retain the massive quality of the plaster of Paris block; the material is relatively fragile and lends itself only to a rather sparse interplay of form and defined space. Even within these limitations students can find countless themes, endless possibilities for individual approaches, and almost unlimited freedom of expression.

One faulty technique which should be mentioned is sometimes stressed in nonprofessional "how-to" or "craft" books. These books occasionally recommend that the beginner concentrate on the profile of his sculpture project before working on the various other parts. Although at first glance it appears that this method readily leads to satisfactory results, in actuality it is a most unsatisfactory approach. As the project progresses it becomes increasingly more difficult to achieve a work which is meaningful when viewed from all positions and not only from one side. There are no shortcuts or tested recipes in sculpture; there is only slow and concentrated effort which requires patience and self-discipline.

A few other sculpture materials can be used in the high school, none of which are too expensive and which can be carved without any special tools, equipment, or skill. These materials are soft fire bricks, lava stones, and soap bars. Soft fire bricks are porous, rough-textured, and uniformly buff-colored; they are quite fragile, can be carved easily, and if necessary can be repaired with synthetic cement. Their most pronounced shortcomings are their shape and size, which are very limiting, permitting only small projects and restricting the choice of theme and expression. By cementing several bricks to form a larger block, this disadvantage can be overcome to some degree. Yet if several bricks are used in this manner, the project must be most carefully planned so that the seams between the bricks will become a contributing rather than a distracting part of the design. Working out such an arrangement is a task which more experienced students may find quite challenging.

Lava stone, which is slightly more dense but of about the same hardness as soft fire brick, can also be carved without special tools or equipment. It is sold in different sizes and shapes and is usually considerably larger than a brick. Natural lava stone has many desirable features, such as its texture and its nonuniform coloring and shape. Instead of working from a preconceived idea or fixed plan, students may be inspired by the characteristics and shape of one particular stone to envision creative possibilities which might not otherwise have occurred to them. The material's most serious shortcoming is that it is not easily obtainable: local building suppliers usually do not carry it. Most of the lava stones come from California, where nearly all suppliers of this material are located.

One other carving material which can be used in the high school is soap. The availability of soap bars and their softness and ivorylike appearance would seem to make this material quite acceptable for sculpture. Unfortunately these desirable qualities are outweighed by rather objectionable ones. The small size of even so-called "large" bars, their uniform, smooth texture, and the very ease with which they can be carved cause students to produce trite knickknacks rather than creating genuinely forceful expressions in three dimensions. The material provides no challenge and its size hampers freedom of ideas; the activity often fails to stimulate students' imagination. It is the imposition of one's will on a strong material, the friction between mind and matter, and the struggle between a vision and its translation into reality which make sculpture such an exciting creative adventure.

Subjects Related to Three-Dimensional Expression

Next to anatomy, volume design is probably the most significant subject intimately related to three-dimensional expression. Volume design is fundamentally the study of relationships between actual volume and space, and the investigation of the structural elements with which space can be defined, unrelated to any subject matter other than stress and balance, rhythm and motion, texture and material. Volume design consists primarily of devising structures in space rather than modeling and sculpturing forms. The underlying thoughts in this approach to design are intellectual; expression of emotion is deliberately avoided, and primarily aesthetic elements are emphasized. Elements such as statics or dynamics are treated free from any immediate connection with reality or usefulness, and are represented as almost abstract concepts. Volume design may also be described as a study of relationships and movements which do not refer to sculpture, architecture, or to any concrete meaning. Studying volume design elements in this isolated and almost abstract manner can be most meaningful when they are considered a basis for understanding space in architecture, sculpture, and aspects of interior or stage design.

The question then is: At what stage in art training should the study of volume design occur? What experiences should have preceded it, and what level of maturity and comprehension should an individual have attained to be able to profit from it? Unquestionably, numerous creative experiences must take place before a person becomes aware that form and meaning are not the same, but are two separate essential factors of any artistic statement. Commonly, young people think and feel for a considerable time that meaning takes precedence over form; only with maturity do they come to realize that attention must be divided equally between them. In volume design, on the other hand, an individual is forced to be preoccupied with form rather than with meaning. To attain a true understanding of the elements of this type of design, he must concentrate on matters which deal primarily with the essentials of form, independent of any emotion and individual expression.

From several points of view volume design can be compared with the study of syntax, semantics, measure, and metrical structure, all of which are closely related to the creation of literature and poetry. If such a study is taken up prematurely, before an individual has an intimate acquaintance with various forms of written artistic expression, it will neither increase or stimulate his creative ability, nor automatically help him to appreciate great writing. Instead he may shrink from becoming deeply involved with more advanced forms of poetry and artistic writing; he may be misled into believing that creating with words is such an extremely difficult process, requiring such thorough knowledge of so many complex subjects, that it is futile for him to pursue any interest he may have had in these fields.

A similar reaction can be expected of high school students if volume design with its underlying abstract concepts is introduced too early. Exercises in this form of design, making students dependent solely on the guidance and judgment of the teacher because they have no means of evaluation, and preventing them from relating personal experiences because these reflect emotions rather than intellectual considerations, can hamper freedom of expression more easily than further it. Unquestionably, students will willingly try to comply with the demands of such exercises, and may even find some pleasure in executing them, for the activity can easily become a playful manipulation of materials, making the difference between pretense and sincere effort hard to distinguish. Still more important, such constructions do not demand any personal involvement or commitment, and can easily degenerate into forms that are merely ambiguous, impersonal, and decorative. The decorative quality in particular often makes these projects appealing to students, as it does not compel them to represent or express anything specific.

It is therefore important to differentiate between principles of volume design, considerations related to materials and their assemblage, and the actual production of examples. The theoretical approaches have many ramifications pertaining to *all* aspects of three-dimensional expression, whereas the constructions of design are often too limited in scope to be valid in related areas. It is taken for granted that an art teacher has had experience in volume design—experimenting with novel or unusual materials, creating constructions with conscious emphasis on different spatial relationships, exploiting various possibilities of mass, and placing stress on ingenuity more than on pleasing appearance. As a result of these experiences the teacher should be equipped to analyze and evaluate all types of students' three-dimensional work, to explain any merit or shortcoming he may find in their creations, to recognize and encourage any signs of originality, and to lend support to their unwitting experimental attempts. At times he may schedule brief, purely experimental sessions for advanced students. The aim of such sessions should be limited in scope and clearly stated. For example, one period might be devoted solely to the many ways of achieving varied textures on different surfaces, another to the discovery of the countless possibilities of obtaining shapes by perforating a solid mass, and still another to the many means by which form can be achieved, or the many ways simple materials (balsa wood, cellophane, and paper) can be utilized to represent mass, or define space.

To avoid misunderstandings, however, it should be strongly emphasized that such experiments are not to lead to the production of decorations or representational images, nor should paper sculpture be regarded as part of such activities. Paper sculpture must be considered a highly specialized and skilled form of creating; it is a means of representation which can easily lead to the production of stereotyped decorations rather than to experimentation or genuine expression. Only a teacher thoroughly versed in paper sculpture can stimulate his students so that they will exploit the medium in an unconventional manner, compose unique designs, and invent ways of utilizing these materials which are neither trite nor obvious. Any such experimental sessions should be aimed at heightening students' sensitivity toward three-dimensional expression, encouraging their exploration of materials, and familiarizing them with problems of creating three-dimensional forms independent of subject matter.

The final question remains: To what extent should unusual or scrap materials be used in the high school for the creation of three-dimensional work? The major issue is whether such exploits are helpful to the understanding and appreciation of sculpture, and encourage the desire to give expression to thought and feeling. On the negative side, the preoccupation with materials can become so important that students neglect the creative aspect, and that the manipulation of materials becomes an end in itself. "I fail to see," wrote Epstein, "how the use of novel materials helps, such as glass, tin, strips of lead, stainless steel, and aluminum. The use of these materials might add novel and pleasing effects in connection with architecture, but adds nothing to the essential meanings of sculpture, which remain fundamental. The spirit is neglected for detail, for ways and means."[105] This neglect is the core of the danger

---

[105] Epstein, *Let There Be Sculpture,* p. 211.

of pure experimentation in volume design. Yet if these activities are not isolated, on the high school level, from other forms of sculpture, but are intimately linked with them, if *one* is used to foster the others, the danger of neglect of the spiritual qualities of this art form can easily be avoided.

IV Subjects Related to Art

Subjects such as art appreciation, stage craft, commercial art, and crafts, while not genuine parts of visual creative art, nonetheless can play a substantial role in the teaching of art in the high school. The responsibility for some of these subjects often is shared by other teaching fields; for example, various crafts are taught in industrial arts classes, or in connection with home economics, and others, like stage and costume design, sometimes are handled by the speech department. Yet because all these subjects are to some degree connected with the visual arts, no art teacher can completely ignore them, although he may give more attention to one than to another, depending on his preparation, preference, and conviction. Some subjects, however, are so closely tied to the creative arts that they are inevitably a part of the high school art program.

Art Appreciation

The subject most closely allied to visual art, found in nearly all high school art curricula, is often referred to as "art appreciation." In many high schools one finds special courses carrying this title, yet the term is not only extremely vague, but literally is not even a subject, because "appreciation" suggests only approval and an awareness of aesthetic values. In other words, the course is an exposure to great art which *may* result in appreciation. But exposure as such is merely one minor and very limited aspect of teaching—it implies that an individual must perceive and comprehend on his own—without the assistance of an informed person—the values to which he is exposed, and this is a demand very few people can meet.

Generally speaking, there are three ways of approaching "art appreciation" on the high school level. Each is different in educational scope and execution. One approach has been emphasized throughout this book: it stresses the close relationship between students' creative efforts and the past and present achievements of great artists, and advocates that studio experiences be intimately linked with the exposure to great art. Students are probably most sensitive and receptive to superior solutions to problems in outstanding artistic achievements while they are attempting to solve their own similar creative problems. If they are exposed to great art works at such a time, their interest in their projects may be heightened, their minds and imaginations may be stirred, and they may create with more verve and vitality than if this means of stimulation had been neglected.

The fear that superior examples might frustrate students seems largely without foundation. After all, thousands of youngsters constantly watch outstanding performances in sports without a loss of interest or faith in their own ability. Fear of overly influencing students also appears unjustified so long as they are shown many examples demonstrating several approaches to a problem, various artistic solutions, different styles and concepts, and numerous ways of handling a medium. Naturally such a selection should never reflect a teacher's preference for or bias toward certain styles or certain artists, but should be chosen objectively. What matters is the appropriateness of the works and their exemplification of quality, profundity, originality, and superior execution. In truth, it is quite unrealistic to be overly concerned about influencing students; teaching is first and foremost a process in which individuals are deliberately and constantly exposed to influences—just being consciously alive is synonymous with exposure to influences. Therefore the question is not "Can or should influences be banned from an art room?" but rather "In which way can they be utilized to be of the greatest benefit to students' creative, intellectual, and social development?" Since students are constantly stimulated by influences and have a longing for ideals and a need for standards, it is in the art room that they should find some satisfaction for these needs and be made familiar with superior examples of great achievements. Ignoring these adolescent desires, or leaving their satisfaction to incidents, casual exposure, or accidental encounters in magazines, on television, or on the street, would constitute default of a teacher's obligation.

Whenever reproductions of great achievements are shown to students, the names of the works and their creators should be mentioned, and questions in regard to the artist, the medium, technique, composition, or subject matter answered fully. However, students' interest should not be dampened by later objective tests. Appreciation of art cannot be measured by testing; it is perceptible only through the manifestation of certain symptoms: an increased willingness to become deeply involved in creative work, a greater effort to leave trite ways in search of fresher expression, and a greater inquisitiveness and heightened interest in the works of great men and the problems connected with visual art.

While a course in art appreciation on the high school level can be approached from a totally different point of view, unrelated to any creative activity, to what degree this would lead to a genuine appreciation of great achievements is open to debate. Still it can serve one important purpose: to contribute to the broad and general education of adolescents. Regardless of their future development, high school students will benefit greatly from having been exposed to aspects of art history and to many media and techniques of visual art. Such a course, therefore, should be primarily informative and cultural; it should consist of familiarizing students, intellectually as well as visually, with various periods of art, with styles and their characteristics, and with art terms such as Gothic or Baroque, impressionism or expressionism. The course should also acquaint them with art media and techniques, enabling them to distinguish, for instance, between an etching and an engraving, and between a gouache and a watercolor. It goes without saying that at the same time students should be exposed constantly to superior art achievements which should help them not only to relate theoretical information, but also gradually to develop affinities for certain artistic works or periods of visual art.

The core of such a course should be built around slides, filmstrips, films, and art reproductions. Its method should consist of illustrated lectures, class discussions, recitations, and reports, in addition to auxiliary reading assignments. Because these lessons must be tailor-made, suited in each instance to a certain student body in a particular situation, the teacher must design his own syllabus.[106] He will then be able to utilize or adapt the available audio-visual and library materials, take advantage

---

[106] Among books which may be helpful for this task are: Hendrik Willem Van Loon, *The Arts* (New York: Simon & Schuster, 1937); Helen Gardner, *Art through the Ages* (New York: Harcourt, Brace & Co., 1948); E. H. J. Gombrich, *The Story of Art* (London: Phaidon Books, 1954), and H. W. Janson, *Key Monuments of the History of Art* (Englewood Cliffs, N.J.: Prentice-Hall, Inc., 1959).

of existing museum and gallery facilities, and incorporate any previous art experiences his students may have had.

There are two possible basic approaches to the teaching of the historical development of art. One begins with the present, and relates or compares contemporary art forms to those of the past; the other begins with the distant past and ends with the present. For young or very uninformed students the first method may be more effective since many contemporary approaches (for instance impressionism, post-impressionism, and expressionism) may be closer to their level of understanding and not too difficult to assimilate. The opposite approach, beginning with the distant past, being more factual and intellectually demanding is also more challenging for both students and teacher. With sufficient audio-visual materials and a careful selection of the most significant aspects of the major art periods, the course can be most informative and fascinating. The history of art, tracing the inventiveness and creativeness of the human mind, is an intriguing subject and can easily capture adolescents' imagination. Whether or not it does depends largely on the teacher's own enthusiasm for the subject, his inventiveness, and his presentation and careful preparation of the material. The preparation consists of the selection of individual topics, of working out a lesson-by-lesson plan, and of gathering appropriate audio-visual material.

In yet a different approach, art appreciation is offered as a supplementary course to American or world history. Here the aim is comparatively broad, as the course pertains to cultural history rather than the visual arts. Its primary purpose is to counteract a misconception which is often inferred or suggested unintentionally in many history classes. It is not uncommon for students to leave such a course thinking that the most significant aspects of man's development are reflected only in his political history, that his political actions are of much greater importance than his spiritual and creative deeds. Also they are frequently left with the impression that to know man's political exploits, his conquests of lands and peoples, the names of leaders, and dates of major events is sufficient to understand the past and the present, and to be well prepared for comprehending and deciding the future.

To counterbalance these possible misinterpretations is one purpose of this art appreciation course. The other is to make students aware of the interrelationship between man's creative achievements and his political existence, to help them gain a proper perspective on man's genius, and to acquaint them with the many great and peaceful accomplishments in the realm of the mind. The course should prove to them that there are things worth striving for other than physical comfort and purely material gains; that countless great deeds, accomplished by sacrifice and under great difficulty, were performed neither for fame nor for personal advantage, but to satisfy an individual's inner need and feeling of moral obligation. This side of man's history is as important as any other, and no student should leave high school without having been confronted at least once with this aspect of his own past.

If it is at all possible, such an art appreciation course should be worked out in cooperation with the teacher of history; his textbook may serve as a guide for the selection of topics and periods, and related factors. Ideally the responsibility for the conduct of the course should be shared by the music, English, and art teachers. There should be liberal use of aids such as recordings of music, drama, and poetry; of slides, filmstrips, and films. The emphasis should be on stimulating students and inculcating the significance of their long cultural heritage, not on teaching facts and training their ability to memorize.[107] A valid sign of success in these lessons is not

---

[107] "If we approach a work of art or nature scientifically, for the sake of its historical connexions or proper classification, we do not approach it aesthetically. The discovery of its date or of its author may be otherwise interesting; it only remotely affects our aesthetic appreciation by adding to the direct effect of certain associations." Santayana, *The Sense of Beauty*, p. 17.

the speedy or accurate recollection of information; it is students' greater inquisitiveness, their expressed desire to want to know more, and their increased ability to integrate cultural information of various accomplishments and ideas with the events studied in their history classes.

Applied Art

A very different group of subjects, intimately related to the teaching of art, depends heavily on factors other than those inherent in creative visual expression. Typical of this group are commercial art, stage craft, and fashion design. These subjects are outer-directed, their products must be conceived with a particular group in mind, and they must serve a definite purpose and appeal to a specific audience. Because of these conditions, the creator of such works is not free and self-directed; he is obligated to please, and his achievements are evaluated by the degree to which they satisfy a requirement and serve their purpose, rather than by how well they express a personal thought or feeling, a stirring idea, or a creative concept. Appropriateness and fitness in terms of function are of major importance; the artist's contribution or excellence is minor.

It is sometimes quite difficult to distinguish between an artist's self-directed action and one which is inner-motivated, and between an outer-directed action and one which is outer-motivated. In this context both forms of motivation mean the particular happening which prompts an action. *Inner* motivation is caused by circumstances over which the artist has no control—an accidental encounter, an impulse, or a sudden vision or idea; *outer* motivation is produced by an external incentive, by a deliberate temptation from the outside, by a requirement to discharge an obligation, or by the desire to fulfill a request.

Self- or inner-direction means that regardless of what prompted the action, the artist is independent in his thoughts, is concerned solely with what he believes or recognizes as right, and assumes the total responsibility for his action and its consequences.

From a historic point of view the cleavage between inner and outer motivation is of much less significance than that between self-direction and outer-direction. Most of the great works of art created until the middle of the seventeenth century were outer-motivated but inner-directed. In many cases when the artist was commissioned to create a work he was outer-motivated, but beyond this point the patron's power or influence did not extend: how the ideas were depicted and the manner in which the work was created and executed were solely the artist's responsibility. The patron was at liberty to accept or reject the work, but was never given the right to interfere with it. Michelangelo was practically forced to create the murals in the Sistine Chapel, yet the concepts and ideas and the manner in which he represented them were entirely his own. In other words, for more than seven years he worked by being outer-motivated but completely self-directed.

Rembrandt is commonly regarded as the first important artist whose significant works for the most part were solely inner-motivated and self-directed. Today the division between fine or free art and applied or servile art is often incorrectly made on the basis of *how* an artist was *motivated:* if he was inner-motivated, his work is automatically classified as fine art; if he was outer-motivated, it is placed in the other category. Such an oversimplification of a rather complex problem is hardly acceptable; many recent and important artistic accomplishments have been outer-motivated. Commissions and competitions are still numerous, and as a result of them excellent paintings, murals, and monuments have been created. Yet the incentive for these creations has come from the outside.

The decisive difference between free and applied art cannot be found in *how* an artist is *motivated,* but in whether he is self-directed or outer-directed. What truly matters is how independently he creates, realizes ideas, interprets concepts, formulates precepts, and represents visions and images. The creation of a self-directed artist reflects a profound idea, a deep understanding, a penetrating meaning. The work of an outer-directed artist often mirrors only shallow thought, an insignificant message, or the most superficial characteristics of forms, persons, or impressions. His preoccupation with wishing to please, to be of service, to comply with requests, rarely permits him to depict more than what is demanded of him, and these demands are the outer-directing elements; they dictate to the artist what he must do, how he is supposed to state it in visual terms, and what limitations he has to accept.

Still, it is not difficult to find outstanding achievements in the realm of the applied arts which have been created by independent, self-directed minds. These works often set examples of styles which are, or must be, followed by others. Their innovators are more than merely trained and highly skilled workers, limited to one field or competent in only one area; they are artists who have a vital interest in all aspects of the visual arts, express themselves in a variety of art forms, and have a superior command of skills.

It is not easy to determine the function and purpose of outer-directed work in the high school because the major objective of art education can be reached more readily through courses emphasizing *inner*-directed work. In many respects, inner-directed more than outer-directed projects force students to make decisions without following precedents, and to solve problems which have more than one solution. Moreover, inner-directed work offers greater opportunities for freedom of expression and demands more imagination and willingness to venture into creative uncertainty than any art form serving a particular and practical purpose. If for any reason a course dealing with some phases of commercial art is offered in a high school, it should be open only to those students who have already acquired a foundation in the creative arts. Such a prerequisite appears necessary because most outer-directed subjects require knowledge and understanding of the basic principles of design, a good visual vocabulary, and considerable skill and training in visualizing thoughts and ideas.

Stage Design

The field in which both inner- and outer-directed work can be most readily combined is stage design. Since a play can be interpreted in many ways and its setting may reflect many different points of view, creating such a decoration entails many choices. Yet stage design belongs to the servile arts because its primary purpose is to be of service to the spoken word, to give concreteness to an abstract thought and reality to an idea. Consequently the chief functions of stage settings are to establish visually the time and the place, of the action, to form a background against which the characters can be effective, to lend an atmosphere which helps actors to be convincing, and to create a mood which will capture an audience.

Because of these requirements, any project in stage design must obviously begin with a careful and thorough study of the play. Ideally any class in stage design should be taught in close connection with classes in English. This form of integration can be of considerable benefit to both students and teachers. The study and analysis of the play could be the responsibility of the English teacher, and the research for and design of the settings and costumes the obligation of the art teacher.

A stage set, like a play, is a condensation of an aspect of reality, a synthesis of a place and a time; it is composed of essentials and fragments which suggest a location, portray a situation, and convey a mood. Only that which distinctly contributes to this end belongs to the design. The criterion for a good stage setting is that it should never be so powerful as to detract from the happenings on the stage, overshadow the action, or take on greater importance than the spoken word. This basic rule should be impressed upon students before they begin to solve a design problem.

Sometimes it is wise to begin the course with a few simple exercises aimed at acquainting students with some fundamentals of stage design. For instance, they should design several interior walls of identical dimensions, each with a window and a door, but each wall representing a different type of home—a dilapidated tenement, a Victorian town house, a modern bungalow, a refined mansion, or a pioneer's log cabin. This type of assignment can be varied still further by designing a wall in a medieval castle, an old church, an ancient cloister, a modern office, an antiquated general store, or a conventional reception room. During these assignments economy in design should be stressed; the aim is to help students discover how little is needed to suggest a locale, provided the most characteristic visual elements are emphasized, possibly dramatized or exaggerated.

Students should not be asked to design a set before they have studied the play thoroughly. The design should be worked out directly in three dimensions in a small model stage rather than on a piece of paper. A stage set, after all, is not a flat illustration of a scene in a play, but a design in space in which possible movement and action must be given as much attention as stationary forms and colors.

Ordinary corrugated cardboard boxes can be transformed into effective model stages, and this transformation is simple enough to permit every student to have his own working model. The models should be made to scale (for instance, one-half inch to one foot) to help students develop a feeling for space and learn to think realistically in three dimensions. Before beginning to design a decoration students should fashion a human figure, representing an actor, in the same scale as their stage models, and use this constantly to determine the appropriateness and effectiveness of their design.

The first phase of designing should consist of cutting out of cardboard and other materials the major parts with which the space is to be divided, such as partitions, elevations, supports, stairs, hangings, backdrops, arches, and pillars. Only after their size, arrangement, and position have been decided should any attention be given to details—colors, the treatment of surfaces, interior and other minor decorations, and stage props. In brief, not before the over-all design is fully developed should particulars be incorporated. The aim of this working method is to encourage students to create directly with media, and to develop ideas by experimentation with materials rather than by designing independently of them, thus remaining unaware of the many possibilities as well as the limitations of the stage.

An intrinsic part of stagecraft is the appropriate designing of costumes for a play; this should be approached from the same point of view as stage design. Here again students should learn to develop their ideas by working directly with materials. First they should fashion simple papier-mâché figures, then create the costumes by experimentation, cutting and draping various textiles and other materials, and fitting these on the figurines. Working in this manner will permit students to see immediately the results of their ideas, and help them discover the potentialities of materials. It should inspire them more than merely designing a costume on paper, without regard to materials, working possibilities, and practical execution.

From an art education point of view, a course in stage and costume design, conducted along the lines indicated, can be of particular value to many high school art programs. Not infrequently a general art course is suddenly interrupted by an urgent request for a stage design or a decoration for an assembly. Often the time for planning and executing the project is so short that it is impossible to transform the request into a worthwhile undertaking. Consequently, students who for the most part are unprepared for such a task hastily produce something without an opportunity to learn anything meaningful or to use their creative abilities. A course in stage design may, to a considerable extent, help to correct this misuse of a general art class; here students are prepared for such projects, learn how to approach them, and are familiar with different ways of designing. Thus instead of merely being a chore, the designing of sets can become a valuable enterprise which gives students an excellent opportunity to exhibit their abilities, newly acquired knowledge, and skill.

Lastly it should be pointed out that some training in the fundamentals of stage design may have considerable value for students who are interested in fields such as architecture, interior decoration, and window display. The experiences of working with space, discovering some of the more uncommon possibilities of dividing it, and becoming aware of the role of color in relation to space are basic and can be transferred to many other creative situations.

Commercial Art

An extremely broad field, predominantly outer-directed, is commercial art; it consists of many different subject areas—advertising art, poster design, lettering, fashion illustration, package design, and industrial design. Each of these subjects is divided into many precise subdivisions, each requiring special knowledge and skill. This obviously prompts the question: Which of these many fields should be selected for teaching in a specialized high school art course, and which should be considered altogether too difficult or too limited to be of value to high school students? This question in turn leads to another: What is or should be the educational purpose of such a course? It is certain that students in the usual nonvocational high school, taking a few art courses among others, can hardly be prepared for skilled labor, let alone for a profession in any of these art fields. Almost all commercial art fields now demand exact technical knowledge and considerable preparation in the visual arts in addition to a thorough general education. It is significant that today most innovators in the field of applied arts, the pacemakers, the creators of new ideas and approaches, not only are artists with a superior command of their craft and a genuine understanding of art, but are also highly educated men. The imitators of styles, and the epigoni, on the other hand, despite great skill are often incapable of producing anything other than what is already established and accepted. They are frequently condemned to follow trends largely because they are so restricted by their limited knowledge, lack of exposure to and experience with many forms of art expression, and highly specialized training. Unless it is built on a solid foundation in the creative arts and on a broad education, a limited training in a narrow, specialized field in the applied arts often seems to hamper rather than further the creative potentialities.

It must be obvious, therefore, that a major objective of any art course, including one dealing with aspects of commercial art, should be to give students a foundation in the visual arts instead of an elementary preparation in a vocational field. To achieve this aim, every art course should provide students with various experiences in visual expression, acquaint them with essentials intimately connected with the creation of art, and impart some knowledge of great achievements—all of which should help them make intelligent choices pertaining to their vocational or avocational future. Such an objective can best be realized in progressively advancing art courses which stress fundamentals of art and pay little attention to outer-directed art forms, as opposed to specialized courses dealing solely with practical applications of art principles, techniques, and skills.

In some nonvocational high schools commercial art courses have been part of the art program for years. Their purpose is taken for granted, their educational value is not questioned, and their method of teaching has not been changed in the past two or three decades. The seemingly useful products resulting from such courses often impress administrators because of their alleged connection with the immediate practicalities of life. Unfortunately administrators are seldom aware that these apparently "practical" works have been executed under conditions and in a manner so amateurish that the little which may have been learned is of no vocational or educational value whatsoever.

Most art teachers, lacking the training in and experience with the production of commercial art, do not instruct their students in the latest practices but in ways and methods which were used generations ago. During the past fifteen years enormous technical advances have been made in producing commercial art works mechanically. To be sure, these advances are independent and outside of any aesthetic considerations; they are mainly intended to improve the mechanical devices for finishing works, to assure their speediest, most accurate, and least costly reproduction, and to substitute for highly developed skill and long experience with technical means, so that more and more semi-skilled labor can be employed in the completion of effective and finished commercial art work. Newly developed devices and aids still require workers who are intelligent, disciplined, and accurate, and can offer some evidence of occupational aptitude and knowledge; otherwise they need no special training outside of what is usually provided at their place of work.

It seems clear, therefore, that a major part of a commercial art course in the high school should be devoted to the teaching of techniques which are current practice. For example, students should learn to work competently with various types of lettering and sign-making guides instead of spending endless hours attempting to master the rudiments of pen or brush lettering. Moreover, they should be well versed in the uses of the many different types of paste-up letters, since most advertising lettering today is no longer done by hand but produced by assembling various cellophane printed letters. A significant part of any commercial art course should be devoted to teaching the essentials of commercial reproduction techniques, such as offset printing, photoengraving, and, above all, the rudiments of typography. Visiting printing plants and advertising departments and agencies, and inviting art directors and designers for lectures should also comprise a significant part of such a course. If possible, the help of professionals should be enlisted in planning or revising a commercial art course because its content and approaches should change with the times. Without outside help it is extremely difficult for an art teacher to coordinate his work with the ever-varying trends, techniques, and demands. The course can be of value to high school students only if it is continually revised and kept up to date, providing them with essential knowledge of current practices and opportunities as well as helping them to discover their own aptitudes. This or a similar approach to the subject should give students a basis for deciding whether or not to enter any of the commercial art fields. Equipping them for such a choice is probably the ultimate justification for commercial art courses in the high school.

Handicrafts

Today only a subtle division exists between crafts and the visual arts; indeed, the line which separates the two is sometimes so fine that it is hard to distinguish between one and the other. It is characteristic of our time that yet another distinction is made between crafts and handicrafts; originally both meant the same—a skill pertaining to artists, artisans, and craftsmen. But at present the term "handicraft" is used to specify the particular manual skill and knowledge needed to create a work in which greater significance is placed on its aesthetic quality than on its possible utilitarian purpose. By contrast the term "craft" is commonly used to characterize any genuine skill which has been acquired for competence in a particular field, be it surgery, watchmaking, acting, or cabinetmaking. "Craft" means technical proficiency, whereas "handicraft" pertains solely to skills which are needed to create artistic and unique as well as useful objects with simple tools. The difference in meaning in the terms "craft" and "handicraft" is largely the result of the ever-growing mechanization and industrialization of the production of objects. Characteristically, the artisan creates his works for the most part by hand, depending mainly on his manual skill and control over rather simple tools, and is responsible for the entire creation from the design to the finished product. He does not work out his ideas and projects on paper, like the designer, or operate complex machines or merely assemble machine-manufactured parts, like the skilled worker in industry.

The distinction between artisans and artists, however, is even less sharp and more complex than that between handicrafts and crafts. Today the artist and the artisan are both inner-directed in spite of the fact that the artisan divides his interest between creating objects which are useful and those which are beautiful and expressive. Originally his first interest was in the usefulness of his products, but industrialization and mass production have done much to change his attitude: expressiveness, originality, beauty of materials, and craftsmanship now are his major concerns, and the practical or utilitarian aspects of his creations have become more or less coincidental or subordinate. As a result, the artisan has become, like the artist, a highly self-directed creator. Exploiting his skill in unique ways, finding new methods of utilizing raw materials, and designing objects which are based on aesthetic considerations and principles rather than on practicalities are the activities which preoccupy the present-day artisan, be he a silversmith, weaver, potter, or bookbinder. It is noteworthy that public interest in the creations of the artisan is focused primarily on their aesthetic qualities; his products are purchased for their artistic merit, rarely for their practical value.

The artists and artisans of our time are concerned with similar problems, and in many respects share the same attitude toward their work. Yet from an art education point of view, the resemblance between them is less important than their dissimilarities. In the disparities between the arts and crafts one may eventually discover the uniqueness of the latter and their place within a high school art program. The artist disregards any utilitarian considerations; his major interest is to evoke ideals and visions, retain and sustain emotions and thoughts. The artisan's interest, however, is much less profound; his concern extends to the excellence of craftsmanship, the display of beauty in design and material, and the functional aspects of his creation. His works may encompass a wide range, from being primarily utilitarian or mainly decorative to purely aesthetic.

The stress placed on appearance and craftsmanship widely separates the handicrafts from the creative arts. In contrast to an artist, an artisan must acquire considerable manual proficiency and exact knowledge before he is able to achieve results which comply with the present high standards of craftsmanship. He must spend years in training, and must practise his craft for a long time before he can hope to master it sufficiently well to work freely and creatively. So long as he lacks this mastery he will merely produce; he will follow trite examples, and at best achieve mediocre results. Usually it takes years before a craftsman conceives new ideas and is able to translate them into concrete examples; these ideas are generally an outgrowth of experience, the mastery of a skill, and a superior knowledge of materials and tools.

At this point handicrafts and art differ considerably. In most areas of visual art the acquisition of dexterity and skills and the act of creating can hardly be separated; they take place almost simultaneously. But in most handicrafts, the learning of skills needed to fashion even a simple piece and its actual production are largely disconnected; they hardly ever occur concurrently but are set apart by time. For example, in jewelry making a student must first learn to saw straight and curved lines, then to file, solder, and polish; he must develop a feeling for metals, discover how they can be shaped, bent, and twisted, and how their surfaces can be treated by hammering, scratching, engraving, or etching. Only after he is acquainted with the many ways of using the material, has acquired some control over his tools, and has gained some understanding of the manifold technical manipulation processes can he begin to create. In fact it is only through these experiences that he will be able to create designs corresponding to the material and utilizing its intrinsic possibilities; it will then grow out of a feeling for and an understanding of the medium, conforming to the criteria of good design.

There is still one other aspect of the difference between arts and crafts which needs to be considered. In the arts the creative process is one in which the artist literally sees his creation grow under his hands; regardless of how long the execution may take, the evolutionary process does not end before he has finished the work. This process continually demands new decisions and the solving of unforeseen problems. The artist needs to devote relatively little effort to technicalities; he can spend most of his time on the ever-changing act of creating. All this is quite different in the crafts; the artisan devotes most of his time to technical manipulation, and gives only a relatively small portion to creating. During the manipulation process he follows established practises, and his mind is occupied with technical problems requiring the recalling of previous solutions. With the exception of the initial, creative phase of the undertaking he has very little opportunity to participate in a genuinely creative act; the major part of the execution of a handcrafted work is production rather than creation.

This characteristic of the crafts is more pronounced in some fields than in others. It is most evident in weaving or bookbinding, and least apparent in pottery. In weaving, for instance, preparing the loom and threading the shuttle are mechanical and time-consuming; the actual weaving is rather slow and almost automatic, though needing constant attention. The operation does not require creative impulses, does not challenge the imagination, and does not confront the weaver with sudden and unexpected alternatives or the need for decisions. Only while planning his project has he an opportunity to utilize his creative ability, and even this he cannot do before he has mastered his craft to a considerable degree, an accomplishment which can be achieved only slowly, often taking years of arduous practise. In pottery it is very different. To begin with, a piece is not planned on paper, as weaving usually is, but is worked out directly by forming the clay. During this stage the potter develops his design, changing, adjusting, or incorporating sudden ideas into his work. If he has acquired adequate skill, he can remain creatively active throughout many phases of the execution of a project. In pottery, learning the manual skills is commonly not completely separated from the creative process, but is largely gained by working creatively with the medium.

From this it can be seen that pottery is the craft which has the closest affinity with art, and no doubt this is why courses in ceramics are offered today in most art departments. In these courses major emphasis is usually placed on the creative and aesthetic aspects of pottery, and less attention is given to a possible utilitarian function. Seen solely from an aesthetic point of view, pottery has much in common with the abstract concepts of art in which the beauty of form and texture, the relationships of sizes and colors, and the interplay of planes and shapes are dominant considerations. So long as these considerations are used as criteria for pottery, the incorporation of this subject into a high school art program is fully justified. Most important, when instructing such a course, the teacher should remember what was valid generations ago, that "the virtue of craftsmen was not, in their eyes, strength of muscle, or nimbleness of fingers. It was a virtue of the intellect, and endowed the humblest artisan with a certain perfection of the spirit."[108]

---

[108] Jacques Maritain, *Creative Intuition in Art and Pottery* (New York: Pantheon Books, Bollingen Series XXXV. 1, 1953), p. 49.

In the final analysis, what truly matters in teaching, be it arts or crafts, is the spiritual value with which a student is confronted, of which he takes possession, and which he learns to appreciate. All other considerations are secondary, for it is not in the practical or material but in the ethical values of art that we find its true educational merits. There are many ways in which students can be helped to acquire these values. They progress toward them whenever they are made aware of the difference between the penetrating and the superficial, excellent and imperfect, real and false, lasting and ephemeral. Also, whenever they are encouraged to make visible what is hidden, bring to light what is in the dark, and make tangible what exists only in their minds—in brief, whenever they are induced to give expression to thoughts and feelings, and are at liberty to transform an insignificant weed into an object of admiration, a decayed piece of wood into a source of delight, a stray cat into a manifestation of dignity and graciousness, and a lonely pauper into a symbol of humanity and compassion. It is also of great help when their creative abilities are challenged, when they are impelled to leave the trite and familiar to venture into uncertainty, and to discover relationships of which they were previously unaware.

Introducing young people to what is of enduring worth and moving them to search for these values is an important aspect of education: it may develop and strengthen those vital faculties and capacities which should eventually equip them to enjoy life deeply and fully, to appreciate and understand man's creative genius, to contribute to the betterment of their fellow men, and give meaning to their own existence.

INDEX

A NOTE ON THE AUTHOR

MANFRED L. KEILER was born in Berlin, Germany, in 1908. He studied at the State Academy, Weimar, where he received his B.A. (1929) and M.F.A. (1931), and did postgraduate work at the Ecole des Beaux Arts, Paris, and the Bauhaus, Dessau. In 1938 he came to the United States, receiving his citizenship in 1944. In 1950 he joined the faculty of the University of Nebraska, where he held the rank of Professor of Art, and Supervisor of Art at the University High School. THE ART IN TEACHING ART was completed in manuscript in the spring of 1960 and Professor Keiler had made his corrections on the first galleys before his untimely death December 1, 1960. Professor Keiler's writings included articles in *Art Education, Everyday Art, College Art Journal,* and other educational publications. He was also the author of ART IN THE SCHOOLROOM, first published by the University of Nebraska Press in 1951. A second enlarged edition appeared in 1955.